The
Economics of
Modern Business

For Ruth and Barbara

The
Economics of
Modern Business

W. DUNCAN REEKIE
and
D.E. ALLEN

Basil Blackwell

338.5
R 327

© W. Duncan Reekie and D.E. Allen 1983

First published 1983
Basil Blackwell Publisher Limited
108 Cowley Road, Oxford OX4 1JF, England

British Library Cataloguing in Publication Data

Reekie, W. Duncan
  The economics of modern business.
  1. Economics
  I. Title   II. Allen, D.E.
  330'.024658   HB171.5

  ISBN 0-631-13115-9
  ISBN 0-631-13116-7 Pbk

Typeset by MHL Typesetting Ltd, Coventry
Printed in Great Britain by T.J. Press Ltd, Padstow

Contents

Acknowledgements

The defects in this text are exclusively our own. However, for the positive qualities our thanks are due to Charles Baird of California State University, Hayward; Falconer Mitchell of Edinburgh University; Brian Summers of the Foundation for Economic Education, Irvington-on-Hudson, New York and P.J. White of Edinburgh for inspiration and comment. Nicola Harris, desk editor at Basil Blackwell and Brian Goodale, freelance copy editor, proved helpful, constructive and fastidious. But our greatest debt is to René Olivieri of Basil Blackwell, without whose entrepreneurial dynamism this book would never have been begun.

1

Plan and Purpose

Economics, perhaps correctly, is not at present held in the highest esteem. This situation contrasts sharply with the halcyon years of 1965–75. In that period economists were seen (and often saw themselves) as possessing the philosopher's stone. Proponents of economics pointed to the unparalleled material welfare enjoyed by the inhabitants of our planet since World War II. Certainly some unattractive pockets of poverty persisted within nations and some countries were poorer than others. But the doctrines of economic growth provided the wherewithal to remedy this. Had not economics pulled us out of the Great Depression? Had not the application of the relevant economic theories provided us with a standard of living we healthily and happily enjoyed? Recent reappraisals of the economic cycle suggest not. Indeed they even suggest the opposite.

So what has been responsible for giving us our present quality of life? The answer is, of course, the one and only wealth-creating section of society: business enterprise. Businessmen, not economists, are responsible for our material welfare. The role of the economist is minor. He can illuminate economic and business activity. He can help us to understand the allocation of resources between firms, within firms and between producers and consumers. In this way he can help, but not guarantee, to make us more effective participants in the business world.

Economists are yesterday's heroes. They have in the past assumed a role they should never have had the arrogance to attempt. They did not and could not deliver what was expected of them. Their true role is to show that businessmen cannot deliver either. We live in a world of scarcity. This requires us to make choices between more and less valued ends. All we can hope to do is make the least bad choices. No course of action will return us to the Garden of Eden. The economist's role is to emphasize this eternal truth and to assist the businessman, the consumer and others to understand the possible outcomes of the relevant choices facing them.

It will be enough if in this book we achieve the modest aim of bringing home the ideas that resources are limited, that nirvana cannot be attained this side of the grave, but that trading and commercial activity can, at least potentially improve our lot. The unsung heroes responsible for our wealth are consumers and producers operating freely in the market-place. It is to promote appreciation of this fact that we have written the book.

The imperfect engine of wealth creation which is Western industry is our main subject of study. In particular we deal with British business. Chapters 2−7 provide a basic economic tool-kit with which to tackle the rest of the book. The kit includes discussion of why firms are the size they are and why they are members of any given industry. Business decisions and the ways in which they are monitored are covered in chapters 8 and 9. Chapter 10 examines how business is owned by the members of society, either directly, or indirectly, through individual savings. Chapters 11 and 12 discuss the nature and evolution of modern British industry; the emphasis there is on manufacturing industry. In chapter 13 the thrust of the examination returns to the market-place and the consumer; marketing, distribution, trading and exchange again take the centre of the stage. Chapter 14 goes on to consider the relationship between employer and employee. This subject aptly follows chapter 13 since, as emphasized there, both employer and employee are the servants of the consumer. Yet, whenever the topic is treated on its own, this truth is often forgotten. The juxtaposition of these chapters ameliorates but does not excise this conceptual problem. Chapter 15 examines the role of the government: does it hamper or hinder the workings of business for the good of the consumer? We do not attempt a definitive answer, but topics covered include conventional ones, such as monopolies legislation, and less conventional but highly topical issues, such as pollution and resource depletion. In that chapter the Coase Theorem (notably absent from other elementary textbooks) is introduced. This theorem goes some way towards removing the authors' ambivalent attitude towards state interference in the workings of the economy.

Wherever possible we avoid abstruse theorizing; we illustrate models with highly relevant practical examples, provide plenty of statistical information, and describe how firms actually take decisions. Business emerges as exciting, interesting and the best (though still imperfect) way of meeting human wants.

2

Setting the Scene

Markets and the Role of Business

Many people believe, as did the mercantilist thinkers in the seventeenth century, that only the seller of a good or service benefits from trade. The buyer pays out money which presumably makes him poorer; the seller receives money, which presumably enriches him. Consequently, business is frequently viewed as an avaricious and less than desirable component of society.

There are two fallacies in this reasoning. The first is the claim that one party to a voluntary trade gains while the other loses. This is not so: barring fraud and miscalculations, both parties gain. Individual valuations differ, and trade occurs if, and only if, both parties anticipate receiving in exchange something of greater perceived value than whatever they give up. Voluntary trading is always carried out in the expectation of improving one's lot, be one the buyer or the seller. In short, buyers and sellers have a common interest; they co-operate, not compete, in trade. Buyers may compete against buyers, and sellers against sellers, but sellers and buyers co-operate for the enrichment of both.

The second error is a direct consequence of the mercantilist view that only the person who receives money in exchange for goods becomes richer. Money has no intrinsic value but only value as a medium of exchange and a store of value. It is something which may be traded later for other things, to use or consume. The ultimate purpose of voluntary trade is to obtain goods and services to consume. Adam Smith put it succinctly: 'Consumption is the sole end and purpose of all production.'[1]

This sounds very fine, but it draws on arguments of 200–300 years ago. Today economists are very fond of saying, 'there is no such thing as a free lunch.' All this means is that all goods (or most) are scarce. If someone gets more of a good then something must be given up (not necessarily by the same person). At its most prosaic, some children get school meals free of charge, but someone (probably the taxpayer) has to forfeit something to make the zero-priced lunches available. Very few goods are genuinely free. Even air is scarce if you are a diver or an astronaut, and clean air is scarce to city dwellers.

Given scarcity, three fundamental economic questions arise. What goods should be produced and in what proportions? How should they be produced and with what technologies? For whom should they be produced and how much of each should members of society get?

These questions arise in every type of community—small or large, free enterprise, centrally controlled or 'mixed'. The third question, 'for whom', logically implies that, given scarcity, there is competition for the limited output. Smith argued that the sole object of production is consumption: but if the goods produced are scarce, who is to consume?

In a centrally controlled (sometimes called *dirigiste*) economy the planners can allocate the output of business by various forms of competition or discrimination. In Hitler's Germany Aryans were given preference over Jews. In the southern USA whites had preference over blacks in restaurant seating and in which parts of a bus they could legally occupy. Taken to the extreme case, if food is allocated by height, beauty, race or political clout, then only the tallest, most beautiful, 'correct' racial groups and politically approved people survive.

In Britain, the businessman who is more articulate and can present his case better to politicians and civil servants may obtain 'selective financial assistance' for investment from the government, while another firm with an identically attractive or even better product concept, but little political nous, will obtain nothing.

In a totally free enterprise economy (i.e. one which is not *dirigiste* but *laissez-faire*) goods are allocated to those who are willing and able to engage in voluntary trade. If in turn those who are willing and able are rewarded on the basis of their productivity, not their sex, colour or race, then the total volume of produced goods available to society to allocate will be increasing, not static. The most productive survive, the least productive do not. This, of course, is no less callous than allocation by decree. Only the favoured group differs. But if the total wealth of the community is increasing then the best of various (imperfect) worlds may be obtained. The handicapped and less well endowed can be aided with ever-increasing amounts of assistance. This can be provided by voluntary charity or by taxation, thus transferring income from one group in society to another. The more productive can earn ever-increasing net incomes for themselves (after tax or charitable donations) and so generate still further wealth for the community. This is the basic rationale for the market economy as against a more autocratic system of resource allocation.

The Mixed Economy

The United Kingdom is often called a 'mixed economy'. It is neither wholly *dirigiste* and centrally planned, nor is it one of totally free enterprise. Actually the name is somewhat misleading since *all* countries are mixed economies;

only the degree of the mixture varies. Thus the USSR has a substantial private sector in taxi-cabs, market-places and agriculture. The USA has significant governmental interests in health, welfare and social security, as well as the more obvious expenditures on defence and policing and less obvious ones on particular industries such as long-distance passenger trains. In Britain, total government expenditure (as a percentage of the Gross National Product (GNP)) has risen irregularly over the century. The impact of world wars is obvious. Less so is the failure of the expenditure to decline in peacetime. And although various welfare measures over the century have been responsible for increasing social (e.g. pensions, sickness and unemployment benefits) and educational expenditures, the rise between 1960 and 1970 is less understandable. This is particularly so when one remembers that the percentages are growing shares of a generally increasing GNP (table 2.1).

Table 2.1 *Government (central and local) expenditure as a percentage of total Gross National Product*

1900	14.3	1950	39.1
1910	12.2	1960	39.2
1920	26.2	1970	47.1
1930	25.0	1980[a]	50.1

[a] Estimate

Source: Barclays Bank Review, 1980

Table 2.2 illustrates how government expenditure is broken down. Social security payments (plus, of course, their administration) account for over one-quarter. The National Health and associated services, together with education, account for a similar proportion. The national defence budget is the next largest recipient of money from government. The remainder are absolutely large but relatively small. The government sector is, of course, an important ultimate customer of business or industry, through one or other of its programmes (e.g. agriculture, fisheries and food; parts of the defence, housing, industry and roads budgets, etc.). Even government programmes such as health and education pay not insignificant sums to (for example) the construction, medicine instrumentation and publishing industries.

The mixed economy, that hybrid of paternalism and free enterprise which exists in Britain, is neither ruthless (as autocratic economies can and have been) nor devoid of concern for others (as totally free enterprise economies theoretically could be). Rather it combines some of the best of both worlds. However, debate can and does exist as to whether the 'mixture' is correct. Is a 'caring bureaucracy' not a contradiction in terms? Would not voluntary charity be more effective? Is government participation too weak? Or too strong? These are legitimate matters of debate, but they will be left to later chapters.

Table 2.2 *Central and local government expenditure (£m)*

Major headings	1980–81 (actual)	1984–85 (forecast)
Defence	11.2	16.4
Overseas aid and other overseas services	1.8	2.5
Agriculture, fisheries, food and forestry	1.4	1.5
Industry, energy, trade and employment	4.2	5.0
Government lending to nationalized industries	2.3	1.1
Roads and transport	3.5	4.5
Housing	4.7	2.9
Other environmental services	3.4	4.0
Law, order and protective services	3.2	4.7
Education and science, arts and libraries	11.4	13.4
Health and personal social services	11.4	15.3
Social security	23.4	35.4
Total	93.5	128.4

Source: The Government's Expenditure Plans, 1982–83 to 1984–85, Cmnd 8494, HMSO, 1982

Business in Britain

For the purposes of this book, the degree to which the economy is or is not 'mixed' is not of primary importance. Rather we are interested in modern British business *per se*, which is to a greater or lesser extent influenced by the state (from ownership and nationalization at one extreme, to taxation of profits or even occasional subsidizing of losses at the other). State influence on industry will be examined in detail later. Here we simply take a snapshot view of industry in the United Kingdom.

Table 2.3 gives some indication of the nature of British industries and their changes in employment, output and share of Gross Domestic Product (GDP) in 1970 and 1980. The table is ranked by number in the British Standard Industrial Classification (SIC) system. There are 27 orders in the SIC and these are further subdivided into 181 minimum list headings (MLHs). Thus food, drink and tobacco (order III) is subdivided into 15 MLHs such as grain milling, biscuits, sugar, brewing and malting, and tobacco; vehicles (order XI) is subdivided into six, including aerospace equipment manufacturing and repairing, and railway carriages and wagons and trains.

It is quite clear from table 2.3 that the *primary* sector of British industry

Table 2.3 *Changes in British industry, 1970–80*

Order (1968, SIC)		% Change		Total employment (000)		% GDP	
		Employment	Output	1970	1980	1970	1980
I	Agriculture, forestry & fisheries	− 20.6	+ 24.1	466	370	2.9	2.2
II	Mining & quarrying	− 16.1	+ 273.3	410	344	1.5	5.6
III–XIX	Manufacturing	− 18.4	− 24.4	8342	6808	32.8	24.8
III	Food, drink & tobacco[a]	− 14.0	− 13.5	792	681	3.7	3.2
IV	Coal & petroleum products[a]	− 18.7	+ 133.3	48	39	0.3	0.7
V	Chemicals & allied industries[a]	− 2.5	− 14.8	442	431	2.7	2.3
VI	Metal manufacture[a]	− 32.4	− 48.0	593	401	2.5	1.3
VII	Mechanical engineering[a]	− 21.7	− 22.2	1106	866	4.5	3.5
VIII	Instrument engineering[a]	− 12.9	− 16.6	163	142	0.6	0.5
IX	Electrical engineering[a]	− 12.1	− 13.8	828	728	2.9	2.5
X	Shipbuilding, marine engineering[a]	− 18.3	− 14.3	191	156	0.7	0.6
XI	Vehicles[a]	− 14.4	− 3.2	842	711	3.1	3.0
XII	Other metal goods[a]	− 14.6	− 19.0	595	508	2.1	1.7
XIII	Textiles[a]	− 35.5	− 38.1	727	459	2.1	1.3
XIV	Leather and fur[a]		0.0			0.1	0.1
XV	Clothing and footwear[a]	− 22.2	− 20.0	455	354	1.0	0.8
XVI	Bricks, pottery, etc.[a]	− 22.0	− 8.3	318	248	1.2	1.1
XVII	Timber, furniture, etc.[a]	− 9.6	− 10.0	271	245	1.0	0.9
XVIII	Paper, printing, etc.[a]	− 15.3	− 21.7	626	530	2.8	2.3
XIX	Other manufacturing[a]	− 13.3	− 14.3	345	299	1.4	1.2
XX	Construction	− 5.5	− 4.3	1339	1263	7.0	6.7
XXI	Gas, electricity and water	− 11.2	− 6.2	391	347	3.2	3.0
XXII	Transport	− 4.6	− 7.0	1572	1500	8.6	8.0
XXIII	Distribution	+ 4.3	− 5.7	2675	2790	10.6	10.0
XXIV	Insurance, banking & finance	+ 29.1	+ 33.8	3854	4975	7.1	9.5
XXV	Professional & scientific services		+ 28.2			10.3	13.2
XXVI	Miscellaneous services	+ 32.1	+ 15.5	698	922	8.4	9.7
XXVII	Public administration & defence	+ 13.3	+ 10.6	3103	3516	6.6	7.3
Total		− 0.001	—	24,753	24,720	100	100

[a] 1979

Sources: Annual Abstracts of Statistics, National Income and Expenditure Accounts

(orders I and II) has suffered a decline in employment over the period. Agriculture's share of GDP has fallen but owing to improved agricultural labour productivity output has increased almost inversely with employment decrease. Mining and quarrying has increased its share of GDP, mainly (although this would only be shown by going down to MLH level) owing to the advent of North Sea oil and gas, which have offset the decline in the coal industry.

Secondary industries other than the manufacturing industries, that is, construction (XX) and gas, electricity and water (XXI), have, on average, remained fairly steady in their contribution to GDP but not in their provision of employment. Manufacturing (III–XIX) as a whole has seen a fall in both output and employment. Within the SIC orders themselves, however, considerable differences are evident. Annual output growth rates have been high in coal and petroleum products, while textiles' share of GDP has fallen (the much more dramatic drop in the case of woollen and cotton goods being only partially compensated for by the growth of the man-made fibre sub-industries). Overall, employment in orders III–XXI inclusive fell by 16.4 per cent.

Conversely, employment in the *tertiary* industries (broadly the government and the distributive and service industries) has risen (by 15 per cent) and their contribution to the GDP by 6.1 per cent.

The reasons for these changes, and a finer analysis of British industry, will be deferred until chapters 4, 5, 8, 9 and 10.

Table 2.3, however, does emphasize one point. All employees are employed in some 'industry'. Sometimes that industry is state-owned, sometimes not. According to some economists this is not of prime importance to an examination of the 'mixed economy'. Rather than the size of the state-owned or controlled sector *per se*, 'it is the public sector activities which do not provide marketed outputs that put particular pressure on the resources of the remainder of the economy. . . . (As these rose) from 41.4 per cent of market output in 1961 to 60.3 per cent in 1974 . . . (they reduced) by nearly one-third the proportion of output that market-sector producers (state or privately owned) could themselves invest and consume.'[2] In the remainder of this book we will be concerned with markets and buyers and sellers, whether state, government, private firms, co-operatives or individuals. We will not be examining the effect of state activities outside the market-place except as they impinge directly on voluntary trading behaviour.

Production

The *product transformation curve* (which shows a firm's potential output combinations) highlights the problem of scarcity. The curve is also applicable to a society and is then usually called a *production possibility frontier*.

We will explain the concept of the product transformation curve by an example (see figure 2.1). Consider a vehicle manufacturing firm which, if operating at full capacity, can only produce at points *A*, *B*, *C*, *D* or *E* in a given period. At *A* it could produce 1000 of the 1.5 litre cars but no 1 litre vehicles in the period. Its manpower and machinery would be fully utilized. At *E*, full utilization results in 1250 of the 1 litre cars being produced but no 1.5 litre cars. At points *B*, *C* and *D* different output combinations of the two types of car are possible. But, because of technological 'lumpiness' in the equipment available to the firm it cannot move smoothly from *A* to any point before *B*. It must switch an entire group of machines over from 1.5 litre to 1.0 litre vehicles in order to operate efficiently. (A moment of thought will establish the intuitive truth of this. It would be extremely costly to switch frequently the programming of metal cutting, boring, stamping and die-casting machines from one size of car component to another.)

The curve is concave to the origin because of the *law of increasing cost* (strictly, we refer here to 'opportunity' cost, which will be discussed on p. 15 below). This law operates in the presence of heterogeneous inputs. This

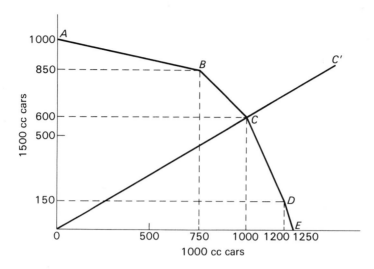

Figure 2.1 *A product transformation curve for a vehicle manufacturer*

simply means that some machinery and men are better equipped or skilled to produce larger cars and vice versa. Thus to move from *A* to *B* the firm must forfeit the opportunity of producing 150 of the 1.5 litre cars in order to gain 750 of the 1.0 litre cars. Each 1 litre car 'costs' the firm 150/750 = 0.2 of the 1.5 litre cars in forgone production. On the other hand, if the firm moves from *C* to *D* it reduces 1.5 litre production by 450 cars and increases 1 litre production by 200 vehicles. Each 1 litre car 'costs' 2.25 of the 1.5 litre cars; there is a substantial cost increase from 0.2 to 2.25. The reason, of course, is that those (differently skilled) men and (differently designed) machines which are best suited to small-car production are transferred first (the *A* to *B* shift) and the least suitable (but most suitable for large-car production) are transferred last (the *C* to *D* shift).

Where on the product transformation curve the firm will choose to produce depends not only on the curve itself, which illustrates costs, but also on the sales revenue the firm can expect to obtain, which determines profits. Later we will see it is also possible to produce combinations other than *A, B, C, D* or *E within* the curve. For the moment, we will restrict ourselves to noting that any point *outside* the curve is technologically impossible. *Within* the curve, given our current assumptions, any point on a ray such as *OC′* implies that the firm is working below full capacity, and doing so with a total car output mix in the ratio of 6 large to 10 small cars.

Exchange

Consumers and producers who enter into voluntary trades act in accordance with seven postulates:[3]

1   For each person some good is scarce.
2   Each person wants more than one good; so given scarcity, choice, competition and discrimination are necessary.
3   Each person is willing to give up some, not necessarily all, of one good to get more (provided that that 'more' is enough) of another. The smallest amount a person would insist on getting of, say, ale to induce him to give up one cake is called the *marginal utility* of that cake measured in ale. It is also the largest amount of ale the other party to the trade would be willing to forfeit to receive one cake.
4   The more a person has of any good, the less valuable is its marginal utility. One glass of ale will quench a thirst. A second will be simply enjoyable. A third may make the drinker feel uncomfortable, and so on. Marginal utility is said to diminish. The reductions in such marginal utility of the cakes and ale are not intrinsic or related to production costs in any way. It may take the same amount of labour to make any one mud cake as it does any one fruit cake. But this is irrelevant in fixing the price at which either type of cake is traded with another person (as under postulate 3). That depends on subjective and *marginal valuations* of the cake in terms of other goods such as ale. Note also that it is the marginal unit which matters to the consumer, not the totality of units.
5   People differ in their tastes and preferences.
6   People are innovative and rational and will try to improve their position by, for example, production and exchange.
7   Decisions taken on the basis of the above postulates may eventually be regretted, or the satisfaction gained may be more than anticipated. No one has perfect knowledge of the future.

Voluntary trade occurs according to these postulates not because people have surpluses to requirements but because people have differing marginal valuations for what they exchange. For example, in figure 2.2 Fred puts a higher marginal value on a pack of butter than does Joe (12 pints of beer against 6) at the initial endowment points of E_F and E_J (12 and 6 pints of beer respectively, and 20 packets of butter each). So mutually advantageous opportunities for trade exist.

Butter will be sold to Fred by Joe until Fred's marginal utility has declined to that of Joe's. Fred values a pack of butter at 12 pints of beer and will gladly buy an extra pack at any price below 12 pints. Joe values butter at 6 pints of beer and will gladly sell a pack for any price above 6 pints. Say Joe and Fred decide to trade at a price of 8 pints of beer. Fred will buy 4 extra packs of butter worth respectively 11, 10, 9 and 8 pints of beer to him, so increasing

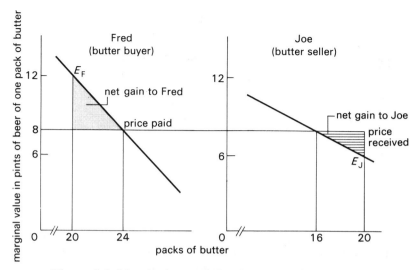

Figure 2.2 *Marginal personal value curves in mutually advantageous trading*

his stock of butter to 24 packs. Joe will sell 4 packs, reducing his stock to 16. He will receive 8 pints of beer for each pack, although they were worth respectively 6.5, 7, 7.5 and 8 pints to him.

In short, Joe will get more beer (as valued by him) than his butter is worth (to him) and Fred will get more butter (as valued by him) than his beer is worth (to him). Both will benefit by an amount equal to the shaded triangles of the diagram. Trade will have benefited both just as if there had been a magical increase in the quantity of beer. Trade is as 'productive' as is manufacture.

The trading continues until both have the same marginal utilities, when no further gains from exchange are possible. Both place the same marginal value on a pack of butter. This can be seen more clearly if Joe's diagram is flipped over 180° from right to left and superimposed on Fred's in such a way that the total length of the base is the total availability of butter (40 packs) (figure 2.3). It is now easy to see that originally Fred's marginal valuation of butter is higher than Joe's and trading continues until they are equal. The intersection point, at a price of 8 pints of beer, is obviously the *point of maximum benefit*. To the left, the gains from trade are not exhausted. To the right, both Joe and Fred are providing each other with commodities they value less than what they are acquiring. (Joe, for example, gives up a pack of butter for 8 pints of beer, but actually values his 15th pack of butter at 8.5 pints; Fred pays 8 pints for a pack of butter but only values his 25th pack at 7 pints).

These marginal value lines can be regarded as *demand curves* (i.e., lines connecting points which show how much beer Fred is willing to give up to

Setting the Scene

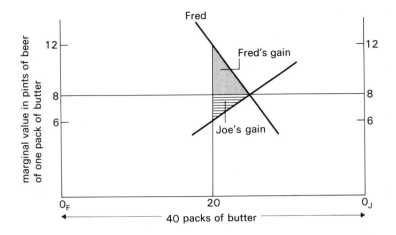

Figure 2.3 *Maximum benefit point and triangles of surplus in mutually advantageous trading*

obtain each unit of the corresponding quantity of butter). In figure 2.3, Joe's demand curve is simply reinterpreted as the *supply curve* of butter to Fred (i.e., a line connecting points which show how much beer Joe must receive to provide each unit of the corresponding quantity of butter).

In conventional textbook analysis, Fred's net gain would then be defined as the *consumer surplus* triangle (i.e., the value from trading obtained over and above what he had paid for the goods). Joe's gain in figure 2.3 would then be *producer surplus*, or *profit* (see later in this chapter). If we now add every individual's demand and supply curves for butter we obtain the *market demand and supply schedules* (figure 2.4). Because barter of butter for beer is inconvenient, time-consuming and unrealistic, the vertical axis is expressed in monetary units.

The demand curve slopes down, other things being equal, because more people will buy at a lower price and also existing buyers will buy more. At a lower price, individuals will substitute butter for other goods, such as margarine, cheese and so on. The supply curve slopes up, other things being equal, because more people will sell butter at higher prices and existing sellers will sell more. At a higher price producers will substitute butter production for other activities such as beef production. The increased real price for butter (provided it is high enough) will encourage this substitution despite the presence and operation of either the law of diminishing returns (see chapter 4) or the law of increasing costs (see p. 8).

The point P_3 in figure 2.4 indicates a position where the price is so high that there is a surplus of *AB* units of butter. At that price sellers will lower their prices to get rid of inventories; some sellers will then drop out of the market, and additional buyers will be attracted in. This process will continue until *equilibrium* is reached at *E*, price P_1. This is called equilibrium since

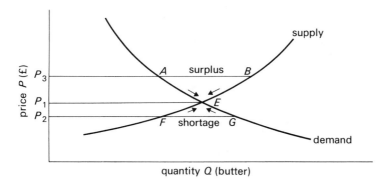

Figure 2.4 *Marked demand and supply schedules*

below that level, at P_2, a corresponding shortage of *FG* would exist. The low price is encouraging high consumption but low production. Unsatisfied purchasers will start bidding prices up, some buyers will drop out of the market and the higher prices will encourage suppliers to increase their quantity supplied until equilibrium is again achieved.

It takes little additional thought to imagine what happens in markets where governments impose price floors of, say, P_3 as with equal-wage legislation, or price ceilings of, say, P_2 as with the rented housing market.

Note that the *P* on the vertical axis of figure 2.4 is relative price, not absolute cash price. That is, the nature of the trade-off must not be forgotten because money is being used. Thus *P* is not cash *P*, but rather cash *P* divided by some sort of average price for all other goods in the economy, as for example, the retail price index (RPI). For reasons of both convention and ease we will simply label the vertical axis *P*, not *P*/RPI which would be both more correct and more meaningful.

This mechanism of voluntary exchange co-ordinates the activities of millions of businesses and even larger numbers of consumers throughout the world. It does so via the presence of differing marginal valuations of products by buyers and sellers. In short, the driving force is the presence of *price differentials*. In a market economy (as opposed to a totally centrally planned *command* society) these price differentials and their movements perform three functions.[4]

First, they transmit information inducing suppliers to produce more (or less) of those items of which there is a shortage (or surplus). Prices do this efficiently since only the information which is important is sent, and only to those who are interested (namely the suppliers of the items, the suppliers of substitutes, the purchasers of the items or the purchasers of substitutes). Traders do not need to know why the price has changed; there could be an infinite number of possible reasons. They only need to know that prices have changed and in which direction. They will then act accordingly.

Second, the information that prices transmit acts as an incentive to producers or to users not only to act but to act efficiently. They will, in order to maximize consumers' surplus or profit, use available resources for their most highly valued uses. If a raw material price rises, manufacturers will be stimulated to economize on the use of that raw material. They will have an incentive to introduce new and less expensive methods of production. If prices rise, consumers will attempt to shift to other patterns of want satisfaction. If they remain high, resources will move into production of the highly priced (i.e. highly valued) commodity. Wages will tend to rise and workers will transfer into that industry whose final product's (higher) price has brought this about.

Third, and this is closely related to the second point, the distribution of income will be affected. Workers and firms in industries producing relatively highly valued goods will earn greater wages and profits than labour and capital elsewhere. Admittedly this is not nirvana. All of us would like to earn the income of Sophia Loren or a diver on a North Sea oil rig. But few of us have Miss Loren's beauty or the courage and strength of a diver. In short, supply is limited but demand is relatively high. But would an oil-rig diver risk his life if the rewards were lower? Probably not. The only alternative, as we said earlier, is to answer the questions, 'what?', 'how?' and 'for whom?', not by voluntary exchange but by coercion.

Business Objectives

The most obvious objective of business is to maximize profit. Whether this is an end in itself, as the bold statement suggests, or whether profit is a measure of how successful the firm has been in attaining some other objective, is another matter. Peter Drucker, in his book *Practice of Management*, argues that 'there is only one valid definition of business purpose: to create a customer.'[5] If a business does not produce what the market wants, it will cease to exist.

Profits, then, are the results of being in business. They test how efficiently a business has 'created a customer' (a topic discussed more fully in chapter 13). All athletes have the sole objective of winning, but different runners aim to run the 100 metres, the 200 metres or the 1500 metres as fast as possible; coming first is the common yardstick of success even though the secondary objectives (the distances) vary. So, in business, the common yardstick of success is profit. The secondary objective is to meet market demand in the firm's selected industry or industries.

What is profit? It is, to the accountant, the difference between sales revenues and costs. But the definition of 'costs' can cause considerable problems. In a profit-and-loss account (see chapter 9) the bookkeeper will deduct wages, raw material costs, rent, fuel costs and so on before arriving at some net figure termed 'profit'. This 'profit' or surplus, belongs to the shareholders who provided the capital in the first place. The economist would claim, however, that only part of this surplus should be regarded as profit. He would claim that the shareholder's capital, had it not been put into the business, could easily have earned interest as a straightforward risk-free loan to, say, a bank. This interest should be imputed and deducted from the accountant's surplus to give the 'true' profit (or loss).

In short, what the provider of capital would have earned anyway, without incurring any of the risks or uncertainties of business investment, should not be included as business or *economic profit*. What would have been earned anyway is the *opportunity cost* of the capital involved.

This then gives us the first hint as to how economists view profits. They not only reward efficiency in meeting market demand, but also recompense businessmen and shareholders for the assumption of *risk* (see chapters 5 and 9). No firm operates in a sure market. The fruit dealer who buys green-groceries early in the morning must resell the same day or his stock will become inedible. He assumes the risk, for example, that rain will not keep his customers indoors and so leave him with unsold produce. The pharmaceutical firm which engages in research to produce a new drug can spend millions of pounds over ten or more years and finally discover that its new product has an unexpected side-effect and so cannot be marketed (as did Fisons Ltd in 1981 with proxicromil).

Thus the theory of profit as a reward for risk also merges into the theory of profit as a reward for innovation—for being the first to introduce a new product or a new, lower-cost process. In such a case, until other firms imitate the innovator, the entrepreneurial firm will earn a profit above those of its competitors. It will have a temporary monopoly until the forces of competition drive down prices and, in the colourful language of Joseph Schumpeter, the 'perennial gale of creative destruction' (i.e., competition from further innovations and imitations) washes away the monopoly profits.

These, then, are some of the theories of the nature of profit. Are they valid? Do businesses maximize profit for these reasons? Indeed, can or should businessmen maximize profits?

In recent years the professional economics literature has been full of articles on why businessmen either do not or should not maximize the profits of their firms. Whether they do is a matter of fact. Whether they should is one of opinion or of judgement. If managers do not maximize profits, even if they wish to, the reasons generally given are that they either cannot (because they do not know how) or they will not (because they prefer to strive for other objectives). If we examine these claims we may be able to judge whether profit maximization is a business goal.

Can business maximize profits?

The earliest attack on the conventional notion of the profit-maximizing businessman came from two Oxford economists, Hall and Hitch, in 1939.[6] They argued, from questionnaire evidence, that managers simply do not have the information to follow profit-maximizing price policies, and that they will accordingly use rule-of-thumb techniques such as the *cost-plus principle* (see chapter 8) to arrive at the price they will charge. In other words, they will not follow the rules of calculus, found in most economics textbooks, to set a price.

But this is not surprising! Businessmen can be successful profit maximizers without either understanding calculus or reading economics primers which purport to predict or explain their behaviour. In everyday life, businessmen make profits because they supply what consumers—you and I—want at prices we are prepared to pay. Businessmen make profits because they understand the market for their products. If they do not, they make losses. Knowledge of the calculus of economics texts is often irrelevant to them. Moreover, since firms produce today for sale tomorrow, it is the knowledge of tomorrow's market which is important to them, not economic theory about today's or yesterday's market data. Tomorrow's market knowledge is entrepreneurial foresight and is available only to those who are alert to the possibility of its existence. Most economists, calculus experts or not, do not even realize that we do not know what information the successful entrepreneur is acting upon.

This type of argument, advanced first by Ludwig von Mises[7] of Austria and latterly by Israel Kirzner,[8] did not quell the enthusiasm of the members of the 'cost-plus' school. Businessmen, they said, were self-confessedly ignorant of their situation. Their admission, in answer to the Oxford questionnaires, of ignorance about the future merely heightened the ardour of the 'they-cannot-maximize-profit' school. Some people might continue to argue that foresight was essential, but businessmen had admitted that they priced on a cost-plus-profit-margin basis.

In 1959, Herbert Simon developed a sophisticated version of this view. He alleged that businessmen operated under conditions of 'bounded rationality' (partial ignorance) and hence 'satisficed' (aimed for a satisfactory profit) and so did not maximize.

Businessmen, of course, had no more read Simon[9] or Mises than they had read or remembered their 'conventional' economics textbooks. It was left to Machlup,[10] of Princeton, to resolve the dilemma. Businessmen, he argued in 1967, could maximize profits *without* full information. Any margin over their accounting costs which they charged was not fixed but varied according to their assessment of the market. In short (successful) businessmen have an intuitive understanding of how to maximize profit even though they cannot articulate it into economists' verbal or mathematical jargon: 'all the relevant magnitudes involved—costs, revenue, profit—are subjective, that is perceived or fancied by the men whose decisions are to be explained.'

But, said the sceptics, are modern business firms not so large that they have a multiplicity of interests and of competing managers? Do not these individuals in turn have differing personal goals? The 'organizational coalition' which emerges not only results in each manager receiving some adequate personal pecuniary or non-pecuniary satisfaction but also, in turn, forces the firm into a non-profit-maximizing position. Machlup pushed this idea tidily to one side when he compared the entrepreneur, or chief decision-maker in the firm, with a car driver. When a lorry has to be overtaken the car driver neither carries out detailed mathematical calculations nor sits down to argue out the pros and cons of how to do it with his fellow passengers. He can successfully solve the problem of how to overtake the truck subjectively and intuitively because he knows how. So the entrepreneur can maximize profits because he knows how. The unsuccessful driver who does not know how will crash. The unsuccessful businessman will make losses.

Does business maximize profits?

The car, of course, can safely pass the lorry in a better or a worse fashion. Can the businessman make profits, not losses, without maximizing profits? Yes, he can, according to many economists. He can maximize his sales, his rate of growth, his perquisites—provided only that he makes 'sufficient' profits.

But the word 'sufficient' gives the game away: 'sufficient' for what? Firms, these writers argue, must avoid take-over. Their profits must be adequate to keep share prices high enough to discourage a take-over bid. If they are not, they will be bought by others with different objectives—for example, the maximization of profits.

Professor Henry Manne[11] argued, in 1965, that incumbent managers will not long be able to depress profits even if they choose. Only a small number of shares must change hands for effective control of even a very large firm to pass to a new owner. He will purchase this control if, in his subjective view, he can get a larger return on the shares than can existing holders. He will believe this to be so if the shares are priced below that price which would reflect the profit-maximizing level of output. Certainly, the use of the Stock Exchange involves costs of brokerage and the like, and this may deter potential purchasers of shares priced low because assets are under-utilized (in the sense of profit maximization). But such *transaction costs* (chapter 13) exist everywhere in real life and must be accepted not as proof that businessmen do not maximize profits but rather as proof that their scope for not doing so is strictly limited.

Yet, this side of the grave, nirvana can only be approached, not attained. One way to minimize the motivation of managers not to maximize profits is, of course, to remunerate them, at least partially, with stock options. Their personal income (and hence motivation) will then depend on the performance of the company's shares and, in turn, on its profitability.

Should business maximize profits?

Firms, say many people, have a duty to be 'socially responsible'. They should spend their profits on anti-pollution devices, safety-improving features, 'preserving jobs', the arts or technology. Alternatively they should reduce their profits by being 'patriotic' and buy from high-cost domestic firms rather than low-cost overseas ones. Or, vice versa, profits should be passed up by refusing to sell to customers from nations whose political regimes we do not like, in favour of customers from countries with whose policies we agree.

Some or all of these goals may be laudable, but they can be achieved (if desired) by legislation which treats each firm equally without fear or favour. This is, presumably, what Milton Friedman has in mind when he says that the 'one, and only one, social responsibility of business . . . (is) to increase its profits so long as it stays within the rules of the game.'[12] He goes on: 'Few trends could so thoroughly undermine the very foundations of our free society as the acceptance by corporate officials of a social responsibility other than to make as much money for their stockholders as possible'.

Why does Friedman take this stance? Is it because businessmen would cease to direct their endeavours according to the price signals of the profit-oriented market mechanism? Prices convey messages to entrepreneurs of what is in short supply and what in surplus. If entrepreneurs interpret the price signals correctly, they make profits until prices are driven down. Forgoing the reward of maximum profits might mean taking business decisions based on other criteria. This, in turn, would mean departing from the system which has made free-enterprise economies the wealthiest in history. And this wealth has always percolated all through such societies and makes the wealthy 'mixed economy' possible. Compared with those in Britain in 1900, it is arguable that no 'average working man' had ever been better fed, housed, educated, enjoyed a higher quality of health or longer life expectancy anywhere else in the world or at any other time in human history. This could also be said in 1980 of relatively free-enterprise America.

No. Material welfare alone is not the reason for Friedman's view. Even if men were materially worse off under capitalism, one suspects he would still hold it. Mises argued that not only does equal treatment under the law maximize each individual's productivity and so his private interests; it also promotes 'the maintenance of social peace' if class privileges disappear and so 'conflict over them . . . cease(s)'.

Even more appositely from the viewpoint of the firm, any failure to maximize profit is the equivalent of taxing the shareholder. The use of the profit cushion to fund managerial objectives of any sort other than that which the shareholder, as an individual, would approve of if he had his own money in his own pocket to dispose of, is the equivalent of allowing A to spend B's money on B's behalf! This is a privilege generally allowed only to parents and governments.

References

1 A. Smith, *The Wealth of Nations* (1776), book 4, chapter 8, Penguin, 1970, p. 516.
2 R. Bacon and W. Ellis, 'How growth in public expenditure has contributed to Britain's difficulties', in *The Dilemmas of Government Expenditure*, IEA Readings 15, Institute of Economic Affairs, 1976, p. 4.
3 This section is adapted from A.A. Alahian and W.R. Allen, *University Economics*, Wadsworth, 1977.
4 M. Friedman, *Free to Choose*, Pelican, 1980, pp. 33–44.
5 P. Drucker, *Practice of Management*, Pan, 1968.
6 R.C. Hall and C.J. Hitch, 'Price theory and business behaviour', *Oxford Economic Papers* 2 (1939), pp. 21–39.
7 L. von Mises, *Human Action*, Henry Regnery, 1963.
8 I. Kirzner, *Competition and Entrepreneurship*, University of Chicago Press, 1971.
9 H.A. Simon, 'Rationality as process and as product of thought', *American Economic Review* 87 (1978), pp. 1–29.
10 F. Machlup, 'Theories of the firm: marginalist, behavioural, managerial', *American Economic Review* 77 (1967), pp. 1–33.
11 H.G. Manne, 'Mergers and the market for corporate control', *Journal of Political Economy* 81 (1965), pp. 110–20.
12 M. Friedman, *Capitalism and Freedom*, University of Chicago Press, 1962.

3

Prices and Demand

Although modern understanding of the role of prices and markets has its ancestry, not surprisingly, in the work of many great economists, not least Adam Smith, it bears strong impressions of the work of Marshall.[1] We shall return, therefore, to Marshall's timeless reminder: 'The laws of economics are to be compared with the laws of the tides, rather than with the simple and exact law of gravitation. For the actions of men are so various and uncertain, that the best statement of tendencies which we can make in a science of human conduct must needs be inexact and faulty.'[2]

We need to bear these warnings in mind as we analyse the workings of prices and markets in this chapter. In many senses, price theory is central to the understanding of economic problems. We saw in chapter 2 that the basis of the economic problem is the choice between alternatives, and to solve this choice the following are needed: a preference scale which guides the act of choice; a knowledge of the terms on which alternatives are available; and an understanding of the volume of scarce resources available. Given this information, the problem of 'the scarcity of given means for the attainment of given ends', as Robbins pithily put it, can be solved.[3] Within the mixed economy the price system has a major role to play in providing a solution via the 'higgling and bargaining' of the market-place.

The term *market* is to be interpreted in a broad sense as referring to any mechanism by which the buyers and sellers of a particular *commodity* are brought into contact. It might be a public place, such as the market for vegetable produce in a local area, or it might be the linkage of dealers in commodities such as Stock Exchange securities, money market instruments, precious metals and the like; such linkages, given the advantages of modern communications, frequently stretch around the world. As long as the prices of the same 'goods' tend to equality quickly, and reflect the forces of supply and demand across the market, then the market functions effectively, no matter what the extent of its physical scope.

The Determinants of Demand

At any particular time the demand for a particular good or service by an individual economic agent—be it a consumer, firm, or household—is likely to be determined by the complex interaction of a number of factors. These are likely to include: the price of the good itself, the prices of other goods, the size of the consumer's income, and the nature of his or her taste. These are expressed in the following formulation:

$$Q^D_{i,k} = F(P_i, P_j, Y_k, T_k) \tag{3.1}$$

Where $Q^D_{i,k}$ is the quantity demanded of good i by consumer k, P_i is the price of good i, P_j is the price of good j, Y_k is the income of consumer k, and T_k is the taste of consumer k.

The problems arise from the difficulty of simultaneously handling the impact of these factors. The normal practice is to isolate the impact of one whilst assuming that the effects of the others are constant—the economist's famous 'other things being equal' or *ceteris paribus* clause—and to continue in this fashion, examining the influence of each in turn.

If we start first with the price of the good, it is probable that, if requested, a consumer could construct a schedule showing how the quantity he would demand of the good would alter as a function of its price, assuming that all the other factors remained constant. In table 3.1 we have constructed a hypothetical individual's demand schedule for apples over a period of a month. It is important to remember that demand is a flow, and measures continuous purchases over a period rather than isolated ones.

Table 3.1 *An individual's monthly demand schedule for apples*

Price of apples (pence per kg)	Quantity consumed (kg per month)
175	0
150	0.5
125	1.0
100	1.5
75	2.0
50	2.5
25	3.0
20	3.5
15	4.0

The First Law of Demand

The normal pattern we woud expect is that the quantity demanded of a good is inversely related to its price; the higher the price the lower the quantity demanded, as shown in figure 3.1. If we added together the individual demand schedule for all the consumers who purchase apples in a particular market, we would have the market demand schedule, and it, too, would display the similar property of sloping downwards from left to right. This is sometimes referred to as the *first law of demand*. It has to be borne in mind that we are concerned here with effective demand, i.e. preferences backed up by purchasing power. Many of us might like to drive round in a Rolls-Royce but not many of us are effectively in the market for Rolls-Royces.

To return to Marshall's caution about the nature of economic 'laws', do demand curves always slope downwards? Liebenstein has demonstrated that this boils down to a basic question about the additive properties of individual demand schedules.[4]

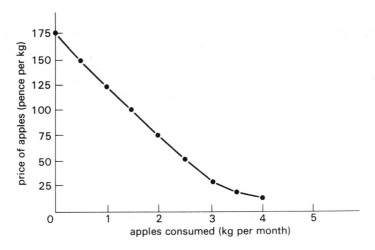

Figure 3.1 *An individual's monthly demand curve for apples*

The additive properties of individual demand schedules

The usual assumption is that individual demand curves can be horizontally summed to produce a market demand curve for the good concerned. This approach assumes that each consumer's satisfaction associated with the consumption of the good is completely independent of the number of other consumers purchasing the same good. Liebenstein terms this approach a functional view of demand, which interprets demand as being based upon qualities inherent in the commodity itself.[5] But what if there are external or non-functional effects? He suggests the following have an impact on utility: (a) the bandwagon effect, (b) the snob effect, and (c) the Veblen effect.

Liebenstein's reservations

The bandwagon effect

The bandwagon effect refers to the extent to which the demand for a commodity is increased because other people are purchasing the same good. It represents the desire to be fashionable. Given this assumption, each individual consumer's demand schedule is likely to be influenced by the level of overall demand in the market. We could analyse this by drawing up such individual demand curves under the assumption that each person thinks that the market demand will be at a given level. The summing of all these demand schedules in the usual fashion gives us a market demand such as curve D_a in figure 3.2. D_a is drawn on the consumer's assumption that market demand wil be OA. On the other hand, if consumers assume market demand to be OB, then D_b is the outcome. And, likewise, D_n is the sum of the individual curves when consumers assume a market demand of ON.

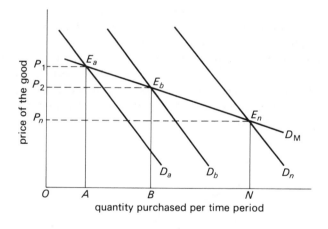

Figure 3.2 *The bandwagon effect*

If consumers are right in their expectation that OA will be the level of market demand, then the price in the market would be P_1 at point E_a. Curve D_a then traces out demand at various market prices, given that assumption. But if market demand turns out to be, say, OB, then as soon as consumers realize this they will start operating on demand curve D_b since this is consistent with the view that overall demand is OB. Again, if they are correct in this, there is only one price which is consistent with demand curve D_b and a level of market demand OB and that is price P_2. Given knowledge of market demand, one point only on each of these 'demand curves' is operative, and a line joining these unique points, marked D_M, traces out the true market demand curve taking into account the bandwagon effect.

The effect in this case leads to a market demand curve which is much more responsive to changes in price (i.e. is more elastic; see later in this chapter) than the simple adding of individuals' demand schedules would suggest.

The snob effect

The snob effect can be seen as the reverse of the bandwagon effect. Once again we assume that the demand schedule of an individual consumer is influenced both by the price of the good and by his estimate of the size of the overall market demand. But in this case the relationship between the size of the market and the quantity demanded is reversed. The snob prefers exclusivity and hence the larger the estimated size of the market the less inclined he is to buy. The analysis proceeds exactly as before. It is assumed that it is possible to draw up an individual's demand schedule on the basis that market demand is expected to be at a particular level, and that all such individual curves can be summed to produce a market demand curve. Thus D_a in figure 3.3 represents the market demand for the good given the consumer's expectation that the overall market size is OA, and so on, as previously. Once again only one price is consistent with curves D_a, D_b and D_n respectively. This is so since consumers switch to the relevant alternative demand curve once they realize that market size is different from either OA, OB or ON. The only difference from the bandwagon effect is that, as the level of market size increases, the true market demand schedule falls more rapidly, at all prices, as some snobs drop out of the market which they regard as becoming less exclusive.

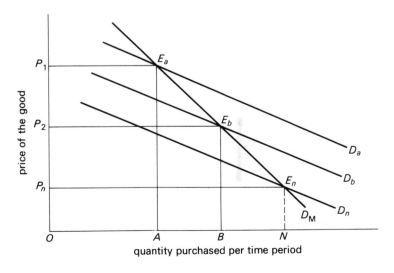

Figure 3.3 *The snob effect*

Once again Liebenstein concludes that simply adding individual demand schedules, ignoring what he calls external effects, leads to an inaccurate estimation of demand and, in this case, demand is less responsive (i.e. less elastic; see later in this chapter) to a price change than otherwise would be predicted.

The Veblen effect

Finally Liebenstein describes the Veblen effect, which is based upon Veblen's theory of conspicuous consumption.[6] Here we distinguish between the good's functional utility and the utility attached to its price; the latter may be considered the conspicuous consumption element. It is this conspicuous component of price which allegedly matters; it is assumed that the higher the conspicuous price the more other people are impressed, and so the greater the satisfaction of the purchaser.

Each consumer has a demand schedule. On the basis of expected conspicuousness of price, prices could be termed P_1, P_2 and P_n, and these curves can be aggregated to produce market demand curves D_1, D_2, and D_n, depending on the conspicuous price. Again, only one point on these aggregated demand curves is relevant, as shown in figure 3.4. If consumers expect the conspicuous price to be P_1, the demand curve will be D_1, but if it turns out to be P_2, they will move up to operate on demand curve D_2, and so on. If conspicuous consumption is an important determinant of demand for the good, the higher the conspicuous price the higher the demand at all price levels. A line can then be drawn through the expected conspicuous price level of each of these demand curves and this produces the 'true' demand curve D_V. The remarkable feature of this demand curve is that it is upward sloping.

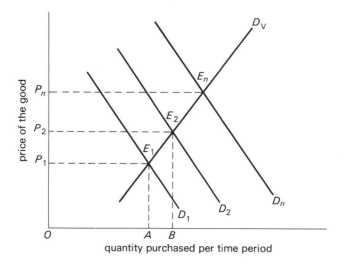

Figure 3.4 *The Veblen effect*

This suggests that an upward-sloping demand curve is conceivable, at least for certain ranges of prices on certain luxury goods. If the price of the good is reduced sufficiently we might expect more normal consumers to enter the market; they will not be concerned with conspicuous effects, the Veblen effect will be reduced to zero, and the customary downward-sloping demand curve will emerge.

Does the 'first law of demand' hold?

We have seen that, in certain circumstances, demand curves might indeed slope upwards, that adding individual demand schedules does not necessarily lead to a clear picture of market demand if there are external effects. It is also conceivable that all these external effects might be simultaneously operating and, to a certain extent, counterbalancing. However, these effects explicitly occur only when other things are not equal, so the first law of demand still holds.

It is true also that short-term speculative effects might lead to a temporary increase in quantity demanded, as people lay in stocks in anticipation of a price rise (the useful role of speculators is dealt with more fully in chapter 7). Even here, however, the first law is not violated, since people are buying more today at a lower price than tomorrow's price is expected to be. We are forced into considering again Marshall's previously quoted analogy of economic laws and the tides. Demand curves usually slope downwards and our customary analysis usually holds, although, like the phases of the moon, markets vary and our analysis will have greater or less force. What is critical is to ensure that the conditions required are met. Thus the market response to a drop in price, other things being equal, is an increase in quantity demanded. The responsiveness of quantity demanded to changes in price is termed the *price elasticity of demand* (see later in this chapter).

Utility and the Theory of Demand

Much of the early work on price theory centred on the use of utility theory. Smith, in his famous water/diamond paradox, pointed out the difference between value in use and value in exchange: 'Nothing is more useful than water: but it will purchase scarce anything, scarce anything can be had in exchange for it. A diamond, on the contrary, has scarce any value in use; but a very great quantity of other goods may frequently be had in exchange for it.'[7] The neoclassicals, then, writing 150 years later, concentrated on the concept of utility as an explanation of the force behind individual consumer demand.

The focus was placed on marginal utility, or the addition to total satisfaction derived from purchasing and consuming an additional unit of a good. The view taken was that 'there is an endless variety of wants but a limit to each separate want', and, thus continued Marshall, 'the total utility of a thing to anyone . . . increases with every increase in his stock of it, but not as fast as his stock increases.'[8]

The basis of the *law of diminishing marginal utility* has already been outlined in the seven postulates on personal utility and valuation discussed in chapter 2.

If we ignore the practical difficulties of measuring utility and make the further assumption that the marginal utility of money is constant, we can shift to thinking in terms of the utility of the last pence spent on purchasing the last unit of a good. If overall satisfaction is to be maximized from the purchase of a bundle or collection of goods in a given period, then it follows that the last pence spent on the purchase of the last unit of any of the goods purchased in the period must yield equal marginal utility. If utilities at the margin are not equal, a rearrangement of the pattern of purchases will increase overall satisfaction. The scope for this will continue until equality is achieved at the margin. Thus we have in equilibrium—when an individual's purchases yield maximum satisfaction—the following condition:

$$\frac{MU_Y}{P_Y} = \frac{MU_Z}{P_Z} = \frac{MU_N}{P_N} \tag{3.2}$$

where MU_Y, MU_Z, MU_N are the marginal utilities of good Y, good Z, good N, etc., and P_Y, P_Z, P_N are the prices of good Y, good Z, good N, etc.

If we concentrate on the equilibrium conditions for two goods, X and Y, we can examine the implications of a change in price of one of the goods. Suppose that initially, at a price of P_{X1} for good X and P_{Y1} for good Y, the equilibrium conditions are met. So we have

$$\frac{MU_Y}{P_{Y1}} = \frac{MU_X}{P_{X1}}.$$

Then the price of good X falls to P_{X2}. If this happens our former equality no longer holds and we have

$$\frac{MU_X}{P_{X2}} > \frac{MU_Y}{P_{Y1}}.$$

Total utility on the part of our consumer can now be increased by rearranging his expenditure pattern. He can now increase purchases of good X so that its marginal utility falls (as we can see from figure 3.5) until it has fallen sufficiently to restore the equality of

$$\frac{MU_X}{P_{X2}} = \frac{MU_Y}{P_{Y1}}.$$

If a fall in the price of good X leads to an increase in the demand for it by an

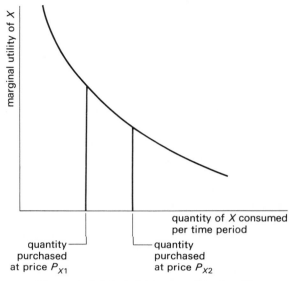

Figure 3.5 *Diminishing marginal utility*

individual consumer, then, other things being equal, it should also hold for all consumers; once again we have established that demand curves slope downwards from left to right. Given that the marginal utility of each extra purchase of good X diminishes, we are led to wonder to what extent the demand for good X increases following a price fall; this leads us back to consideration of the price elasticity of demand.

Price Elasticity of Demand

Price elasticity of demand, usually symbolized by the Greek letter η, is defined as the proportional change in quantity demanded in response to a proportional change in price.

$$\text{price elasticity of demand } (\eta) = \frac{\text{relative change in quantity demanded}}{\text{corresponding relative change in price}}.$$

Symbolically we could define elasticity as follows:

$$\text{elasticity } (\eta) = \frac{\Delta Q/Q}{\Delta P/P} = \frac{\Delta Q}{\Delta P} \frac{P}{Q} \tag{3.3}$$

where Q is quantity, P is price, ΔQ is a small change in quantity purchased, and ΔP is a small change in price.

One of the most convenient properties of this formula is that it is completely independent of the units of measurement adopted, since it is a ratio concerned with proportionate changes. Suppose the price of the good was

Table 3.2 *Market demand schedule for good X*

Price of X (pence)	Quantity of X demanded in market (kg)
100	0
90	100
80	200
70	300
60	400
50	500
40	600
30	700
20	800
10	900
0	1000

initially in pounds; the price change ratio might be, for example, $\Delta P/P = £1/£20$. If we then convert the values to pence, $\Delta P/P = (1 \times 100p)/(20 \times 100p)$; the ratio is unaffected. By similar logic, the unit adopted to measure quantities is immaterial. This is convenient because the price elasticities of any number of products in any price or quantity unit can be directly compared.

Suppose a businessman is selling a product which faces the market demand schedule shown in table 3.2. The graph of this market demand schedule produces the demand curve shown in figure 3.6.

As the relationship between demand for X and its price is a linear one, revealed by the fact that the demand curve in figure 3.6 is a straight line, we

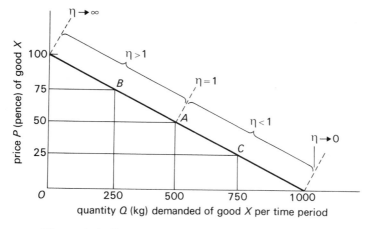

Figure 3.6 *The demand curve for table 3.2, showing elasticity ranges*

could summarize the relationship by writing the appropriate equation:

$$P = 100 - \frac{1}{10}Q. \tag{3.4}$$

In this, admittedly artificial, example we can see that, if nothing is to be demanded, the price will be 100p, and that 1000 kg will be demanded at a zero price. The slope of the demand curve is given by:

$$\text{slope} = \frac{\text{change in price}}{\text{change in quantity}} = -\frac{1}{10}.$$

In this case a fall in price of 1p leads to an increase in demand of 10 kg and so the slope is $-1/10$. The slope is negative since the normal relationship is that a fall in price leads to an increase in the quantity demanded. A straight line has a constant slope which, in this case, can be defined as the ratio $\Delta P/\Delta Q$, the change in price divided by the change in quantity demanded in response to that change in price.

If we return to consideration of the elasticity formula in expression 3.3, we see that this formula uses the inverse of the slope, $\Delta Q/\Delta P$, which in this case is -10. This is a constant, but the other constituents of the elasticity formula, P and Q, are inversely related and their values change as we move up or down the demand curve. From this it follows that elasticity is not a constant but varies as we so move. (This is always the case unless we have a demand curve whose slope changes in such a way that changes in the relative proportions of P and Q exactly offset each other.)

Suppose we wish to calculate the price elasticity of demand at point A on the demand curve in figure 3.6; in this case $P = 50$ and $Q = 500$. Reference to our price elasticity formula gives:

$$\eta_A = \frac{\Delta Q}{\Delta P} \frac{P}{Q} = -10\frac{50}{500} = -1.$$

At point A we see that price elasticity of demand is unitary, i.e. equal to $(-)1$. (The usual convention is to ignore the minus sign; price elasticity of demand is generally negative, given that the quantity demanded is inversely related to price.)

Let us now move to point B, where $P = 75$ and $Q = 250$. Elasticity at this point is:

$$\eta_B = -10\frac{75}{250} = (-)3.$$

Demand at any price elasticity value greater than 1 is referred to as elastic; in fact, all points to the left of A moving up the demand curve would have progressively greater elasticities and elasticity would approach infinity at the top of the demand curve.

Finally we can calculate the price elasticity of demand at point *C*:

$$\eta_C = -10\frac{25}{750} = (-)\frac{1}{3}.$$

At point *C* demand is inelastic, having a value of 1/3. Demand at any elasticity less than 1 is regarded as being inelastic, and as we move down a linear demand curve, to the right of point *A*, elasticity continually diminishes until it approaches zero at the bottom of the curve.

Well, where does all this get us? The point is that price elasticity of demand has important implications for the changes in revenue that a businessman can expect from revising his prices. The demand curve is often termed the *average revenue curve*, since it depicts the price of the good or average revenue per number of units sold that he can expect from placing a given number of units on the market. Total sales revenue is given by price × the number of units sold at that price. If we return to figure 3.6, we can see that, at point *B*, price *P* = 75p and quantity sold *Q* = 250 kg. Total revenue is given by *P* × *Q* = 250 × 75 = £187.50. Total revenue is shown by the rectangle under the demand curve, with its corner touching at point *B*, linking the price of 75p with the quantity demanded of 250 kg.

Suppose now that our businessman has decided to drop the price to 50p but wonders what the effect on total revenue will be. Total revenue now equals 50p × 500 = £250. Total revenue has increased, and in fact at point *A*, where η = 1, it is maximized. This makes sense when we pause to consider the definition of elasticity; it measures the proportionate response in quantity demanded to the corresponding relative change in price. If price elasticity is greater than 1 there will be a more than proportionate response in the quantity demanded. Thus as long as $\eta > 1$, a price cut will increase total revenue. Where η = 1 total revenue is maximized, and any further price cutting when $\eta < 1$ will only serve to reduce total revenue. Indeed, in figure 3.6 we can see that at point *C*, where price has been reduced to 25p, total revenue falls back to £187.5.

It would not be sensible for a profit-maximizing businessman to lower his prices if he is operating in the inelastic range of his demand curve. Some products, such as necessities, will have relatively inelastic demand since they have to be bought whatever the price. Luxury items will have a more elastic demand and so the market will be more price sensitive. Relatively inexpensive products tend to have inelastic demand: if there is a price rise, it is not worth going to the trouble of finding an alternative; (if the price of household salt doubled, this would probably not have a very significant effect on quantity demanded.) Various extreme examples of demand curves of varying elasticity are shown in figure 3.7.

Prices and Demand

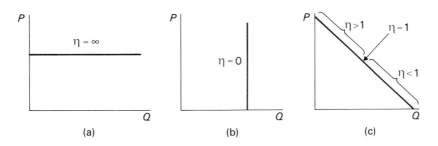

Figure 3.7 *Demand curves of varying elasticity (a) completely elastic (b) completely inelastic (c) varying elasticity (normal case)*

The Second Law of Demand

It is generally accepted that the price elasticity of demand for any product is likely to increase with the time for which a price change persists. There are various reasons why this is likely to be the case. Many purchases are customary or habitual. Consumers have to adjust their spending patterns following a price change, and there will be a certain amount of inertia before they get round to reappraising the relative merits of the various commodities available in the light of the price change. Time is not a free good and there is an opportunity cost for the time spent on seeking market intelligence in terms of the other productive ways in which that time could be spent. Furthermore, markets are imperfect in the sense that information regarding price cuts is not instantaneously available to all, so there will be a lag before the price information seeps through to all potential customers.

A further impact is made by technological considerations. The demand for many products is a derived demand. We do not demand electricity for its own intrinsic merits but for the use to which it can be put in powering electric lights, hi-fi systems, heating appliances etc. There would be a considerable lag before a fall in electricity prices leads to increased consumption via the purchase of electrical central heating, new hi-fi systems and the like.

The *second law of demand* states that price elasticity of demand is likely to be greater in the long run than in the short run. It suggests that the behaviour of demand curves, other things being equal, is likely to vary over time as shown in figure 3.8.

In this figure the initial point of equilibrium is P_1, Q_1 on the initial demand curve D_a. The immediate response to a drop in price from P_1 to P_2 is an increase in the quantity demanded from Q_1 to Q_a. After a passage of time the market behaves as if it is now operating on demand curve D_b rather than D_a and the quantity demanded rises to Q_b. After a further passage of time the quantity demanded increases to Q_c.

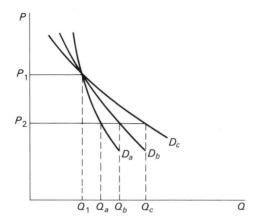

Figure 3.8 *The second law of demand*

We now reconsider our original consumer demand function, expression 3.1. We are reminded that so far we have only explored the impact of the price of the good itself on quantity demanded although, in our treatment of the second law of demand, we moved away from this and examined other long-term effects that actually shift the demand curve. Strictly speaking, changes in the price of the good itself, other things being equal, do not shift the demand curve (in the short term) but lead to movements up or down an existing demand curve. The other factors we shall now consider—the prices of other goods, consumer incomes, and consumer tastes—all lead to shifts in the actual curve itself. We shall first examine the effects of changes in the prices of other goods.

Changes in the Prices of Substitutes and Complements

Changes in the prices of other goods, Y, are likely to have an impact on the quantity demanded of the original good, X, if the other goods are either substitutes or complements. We define X and Y as *substitutes* when an increase in the price of one leads to an increase in the consumption of the other. A typical example would be butter and margarine. On the other hand, some goods—such as petrol and cars—are complements, purchased for joint consumption. We define X and Y as *complements* when an increase in the price of one leads to a decrease in the consumption of the other. An increase in the price of petrol will reduce the demand for cars as more people walk, cycle or use public transport.

The extent to which goods are substitutes or complements can be measured by their *cross-elasticity of demand*, defined as:

$$\text{cross-elasticity of demand} = \frac{\Delta Q_X/Q_X}{\Delta P_Y/P_Y} = \frac{\Delta Q_X}{\Delta P_Y}\frac{P_Y}{Q_X} \qquad (3.5)$$

where ΔQ_X is the change in quantity demanded of good X, Q_X is the original quantity of good X demanded, ΔP_Y is a small change in the price of good Y, and P_Y is the original price of good Y.

Cross-elasticity of demand measures the relative change in quantity demanded of good X in response to a relative change in the price of good Y. Goods which are substitutes will have positive cross-elasticities of demand, since an increase in the price of one will lead to an increase in the quantity demanded of the other. Complements will have a negative cross-elasticity of demand, since an increase in the price of a complement leads to a fall in demand for related goods. If two goods are unrelated, their cross-elasticity will be approximately zero.

Changes in the prices of substitutes can shift the entire market demand curve. An increase in the price of substitutes or a fall in the price of complements should lead to more of the good being demanded at all prices, and therefore the demand curve shifts bodily to the right. This is an increase in demand. A fall in demand would be caused by either a fall in the price of substitutes or a rise in the price of complements. In this case the demand curve would shift bodily to the left.

Changes in Consumer Incomes

The relationship between household expenditure on a good and the level of household income can be illustrated via the use of an Engel curve, shown in figure 3.9. The normal relationship is that increases in income are associated with a rise in expenditure on the good. However, in the case of inferior

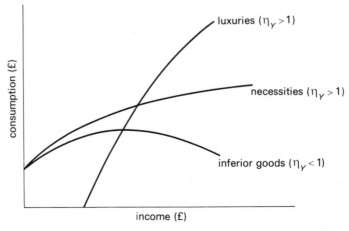

Figure 3.9 *Engel curves for a hypothetical household*

goods, expenditure on the good might fall as income rises. This was pointed out by the Victorian economist Giffen, who argued that the labouring poor in the nineteenth century subsisted on the cheapest diet available—which might consist mainly of bread. A rise in their income would lead not to an increase in consumption of bread but to the substitution of other preferred foods, such as meat, and a reduction in the consumption of bread.

The relationship between changes in income and changes in a consumer's expenditure on a good is measured by the income elasticity of the good η_Y, defined as:

income elasticity (η_Y)

$$= \frac{\text{relative change in the quantity of the good demanded}}{\text{relative change in income}}$$

$$= \frac{\Delta Q_x / Q_x}{\Delta Y / Y} = \frac{\Delta Q_x}{\Delta Y} \frac{Y}{Q_x} \qquad (3.6)$$

where ΔQ_x is a small change in the quantity of good X consumed, Q_x is the original quantity of good X consumed, ΔY is a small change in the consumer's income, and Y is the original level of the consumer's income.

Income and quantity consumed typically move in the same direction, and so in the normal case η_Y is positive. In figure 3.9 we can see that at low levels of income there is no expenditure on luxuries but, once income reaches a sufficient level, expenditure increases on them very rapidly indeed. The income elasticity of demand for cars, audio equipment, air travel, holidays abroad, etc. is likely to be positive and high. The income elasticity of demand for necessities such as basic foodstuffs is likely to be positive but it will have a very low value since, for any given individual or household, there is a limit to the amount of these items required. On the other hand, inferior goods will have a negative income elasticity of demand since consumers will switch to other, preferred, goods as their income increases and they can afford them.

The income elasticity of demand for a manufacturer's product is an important piece of information, particularly when he is trying to forecast levels of future demand (see chapter 7). A low income elasticity means that, to a certain extent, he will be insulated from the vicissitudes of the cycle of business activity in the economy. The manufacturer of foodstuffs can rest assured that, even when unemployment is high and increases in the level of incomes are constrained, people still have to eat. The provider of luxuries will have to pay careful attention to forecasts of the future level of economic activity, and, although he is likely to do well on the upswings, times will be hard on the downswings of economic activity.

Income and substitution effects

Now that we have considered the effects of changes in incomes on demand we can digress for a moment and return to the consideration of the effects of a fall in price of the original good. It is suggested that the effect of the fall in price of a good can be divided into an income effect and a substitution effect. If there is a reduction in the price of a good that a consumer habitually consumes, the effect is similar to an increase in his income. He can buy everything that he did previously and still have some money left to spend if he does not change his expenditure pattern. The fact that he still has some financial resources left leads to an income effect, since the result is indistinguishable from an increase in income.

The substitution effect arises from the fact that the good is now relatively cheaper than other commodities. This leads to an increase in the quantity demanded by the consumer.

The income effect is either positive or negative. We have seen that, usually, increases in income lead to an increase in the quantity demanded, but, in the case of inferior goods, the reverse could happen. Increases in income could lead to the substitution of preferred but more expensive goods. The substitution effect is always positive, but, in the case of an inferior good, the negative income effect could be sufficiently large to overcome this and lead to an overall fall in the quantity demanded after a price fall.

The sum of the two effects will lead to the change in the quantity that the consumer demands in response to the price change.

Changes in Tastes

The factors that shape consumer tastes and preferences are many and varied. They include socio-economic factors—such as age, sex, education, marital status, position in the domestic life cycle (e.g. newly married, a growing family or middle-aged with no child dependants)—and financial factors, such as the disposition of wealth between liquid and illiquid assets. Tastes can change as the result of innovation and advertising (see chapter 13) or, more fundamentally, as the result of changing values and priorities and of rising living standards. Conversely, the existence of stable habits means that the effects of changes in prices, incomes or other variables might be not immediate but subject to a time lag.

Whatever the cause, the effect of a change in tastes in favour of a good is unequivocal; it will move the entire demand curve to the right so that more is demanded at every price level than previously. Conversely, a change in tastes against a good will move the entire demand curve to the left with the reverse effect.

Conclusion

We have now considered all the factors which might affect consumer demand for a good. These included the prices of substitutes and complements,

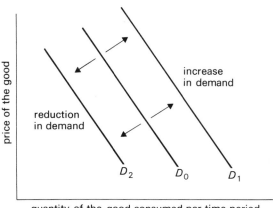

Figure 3.10 *Shifts in demand*

changes in consumer income, and changes in consumer tastes. Their effects are summarized in figure 3.10.

In figure 3.10 the original demand curve is D_0. If there is an increase in demand, it moves to the right, to D_1. If there is a decrease in demand, it moves to the left, to D_2. The factors which could cause such shifts are summarized below:

Decrease in demand	*Increase in demand*
(a) Fall in the price of substitutes	(a) Rise in the price of substitutes
(b) Rise in the price of complements	(b) Fall in the price of complements
(c) Fall in consumer income (normal goods)	(c) Rise in consumer income (normal goods)
(d) Change in tastes against the good	(d) Change in tastes in favour of the good

These effects must not be confused with the effect of a change in the price of the good itself. This leads to movements up and down the original demand curve, not to shifts of it.

There are a few other obvious factors which will also contribute to a determination of the overall size of the market itself. Demographic and socio-economic factors are obviously important: for example, the overall size of the population and its distribution into age groups; the distribution of income and the relative proportions of the various income groups; the age structure of the population; the incidence of marriage; and preferences in family size. All these factors will influence the number of potential consumers in a market.

The geographical area of a market will depend on the price of the commodity and the cost of transportation. The higher the price, the larger the area of supply but the less concentrated the likely demand. The qualities of the product have a major influence. High-value, non-perishable, cheaply transportable commodities—such as financial securities, precious metals, currencies, etc.—will have one market which effectively spans the world, in the absence of artificial restrictions. Bulky, perishable commodities will have markets that are more localized, but even here advances in transportation and refrigeration mean that Spanish tomatoes and French lettuces can vie with local varieties. Perhaps a better example is given by the housing market, which is usually local. The costs of transportation of tenants is relatively high, yet, even so, commuters travel long distances to London. Nevertheless, there are substantial regional disparities in housing prices, reflecting local differences in supply and demand.

In the next chapter we consider the supply side rather than the demand side of markets. This involves us in considering production and cost. The car markets of Edinburgh and London are, from the viewpoint of buyers, considered as separate—but not from the viewpoint of manufacturers, who will perhaps have one production plant to serve the entire British Isles. However, the various factors which affect the extent of markets will be considered more fully in chapter 7, which considers demand forecasting.

References

1 A. Marshall, *Principles of Economics* (1890), Macmillan, 9th edn, 1961.
2 Marshall, *Principles of Economics,* book 1, chapter 3.
3 L. Robbins, *An Essay on the Nature and Significance of Economic Science,* Macmillan, 1935, p. 36.
4 H. Liebenstein, 'Bandwagon, snob and Veblen effects in the theory of consumer's demand', *Quarterly Journal of Economics* (1950), pp. 183–207.
5 *Ibid.*
6 T. Veblen, *The Theory of the Leisure Class* (1899), Allen & Unwin, 1971.
7 A. Smith, *The Wealth of Nations* (1776), Penguin, 1970, book 1, chapter 4.
8 Marshall, *Principles of Economics,* book 3, chapter 3.

4

Production and Costs

The economic theory of production provides a complement to the theory of demand. Given the firm's objectives and given the level of demand, what is the optimum level of output for the firm? Given current knowledge and available technologies, what is the optimal production process? What is the most suitable mix of factor inputs? How will costs vary if output is expanded? Will this involve a change in the use of factors, and how will changes in the prices of factors affect their optimum combination? One of the fundamental rationales for the use of a market system with a pricing process as considered in chapter 2 is that firms compete in their use of factor inputs, react to relative price changes, and continually strive to use their inputs as effectively and efficiently as possible. The theory of production and costs provides an analysis of how price signals should be translated into effective production decisions, so that not only are markets provided with what they demand but also production is by least-cost methods.

Production and the Concept of Value Added

Production is the process of transforming resources into finished products in the form of goods and services. It is an activity which creates or adds value. It applies as much to service, distribution and storage functions as to the process of manufacture. Utility or value can be added by changes in ownership, location or time as well as form. Coal at the bottom of a mine in the middle of summer might not be of much use to you, but once it has been mined, graded, stored until the winter, delivered by the coalman to your door, and has ended up sitting at the back of your grate on a frosty night, it has considerable value. To take another example, consider 2 kg of wheat ultimately selling as a loaf of bread to a housewife for 35p. Assume the chain of sales and intervening processes takes place as detailed in table 4.1.

The value to the miller of 2 kg of wheat is 12p. That is what it is worth to him (otherwise he would not willingly part with 12p to obtain it). The miller in turn converts the grain into flour. How much effort he spends in doing so

Table 4.1 *Production and value added*

Transactor	Selling price (p)	Value added (p)
Farmer	12	12
Miller	20	8
Baker	30	10
Grocer	35	5
Total	97	35

is irrelevant. What is relevant is that the baker is willing to part with 20p to get the flour. The baker believes that the miller has added value of 8p to the grain. The baker converts the flour into bread and sells it to the grocer for 30p who in turn sells it to the housewife for 35p. Again, this 5p does not reflect the costs incurred by the retailer, it reflects what the housewife is willing to give up for what the retailer does (otherwise she would purchase the bread from the baker at 30p). She values the retailer's service (convenient opening hours, location, car parking facilities, the provision of convenient selling quantities, the opportunity to purchase other items simultaneously) at 5 pence. This analysis is exactly in line with our discussion in chapter 2 of marginal personal valuations and the rationale for trade and exchange. In economics, value is subjective and bears little or no relation to production cost.

Value added at each stage equals selling price received at that stage less the amount paid for the intermediate product. More accurately it equals:

sales − (material + fuel purchases)

which in turn is identical to:

wages + rents + interest payments + profits (gross of corporation tax).

Nevertheless, to keep the arguments straightforward we will consider production largely in the context of the manufacturing process.

The processes of production add value to goods by transforming them in the manner required by consumers. By this means a fund of value is created, by virtue of which factors can be rewarded. Payments are made for raw materials and components, for labour (in wages and salaries), as well as for rents, taxes, etc.

The experience of costs and the adoption of production processes will vary both across and within industries. Firms of differing size in the same industry may use different methods of production, have differing combinations of

Table 4.2 *Output and costs in manufacturing industry, 1974–78*

	Enterprises	Sales and work done (£m)	Gross output (£m)	Purchases (£m)	Increase in value of stocks (£m)	Cost of services (£m)	Gross value added at factor cost (£m)
1974	84,514	80,013	85,153	49,821	1,963	5,950	31,345
1975	86,722	91,243	93,048	53,760	87	6,984	32,390
1976	89,522	110,485	113,170	67,626	1,773	8,484	38,832
1977	90,154	129,484	132,030	78,581	923	10,380	43,992
1978	89,203	140,920	142,980	83,001	930	12,269	48,640

Source: Business Monitor, 1978, cited in *Report on the Census of Production*, 1978, table 1

inputs and levels of efficiency and, therefore, experience different costs. A rough outline of the composition of production costs in manufacturing industry is given in table 4.2.

In this table the difference between annual sales and gross output is made up of changes in the value of stocks of finished goods and work in progress. Purchases include the costs of raw materials, components, semi-manufactured goods and workshop materials, etc. The increase in the value of stocks shown refers to increases in the value of materials, stores and fuel, not to finished and semi-finished goods. The cost of services includes industrial services, such as payments to other firms for work done, repairs, maintenance and contracts sublet, and non-industrial services, such as rents on property and buildings, hire charges for machinery and vehicles, payments of royalties for the use of patents, etc. Thus, by deducting from gross output the purchases and the cost of services, and adding the increase in the value of stocks, we are left with gross value added at factor cost. From this fund wage costs would have to be met, plus all depreciation charges required to maintain the value of equipment, plus payments to providers of capital and to the government in taxation.

The Use of Production Functions

A *production function* is the term given by economists to the technological relationship between the rates of inputs of productive factors and the rate of output of production. To employ production functions it has to be assumed that the state of knowledge and technology is given; if it were not, the relationships between inputs and outputs would be altered by technological advance, leading to more efficient production techniques. It is also assumed that, given production functions, firms utilize their factor inputs at maximum levels of efficiency. The production function could be written as follows:

$$Q = f(A,B,C,D, \ldots). \tag{4.1}$$

This is simply a symbolic statement of the fact that the output Q is the maximum amount which can be produced for a given numerical set of amounts of factor inputs A, B, C, D, etc. The way in which output changes in response to changes in the values, relative and absolute, of these inputs will vary according to the precise numerical formulation of this equation.

The Law of Diminishing Returns

A basic economic assumption underlies the production function. This is *the law of diminishing returns*. It states that as more and more units of one factor are applied, all other inputs being held constant, a point will be reached at which successive additions of that factor will yield diminishing marginal increments to total output.

If we start with a fixed input, say A_1, of factor A, and proceed to add successive units of B, at first production rises very rapidly (see figure 4.1); then the rate of increase slows as diminishing returns set in at B_0. Finally a maximum is achieved, in this case at Q_1, where an optimum combination of A_1 and B_1 units are combined. If further additions of B were made beyond this, total output would not increase and would begin to fall again. This makes intuitive sense. A trite example would be an attempt to increase crop yield from a window box by ever greater applications of labour and fertilizer. Clearly, after a certain point, such foolish efforts would be counter-productive. Figure 4.1 shows the effect of diminishing returns.

This analysis leads naturally on to consideration of the *short run*. This is a conceptual interval of time during which one factor input, usually considered to be capital, is fixed, whilst other factors are variable. This makes sense in that it usually takes much longer to alter capital inputs, in the form of industrial plant and machinery, than it does to alter inputs of labour and raw materials. The short run is not a fixed period of time, and will vary considerably from case to case and industry to industry. At one extreme, if we took

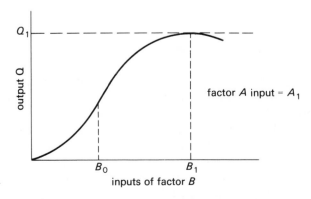

Figure 4.1 *The law of diminishing returns*

the example of the garment industry, a small operation making up garments might be able to increase the number of sewing machines it employs in a matter of weeks. On the other hand, in the electricity generating industry it might take more than a decade to introduce a new nuclear power plant. In the consideration of costs in this chapter we shall concentrate on the analysis of the short run, for which we have assumed that there is a constant state of technology and that one factor input, capital, is fixed. This can be contrasted with the *long run*, in which all inputs are variable, and the *very long run*, in which technology is subject to change; these circumstances will be considered in the next chapter.

Short-run Costs

As the input of the fixed factor is, by definition, unaltered in the short run, its cost is unlikely to alter. Typically *fixed costs* might include rentals on leased machinery, interest on capital, rates, and the salaries of those employees who cannot be laid off as output is reduced. *Variable costs* might include raw material costs, the variable part of power and water charges, commissions on sales, and some wage costs. The behaviour of total, fixed and variable costs in the short run is shown in figure 4.2.

By definition, fixed costs are constant in the short run, and so they are shown in figure 4.2 as being invariant with output. The behaviour of variable costs reflects the law of diminishing returns. At first, variable costs rise fairly rapidly because too few variable factors are being combined with the fixed factor, and the combination is not efficient. As a more effective level of combination is attained, variable costs rise less rapidly as output is increased. Finally, as an ever greater input of variable factors is combined with the fixed factor, diminishing returns set in and variable costs rise rapidly again.

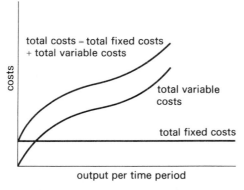

Figure 4.2 *Total costs in the short run*

From the basic cost functions shown in figure 4.2 others can be derived which are of considerable analytical use. For example, *average fixed cost* (*AFC*) is simply the fixed cost per unit of output:

$$\text{average fixed cost } (AFC) = \frac{\text{total fixed cost}}{\text{output}} = \frac{TFC}{Q}. \tag{4.2}$$

Likewise, *average variable cost* (*AVC*) is the variable cost per unit of output:

$$\text{average variable cost } (AVC) = \frac{\text{total variable cost}}{\text{output}} = \frac{TVC}{Q}. \tag{4.3}$$

Similarly, *average total cost* (*ATC*) is obtained by dividing total cost (*TC*) by output:

$$\text{average total cost } (ATC) = \frac{\text{total cost}}{\text{output}} = \frac{TC}{Q} = \frac{TFC + TVC}{Q}. \tag{4.4}$$

Marginal cost (*MC*) is the rate of change of total cost with respect to changes in output. It is measured by the gradient of the total cost curve at any particular point representing a given level of output:

$$\text{marginal cost } (MC) = \frac{\Delta(TC)}{\Delta Q}. \tag{4.5}$$

But, as total fixed cost does not change, it is only affected by changes in variable cost; thus:

$$\text{marginal cost } (MC) = \frac{\Delta(TVC)}{\Delta Q}. \tag{4.6}$$

Marginal cost is obtained by deducting the total cost at any given output from the total cost immediately preceding it and dividing by the change in

Table 4.3 *The behaviour of short-run costs*

1 Units of variable input	2 Units of fixed input	3 Total output	4 Total fixed costs (£2.50 per unit)	5 Total variable costs (£1 per unit)	6 Total costs (4 + 5)	7 Average variable costs (5 ÷ 3)	8 Average fixed costs (4 ÷ 3)	9 Average total costs (7 + 8)	10 Marginal costs (from 6 and 3)
		Q	TFC (£)	TVC (£)	TC (£)	AVC (£)	AFC (£)	ATC (£)	MC (£)
0	2	0	5	0	5	—	∞	∞	—
1	2	4	5	1	6	0.25	1.25	1.5	0.25
2	2	9	5	2	7	0.22	0.55	0.77	0.20
3	2	15	5	3	8	0.20	0.33	0.53	0.17
4	2	22	5	4	9	0.18	0.23	0.51	0.14
5	2	26	5	5	10	0.19	0.19	0.38	0.25
6	2	28	5	6	11	0.21	0.18	0.39	0.5
7	2	29	5	7	12	0.24	0.17	0.41	1.0

output. The behaviour of cost schedules for a hypothetical firm is shown in table 4.3.

A set of cost curves which behave in a manner consistent with what is implied by the data in table 4.3 is shown in figure 4.3. As fixed costs are constant, total fixed costs at any point on the average fixed cost curve (*AFC*) must be constant. In terms of figure 4.3, total fixed costs $(TFC) = AFC \times Q = (TFC/Q) \times Q$. In figure 4.3 a perpendicular drawn up to the *AFC* curve at a given level of output, and then across from the curve at right angles to the vertical axis, shows the *AFC* of producing that level of output, and the area enclosed in the resulting rectangle is the *TFC*. The two rectangles produced by the dotted lines in figure 4.3 will always have the same area, as will any other similar rectangle, and this is equal to the value of total fixed costs. The only curve which displays this required property is termed a rectangular hyperbola, and the *AFC* curve is thus always a rectangular hyperbola.

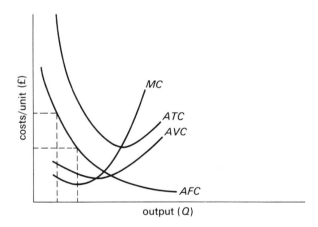

Figure 4.3 *Average and marginal costs in the short run*

Marginal cost is equivalent to the slope or gradient (obtained by taking the first derivative) of the total variable cost curve, as was implied in expression 4.6. It follows from the behaviour of average and marginal quantities that whenever *MC* is below *AVC*, average variable cost must be falling. It reaches a minimum where *AVC* = *MC*, and as soon as *MC* rises above *AVC*, average variable cost starts to rise. Average total cost is the sum of average variable costs and average fixed costs: *ATC* = *AFC* + *AVC*. This can be seen in table 4.3. Similarly, it follows from the nature of the curves that the marginal cost curve always passes through the minimum point of the average total cost curve.

We have now reached a stage where we have a basic tool-kit which can be applied to analyse the factors determining supply and demand; it will be utilized in the next chapter when the theory of the firm is examined more closely. However, in order to develop these basic principles and concepts we have smoothed over and ignored a number of practical difficulties. For example, it has been assumed that information about company costs is readily at hand. Yet it will be seen in chapter 9, when various accounting issues are broached, that the assessment of company costs is by no means a straight-forward, unequivocal matter.

Similarly, in the development of our treatment of costs it has been assumed that it is possible to switch continuously between the various factor inputs to achieve the most efficient method of producing a given output. In the final section of this chapter we shall move away from this to an examination of the use of linear programming, which provides a very powerful method of analysing the behaviour of costs and output under much more restrictive conditions than previously assumed.

Linear Programming

Linear programming is a powerful analytical technique which can be used to determine the optimal solution to maximization or minimization problems. It is particularly useful in its ability to handle 'constraints', which limit the courses of action available to the decision-taker. These are a common feature of the environment in which businessmen have to operate. The technique can be applied in a great number of decision areas—including the determination of the optimum factor input mix, product distribution analysis (taking in decisions such as plant location or delivery routing), and the design of promotional mix in marketing activities—to mention but a few. We shall concentrate on its use in the analysis of the behaviour of production and costs.

Linear programming, as its name suggests, involves a basic assumption that all relationships between variables are linear. If costs are to rise linearly with increases in output, two conditions are required: (*a*) the firm's *production function* must be linear homogeneous—i.e. factor inputs will be optimally combined only in constant fixed proportions—and, furthermore, there are *constant returns to scale*, production being equally efficient whatever the level of output; (*b*) there must be *constant factor input prices*. If all the above conditions are met, total costs will rise linearly with increases in output.

The assumptions may seem unreasonably restrictive, but in practice, over limited output ranges, the treating of factor input prices as constant will frequently be quite justifiable. A further point in favour of linear programming is that the method assumes there are a limited number of processes in which factor inputs can be combined to produce a given output, rather than the continuous substitution of standard economic analysis. The existence of *constraints* on resources is also quite likely in the short term. Examples of this might include shortages of given types of equipment, limitations on warehouse space, shortages of raw materials, or even a lack of skilled labour.

The technique handles the setting of upper boundary limitations on various inputs with great ease.

To illustrate, suppose that a firm is producing a single product using inputs of two factors, L and K. Further assume that there are three alternative production processes, A, B and C, available to the firm, which use different fixed proportions of inputs K and L to produce the product. Figure 4.4 shows three process rays, drawn through the origin, which link points representing successive units of output and use the two inputs in the appropriate proportions. Thus, A_3, B_3 and C_3 all represent three units of output, but are produced by processes A, B and C respectively, using differing quantities of inputs K and L, as indicated by their positions on the KL plane and measured on the two axes.

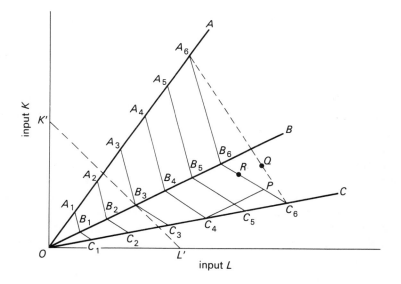

Figure 4.4 *The determination of the least-cost method of production*

Because there are constant returns to scale, OA_1 is equal to A_1A_2, A_2A_3 and so on. Similarly $OB_1 = B_1B_2 = B_2B_3$ etc., and $OC_1 = C_1C_2 = C_2C_3$. This follows since the same proportionate increases in factor input, by definition, produce a constant proportionate addition to output.

If we join up the points of equal output, say A_6, B_6 and C_6, we have mapped out the combinations of inputs which produce an output of six units. This equal product 'curve' is termed an *isoquant*. A similar exercise for outputs of 1, 2, 3, 4 and 5 units produces the set of isoquants shown in figure 4.4.

The argument requires some further clarification. Each point on B_6C_6, for example, represents a combination of processes B and C which produces the same output as OB_6 units of process B or OC_6 units of process C. This is illustrated by taking any point P on line B_6C_6 and drawing a line through P

parallel to *OB* (a similar result would be obtained by drawing a line parallel to *OC*). With the point *P* chosen in figure 4.4, this line intersects *OC* at C_4, indicating that four units should be used using process *C* and the remaining two using process *B*. This follows because $C_4P = B_4B_6$ which are opposite sides of the parallelogram $B_4B_6PC_4$, and because $B_4B_6 = OB_2$. (The argument also involves the further assumption that using both processes simultaneously will neither enhance nor detract from either's performance.) We are also assuming that the firm is unable to combine *K* and *L* in ratios that lie either above production process ray *OA* or below ray *OC*. It can further be shown that the isoquants in figure 4.4 represent the most efficient ways of combining production processes to produce a given output.

Suppose we combined processes *A* and *C* to produce an output of six units. The dashed line in figure 4.4 joining A_6 and C_6 shows the combinations of the two processes that would do this. A point *Q* on this line shows a combination of the two processes that would produce six units. But there are combinations of *B* and *C* on B_6C_6, such as point *R*, which will also produce six units using fewer inputs since the sum of *K* and *L* needed to achieve *R* is less than to achieve *Q*. Clearly A_6C_6 is suboptimal and would never be considered. This also demonstrates that linear programming, even though it involves an assumption of constant returns to scale, can handle the type of diminishing returns associated with a diminishing marginal rate of substitution of one input for another.

To demonstrate how the cost of the production process can be minimized using this analysis, we have to consider 'isocost' lines. These link points of equal expenditure on factor inputs, and one such line is represented in figure 4.4 by the dashed line joining *K'* and *L'*. Given the prices of factors *K* and *L* and a certain amount of money expenditure, we could either spend it all on factor *K*, purchasing *K'* of it, or on *L*, as indicated by *L'*, or on combinations of the two which involve the same expenditure and plot along *K'L'*, process *B* is optimal and, given our expenditure level, the best we could achieve would be to produce three units of output using process *B* as indicated by the intersection of *K'L'* with point B_3. Any other combination of inputs would involve the same expenditure but would produce less than three units.

We have assumed so far that there are no constraints imposed on the ability of the firm to obtain factor inputs at constant prices. This is unrealistic, and firms are likely to have only limited access to floor space, machinery, labour, etc. at any given time. In figure 4.5 it is assumed that constraints limit the maximum amounts of *K* and *L* available to K_c and L_c.

The production possibilities now open to the firm are represented by the shaded area in figure 4.5, which is bounded by the process rays *OA* and *OC* and the two constraints. This shaded area is termed the *feasible space*. Clearly, if the firm wishes to maximize output, it should operate where the feasible space touches the highest attainable isoquant—point *S* in the diagram. The combination of processes *B* and *C* required to achieve this output can be found by constructing the appropriate parallelogram, as illustrated in figure 4.4.

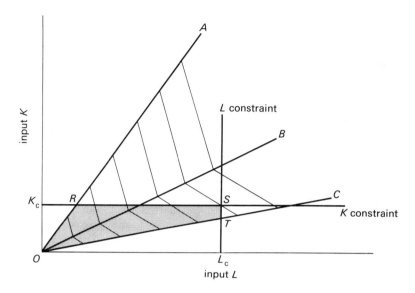

Figure 4.5 *The determination of the least-cost method of production subject to constraints on inputs*

To further illustrate the versatility and practicality of linear programming we will consider the geometrical solution of another simple problem. Suppose the firm in question produces two products, *C* and *D*, which use different combinations of three inputs, *K*, *L* and *M*, in the process of production. The firm is subject to constraints on the availability of all three inputs and, subject to these, wishes to maximize the profitability of the combined output of *C* and *D*. The question is: what output mix, given the constraints and differing contributions to profits from the two products, will do this? This type of problem is commonly faced by, for example, oil refiners, food processors, timber processors, etc.

This typical linear programming problem involves the following standard elements which will be considered briefly in turn: an objective function, a set of constraints, and non-negativity requirements.

The objective function

The objective function is usually concerned with either cost minimization or, as in this case, profit maximization. As we are in a short-run situation, fixed costs can be ignored, since they will be incurred no matter what decision is made. For this type of problem, therefore, 'profits' are '*contribution profits*' (total revenue minus variable costs). (For further discussion of profits and contribution analysis, see chapter 9.) The unit contribution of each product is its selling price minus the average variable costs of production. Suppose this is £0.5 for *C* and £1 for *D*. The objective function can be written as:

$$\text{maximize } \Pi_c = £0.5Q_C + £1Q_D \tag{4.7}$$

where Π_c is total contribution profit and Q_C and Q_D are the respective quantities of C and D produced.

The constraints

The constraints will depend on the absolute limitations on the amounts of K, L and M available in each period. Suppose that these are 10, 15 and 12 respectively. Knowledge of these, together with the factor input requirements of the production processes for the two products, are all that we need to develop the constraint equations. Let us suppose that 1, 2 and 0 units of K, L and M respectively are needed to produce C, and similarly 4, 3 and 6 to produce D. We know that the constraints on the availability of inputs are $K \leqslant 10$, $L \leqslant 15$ and $M \leqslant 12$. These can be combined with our knowledge of the production input requirements to produce the following constraint equations:

$$1Q_C + 4Q_D \leqslant 10 \tag{4.8}$$
$$2Q_C + 3Q_D \leqslant 15 \tag{4.9}$$
$$6Q_D \leqslant 12. \tag{4.10}$$

The non-negativity requirements

In the geometric analysis which follows we will obviously limit ourselves to answers which involve positive outputs. However, linear programming problems are usually much more complex than our simple example; even so, they can be solved rapidly with a computer and the appropriate algorithm.[1] However, a computer would not baulk at providing a mathematical 'solution' which involved, where 'appropriate', negative outputs, even though they make economic nonsense. To avoid these potential embarrassments, positive solutions are specified as part of the system of equations, as shown below:

$$Q_C \geqslant 0 \tag{4.11}$$
$$Q_D \geqslant 0. \tag{4.12}$$

To obtain a geometric solution for our simple problem, the first step is to draw a diagram, on a plane representing outputs of C and D, of our constraint equations 4.8, 4.9 and 4.10. This is done in figure 4.6.

The constraint equation which results from the limitation of the input of K to a maximum of 10 units per period is given in expression 4.8. We know that this could be used to produce: either 10 units of C and no D, as marked by the point of intersection of the line representing the K constraint with the vertical axis; or, at the other extreme, 2 units of D and no C, as marked by the intersection of this line with the horizontal axis; or a combination of C and D which plot along the line joining these two extremes. The lines representing the other constraints are developed on a similar basis, and together

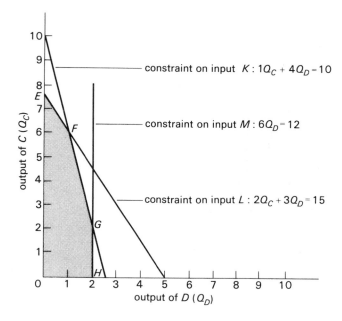

Figure 4.6 *Determining the feasible space*

they enclose the feasible space—the shaded area *EFGH* in figure 4.6. It is obvious that the solution of maximum profitability will lie somewhere along the boundary of this area, and the key points to examine are the corner solutions at *E*, *F*, *G* and *H*, since combined output is maximized along this boundary.

In figure 4.7 we have taken the previous diagram (figure 4.6) and added a set of iso-profit-contribution (Π_c) lines. These show the particular combinations of outputs of *C* and *D* which make the same contribution to profits, and are based on expression 4.7. The point on the boundary of the feasible space which just touches the highest iso-profit-contribution line is the optimum solution. This is point *F* in figure 4.7. At this point, six units of *C* and one unit of *D* are produced, yielding a total contribution to profits of £4—the maximum attainable under the circumstances.

These simple examples give no more than a hint of the tremendous versatility and potential of linear programming techniques, which are now a well-established part of the decision-maker's tool-kit, since optimization problems subject to inequality constraints are a frequent feature of both business and governmental problems.

The nature of each firm's experience of costs will determine both its and, in aggregate, the industry's response to changes in market conditions. These factors, taken together with the analysis of demand conditions in chapter 3,

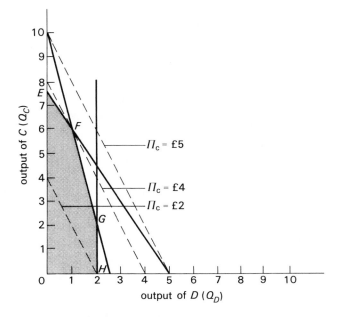

Figure 4.7 *The graphical solution of a linear
programming problem*

provide an analysis of how an equilibrium of demand and supply conditions
is determined in the market.

In addition, we have now seen how the pure theory of costs can be applied
to decisions at the firm level using the technique of linear programming,
which is derived directly from a restricted version of the production function.

References

1 See, for example, W.J. Baumol, *Economic Theory and Operations Analysis*,
  Prentice-Hall, 3rd edn, 1972.

5

Market Structure and Business Conduct

Why do firms exist? What is unique about them? What is meant by market structure, and what is its relationship with competition, monopoly, pricing behaviour of firms and other business activities? These are the questions we attempt to answer in this chapter.

The Theory of the Firm[1]

First, firms are collections of people—owners, managers and employees—with (at least in principle) the owners telling the others what to do. Orders are given and received. The people involved do not perpetually make and renew contracts with each other as buyers and sellers do in the outside market. There is, instead, a hierarchy.

Second, firms often have team activities. When groups work together (a) it is often difficult to determine the contribution of each individual and (b) the total output is larger than it would be if each individual acted independently.

Third, owners, unlike employees, are not paid directly for their time or services. Rather they receive the right to the firm's residual surplus, or deficit, of revenues over costs. (Managers often blend the roles of owner and employee if they receive, in addition to a salary, earnings linked in some way to profits.)

So much for the characteristics of the firm as a hierarchy. Why, however, does this replace the outside market? Why would the costs of buying and selling semi-finished goods on a production line, in transactions between independent people renting space on a factory floor, exceed the costs of organizing a firm? Put this way, the question seems trite and the answer obvious. But in fact neither is the case; if the answer was *universally* obvious, then all outside market transactions would cease and all activities would be organized into one giant firm. The question is why in some cases firms exist, and in others they do not.

One reason has already been given. Team activity is often more productive in the aggregate than individual activity. But this itself poses a problem only the firm can solve. Since it is difficult to measure the input of each individual it is easy for an individual to shirk or do less than his part. The loss in output is shared by all team members and cannot be traced to the shirker. He bears less than the full cost of his action; thus each person in a team tends to shirk more than he would if he were self-employed and bearing all such costs. (This is simply an application of demand theory: the lower the cost or price of shirking, the more shirking will take place.)

It is, therefore, sensible to have a *monitor* to observe the behaviour of the team members, evaluate their contributions and so minimize shirking. The monitor (or manager) must in turn be monitored. The problem of monitoring the monitor is often solved by giving him a reward linked in some way to the residual earnings of the firm. The more successful the monitor, in turn the more his share of firm profits will be. Thus the owner−manager−employee, or firm, relationship comes into being for the purposes of team production and consequential monitoring.

A second reason for the existence of firms is the differing willingness of people to bear risk. Some individuals are more or less *risk-averse* (that is, wary of risk) than others. Very few people will actually be *risk-preferrers*, that is, prefer a risky situation to a non-risky one. Since people have different degrees of aversion to risk they must be paid more or less to assume any given risk. Thus, owners can be deduced to be more willing to assume risk than managers or employees. This may be where their comparative advantage lies.

This will be partly a psychological phenomenon and partly one of wealth. If an individual has wealth of £10,000 he will be more wiling to risk £1000 than someone whose life savings amount to £1000. In turn, potential owners may not have the skills of management which potential monitors have. They would prefer to hire managers rather than do it themselves. Their asking price for a management salary would reflect this and be relatively high. (This is merely a restatement, for different commodities—risk aversion and management skills—of the arguments put forward in figure 2.2 for Joe and Fred, who had different stocks of, and psychological preferences for, beer and butter.)

This phenomenon, in turn, leads to what is often called the 'divorce of ownership from control'. Managers are frequently not owners of the firms they manage. Entrepreneurs can be presumed to assess the trade-offs of this situation. The cost savings in raising capital must be offset against the less rigorous, but also less expensive, management which will be installed if monitors own little or nothing of the firm they manage.

Firm Types and Market Structure

Traditionally, economists subdivide firms into two major categories: *perfect competitors* and *monopolists*. Both perfect competition and monopoly have

Table 5.1 *Conditions and results for perfect competition and monopoly*

	Conditions	Results
Perfect competition	1 Large number of firms 2 Independent action by firms and consumers 3 All firms produce basically identical products 4 Firms can enter the industry easily 5 Buyers and sellers have all relevant information about the market offerings each makes	1 Lowest-cost producers supply the product 2 Consumers pay the lowest price consistent with cost 3 Producers have no discretion in the price they set
Monopoly	1 A single seller and/or 2 The presence of restrictions on the entry of new firms to the market	1 The firm (or firms) has some degree of 'monopoly power' which permits it (them) to determine price

conditions which determine their existence and results which arise from this existence. Table 5.1 summarizes these conditions and results.

This table, however, requires a number of qualifying statements. First, the condition of complete information under perfect competition has been attacked on the grounds that it should be regarded not as an assumption but rather as a consequence of competition.[2] Thus, competition in athletics, the writing of poetry or industrial production can be seen as a totally futile process if one already knows the fastest runner, the best poet or the most efficient producer of a good or service to meet demand.

Second, *price taking* (the absence of pricing discretion) is not unique to perfect competition; relatively monopolistic markets may have price-taking characteristics. In real life, information is not freely available. Firms do not always know what values consumers place on various products, especially those not yet produced. Competition, then, often takes the form of introducing a new product with the hope that consumers will value it more highly than its cost, and that other firms will not immediately enter—thus allowing the first firm a chance to earn some innovational profit.

For example, in the beer industry in the 1970s, the main problem was to decide just how far, if at all, the trend from ale to lager was going to go. In the early 1960s only a small amount of all beer produced was lager. By 1973 this figure had risen to 14.8 per cent and by 1978 to 27 per cent. Those brewers who did not correctly forecast this change in consumer taste (brought about partly by the familiarization with lager owing to an increasing number of foreign holidays), and so failed to build lager breweries to meet it, became less profitable than those who did.

It is this rivalry to produce the commodities most highly valued by consumers (relative to cost, since that is how profits are earned) which results in the benefits of competition from the consumer's viewpoint—namely, the ability to choose from among alternative suppliers. Thus the results of this process are similar to perfect competition, where firms are price takers. Only those goods survive for which consumers are willing to pay; the price paid approaches production costs, and only the lowest-cost producers stay in business. Thus, while the beer, motor-car and oil industries do not meet the conditions of perfect competition, the price-taking model can often still be used to analyze them, and can frequently be just as effective as more realistic (but more complex) models of industrial structure.

Third, in the case of monopoly the condition of there being a single seller is often an adequate one to produce the results implied by table 5.1. The National Coal Board is a single seller of coal. But if the NCB's product is defined as 'energy', then it is only one of many sellers which must compete against several companies in the oil, gas, nuclear power and electricity industries. The falling price (relative to that of coal) of oil and gas in the 1950s, 1960s and early 1970s resulted in large swings in demand away from coal. Is the NCB, then, a single seller if we define the commodity this widely? Similarly, if a commodity is defined narrowly, everyone is a single seller. Only the hairdresser at the corner of the high street can produce that precise service in that precise place. In short, the condition for monopoly, that is, that there should be a single seller, is often somewhat vague and unhelpful.

Fourth, the presence of *entry barriers* and restrictions on new sellers in a market can be a more helpful guide to the conditions necessary for the results of monopoly. The concept is old, and generally the restrictions are the result of government or other regulations. The powerful East India Company had a state-granted monopoly to trade to India until 1813, a privilege which lasted for over a century. This company has now disappeared but a contemporary trading giant, with exclusive rights which lasted till a later date, continues to exist in the Hudson's Bay Company.

But even when there are many sellers, artificial restrictions can exist. For example, doctors and teachers must be registered and only they may be employed in the state sector of health or education. Taxi-cabs must be licensed by the local authority; as a consequence, they are not permitted to ply for traffic outside a specified area. Thus at most airports in Britain a taxi may drop off a passenger but, unless the cab is appropriately licensed, must return empty to base, whereas another taxi may pick up a fare but must return to the airport empty. Lawyers, and until recently, long-distance bus operators, must also be licensed. So, too, must publicans and hotel keepers serving alcohol. Entry restrictions are also placed on airlines wishing to fly on certain routes, on television broadcasting companies, and on messenger services that might wish to carry letters and might thus infringe the Post Office's monopoly. Consequently, a closed market can exist whether sellers are few or many.

Fifth, monopoly can be examined from the viewpoint of its outcome rather than its preconditions. Firms are often *not* price takers. They can raise prices and retain most of their sales. They do not take prices as given but rather have to seek out the best price to maximize their profits. Such firms have a degree of monopoly power and can be deemed to be *price searchers*. Since 'monopoly' is such a difficult word to define, the term 'price searcher' may be a more accurate one to describe the situation in which a firm faces a downward-sloping demand curve.

Why, in the absence of legally imposed entry restrictions, do some industries contain many price-searching firms and others only a few? The answer depends on demand and cost conditions. On the demand side, consumers may prefer to have a large or small choice of alternative products. Provided they value a range of choice highly enough to pay for the costs of providing it, then a large number of price-searching firms will emerge. The restaurant industry is an example of this. Eating-out establishments range from the large to the small, from the expensive to the inexpensive, from the gaudy to the subdued, from those with wide to those with restricted menus, and so on. Alternatively, on the cost side, it is the presence or absence of *economies of scale* which determines whether there are many or few price-searching firms. If a large, rather than a small, number of firms exists in an industry—and their costs are significantly higher than they would be if their numbers were fewer—then clearly there is an incentive for firms to grow in order to achieve the benefits of lower unit costs; other firms will then either disappear through merger or closure. The concepts of scale economies and product differentiation will be discussed in more detail later in this chapter and in chapter 6.

To summarize thus far, table 5.1, which classified market structure, can be recategorized as in table 5.2.

Industries can thus be judged by whether or not there are legal barriers to entry (open and closed markets) and by whether or not firms in them have market power (price takers or price searchers). Thus there are no legal barriers to becoming a football star, but because Kenny Dalgleish has few close substitutes he can command an extremely high salary. If there were many footballers of Dalgleish's skill and talent, he would be unable to command a salary much above that of the next best alternative job he is competent to do.

Table 5.2 *Market structure classifications*

1 *Open market price takers* e.g. foodstores, motor-car component producers, yarn and textile manufacturers	2 *Closed market price takers* e.g. licensed restaurants, liquor retailers, taxi-cabs, road haulage firms, lawyers, doctors
3 *Open market price searchers* e.g. motor-car firms, film and sports stars, aluminium producers	4 *Closed market price searchers* e.g. British Telecom, electricity boards, airlines (at least within Britain and Europe), patent holders

In fact, the price he can charge for his services over and above their cost of production (in other words, his monopoly power) is probably considerably greater than, say, a car firm or an aluminium producer. If Ford or British Aluminium charged significantly higher prices than production costs, then custom would quickly move to Talbot, Fiat or Datsun or, for aluminium, towards Alcan.

Not only does the degree of monopoly power—as measured by the obviousness of whether a firm is a price taker or searcher—vary along a spectrum, but so also does the degree to which legal entry barriers are important. Thus, obtaining a taxi licence is easier than obtaining a licence to practise medicine, which, in turn, is easier than obtaining the right to run an alternative telephone service. We will now examine price takers and searchers more analytically.

Price takers

A firm which is a price taker has a demand curve which can be regarded as a horizontal line. This may seem at odds with what we discussed in chapters 2 and 3, where it was asserted that demand curves always slope down and to the right. The paradox is resolved by remembering that no individual seller in a price-taking market is large enough, relative to the market's size, to have any significant effect on the good's market price. The point is *not* that the seller believes that the price will never change, but rather that each seller assumes that nothing he can do *individually* can change the price. In fact, even one seller withdrawing or adding his supply to the market will shift the intersection of supply with demand and so raise or lower the market price. But the movement will be so imperceptible that, in reality, the seller can disregard it, and therefore—for exposition purposes—we can legitimately do so as well.

The facility of drawing a horizontal demand curve is useful since it permits

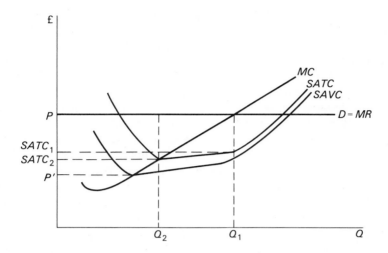

Figure 5.1 *Demand curve, and maximum profit and minimum cost points, for the individual seller in a price-taking market*

us to describe another concept using the same line. This is *marginal revenue (MR)*, which is the addition to total revenue that a firm gains when it sells one more unit of output. Clearly if price is unchanged, no matter what number of units is sold, marginal revenue is equal to price. With this information, and the cost curves of chapter 4, we can now establish at what level of output a price taker will choose to produce. To do this we assume that the firm is a profit maximizer, i.e. that its profit equals total revenue less total costs, and that costs are correctly calculated to include all opportunity costs (e.g. forgone interest on capital employed is correctly imputed as discussed in chapter 2). Figure 5.1 shows that the firm, if it produces at Q_1 (the level at which marginal revenue equals marginal cost), will earn economic profit (i.e. profit over and above what it could earn elsewhere) of $(P - SATC_1)$ per unit, or, in total, that unit profit times Q_1 (which can be represented by the rectangle of width Q_1 and height of $P - SATC_1$). (*SATC* refers to *short-run* analysis.)

Q_1 is, in fact, the output level that gives maximum profit. It might at first be thought that Q_2 (the level at which average total cost equals marginal cost) would be the profit-maximizing output. This is not so. Certainly Q_2 is the level of minimum unit costs and unit profit $(P - SATC_2)$ is larger than $(P - SATC_1)$. But the volume sold, Q_2, is so much less than Q_1 that total profits are less. The area of the profit rectangle $(P - SATC_2) \times Q_2$ is less than $(P - SATC_1) \times Q_1$. We can use logic to prove this. At Q_2, if one unit more is produced, then total revenue (*TR*) increases by *MR*. Simultaneously, total cost (*TC*) increases by *MC*. But total profit is $TR - TC$ and, at one unit more than Q_2, *MR* is larger than *MC*, so profit, $TR - TC$, becomes greater.

This increase in total profit after Q_2 continues as long as $MR > MC$—that is, right up to Q_1, when $MC = MR$. After Q_1, $MC > MR$ so $TR - TC$ begins to fall. Q_1 is thus the level of maximum total profit (albeit not the level of minimum unit costs).

Figure 5.1 also indicates at what level of costs and output a firm should close down its operations. Thus a price taker can be seen as having three sequential decisions to take. First, should it or should it not stay in business? If the price is expected to be at $SATC_2$ or above, then it should. All the costs of being and staying in business will be covered. Second, if the answer is positive, should the firm continue to operate or not, that is, continue not just owning its assets but using them? Since a decision has been taken to continue incurring fixed costs, only variable costs should now be considered. If price is above P' (the level at which average variable cost equals marginal cost) then it should temporarily discontinue operations. If price is below P', it should temporarily discontinue operations. If price is expected to be below $SATC_2$ permanently, then the assets should be sold off and owners and employees should put their resources to better alternative uses.

Third, if the owners decide to continue operating, at what level of output should they produce? The answer is at the level where marginal revenue (or price) equals marginal cost.

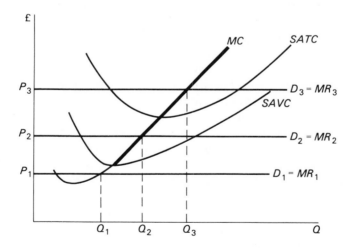

Figure 5.2 *Supply curve and operating decision points for the individual seller in a price-taking market*

The answers to these three questions help us to derive the price-taker's supply curve—i.e., how much such a firm will be willing to supply at a range of prices. As long as the firm is operating, its supply curve will be the same as its MC curve. (In figure 5.2 this is the thicker portion of MC lying above $SAVC$.) At price P_1 the firm will take a decision not to operate since the price does not even cover variable costs. At P_2 it will operate (at least temporarily) producing an output of Q_2 where $MR_2 = MC$. Similarly, at P_3 it will happily operate, this time on a continuous basis, at Q_3, where economic profits can be earned.

Figure 5.3(a) shows the supply curve for a typical firm in a price-taking market. If the industry is composed of, say, 100 such firms then at a price of £20 each firm would be willing to supply 400 units, and so the industry would be willing to supply the sum of all the firms' quantities supplied, namely 40,000 units. A similar aggregation exercise could be performed at all price levels, and so the industry's supply curve (the horizontal sum of all firms' supply curves, ΣMC) would be obtained (figure 5.3(b)). In reality, of course, it is unlikely that all firms would have the identical MC curves assumed for the representative firm. If nothing else, managerial efficiencies would differ and each firm's MC curve would lie at a different level. Nonetheless, the principle of horizontal aggregation would remain unaltered. Only the graphical and numerical neatness and proportion of figure 5.3 would be forfeit.

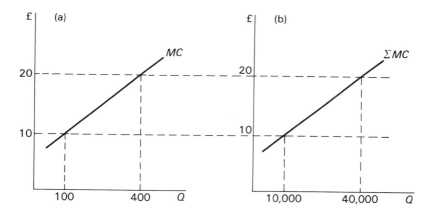

Figure 5.3 *Supply curves in a price-taking market for (a) a typical firm (b) the industry of 100 firms*

Thus we have now obtained, in a different manner, the supply curve discussed in figure 2.4. Supply can also be considered, as we saw in figures 2.2 and 2.3, to be simply a variant of the way we regard demand. In a price-taking market for good X, the firms in the industry merely put lower marginal valuations on X (in terms of money) than do the buyers of X and continue to do so until the market price is reached; at this point trading ceases, since the industry's marginal valuation (i.e. its aggregate marginal cost) is now higher than that of potential buyers. With this in mind it is not surprising that three important concepts relating to demand can also be applied to supply.

First, *supply* has an *elasticity* just like that of demand and it is measured in an analogous manner; namely, the elasticity of supply is equal to the relative change in quantity supplied divided by the relative change in price that caused the change in quantity:

$$\text{elasticity of supply} = \frac{\Delta Q_s/Q_s}{\Delta P/P}.$$

Second, as with demand, long-run supply is more elastic than short-run supply. Third, as a demand curve always slopes down and to the left, so a supply curve always slopes up and to the right.

Figure 5.4 shows diagrammatically the difference between long-run and short-run supply elasticity. The causes are similar to those for demand elasticity variations over time. Firms do not make a total response to a price change instantaneously. Existing firms will raise output in response to a price rise but, in the short term, will do so by using existing plant. In the long term they may plan, design and build larger plants, but this takes time. Similarly, a higher price will tempt new firms into the industry, but that also cannot happen instantaneously. So, in the short run, a price rise from P_1 to P_2 may increase the quantity supplied to only Q_2 (from Q_1); in the long term, however, the overall increase would be $Q_2' - Q_1$.

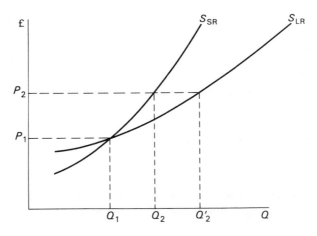

Figure 5.4 *Long-run and short-run supply elasticity*

Figure 5.5 explains these points more fully. First, the price rise does not 'just happen'. Something independent of supply must cause it. Demand in the industry (figure 5.5(b)) increases from D_1 to D_2, causing the equilibrium price to rise from P_1 to P_2. Originally, the representative firm (figure 5.5(a)) was producing q_1 units at P_1 and making only 'normal' (i.e. zero economic) profits. In the short run, the response to the price rise is limited to what existing firms can accomplish in their existing plants. The representative firm consequently increases its output to q_2. The long-run response to this is that new firms enter and existing firms expand in size. As new firms enter, the industry short-run supply curve shifts to the right (S'_{SR}). This reduces the price to P_3. If this was all that was happening, entry would continue until, for the representative firm, the price had fallen down MC to P_1 and quantity had been restored to q_1. (Since the intersection of P_3 ($= MR$) and MC is where existing firms continue to make economic profits, because $P_3 > SATC$ at that output level). But other things are not equal. P_1 is not the long-run price and S_{LR} is not horizontal. The reason is that, as other firms enter the industry, the demand for the *inputs* which firms use rises and so input prices rise. This causes costs to rise and $SATC$ moves upwards to $SATC'$, and MC to MC'. Now at P_3 there is no incentive for a still further set of new firms to enter the industry and each of the (still increased in number) representative firms now produces q_3 units.

Note that if the expansion of industrial output *lowered* input prices, then the cost curves would fall and the long-run suply would be downward sloping. This could happen, for example, if the output change was so great that other economies could be reaped. Thus, if an industry grew dramatically it might be feasible to organize special training courses for employees. This could improve their efficiency and productivity and so lower the cost of labour per unit, even with a higher wage rate.

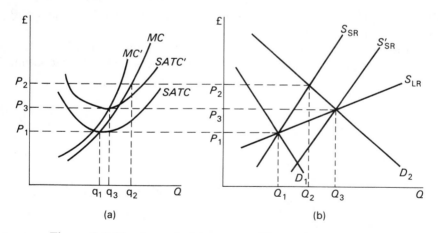

Figure 5.5 *Short-run and long-run effects of a price rise on (a) a typical firm (b) the industry*

Price searchers

In contrast to price takers, price searchers have a pricing problem. For them, price and marginal revenue are not identical; this is because of the downward-sloping demand curve which they face. As a consequence of this, the addition to total revenue from selling one extra unit is less than the price at which it is sold. The price taker did not experience this. If he sold 10 units,

Table 5.3 *A price-searcher's demand schedule, total revenue and marginal revenue*

P	Q	TR	MR
10	1	10	
			8
9	2	18	
			6
8	3	24	
			4
7	4	28	
			2
6	5	30	
			0
5	6	30	
			−2
4	7	28	
			−4
3	3	24	
			−6
2	9	18	
			−8
1	10	10	

his receipts were 10 times the market price; if 11, then 11 times that same market price, and so on.

But a price searcher can only sell more if he lowers his price. Table 5.3 illustrates this and figure 5.6 plots a typical price-searcher's demand and marginal revenue curves.

Bearing in mind that the firm's objective is to maximize profit $(TR - TC)$, then again the profit-maximizing price, as with the price taker, is that output

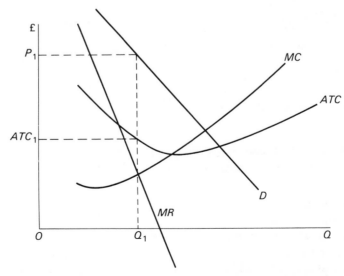

Figure 5.6 *A price-searcher's demand and marginal revenue curves*

level where $MR = MC$. To the left of such a point—at level Q_1 in figure 5.6—additions to total revenue exceed additions to total cost for each extra unit produced; to the right of that point, the reverse holds. Consequently, P_1 should be chosen as the profit-maximizing price.

Several inferences can be made from this diagram. First, the firm is making economic as well as normal profits (the economic profits are given by the rectangle $(P_1 - ATC_1) \times (Q_1 - O)$.) Second, the profit-maximizing price could (but need not, as is the case here) be a price which results in an output producible at minimum ATC. Such an outcome would be pure coincidence. Third, the economic profits the firm makes need not be positive. They can be negative or losses. All that the $MR = MC$ condition results in is profit maximization (or loss minimization). The profit rectangle in figure 5.6 is only a graphical coincidence. One need look no further than British Leyland, a price-searching firm aiming to maximize profits, which is kept from bankruptcy only by continuous injections of government-provided money taken firstly from the individual citizens of the country. Fourth, no matter how low costs are, a price searcher will never produce where its demand curve is inelastic.

To illustrate the last point, recall our discussion of elasticity in chapter 3. A demand curve is inelastic if a price reduction results in a total revenue fall (i.e., MR becomes zero and then negative). Graphically, since costs, including MC, can never be negative, MC will never equal MR when MR is negative and so the statement is true. Logically it would be stupid for a profit-maximizing price searcher to increase output (thus increasing total costs) by lowering total revenue (thus reducing profits). This is shown formally in the next few paragraphs.

Marginal revenue and demand elasticity

In our simple example in table 5.3, we used discrete price changes of single units. If we had assumed, as is customary in developing this type of analysis, that both the price and the quantity demanded can be altered by very small amounts, then calculus can be utilized to analyse the behaviour of our demand function. We shall briefly consider how calculus can be applied to the analysis of these functions; those not mathematically inclined should be able to follow the verbal explanations of what follows.

$$\text{total revenue} (TR) = \text{price} \times \text{quantity} = PQ \qquad (5.1)$$

Marginal revenue is the change in total revenue which results from selling one extra unit of output. This is not the same as the price at which the last unit is sold, since—unless the demand curve is horizontal—the price of all units sold must be reduced in order to sell an extra unit. It is measured by the gradient of the total revenue curve. This can be found by differentiating the expression for total revenue with respect to quantity, i.e.:

$$\text{marginal revenue} (MR) = \frac{dTR}{dQ} = P\frac{dQ}{dQ} + Q\frac{dP}{dQ}$$

$$= P + \frac{QdP}{dQ}. \tag{5.2}$$

There is a very close link between marginal revenue and price elasticity of demand. Remember that price elasticity measures the proportionate response in quantity demanded in response to a proportionate change in price, and the formula was

$$\eta = \frac{dQ}{dP}\frac{P}{Q}.$$

If we extract P from our expression for marginal revenue in equation (5.2) we obtain:

$$\text{marginal revenue} (MR) = P\left(1 + \frac{Q}{P}\frac{dP}{dQ}\right) = P\left(1 + \frac{1}{\eta}\right). \tag{5.3}$$

Expression 5.3 shows that marginal revenue is equal to price times (one plus one over price elasticity of demand). What happens when price elasticity of demand is unitary? When $\eta = (-)1$ the expression in brackets in equation 5.3 becomes zero and, therefore, marginal revenue is zero. This is also the point at which total revenue is maximized. This follows since marginal revenue equals the gradient of the total revenue curve and, when the total revenue curve is at a maximum, its gradient will be zero. This is because, at that point, the curve is neither increasing nor decreasing. The implication of this is that businessmen, if they are profit maximizers, will behave in setting their prices as if they are operating on the section of the demand curve where elasticities are greater than one. There is little point in cutting prices if the result will be a drop in revenue.

This last point is particularly interesting since it gives the lie to so many casual denunciations of industrial pricing practices. Consider the petrol industry. People are often heard to say: 'Of course, they can and do raise their prices to maximize their profits. They can do this because petrol is a necessity, there is no price sensitivity (i.e., demand is inelastic).'

Our analysis shows that if the price elasticity for petrol is this low then firms cannot be maximizing profits; or, if they are, then price sensitivity is not so low as the casual gossip suggests. Probably both explanations have some validity. When petrol prices rose in the 1970s short-run usage of cars did drop off, and in the long run car firms have been expending considerable effort in making the increasingly fuel-efficient cars which replacement buyers have been demanding. In short there is some price sensitivity in the petrol market.

Nevertheless studies do show that it is very low. It can only be low (i.e., well below 1.0) if firms are *not* profit maximizing. Since the petrol market is not closed, and as there is not a single seller, this suggests that firms have been continually competing with each other, not of course to raise prices but to lower them. Naturally, they would have liked to act as a single seller in a closed price-searching market and maximize profits by raising prices to the profit-maximizing, demand-elastic range, but they have been unable to do so owing to the forces of competition.

What confuses the issue is the problem of rising prices caused by government taxation in the UK, raw material price increases in the oil-producing countries, and the general level of inflation itself which makes it difficult to sort out what, in fact, is happening to any one good's real or relative price.

We have seen that the demand curve for price searchers might lie above or below *ATC* so that the firm could make economic profits or losses. This is true in the short run. As with price takers, it is not true in the long run. Profits and losses both tend to disappear as either the number or the size of firms in the industry changes. That, of course, depends on entry not being closed by some restriction or barrier to entry and/or exit. Figure 5.7 shows the impact of both time and entry on the firm of figure 5.6. Because of the incentive of profit which the firm in figure 5.6 is making, firms which discover they can make an acceptable substitute enter the market and the original firm's demand curve falls, becoming more price elastic ($D_{SR} \rightarrow D_{LR}$). Corresponding price and quality changes occur if the firm is to continue maximizing profits at $MR_{SR} = MC \rightarrow MR_{LR} = MC$. If the process continues without any substantial shocks, such as a major product innovation, taste change or cost-reducing

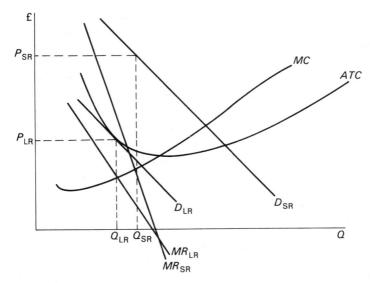

Figure 5.7 *Impact of time and market entry on the price-searching firm of figure 5.6*

process innovation, then there is a tendency for the firm to end up in a situation where the best that can happen is that price covers costs at P_{LR}. At any output other than Q_{LR}, the firm makes a loss.

Product Differentiation and Research and Development

Both price searchers and price takers tend to earn no more than normal profits. One way to alter this is to close the market so that competitive entry does not occur; restrictive practices and legal barriers (see chapter 11) are methods of doing this. A second way is by advertising (see chapter 13), which can produce a taste change. A third is to engage in research and development in order to obtain a unique product (and so a unique demand curve) or a lower-cost process for a given product and demand curve.

What is research and development (R & D)? It can be seen as a spectrum stretching from basic research through applied research to development. Basic research is an attempt to increase pure scientific knowledge, and typically occurs in universities or other centrally or charitably funded bodies such as the research councils. An example of basic research was Hertz's experiments with the wireless transmission of sound waves in the nineteenth century, which occurred long before Marconi invented his radio. That was applied research: a deliberate attempt to invent, given the state of knowledge, and begun with a particular application in mind.

Applied research may be divided into two. First, background applied research is carried out to increase or refine the store of know-how on which future applications can draw (e.g. studies of the causes of the common cold may lead to the discovery of a cure). Again this tends to occur in the universities or the research councils but occasionally in industry also. Second, product or process-directed applied research is carried out to obtain a product or process within predetermined commercial criteria. This occurs mainly in industry or industrially funded research associations. A new aircraft design or the application of industrial robots for a production line are examples of this.

Development is the adaptation of a newly acquired product or process to the ruling demands of the market-place. Development generally occurs in an industrial environment and examples might be the constructing, testing and refinement of a prototype aircraft, or the test of a chemical to ascertain that it is safe for human consumption.

This R & D spectrum results in technical change—but barriers to the enjoyment of such change can occur at several places. For example:

1   A lack of scientific knowledge can hinder invention. For example, a lack of true understanding of the causes of cancer means that the search for a cure is not well defined, but rather that effort is dispersed and thus less effective than it might be.

2   The hovercraft, conversely, was invented long after the requisite know-how was available; what was lacking was an inventive 'act of insight'.

3   A lack of development can hinder innovation. Penicillin provides a classic example. Fleming discovered its anti-bacterial activity in 1928, but his discovery lay dormant as merely a fact in the scientific literature of the day. It was not until 1939 that Florey and Chain did further development work on it which led to its eventual innovation in 1943 as a marketable product.

4   After innovation occurs, diffusion can be tardy.

(*a*) For example, there was a failure of horizontal diffusion in the motor industry when firms in the same industry (albeit in America) did not adopt the innovations of disc brakes and radial tyres until long after they had been available in Europe.

(*b*) Vertical diffusion may be impeded if customers in the industry fail to make use of an innovation. Thus, long after anti-depressant drugs had been made available, the medical profession continued to prescribe tranquillizers. This was because depression was not regarded as a disease or clinical entity in most medical schools at the time. This situation is now rectified in formal medical education after intensive advertising by the pharmaceutical firms involved to overcome the inertia and ignorance of existing prescribers.

(*c*) Lateral diffusion into apparently unrelated fields may not occur because of a lack of entrepreneurial vision. Thus while Marconi became synonymous with the wireless telegraph, he failed to perceive the potential of radio broadcasting as a news and entertainment medium. It was left to firms such as RCA to exploit this to the full.

As Schumpeter emphasized, however, one way to encourage innovation and diffusion is to formally conduct R & D on a routine basis. This has taken place in industry over the last few decades, and, as figure 5.8 indicates, R & D expenditure is at present over 2 per cent of GDP in the UK. The figure is divided into three: large R & D performers (where the amount spent is large in both relative and absolute terms); medium performers (where the R & D intensity relative to GDP may or may not be less than in the first group, but where the absolute resources devoted to R & D are less); and small R & D performers (low both in R & D intensity and in resources spent on R & D). (The USA's steep decline reflects the wind-down of the space exploration programme since the moon landing in 1971.)

Table 5.4 shows in which sectors of the economy R & D expenditure is incurred. By far the greatest proportion, some 58 per cent is spent by private industry. The next largest spender is the government sector, at 21 per cent, followed by the academic institutions at over 9 per cent.

Table 5.5 shows the sources of finance for R & D expenditure. A comparison of Tables 5.4 and 5.5 illustrates that a high degree of cross-

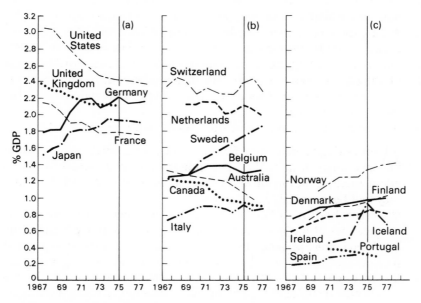

Source: *Science Resources Newsletter*, 1980, OECD, Paris.

Figure 5.8 *R & D expenditure as a percentage of GDP (a) large R & D
performing countries (b) medium R & D performing
countries (c) small R & D performing countries*

Table 5.4 *R & D expenditure in Britain: users of finance, 1978*

Sector carrying out the work	£m	%
Government:		
Defence departments	331.0	9.4
Civil departments	271.8	7.8
Research councils	152.3	4.3
Local government	3.0	0.1
Total (government)	758.1	21.6
Universities and technical colleges	317.7	9.0
Public corporations	212.5	6.1
Research associations	50.5	1.4
Private industry	2061.0	58.7
Other	110.6	3.2
Total	3510.3	100.0

Source: *Annual Abstract of Statistics*, 1981

Table 5.5 *R & D expenditure in Britain: sources of finance, 1978*

Sector providing the funds	£m	%
Government	1651.4	47.0
Universities, etc.	28.4	0.8
Public corporations	259.7	7.4
Private industry	1292.4	36.9
Others	278.4	7.9
Total	3510.3	100.0

Source: *Annual Abstract of Statistics,* 1981

subsidization exists. While the government *performs* one-fifth of the UK R & D effort, it *finances* nearly one-half. The academic institutions spent over £300 million but provided less than £30 million of this from their own funds: the remainder came from government bodies, industrial grants and contracts, and donations from charitable foundations.

It was conceptually convenient in the R & D spectrum to distinguish between basic research, applied research, and development, but in practice the various stages may be extremely difficult to separate. The dangers of isolating the stages in practice, with a possible resultant blockage in the process of technical progress, are underlined by the actions of some of the practitioners. Universities establish industrial liaison departments; one of the principal motivating factors is the failure of much university research activity ever to reach the development stage, to say nothing of innovation and production. At the other end of the spectrum, many industrialists show an awareness of the necessity of R & D continuity and allocate a portion of their R & D budget to basic research either in-house or by grants to a university.

Table 5.6 shows the distribution of the British R & D effort across the three stages of the R & D spectrum. The table indicates that 70 per cent of all basic research is performed by certain government establishments and the academic sector. It further indicates that the bulk of academic research is basic, with little continuity through to development. This is similarly the case with applied research, where over 50 per cent is performed by private or public industry and the research associations. Development is not the most important activity of the research councils but is a characteristic of research association activity.

Well over 70 per cent of all development expenditure is incurred by industry, private or state-owned. In like manner, almost three-quarters of industrial R & D expenditure is allocated to development activities.

Looking at the nation's entire R & D effort, one-eighth is basic research, one-quarter is applied research expenditure and the remaining five-eighths

Table 5.6 *Expenditure distribution by nature of R & D activity in the UK*

Sector carrying out the work	Basic research (%)	Applied research (%)	Development (%)	Total[6] (%)
Government:				
Defence[a]	0.6	2.2	7.1	13.9
Civil	1.2	3.8	5.3	10.3
Research councils	2.6	1.4	0.02	3.7
Total (government)	4.4	7.4	12.4	27.9
Universities	4.2	4.2	0.0	8.4
Technical colleges	0.1	0.1	0.02	0.22
Public corporations	0.2	2.4	2.1	4.7
Research associations	0.2	1.0	0.4	1.6
Private industry	2.1	13.2	4.0	59.2
Others	0.7	0.9	0.3	1.8
Total[b]	11.4	26.6	62.0	100.0

[a] Some defence expenditure is non-allocable, and so the defence subtotal and the government total exceed the sum of the individual figures.
[b] Totalling discrepancies are due to 'rounding' errors.

Source: Statistics of Science and Technology, Department of Education and Science, 1970

development. The table begs two questions. Why should this be the distribution of R & D expenditure? Further, should this be regarded as the optimum for inducing economically desirable technical change?

R & D is an inherently risky activity of uncertain outcome. The nearer to the basic research end of the R & D spectrum is the activity, the greater is the uncertainty of object. The nearer an R & D project approaches development, the more accurately can remaining future costs be assessed, realizable goals defined and the probability of failure reduced. Commercial potential and technical feasibility are almost unknown at the basic end of the spectrum; the predictability of both tends to certainty the nearer the completion of the development process. This being the case, it is to be expected that profit-motivated industrialists who decide to spend on R & D will tend to incur that expenditure in those portions of the R & D spectrum where a return will be achieved sooner rather than later—at a lower rather than a higher risk—and where the object of the expenditure is definable and of known value rather than vague or uncertain. This is, in fact, the pattern of industrial R & D spending.

The predominance of basic research in the universities is also subject to intuitive explanation. Once a major scientific breakthrough has been made in a project in a university the need for profitable exploitation is absent, and other motivating factors, such as scientific interest *per se*, are not so strong in carrying a knowledge increase through to a usable innovation as they are in encouraging further basic research.

The dominance of development expenditure is equally to be expected. Development costs more than basic research. In development, the scale of R & D operations may be approaching full-size factory operation, or a project which has not yet progressed beyond the drawing-board may have to be transferred to a full-scale mock-up model. Crude principles discovered earlier in the spectrum may have to be refined or altered to meet marketing or production constraints which, in turn, may require more sophisticated equipment and more scientific disciplines, represented in larger teams of research workers. In multistage processes, stage efficiencies observed in the laboratory may be completely unacceptable in production itself, particularly with a high-priced raw material or low-priced end product. For example, a three-stage process with a 50 per cent yield at each stage will yield at the end of stage three only 12½ per cent of the original (but now processed) raw materials. In a process with many more stages than three, the development problem of getting a high final stage output can be extremely costly to overcome.

Most industrial R & D activity occurs in what are frequently called the science-based industries such as chemicals, electronics, aerospace and engineering. Table 5.7 indicates that only some of R & D expenditure within manufacturing industry occurs in the more traditional craft-based industries. The inter-industry pattern of R & D effort is determined in part by the vast differences in the amounts and value of equipment required in different fields. For example, while the aerospace industry absorbs 19 per cent of all industrial R & D expenditure it accounts for only 13.6 per cent of the qualified man-power in industrial R & D. This is largely due to the relatively large sums

Table 5.7 *Expenditure on R & D within manufacturing industry, 1978*

Product group	Total expenditure (£m)	(%)	Product group	Total expenditure (£m)	(%)
Food, drink, tobacco	82.3	3.7	Scientific instruments	45.4	2.0
Chemicals, allied products	431.8	19.3	Electrical engineering	751.3	33.5
Iron, steel	32.5	1.5	Motor vehicles	130.0	5.8
Non-ferrous metals	13.3	0.6	Aerospace	424.9	19.0
Mechanical engineering	181.9	8.1	Leather, textiles, etc.	31.0	1.4
Glass, building materials, etc.	26.1	1.2	Timber, paper, publishing, etc.	17.2	0.8
Ships and marine engineering	18.8	0.8	Others	29.8	1.3
Other metal goods	23.1	1.0			
All manufacturing industry				2255.1	100.0

Source: Business Monitor, 1980

Table 5.8 *Qualified manpower engaged in private
manufacturing industry, 1978*

Industry	R & D manpower	
	(men, 000s)	(%)
Food, drink, tobacco	2.2	3.4
Chemicals, allied products	12.0	18.3
Metal manufacture	2.6	4.0
Mechanical engineering	5.1	7.8
Electrical engineering and electronics	26.4	40.4
Vehicles, etc.	4.0	6.1
Aerospace	8.9	13.6
Textiles, clothing, etc.	1.0	1.5
Other industries	3.2	4.9
Total manufacturing	65.4	100.0

Source: Business Monitor, 1980

required for prototype construction and to their relatively early appearance in the R & D process. Chemicals, conversely, employ 18.3 per cent of the qualified manpower in industrial R & D but accounts for 19.3 per cent of the expenditure incurred. Much chemical research can be performed with relatively inexpensive equipment in the laboratory and the appearance of expensive pilot plants is a relatively late phenomenon in the R & D process.

Differences of this nature, however, do not alter the basic concentration of R & D in the science-based industries as a whole. Table 5.8 shows 80 per cent of all qualified manpower in R & D to be concentrated in such industries. Not only do such industries perform more R & D absolutely than the craft industries, they also have an above-average propensity to conduct R & D. Using the ratio of R & D expenditure to sales, table 5.9 indicates that the greatest density of R & D effort occurs in the chemical, electrical, aerospace and associated industries. (The low figure for mechanical engineering is a noteworthy exception.)

There would appear to be two complementary reasons for the absolute concentration of R & D in the science-based industries—profitability and cost differences.

A science-based industry is able to utilize more promptly and effectively any change in its related body of technical knowledge. Where an industry's closest related science is relatively far removed, as in the craft-based industries, then discoveries may be initially inapplicable and tardy in providing any net financial return for the outlay required for R & D.

Table 5.9 *Gross expenditure on R & D as percentage of sales in manufacturing industries, 1978*

Industry	%
Food, drink, tobacco	0.44
Chemicals and allied industries	2.24
(pharmaceuticals)	(10.38)
Metal manufacture	0.46
Mechanical engineering	0.93
Electrical engineering and electronics	7.18
Vehicles, etc.	1.45
Aerospace	18.52
Textiles, clothing, etc.	0.39
All manufacturing industries	1.61

Source: Business Monitor, 1980

For example, chemistry is far removed from the traditional leather goods industry. The chemical discovery of plastics which could be used as leather substitutes was largely ignored by the leather industry. The plastics were initially unattractive and synthetic in appearance and had little capacity for hard wear. To alter this the leather industry would have had to incur large initial outlays on R & D teams, already in existence in chemicals, acquire know-how on plastic manufacture, and develop a product with the intention of replacing, rather than supplementing, the raw material already in use. The net profitability gain from such an exercise, at least in the short to medium run, would almost certainly have been negative. Consequently it was a chemical company, Du Pont, which first developed a plastic possessing the necessary pliability, durability and quality of appearance to compete with leather as a material for shoe manufacture.

The costs of R & D performance may be relatively high if an industry does not possess a well-developed scientific base. The possession of a scientific base implies an existing body of well-ordered and verifiable knowledge and information. The approach to an applied research problem can, in such circumstances, be systematic rather than empirical. That is, a definite goal can be worked towards from this foundation of knowledge by the use of strictly disciplined scientific thought, or deductive 'paper-and-pencil' techniques.

Where no scientific base is present, however, the approach to a research problem will tend to be empirical or random in nature. Solutions to the problem must be sought by trial-and-error experimentation rather than by deductive thought. The empirical approach is, therefore, relatively more

Table 5.10 *Summary of the case for an association between market structure and innovation*

Arguments in favour of high concentration	Major reservations
(A) *Cost of resources.* Market control raises profitability and reduces the demands on management, thus implying a lower opportunity cost of resources devoted to R & D. (B) *Risk.* Reduced short-run price competition provides greater security and permits a longer time horizon for research.	There may be financial advantages *for enterprising firms,* but the opportunities may not be realized if the incentive to innovate is impaired (see (C)—(E) below). Further, the relevance of financial advantages may vary with the scale of the technology.
(C) *Competitive incentives.* The risk of retaliation discourages oligopolistic price competition. Non-price competition is thereby encouraged, being less readily matched by competitors.	Non-price competition may give way to collusion unless the technology offers large gains from innovation. If one firm can appropriate these gains, the *initial* market structure may be irrelevant.
(D) *Market share incentives.* A large market share implies a greater absolute gain from any given proportionate change in costs or revenues. Therefore the costs of R & D are more easily recovered.	(i) Market leaders may gain less if new products replace existing products. (ii) Monopolists may bias the choice of innovations so as to preserve their dominance.
(E) *Risk of imitation.* Market dominance reduces the risk of imitation by competitors, and enables market leaders to retain the benefits of innovations.	Given that dominant firms may seek to delay innovations competing with established products, they may prefer a 'fast second' strategy, using market dominance to take over the proven innovations of smaller competitors.
(F) *Size of firm.* (A)—(E) may be reinforced if the monopolists or oligopolists are also large firms. Potential benefits include: (a) Indivisible innovations may require an absolutely large volume of resources. (b) Economies of scale may exist in the R & D process if specialized staff or equipment are required. Large firms are then more able to finance the optimum scale. (c) Economies of scale in marketing or production may enable large firms to exploit innovations more profitably. (d) The risk of failure of an R & D programme may be reduced if the number of independent projects in that programme can be increased. (e) Large firms may have a more diversified product range, giving more scope for the internal exploitation of new discoveries.	The benefits of size may be exaggerated. Reservations include: (i) Large firms may stifle creativity, and restrict invention and discovery. (ii) Advantages of size are more significant for development than for research, and may vary between industries. (iii) If there are no economies of scale in the R & D process, small firms with lower overheads may be more cost-effective and more flexible. (iv) Many small firms do no R & D. The owner-managers of those which do may be more highly motivated and less averse to risk than the salaried managers of large firms. (v) Diversification may encourage basic research, but is less relevant for targeted R & D. If there are economies of scale in R & D, a diversified firm may dissipate its resources over too wide an area.

Source: R.W. Shaw and C.J. Sutton, *Industry and Competition,* Macmillan, 1976, p. 203

expensive, requiring costly experiments comparatively sooner and more frequently than the systematic approach.

Having said this, one must not play down serendipity, the chance discovery of the highly trained observer. Without serendipity and Fleming's expertise, penicillin would have remained an unwanted mould growing in a glass jar in St Pancras.

If technical progress and R & D are regarded as desirable, is there any particular type of firm or industrial structure which will tend to encourage the activity? This question can be asked independently of the presence or absence of a scientific base in any given industry. It depends also on whether firms are price takers or searchers, on whether there are scale economies or not, on whether the firm is vertically integrated or not, and whether the industry is or is not highly concentrated. Scale and integration will be discussed in chapter 6. Market concentration will be deferred until chapter 11. In the meantime, table 5.10 summarizes the various (and often conflicting) answers to the question of the relationship between structure and innovation. It is suggested that the reader cross-refers to this table from time to time when studying the relevant parts of the rest of this book.

References

1 These pages draw on A. Alchian and H. Demsetz, 'Production, information costs and economic organisation', *American Economic Review* 62 (1972), pp. 777–95.
2 F.A. Hayek, 'The use of knowledge in society', *American Economic Review* 35 (1945), pp. 519–30.

6

Scale and Firm Growth

Why do firms grow? What determines the rate and direction of their growth? What is the phenomenon of scale economies to which we referred in chapter 5? We shall now consider the answers to these questions.

Economies of Scale

Economies of scale (or *increasing returns to scale*) is a phrase often used very loosely. A precise definition might relate to a hypothetical plant or firm. If technology is assumed constant, and all inputs (labour, materials, plant size itself) are increased by a given percentage but output per period of time rises by more than that percentage, then scale economies are present. *Decreasing returns to scale* (or diseconomies of scale) arise when all inputs are increased by a certain proportion but output rises by less than that proportion. *Constant returns to scale* are then self-explanatory: output rises or falls in the same proportion as inputs.

Note that, in the definition, all factors are variable—the scale changes— hence the term 'returns to scale'. This contrasts with the law of diminishing returns (or, as it is sometimes known, *returns to factor*) where at least one factor or input is held constant.

Geometrically this is one major distinction between short-run and long- run average cost curves. The short-run curve is composed of a unit fixed cost curve (for a non-varying input) and a unit variable cost curve. It has a U-shape for two reasons. First, fixed unit costs are spread more thinly over an increasing output. Second, after a point, diminishing returns set in and the marginal cost curve begins to rise; the rate of decrease of the unit variable cost curve slows, ceases to fall when it equals marginal cost, and then rises.

In the long-run case there is no fixed cost curve because all factors are variable. The long-run average cost ($LRAC$) is the so-called envelope of the short-run curves. It does *not* show a line joining the bottoms of the Us of each possible short-run curve. Rather it shows, to quote Pratten, 'the lowest possible cost of producing at any scale of output after all possible adaptation

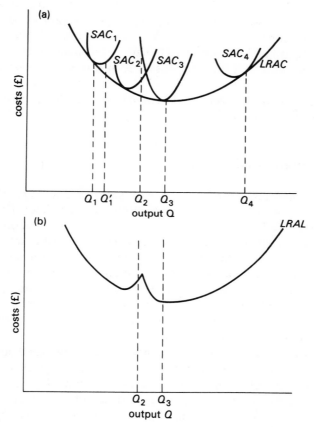

Figure 6.1 *Long-run average cost curve (a) general form, joining*
short-run curves for four plants (b) given that output
requirements fall between the points of tangency of
short-run cost curves for possible plants

to that scale has taken place'.[1] To join the bottoms of all the Us by any smooth curve would in fact be a geometric impossibility.

Figure 6.1(a) summarizes our discussion to this point. The figure shows short-run curves for four possible plant sizes and the long-run envelope scale curve. Economies of scale are present as we move from plant size 1 to plant size 3; the *LRAC* slopes down. At plant size 4 diseconomies set in. Only at Q_3 do the minima of a short-run and the long-run curve coincide. Thus in the case of plant 1, with short-run average cost SAC_1, Q_1' is the minimum but Q_1 is the point of tangency.

To return to Pratten's definition: the *LRAC* shows the lowest cost of producing at any scale after all adaptations have taken place. If for technological reasons it is not possible to build a plant between sizes 2 and 3 then the cheapest way of producing Q_2 is plant size 2. Plant size 3 could also produce Q_2 but at a higher cost; the line of output Q_2 cuts SAC_2 at a lower point than SAC_3; the envelope curve, would in fact, have the tilted-W shape of figure 6.1(b). The right-hand portion of SAC_2 and the left-hand limb of SAC_3 form the centre peak of the W, for as long as the former is below the latter and vice versa.

If plant of any size between 2 and 3 *could* be built then the original smooth envelope could indeed be drawn.

Sources of Firms' Scale Economies: the Static View

The first detailed analyses of the sources of scale economies and their implications were made by Professor Sir Austin Robinson in his book *The Structure of Competitive Industry* in the 1930s,[2] and by Professor P. Sargent Florence in his *The Logic of British and American Industry*.[3] Although both these books are now somewhat elderly their basic insights remain unsullied. Robinson emphasized the concept of the optimum size of firm. He analysed the five criteria of technique, management, finance, marketing and risk. Each of these could have different optimum scales of operation and the reconciliation of these optima was essentially an exercise in organizational logic and was a major managerial task.

In brief, Robinson was emphasizing that scale economies and diseconomies can produce $LRAC$ curves for one firm, but the foot of the U need not be at the same output level for different corporate functions. Figure 6.1 basically referred to the plant or factory, not to the firm as a whole. It referred only to technique, not to management, finance, marketing or risk. We will return to these other criteria below.

Specialization

The larger the output the greater will be the opportunities for, and advantages of, specialization of both men and machinery. Adam Smith noted that the division of labour in a pin factory permitted increased efficiency owing 'first, to the increase of dexterity in every particular workman; secondly, to the saving of time which is commonly lost in passing from one species of work to another; and lastly to the invention of a great number of machines which facilitate and abridge labour and enable one man to do the work of many'.

Increased output may enable firms to employ staff with special skills in engineering, production, marketing, finance or information processing. Smaller firms may have neither the resources to pay for nor the number of tasks to fully occupy and utilize some specialists. They consequently may then have to make do with less well trained personnel whose lower efficiency is not compensated for by proportionately lower remuneration.

The principle of multiples

Sargent Florence argued that scale economies could arise from three principles: multiples, bulk transactions and massed reserves. The principle of
multiples is also often called the problem of indivisibilities. The economies
available from specialization depend upon the specialists being fully utilized
in their speciality up to capacity. (It is somewhat inefficient to use a highly
qualified accountant or market research specialist for two and a half days
out of five, and, because inadequate work is available, to employ them as a
bookkeeper or delivery man respectively on the remaining two and a half
days.) But the capacity of different specialists is not identical, and they are
often indivisible or non-transferable. Thus an accountant can rarely be
transferred to a market research man's desk and perform the job with the
same competency as a marketing specialist. When capacities vary as well as
competencies the problem of indivisibilities arises.

Consider the can-making process outlined in table 6.1. The greater the
productive capacity of any one indivisible and specialist resource (in this
case, the cutter) the greater is the necessary multiple of the others to ensure
that the lowest common multiple (LCM) throughout is attained.

The principle of bulk transactions

This saving can be subdivided into at least three categories. Most obviously,
as Sargent Florence pointed out, 'the total monetary, physical or psychological costs of dealing in large quantities are sometimes no greater . . . than

Table 6.1 *Can-making process*

	Steel cutters (i.e. cutting rectangles of metal)	Moulders & solderers (i.e. shaping hollow cylinders	Capping machines (i.e. fixing end on to tin can cylinder)
Capacity in tons of strip steel equivalent per hour	30	5	10
Number of machines required to have each fully utilized	1	6	3

the costs of dealing in small quantities; and hence the cost *per unit* becomes smaller with large quantities.' A salesman makes very little, if any, extra effort when he negotiates an order for several thousand units than if the order were for several dozen. The same holds for a firm's purchasing agent and also for the accounting department which maintains records of the transaction.

Second, there is what Austin Robinson called the *integration of processes*. In a sense this is the opposite of specialization and the division of labour. It occurs where output is large enough to justify the cost of one large sophisticated machine (a form of indivisibility) which can carry out a series of formerly consecutive processes simultaneously. This eliminates transfer time from machine to machine of the work in progress. And it eliminates the labour and time required to set up the work on each of a series of successive specialized machines.

Third, there are the *economies of increased dimensions*. For many types of equipment both initial and running costs increase less rapidly than capacity. Tanks, pressure vessels, ships, blast furnaces and other static and mobile containers are examples of this form of economy. Any cubic container whose external dimensions are doubled has its volume increased eight times but the area of its surface walls will only have increased fourfold. This reduces material and construction costs and, where appropriate, heat loss and surface, air or water resistance per unit. Fuel economies are thus gained. Moreover, the labour input required to operate a large machine seldom rises in proportion to that required to operate a small machine with an identical function. For example, a 100-seater plane flying from London to Berlin has a flight deck crew of two: this number is unchanged when the size of plane increases to a 250-seater.

The principle of massed reserves

What Pratten calls *the economies of massed resources* is a scale economy dependent on the law of large numbers or the insurance principle. The economized resource can be any for which demand is uncertain or risky. For example, a firm using several identical machines will have to stock proportionately fewer spare parts than a firm with only one, since the larger firm can assume that all of its machines are unlikely to break down simultaneously for the same reason. Similar economies can exist for raw materials, for finished goods in a central warehouse servicing the fluctuating demands of a chain of retail shops, for labour and for monetary resources.

Sources of Firms' Scale Economies: Dynamic Economies

So far we have assumed that technology is constant—that there is an absence of learning within known technologies—and that no economies of growth

are obtainable by firms. We will now drop the second of these two assumptions. For the first, it is obvious that technology can lower costs, but it is difficult from this alone to conceptualize scale economies, other things being equal. Moreover, there is still no definite consensus among economists as to whether larger or smaller firms are more technologically progressive.

Learning curves

Armen Alchian[4] has argued that 'as the total quantity of units produced increases, the cost of *future* output declines.' This is not the same as saying that unit costs fall as output rises. Rather it is akin to Adam Smith's increasing dexterity due to division of labour; people 'learn by doing'. The whole *LRAC* is lowered as a consequence of production. It is not simply that the *LRAC* falls along its length as output rises, but rather that as output rises, then at any future output the *LRAC* will have fallen. This phenomenon is known as the learning curve (figure 6.2). Clearly firms will move further and faster down the learning curve the higher is their output in any given period.

Since the 1930s the aircraft industry has found the 80 per cent curve (i.e. a 20 per cent reduction in labour costs) to be a fairly exact estimator of its past experience in the construction of aeroplanes. Where machines play a larger part of the production process the 90 per cent curve may be more appropriate. And where machinery is automatic, no learning can be expected. Once a learning curve has been established it is clear that (a) it can be used to forecast labour requirements in the future given assumptions about future production schedules and demand levels, and (b) it will have more impact on a firm with a large rather than a small throughput, all other things including time remaining equal.

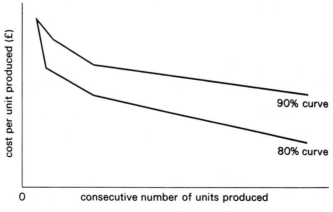

Figure 6.2 *Learning curves*

Economies of growth

Economies of growth were first described at length by Edith Penrose in *The Theory of the Growth of the Firm*.[5] At first glance they seem easy to understand; but the motives for firms growing are many and varied. The unique aspect of economies of growth as a scale economy is that a given firm, *irrespective of its size*, is able to put additional output on the market at a lower unit cost than any other firm. This is then an economy of scale arising from growth to a size, not an economy of scale arising from a size level. Clearly, to be a valid concept it can only apply to a particular firm which can take advantage of a unique opportunity in supply or demand conditions. It applies to the opportunity rather than the firm, even though it is a firm that perceives and acts on the opportunity. For example a book publisher may suddenly have the opportunity to sign on a best-selling author. If he does, his throughput will increase dramatically and his unit costs will fall, for example via the principle of bulk transactions; but such unit cost reductions through growth are available only to that one publisher, not to each firm in the industry. Other firms may wish to have a best-selling author on their list but this, and therefore growth, is not always possible.

Sources of Scale Diseconomies

Indivisibilities

The principle of multiples indicates that firms should be large enough to achieve a level of output where at least one large and indivisible specialized resource can be used, and so attain the least common multiple (LCM) of all inputs. Conversely, since the specialized input is 'lumpy', if output rises beyond levels which are not common multiples of all input types then some of the indivisible factors may again become under-utilized.

Technical factors

Technical factors are unlikely to produce diseconomies of scale. If inefficiencies arise as a result of over-large plant size then they can be overcome or avoided by replicating units of plant of a smaller, optimum size. One example of this is turbine blades. If an over-large turbine is constructed the ends of the blades will travel at a speed near to that of sound. The strains and stresses then imposed on the blades increase more than proportionately with turbine capacity.

In short, technical factors are more likely to limit the sources of scale economies than to act as a source of diseconomies. At worst, constant returns to scale via replication are attainable.

Managerial factors

However, replication of technical inputs leads to problems in other spheres. Hence Robinson's stress on the need to reconcile the optima of the criteria of technique, finance, risk, marketing and management.

When diseconomies of scale arise they are more likely to be associated with the human and behavioural problems of managing a large enterprise. Consider what Williamson[6] calls the *U-form organization* of figure 6.3. This is a highly simplified organization chart or managerial hierarchy. The functional managers of manufacturing, marketing and finance are all responsible to the chief executive. If any of the three wishes to communicate with the other he must follow the formal chain of command and pass his message through the chief executive, whose function is co-ordination. This will be a time-consuming business wrapped in red tape but, given a large organization with several hundred managers, such indirect co-ordination may be the only practical method of avoiding chaos.

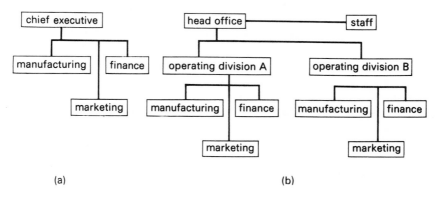

Figure 6.3 *Organizational forms (a) unitary or U-form
(b) multidivisional or M-form*

The chief executive, however, can only co-ordinate a limited number of subordinates, and if the organization grows too large then another layer of management may have to be inserted. This lengthens the chain of command, and the chief executive, in order to communicate further down the hierarchy, must pass his message through an intermediary. This increases the costs of communication and also introduces the problems of possible message distortion or misinterpretation, with corresponding implications for organizational efficiency.

These arguments are embraced in Williamson's concept of 'control loss'.[7] The decisions taken by a top executive must be based on information passed across a series of hierarchical levels. In turn, the instructions based on this information must be transmitted through these successive stages. This transmission results in a serial reproduction loss, or distortion, of both the information and instructions. This will occur even if those individuals forming the hierarchy have identical objectives. Increases in the scale of the hierarchy result in a reduction in the quality of both the information reaching the top co-ordinator and of the instructions passed down by him to lower-level personnel. Moreover, since the capacity of the top administrator for assimilating information and issuing instructions is limited, he can, beyond a certain point, only cope with an expansion of the hierarchy by sacrificing some of the detail provided before the expansion. Thus the quantity of information received and transmitted per unit of output will be less after expansion than before. This is the phenomenon of control loss. As a result it can be argued that functional units will not adhere as closely to the top administrator's objectives of cost minimization as they did before expansion of the firm's output.

To overcome or mitigate such diseconomies the *M-form organization* has been suggested. Responsibility for day-to-day decisions, and even longer-term decisions, is left to the operating divisions (provided only that they do not step outside some predetermined remit such as product groupings or geographical areas). This reduces the information flows to and from head office. The chief executive can concentrate his efforts more on overall strategic planning, assisted by a specialist staff. Divisional managers do not have the conflict of objectives they might have in a U-form organization, where for example the production manager may wish to simplify the product line while the marketing manager may wish to broaden it. Moreover control is enhanced since each division can be run as a mini-firm and profit centre in its own right. This is much more difficult, if not impossible, in a U-form organization. In the M-form organization rewards, punishments and incentives to management and staff can be allocated more accurately according to productivity. For these reasons, M-form firms do not suffer from the same diseconomies as do U-form firms of a similar size.

Finally, there are the problems of morale and motivation of both management and labour force. It is often argued that the *esprit de corps* of a small firm is greater than that of a large. The labour force is more closely identified with the small firm and this results in improved productivity and greater overall loyalty to the organization. Management in the large firm may feel more secure and better insulated from competition than in the small; this may provoke a sluggishness and a lack of enterprise which are less likely in managers who see the possibility of being put out of business as a real threat. (We will discuss this type of inefficiency in more detail in chapter 11.)

Given these economies and diseconomies—the varying optima in technique, risk, marketing, finance and management—how in fact do firms adjust their size to attain optimal scale? Can they do so? Or can they merely attempt to? It is to these factors we now turn.

Reasons for and Methods of Growth

Firms grow for a variety of reasons. Growth may be an objective in itself; managers may like the apparent security large size brings. On the other hand firms may grow so that they can achieve a size, neither too large nor too small, that reconciles the optima of the five criteria of technique, risk, marketing, finance and management. Sometimes this requires that the firm grows so that it is large enough, say, to reap the scale economies of a large marketing team. On other occasions the firm may simply hive off certain activities, either because they would require the firm's other functions to be inordinately and uneconomically large and costly, or because the firm can never hope to use the function at a frequency that would allow it to minimize costs. In short, some of the criteria may reach the point of decreasing returns to scale before the others achieve such economies to the full. The finance function is a good example of this. Firms, for example, have to be large to bear the costs of a Stock Exchange flotation even once in a period of years. Only a specialist finance house performing such an operation regularly and frequently can minimize such costs, and the firm, no matter how large, will generally subcontract the task to such a specialist.

Firms can grow in three main ways. They can expand their existing operations in their current product fields; they can extend their activities into wholly unrelated areas (*diversification*); or they can begin to carry out different but successive stages in the production of their original product (*vertical integration*).

Vertical Integration

Vertical integration can be either backwards or forwards in nature. *Backward integration* is where the firm commences manufacture of products previously purchased from others in order to utilize them in making its original product line. An example of this type of activity would be the acquisition by a tea firm like Typhoo (Cadbury–Schweppes) of a tea plantation. *Forward integration* occurs when the firm moves nearer to the final market for its product and carries out a function previously undertaken by a customer. An example of forward integration is the ownership of many high street shoe shops by the manufacturing British Shoe Corporation.

Causes of vertical integration

Security

Traditionally the most frequently cited reason for vertical integration is a search for security (Austin Robinson). When manufacturers are outbidding each other for supplies because demand conditions are high it may make sound sense to integrate backwards and so have an assured source of materials of a quality and a quantity one can dictate. A major reason for the Shell Transport and Trading Company integrating backwards with the Royal Dutch Petroleum firm to form Royal Dutch/Shell in 1907 was the fact that Royal Dutch was rich in gasoline supplies, while Shell Transport's relative strength was that of a bulk transporter and merchandiser. In 1903 Shell had run into difficulties. Its Borneo kerosene was of poor quality and its refinery at Balik Papan was giving trouble, and the (independent) field of Moera Enim was unable to fulfil its contract. The outcome was vertical integration.

Conversely, if demand is slack and manufacturers are competing for business, it can clearly appear to be sensible to integrate forwards and so be assured of 'customer' loyalty. This was one major reason for the ubiquitous takeovers of independent bakery firms by the large flour millers such as Spillers, Rank Hovis McDougall and Associated British Foods in the 1950s and 1960s. Rising affluence in these years was reflected in a declining per caput consumption of bread and flour confectionery, as people began to eat more meat products at their evening meals. To attempt to retain outlets for their flour in this declining market the millers integrated forward by buying large numbers of retail outlets.

Efficiency

Where vertical integration results in cost reductions it is a form of scale economy since, other things equal, an integrated firm is larger than a non-integrated one. Four main sources of savings are possible. First, there are *engineering economies*. The classic example of these is the combining of iron production with rolling mill operations into a single, integrated steel manufacturing process. The need to reheat the iron is removed if the processes are carried out in quick succession.

Second, *marketing economies* are achieved and delivery charges reduced if plants are located in close proximity. Savings are also possible without physical nearness. Advertising and sales promotion expenditure can be pruned when the loyalty of 'customers' is guaranteed. Economies also arise when transactions are continually carried out by the same groups of individuals. Negotiation effort can be reduced when transactions are frequent. Repetition permits the development of routine, reliable and so low-cost information flows. Risk of faulty decisions also falls and decisions in the integrated firm are thus improved.

Third, *financial economies* are achievable in an integrated firm. Capital costs are lower when stocks can be held at lower levels than they would be in separate companies. An integrated firm can co-ordinate production and consumption rates in its various stages and so minimize the need to hold stocks for unforeseen contingencies.

A firm can also find it easier and cheaper to raise capital if it can gain investors' confidence by reducing risk and informing them how this has been achieved. For example, in the 1920s and 1930s film companies in the USA had to raise money to finance the manufacture of films. Loans, however, could generally only be raised against the security of a distribution contract from one or more of the major cinema chains. Given that the film was still unmade and so to some degree an unknown quantity this was no easy task. The situation was a major stimulus to the makers to integrate forwards to owning their own cinema groups.

Finally, *administrative economies* are possible. To the extent that successive stages of production, each with an individual administrative framework, can be combined under a single unit of supervision, there are obvious savings to be made by vertical integration.

Predatory reasons

Predatory causes of vertical integration can be seen as the desire for security writ large. Forward integration can secure a market but it can also foreclose it to competitors. One cannot buy Younger's beer in a pub owned by Watney. Backward integration can guarantee a reliable source of supply, but it can also prevent rivals gaining access to that source; or it can ensure that their costs are raised disadvantageously if the price charged to them is higher than the price set in an intra-firm transfer.

Deterrents to vertical integration

Vertical integration can yield benefits, but like most other activities it also has a cost. The rational businessman who calculates that the costs exceed the benefits will not undertake vertical integration as a means of growth or of reconciling the optima of the five Robinsonian criteria.

Clearly, a firm which is integrated backwards may find itself at a disadvantage in times of low demand. It will have forfeited flexibility in its purchasing policy. Production runs in earlier stages may become too short to achieve minimum unit costs. Relative to outside sources of supply it may also find itself committed to the use of obsolete production techniques.

Conversely a firm which is integrated forwards may find itself, in times of high demand, tied to relatively inefficient and poorly located markets or outlets. The advantage of a 'secure market' may be a disadvantage when demand conditions change.

The administrative costs of co-ordinating successive stages of production may be greater than the savings which result from the integration. Moreover, to the normal difficulties of co-ordination will be added the costs of acquiring skills in a relatively strange technology, be it at a stage of production preceding or succeeding that in which the existing management team have their expertise. Quite apart from the learning costs, which can be overcome in time, the administrative skills required for additional stages could prove to be incompatible with those already possessed.

In addition, a decision to expand by integration diverts corporate resources and funds from alternative courses of action. For example, they can no longer be used to expand a product line and so gain for the firm the advantages of diversification such as risk spreading. Similarly, the opportunities to expand in the same product area (*horizontal integration*), and the gains from scale economies that go with this, are forgone. In short, there are opportunity costs.

Alternatives to vertical integration

Integration is not costless. But some of its advantages in terms of the reconciliation of the optima of the five Robinsonian criteria (and elaborations on these savings) can be obtained without full, formal integration. We have already mentioned, as an example, that even giant firms use specialist financial service houses when undertaking a share flotation (or, for that matter, simply use a bank for borrowing rather than directly accepting deposits from the public). There are three main alternatives discussed below.

First, in *partial vertical integration*, the firm vertically integrates a sufficiently large proportion of its business to obtain the benefits desired but stops short of total integration. One example of this is provided by the Walls ice cream division of Unilever. Walls is also in the transport business with a large fleet of refrigerated trucks. In order to avoid having large numbers of expensive lorries lying idle in winter (when demand is low), Walls owns only a basic fleet and in times of high demand rents refrigerated vehicles from a hire company such as Avis.

Second, *exclusive franchising* involves the granting of sole rights to resale to a particular customer in a specific trade or locality. It may include the granting of special discount rates to ensure that the outlet is, in turn, exclusively loyal to the supplier. This system provides many of the economies in transportation and promotion which are obtained by ownership of outlets without the associated costs of capital outlay and day-to-day management. Moreover, a poor dealer can probably be dispensed with and replaced more readily than a poorly located but wholly owned retail site. Motor-car distributorships and dealerships are common examples of this type of franchising operation. To protect their own image, car manufacturers tend only to award franchises to garages who guarantee to adhere to certain standards of stock and spare part holding, and who can provide specified engineering and service facilities.

Finally, a firm may be able to exercise considerable buying strength or *countervailing power* if it is large and faced with an unconcentrated supplying industry. It can possibly force prices down to near-competitive levels. Simultaneously, it can ensure that supplies are tailored to its own specification and requirements. This is a relationship not unlike that which Marks and Spencer had for many years with the highly fragmented garment manufacturing industry. Conversely, large specialized firms can charge a relatively high price to diffuse purchasers and so provide much the same profit increase as would formal forward integration. Examples of this occurred in the 1960s when for a short time some large confectionery and tobacco firms refused to deal with certain supermarket chains, preferring to obtain higher prices from and award lower discounts to small retailers.

Diversification

Diversification refers to the extent to which a firm produces a variety of different kinds of output. Sometimes it is referred to as *lateral integration* to distinguish it from vertical integration which could (at least semantically) be included in the above definition. Diversification, like other company activity, reflects the firm's desire to achieve certain objectives. For example, the profit-maximizing firm will diversify rather than expand its existing activities if the former course promises the higher rate of return. Another major reason is (again) to attempt to reconcile the optima of the five Robinsonian criteria of risk, management, technique, marketing and finance. For example, in the case of risk, if the probability of loss in market A is 0.2 and in market B is 0.3, then the probability of loss in both simultaneously is 0.2×0.3, namely 0.06. The probability of an extreme occurrence in all markets simultaneously is always very much less than the probability of such an occurrence in any single market. Diversification then can be prompted by the desire to avoid having all the firm's eggs in one basket. It may also be the consequence of the emergence or perception of a previously unavailable profit opening.

What are the *economies of diversification*? The major one is what Penrose called 'the continuing availability of unused productive services'. Briefly this can be subclassified as follows.

First, there is the *balance of processes* (or the reconciliation of the optima of all the Robinsonian criteria except risk). This is the principle generally explained by reference to the size of manufacturing plant required to utilize fully a range of machine types with differing and indivisible throughput capacities (see table 6.1). Overall, throughput must be large enough to equal the least common multiple (LCM) of the various maximum outputs from each machine type. If we take this principle further and consider the whole range of resources in a firm (managers, accountants, market researchers, sales force workers, engineers, research and development staff, and so on) it becomes apparent that to utilize fully all of these resources, human and/or physical, the LCM will be very large indeed in terms of output. In the presence of market saturation and the like it is not surprising that diversification may often prove to be the most profitable way to achieve this large LCM.

Second, in addition to avoiding 'idleness in resources' by failing to reach the LCM there is the very similar economy of *fully utilizing specialized services*. For example, if two products have common costs a firm specializing in one product may diversify into the other so that it can achieve economies at the stage of common cost. This need not mean taking up slack as in the previous case; it can do, but it can also include the attainment of any scale economies available at that point of common cost. Thus, a tinned soup manufacturer with his own tin can factory may diversify into tinned fruits in order to achieve further traditional scale economies in the essentially service factory which produces the tin containers.

A third economy of diversification (or *economy of scope* as these savings have recently come to be called) is the *avoidance of risk*, which we have already mentioned. Over time the sales levels of a firm can be affected by seasonal, cyclical and irregular factors, and by the direction of the overall market trend itself. If the trend is falling, a specialized firm will clearly wish to diversify so that its total sales will not decline along with those of its primary market. However, this is diversification for the sake of survival rather than diversification in order to minimize risk and uncertainty. Diversification to minimize the impact of seasonal, cyclical and irregular factors on the firm's health would, however, fall into this category.

Firms producing seasonal goods will diversify to keep their plants fully utilized for the whole year; or to avoid having to build up stocks in seasons of lean demand; or to avoid the need to shed and re-engage labour. None of these are costless alternatives. The ideal form of diversification in this instance is obviously to produce goods with a seasonal fluctuation inversely related to that of the original product (e.g. Christmas card firms may diversify into summer postcards, and also attempt to encourage demand for cards at less popular festivals such as fathers' and St Valentine's days).

In a similar manner, firms in industries typified by a cyclical pattern of demand may diversify into products with a sales pattern the reverse of the original. This may not prove as easy as with seasonal fluctuations, given the relative lack of predictability of economic *vis-à-vis* seasonal fluctuations. Another way to obtain a sales cushion is to diversify into a cyclically stable industry. This was one of the motivations behind the merger between Redland (a cement firm subject to the volatility of the cyclical construction industry) and Purle (a firm specializing in the disposal of industrial waste, a stable industry with a rising trend). The fact that Redland also owned derelict quarry sites which were ideal for the dumping of refuse was an added bonus.

Irregular factors, of course, are wholly unpredictable. Diversification to avoid such uncertainty rests on the desire of the firm to avoid having all its commercial eggs in one basket. External market opportunities change and this, coupled possibly with one or more of the other motivating factors, may induce diversification. One obvious example of this two-edged motivation for diversification is the possession of a research and development department. This provides the firm with a built-in engine of diversification which is constantly producing new technological ideas which need not be related to the firm's original market. An illustration of this is how the large Swiss chemical firms, originally founded by Huguenot refugees from France, moved from weaving into dyestuffs. The chemical research required to produce new dyes for woven garments proved also to produce molecules which could be used for human and veterinary medicines, and for animal and plant feedstuffs.

Another example is the possession of marketing expertise. This may be an under-utilized specialist resource merely awaiting an opportunity to arise in order to exploit it by diversification. Thus possession of the financial where-withal, desire to grow, expertise in the mass marketing of consumer durables, plus a respected brand name in the field, resulted in Hoover diversifying out of vacuum cleaners into washing machines, refrigerators, dishwashers and other household equipment.

Similarly, production know-how in fermentation techniques coupled with the growth of the pharmaceutical market after the discovery of penicillin resulted in the Distillers' Company moving into the large-scale production of fermented antibiotics in their custom-built Liverpool factory.

References

1 C.F. Pratten, *Economies of Scale in Manufacturing Industry*, Cambridge University Press, 1971.
2 E.A.G. Robinson, *The Structure of Competitive Industry*, Cambridge University Press, 1931.
3 P.S. Florence, *The Logic of British and American Industry*, Routledge & Kegan Paul, 1972.
4 A. Alchian, 'Costs and outputs', in *The Allocation of Economic Resources: Essays in Honor of B.F. Haley*, Stanford, 1959.
5 E. Penrose (1959), *The Theory of the Growth of the Firm*, Blackwell, 2nd edn, 1980.
6 O.E. Williamson, *Corporate Control and Business Behaviour*, Prentice-Hall, 1970.
7 O.E. Williamson, 'Hierarchical control and optimum firm size', *Journal of Political Economy* 78 (1967), pp. 359–87.

7

Forecasting

The basic economic tool-kit which has been developed in the first chapters can be applied in the analysis of those interrelated sets of problems concerning production, investment, pricing, financing and marketing, and all the other decisions faced by companies engaged in economic activities, which collectively comprise the corpus of business economics. A central feature of this has been a development of the role of markets and an appreciation of the forces lying behind supply and demand. It will have been readily apparent that a considerable amount of simplification and some quite far-reaching assumptions are required merely to hoist our conceptual apparatus into place before it can be put to any practical use.

One key assumption, previously mentioned yet not fully considered is the role of information in business decision-making. Most economic models assume the existence of adequate information, yet information is a costly and scarce resource. Businessmen typically have to take decisions in the absence of complete information. Indeed, the bearing of risk and the acceptance of the consequences of decisions taken under risky conditions are key aspects of the role of the business entrepreneur and the normal functioning of the free-enterprise system.

In this chapter we will begin by looking at some of the ways in which forecasting techniques can help to provide information which will to some extent 'pierce the veil' of the always uncertain future. In particular we shall examine some of the methods available for forecasting demand conditions. Information is rarely likely to be completely adequate. Even in the case of information about the firm's costs, as we shall see in chapter 9, accountants are not in complete agreement about how certain costs should be defined, measured and apportioned. Cost information too, is hedged around with uncertainties.

We shall then proceed to look at the implications of uncertain information for firms' demand curves and the ways in which this uncertainty can be reduced, in certain cases, by *forward trading*. In chapter 8 we discuss pricing policies and the likely implications of different business objectives for the firm's pricing and output decisions.

Forecasting

In an uncertain world most business and economic decisions rest upon forecasts of future conditions. These will take place at all levels of economic activity, in both the private and the public sectors, and will include both long- and short-range projections. Methods of forecasting may be roughly categorized as follows:

(a) Opinion polling
(b) Mechanical extrapolations
(c) Barometric techniques
(d) Statistical and econometric methods.

If a company is about to embark on a forecasting exercise (although in reality this is likely to be a virtually continuous activity), the obvious point of departure is a sales forecast; following this, the economist can move into other contingent areas of corporate forecasting and planning.

Future sales forecasts might be in terms of the short (say three months), medium (one year) or long run (perhaps five years). We have defined the terms along fairly standard lines though definitions will obviously vary between industries and companies.

Figure 7.1 gives a simple illustration of how sales might vary over time. In this figure the long-run trend is upwards, though in the short term seasonal variations produce cyclical sales patterns with pronounced downward swings in the early part of the year. The forecaster must therefore be careful not to be fooled by seasonal variations and not to ignore their timing and implications. Short-run forecasts assist the timing of decisions and can be used as a means of monitoring and controlling decisions based on long-term forecasts.

In the case of medium-term forecasts the direction of trend is the most important feature. This could have implications, for example, for the firm's

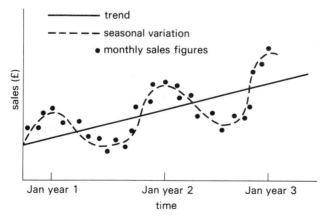

Figure 7.1 *The behaviour of sales figures*

employee recruitment and training policy, and, if confirmed in the long run, for corporate investment plans and the firm's entire long-run strategy.

Forecasts might be further categorized in terms of their scope. Forecasts of the future performance of the entire economy will have implications for individual industries. Market demand forecasts (e.g. for the entire car industry) will give the company an indication of industry prospects. Even if the prospects for the industry are favourable, this is cold comfort if the bulk of trading activity is to be undertaken by rivals. Company demand forecasts (e.g. for the British Leyland Motor Company) give a guide to the company's likely market share. Given these, the company will wish to make product line forecasts (e.g. Mini Metro or Bounty/Acclaim), to decide which products should be given relative priority in company production operations.

Forecasting techniques vary widely in their accuracy and sophistication. The most accurate technique is to be preferred, subject to the availability of data, expertise and finance and to the nature of the forecast required. There is little point in engaging in a sophisticated and expensive operation if a simple polling of sales branches would produce the required information.

Opinion polling

The assumption here is that by asking people who are likely to be directly involved, such as consumers or the sales force, attitudes and opinions which affect economic decisions can be assessed and predicted in advance. This is a subjective method of forecasting made up largely of a weighted or unweighted averaging of expectations and attitudes. Survey techniques might include the use of interviews, personal or by telephone, or mailed questionnaires.

Consumer surveys

Surveys of consumer intentions via market research sample surveys are costly exercises. The results are not guaranteed in that people might not wish to divulge their intentions, or might respond in the best of faith and then subsequently revise their views and behave differently. An extreme illustration of the fluidity of intentions is given by the experience of pollsters assessing voting intentions on the run-up to an election. The technique might best be used as a back-up to other methods or in situations where there are no other data available, such as a new product launch. Nevertheless this type of survey is used frequently in a number of areas, including the Confederation of British Industry's (CBI) regular surveys of businessmen's capital expenditure intentions.

Sales force polling

Sales forecasts developed from information provided by the sales force—

those closest to the market—are straightforward and cost-effective ways of utilizing professional knowledge. Yet the results may be dependent on 'guesstimates' which may reflect the relative optimism or pessimism of individual staff and be biased by their own preferences with respect to desired sales quotas. The individual's view of the market is likely to be a partial, incomplete one, and at best the results of such surveys will need to be carefully revised and monitored in the light of previous experience and future expectations.

Panels of experts

Consulting the views of outside experts or specialists might be appropriate in certain circumstances, perhaps in the case of complex new technological developments where data are not available. For example, at the moment no one is quite sure about the full implications of the advent of cable television and the attendant information revolution for matters such as consumer behaviour, personal communications and the location of the office at home or at work. Telephone or postal contact with a cross-section of expert opinion is cheap and straightforward, and may give either the benefits of a balanced cross-section of opinion or a consensus of ignorance.

Test marketing

Test marketing can be potentially useful in the forecasting of sales in either a new product launch or the introduction of an existing product in a completely new market area. The method involves finding a test area which typifies the planned new market in microcosm; the appropriate socioeconomic classes, income and age groupings etc. should be well represented in the test area. Similarly the test launch of the product in terms of the type and scale of advertising must replicate the planned major launch. If the test has been correctly designed and is operated for a period sufficient to reflect not merely novelty purchasing but also regular buying habits, then the response in the test area should give a good guide to the likely success of the launch. However, it is very difficult to accurately model the full launch and there is the further disadvantage of the full disclosure to rivals of the company's intentions.

Mechanical extrapolations

This is probably the most frequently adopted method of forecasting. It involves the basic assumption that past patterns of economic behaviour will continue to the extent that past behaviour can be used to predict the future. It has the attraction of also being relatively cheap in that the company is likely to possess most of the relevant historical information.

Trend fitting by eye

At its simplest this might consist of taking a time series of historical sales figures, such as that shown in figure 7.1, and fitting a trend line to it by eye. This can then be used to read off sales predictions for the required future dates.

Ordinary least-squares linear regression

The ordinary least-squares (OLS) technique uses a mathematical formula to produce a line of best fit relating the dependent to the independent variables for data such as those of figure 7.1. When used to fit a line summarizing the relationship between variables the technique also provides a measure of the explanatory power of the relationship on the basis of the relationships observed in the original data. If sales follow a constant growth pattern we might have the following equation, estimated via OLS regression, which could be used to predict in some future year T:

$$\text{sales}\,(Q_T) = a + bT. \tag{7.1}$$

The constants a and b in this equation will have been estimated using *regression analysis* on past data, and to utilize the expression to forecast sales we merely have to insert the year number T for which the forecast is required. (Regression analysis, a set of statistical techniques used to quantify the relationship between two or more variables, is outside the scope of this book. The reader is referred to any standard statistical text for further details.) Although the method can encompass non-linear relations by using the logarithms of appropriate variables, it is perhaps more useful for long-term rather than short-term forecasting. It cannot pick up cyclical turning points or fluctuations, as the underlying assumption is one of constant proportionate change.

Time series analysis

More sophisticated versions of time series analysis than that just considered will allow for the influence of seasonal and cyclical factors as well as the basic trend. For it is usually argued that a time series of movements in a variable over a long period is typically made up of the following elements:

(a) Trend T
(b) Seasonal variations S
(c) Cyclical fluctuations C
(d) Irregular movements I

The *trend* is a smooth upward or downward movement of the time series over a long period. The *seasonal variations* are, as common sense suggests, cycles within a calendar year which mainly tend to reflect the weather and customs. Thus department stores might expect peaks in sales activity to coincide with certain holiday periods, Christmas in particular. *Cyclical fluctuations* are movements in the business cycle which produce recurrent peaks and troughs in business activity around trend levels; the fluctuations may have a periodicity of varying numbers of years depending on the industry being considered. Finally, *irregular movements* are short erratic movements in the time series resulting from the random shocks produced by non-predictable events. For example, the sudden rise in OPEC oil prices must have led to irregularities in certain time series.

The usual practice adopted in the construction of forecasting models is to assume that the time series can be decomposed into the four previously mentioned components on an additive or, more conveniently, a multiplicative basis. These two constructions are as follows:

$$\text{time series} = T + S + C + I \tag{7.2}$$

$$\text{time series} = TSCI. \tag{7.3}$$

We shall now look at some methods of analysing each of the components in turn.

Seasonal variations may be estimated in a number of ways. One popular method is the *ratio to trend method*. If the trend analysis of sales suggests a June figure of 17,925 units, the estimate can be adjusted for seasonality. Assume that over the previous four years the trend model predicted June sales figures as shown in table 7.1. These show that, on average, June sales figures have been 10 per cent higher than that predicted by trend. Hence the current forecast for June sales should be seasonally adjusted upward by 10 per cent.

Table 7.1 *Ratio to trend seasonal adjustments*

Year (June)	Forecast	Actual	Actual/forecast (%)
1977	15,825	17,249	109
1978	16,350	18,312	112
1979	16,875	18,225	108
1980	17,400	19,314	111
1981	17,925	—	
			average 110

Cyclical variations can likewise be accounted for by the construction of an index. Annual sales figures will contain the influence of both trend and cycle, designated TC. If the original data are divided by trend T, a cyclical relative index C' is produced. Thus we have

$$\left(\frac{TC}{T} \right) 100 = C'.$$

One method of eliminating the irregular component I from the time series is termed *exponential smoothing*. It is also frequently used with raw data as a forecasting technique in its own right. Exponential smoothing methods are basically a refinement of the moving average technique. The basic exponential smoothing forecasting equation for one period ahead is:

$$\text{forecast sales}_{t+1} = \alpha \, \text{sales}_t + (1 - \alpha) \, \text{forecast sales}_t \qquad (7.4)$$

Where α is a smoothing constant with a value between 0 and 1, i.e. $0 < \alpha < 1$. The expression tells us that forecast sales for time $t + 1$ are made up of two components—the level of sales in the previous period multiplied by α, plus the forecast sales for the previous period multiplied by $(1 - \alpha)$. The forecast sales for the previous period were made up in a similar fashion, and so we have the recursive relationship shown in the basic equation:

$$\text{forecast sales}_{t+1} = \alpha \, [\text{sales}_t + (1 - \alpha) \, \text{sales}_{t-1} + (1 - \alpha)^2 \, \text{sales}_{t-2} + \dots \text{etc.}]$$
$$(7.5)$$

The weights $\alpha, \alpha(1 - \alpha), \alpha(1 - \alpha)^2, \dots$ etc. sum to one and decline exponentially since α is a positive constant between 0 and 1. The value of α determines the rapidity with which the system reacts to change. If α is very small then little weight is given to current sales, but the nearer it approaches 1 the greater the weight placed on current sales. If α equals 0.3 the weights attached to the sales of previous periods are calculated as shown in table 7.2.

Table 7.2 *The calculation of weight in an exponential smoothing exercise*

Time period	Calculation of weight	Weight
t	0.3	0.3
$t - 1$	0.3×0.7	0.21
$t - 2$	$0.3 \times 0.7 \times 0.7$	0.147
$t - 3$	$0.3 \times 0.7 \times 0.7 \times 0.7$	0.103
all others	etc.	0.240
	total	1.000

Barometric techniques

The mechanical methods of forecasting rely on future conditions being an extension of past ones. Barometric techniques, on the other hand, assume that present happenings can give an indication of future events. The foundation of the process is based on the observation that there are lagged relationships between many economic time series. This results from the fact that various economic activities are likely to take place at different stages within the business cycle.

Leading indicators are those which tend to herald future changes in the course of business activity. For example, at the start of an upswing of the cycle we might expect to see company order books 'improving', and the resultant improved optimism will lead companies to start adding to their stocks of raw materials, components etc. The behaviour of these variables in aggregate can be used as leading indicators, as shown in figure 7.2.

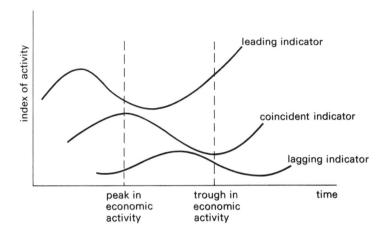

Figure 7.2 *Indicators of economic activity*

Coincident indicators move in step with the cycle; examples of these might include aggregate levels of sales, employment and industrial production. Finally, there are *lagging indicators* which trail behind the level of economic activity; amongst these we might include capital expenditure on new plant and equipment, or the general level of consumer credit outstanding.

Unfortunately, although it is possible to isolate various leading indicators the direction of movements in each does not presage movements in economic activity with complete accuracy. Even if their movement is in the 'right' direction there is the further problem that the lead time between their behaviour and the ensuing change in economic activity is not likely to be constant. Finally, they give little indication of the magnitude of changes in the offing.

One means of meeting some of these deficiencies is to examine the behaviour of a group of leading indicators. *Composite indices* can be formed by taking a weighted average of the behaviour of several leading indicators. Another approach is to form *diffusion indices*, which reflect the percentage of leading indicators that are moving in the same direction at a given time. These approaches at least help to get rid of random fluctuations or *noise*.

Statistical and econometric methods

The behaviour of sales obviously depends on a large number of factors as well as the passage of time. Major influences are likely to include changes in price levels, advertising expenditure, income levels, the age composition and size of the population, and so on. Statistical and econometric methods, similar to those used in time series regression, can be used to analyse the economic relationships between variables.

This approach has a number of advantages. It forces the forecaster to try to build logically consistent prediction models which take into account causal relationships between economic variables. Once a model has been constructed it can be modified and refined in the light of experience. The forecasting process is no longer quite so *ad hoc*. Models built in this fashion should give an indication of both the magnitude and the direction of changes in forecast variables and help to explain the behaviour of economic phenomenon. This is very important since the management has a degree of control over some of the variables which, for example, control sales. If they can assess the impact of changes in their pricing or advertising policy they can revise their strategies much more effectively. On the other hand these methods are likely to be relatively costly and time consuming in their development. They provide an extreme contrast with naïve models based on back-of-the-envelope calculations and should only be used if they are cost effective. If conditions are relatively stable it may be possible to obtain reasonably accurate predictions from 'no change' or 'constant growth' models which make these respective assumptions about the behaviour of the variable concerned. But where changes are frequent and irregular, much more complex models will be required.

Single-equation models

Many of the firm's forecasting problems can be solved with a single-equation econometric model. The first step in the construction of such a model is to specify the hypotheses which purport to explain the relationships between the variables in question. These are set out in an equation of a form suitable for econometric testing. In the construction of a model to be used for forecasting the sales of a good, we might hypothesize that demand for the good Q_D is determined by the price of the good P, the prices of substitutes S, personal disposable income Y, population Pn and company advertising expenditure A. A linear model expressing this relationship could be written as follows:

$$Q_D = a + bP + cS + dY + ePn + fA + g. \qquad (7.6)$$

Regression analysis can then be applied to estimate the parameters of the equation—the values of *a, b, c, d,* etc. Once established the model can easily be used for forecasting by substituting the expected values of the independent variables into the equation; these are the values of *P, S, Y* etc. The result will be a forecast of the value of the dependent variable Q_D. Additionally the model gives the businessman the opportunity of experimenting to test the predicted results of various strategies. He can obtain the model's answers to questions about the likely effects of changing any of the independent variables under his control. For example, he might be interested in the possible results of doubling advertising expenditure.

Simultaneous equation models are resorted to when the interrelationships between variables in the model are so complex as to be beyond the capabilities of single equations.

A number of statistical problems can arise which must be overcome before any confidence can be placed in the predictions of the single-equation model. A brief indication of some of these difficulties follows.

Missing variables

In expression 7.6 the last term *g* is an error term included to account for the fact that the model is unlikely to fit the data exactly; there will be discrepancies between the values suggested by the model and actual observed values. The assumption behind the regression techniques applied to estimate the parameters of the model is that successive values of the error term are independent and average out; they thus have an expected value of zero. However, this is not necessarily the case; successive values of the error term might be related, thus showing a pattern of movements. In this case they are described as displaying *autocorrelation*. One possible cause of this is the omission of an important variable from the equation being estimated. If the missing variable behaves as an economic variable and has a regular influence on the data, the error term could behave systematically. This may mean that in reality the model explains the behaviour of the data less convincingly than the standard measurements indicate.

Multicollinearity or intercorrelation of variables

In the use of regression analysis it is assumed that the independent variables *P, S, Y* etc. in expression 7.6 are truly independent of one another. If this is not the case and two or more of them are correlated, then multicollinearity is said to be present. In this situation it is difficult to ascertain which of the variables has the explanatory power, and the estimated coefficients attached to them are likely to be inaccurate. The easiest way round the problem is to omit all but one of the variables which are linked together.

The identification problem

It is very difficult to be certain in statistical efforts to estimate demand that success has been achieved. Suppose that we are trying to estimate the demand curve for the product shown in figure 7.3. The data available on price charged and quantity purchased at different points in time appear to produce a convincing downward-sloping demand curve. Yet we cannot be sure of this unless we have additional information. It will be recalled from the discussion in chapter 3 that a demand curve only holds good if all other factors which affect demand are held constant; otherwise it will move about. It may be that our observed points on the line *EF* are all on the same demand curve and represent various points of market equilibrium attained as supply conditions change. This is shown in figure 7.4. If this is the case, and demand conditions have not changed, *EF* is a genuine demand curve.

On the other hand, non-price variables in both the supply and the demand functions may have changed between the data points. Perhaps new machinery has been installed between observations and the supply curve has moved downwards to the right, reflecting the increased efficiency in production. Perhaps at the same time the prices of substitute goods for *X* have risen, so that the true demand curves for good *X* have also shifted downwards to the right. This is shown in figure 7.5. In this case both demand and supply conditions have altered between observations. Our points on *EF* are a meaningless hybrid of different sets of equilibrium demand and supply conditions.

If it were assumed that *EF* is the genuine demand curve, wildly inaccurate forecasts could result. Suppose that the current price is PX_1 and the firm is considering lowering its price to PX_2 in the hope of obtaining an increase in

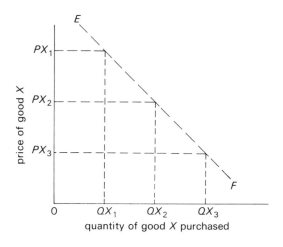

Figure 7.3 *A plot of price/quantity combinations*

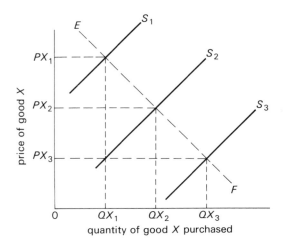

Figure 7.4 *A stable demand curve and shifting supply conditions*

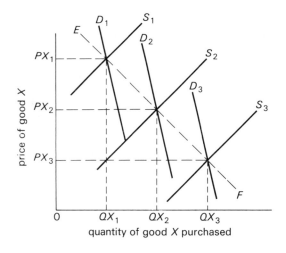

Figure 7.5 *Shifting supply and demand curves*

sales of $QX_1 - QX_2$. If in fact demand conditions are given by D_1, a much more inelastic demand curve than the one 'estimated', the firm will suffer a very poor response in sales and might be better served leaving the price as it is.

We are back to Marshall's analogy of the two scissor blades, supply and demand, which jointly determine price. We basically have two simultaneous relationships and identification of the demand curve is only possible under certain conditions.

For a start, identification is impossible if neither demand nor supply conditions have changed during the period of observations. In this case,

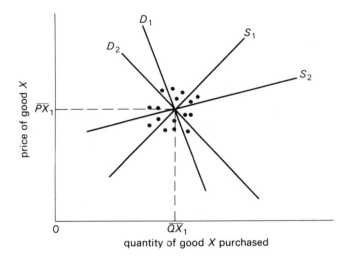

Figure 7.6 *Demand and supply conditions unchanged;*
identification impossible

depicted in figure 7.6, perhaps only one of our pairs of observations lies on the true intersection of the two curves, and all the others merely reflect temporary disequilibrium disturbances. The bar indicates the mean of the observations. We could fit any number of supply and demand curves through the points shown in the diagram. Here we have only one point, with co-ordinates PX_1 and QX_1.

If we had two points we could draw in a line. If demand conditions remained constant and if supply conditions changed, a number of points of equilibrium would be produced along one demand curve and the curve would be identified. If the converse happened—demand conditions altered but not those of supply—we would not be able to identify the demand curve (though the supply curve would be determined).

Finally, it is possible to identify the demand curve if sufficient information exists to explain why and by how much each curve has shifted between observations. By way of example, for an agricultural product the position of the demand curve might be affected by personal disposable income Y, and the position of the supply curve might be affected by temperature T. A simultaneous equation estimation procedure can then be used to estimate the relationships between the four variables—price (P), quantity (Q), personal disposable income (Y) and temperature (T). It is possible to obtain equations representing both supply and demand functions separately if each simultaneous equation contains a variable that does not appear in the other. In our example we have

$$Q_D = a_1 + a_2P + a_3Y \tag{7.7}$$

$$Q_S = b_1 + b_2P + b_3T. \tag{7.8}$$

where a_1, a_2, a_3, b_1, b_2 and b_3 have been calculated from past data relating to the variables as in equation 7.6 above. This pair of simultaneous equations fulfils the requirements and they are duly identified as demand and supply equations respectively. Given forecasted values for P, Y and T, Q_D and Q_S can then be found without the danger that the identification problem will result in inaccurate estimates for either Q value.

If the identification problem cannot be solved, the analyst has to fall back on other forecasting techniques such as barometric indicators or opinion polling.

Uncertainty and Demand Curves

The discussion of forecasting techniques and demand curve estimation procedures in the previous section will have suggested that a firm's knowledge of its demand conditions is not quite as straightforward and unequivocal as the demand curve in a typical textbook analysis might imply.

In practice a typical firm that is a price setter will probably be operating in an environment in which information about equilibrium prices and quantities is a scarce, costly commodity. Firms are unlikely to possess full information about the quality and price of their rival firms' products. Customers will not be fully informed of the selling prices right across the market.

Suppose that a typical company obtains information about the demand for its product by observing how sales perform at the current price. If it has been in operation for some time, it will have an accumulation of this information plus, presumably, knowledge of its own cost structures. It should eventually be in a position to determine roughly what price is optimal for its operations. The position of a firm with imperfect knowledge of its demand conditions is shown in figure 7.7.

If the firm knew its costs and demand conditions perfectly, and was a profit maximizer, it would equate its marginal revenue with its marginal costs and sell output Q_0 at price P_0 (figure 7.7(a)). But if the firm was uncertain about its demand conditions, Q_0 could be viewed as the mean of a normal probability distribution (the continuous curve in figure 7.7 (b)). The uncertainty is shown by the shaded band drawn around the demand curve in figure 7.7(a). At a price P_0 the firm would expect sales to vary about an average of Q_0. The extremes of the variation are given by the intersections of a horizontal line drawn through price P_0 and the two edges of the shaded band around the demand curve in figure 7.7(a). These intersections also determine the two extremes of the probability distribution around Q_0 in figure 7.7(b). It follows that the marginal revenue curve is similarly uncertain, and it too is enclosed by a shaded band.

Suppose that in a given period the firm starts to observe sales of Q_1 at price P_0. Does this mean that it will immediately alter its price? It is unlikely to change its price unless it thinks demand conditions have altered and that Q_1

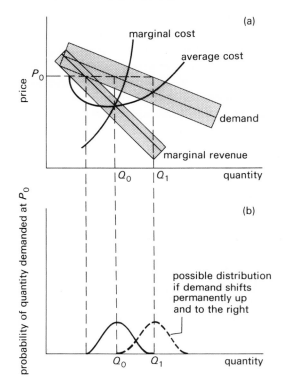

Figure 7.7 *The position of the firm facing uncertain demand*

is the centre of a new distribution, marked by the dashed curve line in figure 7.7(b). It will need to observe steady sales around Q_1 before it is convinced of this. When this happens and it decides that demand conditions have altered it will revise its price accordingly as the new demand and marginal revenue curves suggest.

Although firms typically face uncertainty about demand conditions there are certain strategies that help to diminish these risks. Indeed, in certain cases markets are organized to this end. This leads us to consider futures markets and hedging.

Futures markets and hedging

Many contracts are made in advance of delivery. Whenever something is ordered, rather than purchased on the spot, a forward or futures contract is involved. Organized futures markets exist in commodities of all kinds, foreign currencies and financial instruments. One of the advantages of a futures contract is that price uncertainty is removed, since the price is decided at the time the order is made, though the 'good' concerned may not be delivered until months later.

For example, a producer may wish to sell a crop of wheat in eight months' time but may be unsure about the price at which he will be able to sell it. A buyer may be looking for a delivery of wheat at the same time. The existence of a futures market with standardized procedures and contracts will enable both to enter into an agreement immediately. The agreement will specify the grade and quantity of wheat, the point at which the producer will deliver in eight months' time (when the contract becomes due), and the guaranteed price. The relative positions of the buyer and seller in such a contract are shown in figure 7.8.

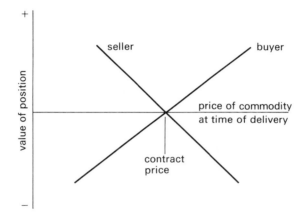

Figure 7.8 *Positions in a futures contract*

The profit of the buyer or seller depends on the actual price of the commodity at the time of delivery. If wheat prices slump following a bumper crop then the seller will profit, but the gains are reversed if the price of wheat exceeds the contract price. By entering into the contract the seller has removed the uncertainty of the price at which he will sell the wheat, but not the risk attached to future price fluctuations.

However, if he already owns a stock of wheat when he enters into the contract he is said to have *hedged* his position. The value of his stock of wheat will increase in step with changes in the price of wheat at the time of delivery. The value of the futures contract will move in step in the same direction but the farmer is 'long' in wheat (he possesses it) and 'short' on the futures contract (he has sold it). Gains on the futures contract will go to the purchasing speculator if prices move up. Thus, from the farmer's point of view, the two movements offset one another and he has hedged away his risk.

His overall position is the same if prices fall. The value of his stock of wheat goes down but he gains on the futures contract and again the two movements cancel out. When he hedges the farmer makes a two-way bet and thus gets rid of risk. The purchaser of the contract makes a one-way bet; if prices rise above the contract price he gains, but if they fall below he loses.

Thus the 'speculator' performs a valuable function in commodities markets—he enables other operators to hedge away risk. However, he does not play this part for nothing and the pattern of futures contract prices in relation to actual commodity prices should be such that on balance he receives a reward for bearing risk. Thus it is argued that typically the futures contract price should be less than the expected spot price (price of the commodity at the time of delivery); this phenomenon is termed *normal backwardation* and generates the speculator's return.

Thus by taking the appropriate positions in futures markets, price uncertainty of the kind considered in the previous section can be removed. In chapter 8 we shall look at various other factors which are likely to affect the manner in which a business sets its prices, including the overall objectives of the business.

8

Pricing Policies

In chapters 3 and 4 we examined the theory of prices and costs. However, the realities of business life often (although not always) make such theories rather less than useful. In this chapter we look at pricing decisions starting from the ground up, as it were, and then refine our discussion in the light of the earlier chapters.

Cost-plus Pricing

Many businessmen have claimed to use this technique. It involves finding the direct costs of the product (e.g. labour and materials) and adding a charge for indirect costs. This charge is estimated by allocating the firm's overheads to the product using some pro rata formula per unit; the unit is based on an arbitrary yardstick such as man- or machine-hours used or floor space occupied. For example, if product A occupies 40 per cent of the firm's factory space then 40 per cent of the firm's overheads are allocated to that product, whether or not this is an accurate measure of A's usage of central administrative services, research and development or other company overheads. To direct plus indirect costs is added a further sum from profit, usually some percentage of these total unit costs.

The cost-plus method could be called the accountant's way of solving pricing problems. It has the advantage of apparent safety by deliberately attempting to set prices above a loss-making level. Economists have some severe reservations about cost-plus pricing, however. First, it ignores demand. Consumer wants and willingness to pay (which are totally unrelated to a firm's cost structure) are completely neglected. Second, it takes no account of either existing or potential competition. Competitors need not stand idly by and allow a firm to set a price at a cost-related level without in turn reacting by shifting (or even maintaining) their own price levels and so affecting the first firm's sales and profits. Third, as already suggested, there is no unimpeachable basis for allocating overhead costs to different products in a multiproduct firm. Fourth, the cost concepts used may be irrelevant for any given pricing decision. Opportunity costs are ignored; that is, the firm does not ask itself what is forgone in terms of some alternative use of its facilities. The profits forgone by producing product *A* rather than product *Z* are not considered. Nor is any account taken of marginal costs. In certain circumstances these may be far more important than actual total costs. Thus if a firm has spare capacity it may well be better to sell at a price below full costs, and so make a contribution to overheads, than to charge a higher price (albeit one which nominally covers total costs) and discourage custom, so making no sale and, therefore, incurring a larger loss.

The latter point is illustrated in figure 8.1. Any price above P_2 calculated on a cost-plus basis could earn the firm a profit provided the firm was working at full capacity (defined as minimum *SATC*) and producing Q_2 units. However, if the firm was working at less than full capacity because, say, demand was depressed, then price could be lowered below P_2, where a loss would be inevitable no matter what quantity was sold. None the less, provided the fall in demand is restricted to the region Q_2 to Q_1 then the firm should price at marginal cost, i.e. where appropriate between P_2 and P_1. At a price below P_1 the firm would not even cover its direct costs of labour and materials, but above P_1 it would and in addition would earn a surplus which would contribute to overheads and thus minimize losses.

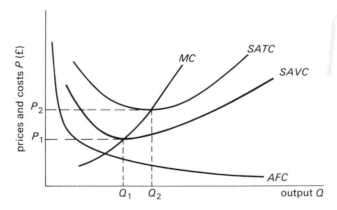

Figure 8.1 *Pricing and the firm's shut-down point*

Another way in which the cost concepts used in cost-plus pricing may be inappropriate is that they will generally be current historic costs. Clearly since the firm wishes to continue in business for more than one transaction the figures employed should be future or replacement costs.

Consider a simple example. A retailer with no overhead or labour costs buys in 100 widgets for £90 and adds 10 per cent to arrive at his selling price. He subsequently sells the product for 99p and makes an apparent total profit of £9. He subsequently goes to replenish his stocks but finds that in the interim the price of widgets has, for some reason, risen to £100 for 100 units.

His cash resources, however, extend only to £99, the receipts from the sales of his original widget purchase. Unless he now borrows additional capital he must, because of his original pricing decision, either contract his business or cease trading. In short his apparent profit is fictitious. The 10 per cent margin he added to costs should have been added not to his current or historic costs but to his future costs.

Finally, cost-plus pricing is illogical since it is based on circular reasoning. Costs vary with output. According to cost-plus pricing principles, price should therefore change as output (and so costs) rises or falls. But in fact output (what the market is prepared to purchase) depends on what price is set.

However, there are arguments in favour of cost-plus pricing. In tendering for a one-off contract it indicates to the seller the minimum acceptable price necessary to avoid a loss. Second, in many cases it may be the only practicable pricing mechanism if demand conditions, competitors' possible reactions and future cost conditions are all totally unknown. Third, its seeming popularity may be illusory in any event. Although businessmen may examine costs very carefully when they set price, the actual 'plus' or mark-up component added to costs to obtain price may well vary and be subject to considerable discretion. When demand conditions are high or demand is inelastic, the mark-up may well be much greater than when demand is very elastic, competitors' rivalry is a serious threat, or market conditions are tight. Thus cost-plus pricing may not be so ingenuous as it appears at first sight and may well approach the profit-maximizing behaviour the normative business economist would recommend.

Pricing and Scale

In figure 8.1 we saw how firms might reduce price to utilize spare capacity in order to minimize losses. In the long run, of course, such a firm would close down. Conversely, if the firm was operating at an output level well beyond Q_2 it might in the short run find that maximum profits could be earned at a price well above P_2. This situation is shown in figure 8.2 at price P_3, output level Q_3, on demand curve D.

In this case, however, the firm is operating beyond full capacity and it may, in the long run, estimate that it would be more profitable to construct a larger plant to reap the benefits of such economies; this is shown by the larger plant size $SATC'$, with output and price remaining at Q_3, P_3. If demand is relatively price elastic then price itself could be reduced and still further cost reductions achieved; for example, price could be reduced to P_4 and output increased to Q_4 if plant size $SATC''$ were constructed.

The course of action chosen will, of course, depend on the profitability of each. It will also depend on the elasticity of demand. Thus if demand had been relatively inelastic, such as indicated by D', then at no point on D' would it be feasible to consider constructing plant size $SATC''$. No price

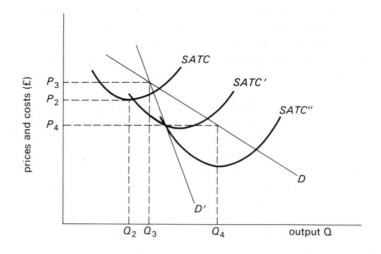

Figure 8.2 *Pricing and scale*

reduction, of whatever size, would increase the quantity demanded to a break-even level, let alone a profit level, with such a large plant.

A good example of scale economies being fully exploited by price reductions is given by the airline industry. Although wide-bodied, high-capacity jet aircraft had been in use for several years no airline was fully tapping the market potential. Planes were crossing the Atlantic often with 40 per cent or fewer of their seats occupied. (In terms of figure 8.2, the position was that of P_3, Q_3 and *SATC"*.) Laker Airways was the first to realize how price elastic demand was, and although the firm had substantial government opposition to overcome it was eventually permitted to lower prices to a P_4 position. Fears that the demand curve would be like D' proved groundless.

Pricing and the Product Life Cycle

Most products generally have an S-shaped life cycle of the kind depicted in figure 8.3. The unknown factors are the scales of each axis and the turning-points, rates of growth and decline of the S. These depend on variables such as technological progress, the willingness of the market to accept a new product, and the ease with which imitative products can or cannot be introduced. The strategic pricing decision is whether to adopt what Joel Dean termed a skimming price policy, a penetration policy, or some other policy in between these two extremes.[1]

A *skimming* policy is one of relatively high prices plus heavy promotional expenditures in the early stages of the life cycle. Lower prices are progressively adopted at later stages. This policy is usually adopted for a product which is

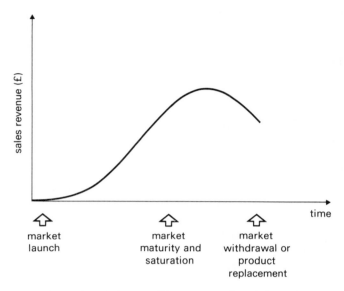

Figure 8.3 *Sales profile over product life cycle*

a major departure from previously available alternatives. Classic examples are ball-point pens, pharmaceuticals and pocket calculators.

Skimming policies will tend to be successful in given circumstances. One such circumstance is when demand is price inelastic early in the life cycle. For example, consumers may be willing to pay relatively highly for a novelty (of whatever kind, be it a life-saving drug or an entertaining Rubik cube), perhaps because the novelty itself makes it difficult to estimate a 'fair' price. Second, sequential skimming over time breaks the market up in ascending order of price sensitivity. Thus the most profitable 'cream' can be skimmed from each successive segment as price is progressively lowered. Third, if elasticities are unknown skimming is a good 'water-testing' approach. Prices can be quickly dropped if they are pitched too high. If they are pitched below the most profitable level, considerable goodwill may be forfeited if the firm then tries to rectify its error by raising prices. Finally, if the firm requires a high cash flow quickly then skimming may be the optimal alternative (for example, to cover outlays already made on research, retooling or promotion). Certainly this extends the time it will take to commence moving up the S, but if cash is unavailable elsewhere there may be no alternative.

Instead of skimming, firms can pursue *penetration* pricing policies. Here, low prices would be used to maximize instantaneously the penetration of a mass market. Clearly, this should be adopted with a view to long-run rather than short-run profits, since although the lower left limb of the S is truncated it still requires a non-negative length of time to achieve the full volume potential of the market. Moreover, penetration pricing requires that demand elasticity is high. If it is not then a low price will merely result in both a low volume and a low total revenue. In short, penetration pricing does not have the bet-hedging advantages of skimming. Thus penetration pricing is inappropriate when a product will not readily be widely adopted because of consumer caution or unfamiliarity. If these are not present, however, and if demand is elastic, then penetration pricing can be attractive; this is even more true if there are substantial benefits to be obtained from scale economies. In addition, penetration pricing is a useful competitive device to discourage potential competitors. As a 'keep out' warning it can reduce the attractiveness of a market to others, since they too must approach or undershoot the innovator's price (or produce a better product). If the market is very large, of course, then even a low price may not be an effective entry deterrent. Thus Librium and Valium (tranquillizer drugs, and exceptions to the general rule that most new major medicines are priced relatively highly), although priced at or below the level of other tranquillizers, did not discourage continuous further entry into that market.

When market maturity arrives the pricing decision becomes much more closely bound up with market structure and the numbers and types of competitors. These are issues we considered in chapter 5.

Sealed Bid Pricing

When firms tender for contracts under a sealed bid system the main problem is estimating the probable bids of competitors. 'Guesstimates' of these can be obtained from a variety of sources. What sort of level of bids have they submitted in the past? What are their current cost levels? Does trade gossip suggest they are working above or below full capacity? Is their plant and equipment modern and low cost or obsolete and costly to operate? Alternatively, even if their plant is modern and their variable costs low, was the capital cost so great that they must keep the plant in continuous operation to recoup their fixed costs? In short, how keen are they to obtain business? With this sort of information a pay-off matrix of the kind shown in table 8.1 can be constructed. Here we have hypothetical data with four price choices and an assumed unit cost of £8.

Profits, over time, will be maximized with the £11 bid. Over a run of contracts we assume that we will win 70 per cent of them with bids of £11 and lose 30 per cent. This provides an average or expected profit for every contract we bid for (whether we win it or not) of £2.1 per unit. Obviously this type of analysis is only useful if market conditions are fairly repetitive; this need not be the case. In addition, if our firm requires certain or near-certain profits in the short run then a bid of £10 or less should be made. This will not maximize long-run profits but it will generate near-certain business.

In the final section of the chapter we shall examine how the various alternatives for the firm's ultimate goal might affect pricing decisions.

Table 8.1 *Sealed bid pricing*

Bid (1) (£)	Profit (2) (£)	Probability of our bid winning the contract (3)	Expected pay-off (2) × (3) (£)
10	2	0.9	1.8
11	3	0.7	2.1
12	4	0.5	2.0
13	5	0.3	1.5

Alternative Business Objectives

As suggested above it appears to us that there are good reasons why business-men do attempt to maximize profits (achieved by satisfying consumers). None the less the various alternative theories of business objectives will now be amplified and the reader left to judge for himself.

Profit maximization

Figure 8.4 shows the typical accountant's break-even chart, with a fixed cost (*FC*) irrespective of output, and a variable cost rising as output increases.

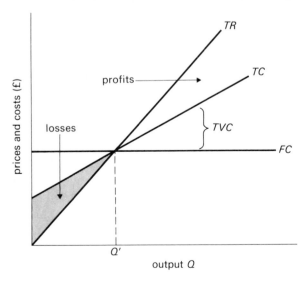

Figure 8.4 *The break-even chart*

Total variable cost (*TVC*) is assumed uniform and rises in proportion to output, and hence total cost (*TC*) is a straight line. Total revenue (*TR*), or sales, is also a straight line and assumes a constant price irrespective of quantity sold. The firm breaks even at output level *Q'* and the further to the right it can move the higher are its profits.

The economist takes issue with this. Detailed reasons will be provided in later chapters, but a brief discussion follows. In essence, *TR* is assumed to be curved since to sell even more (other things like advertising held constant) then price must be reduced. After a point price will have to be reduced so far that the volume increase will not compensate for the price reduction and sales value will fall. *TVC* rises but not uniformly. For a period it rises slowly and then rises more rapidly as the variable inputs (such as labour and materials) begin to cost more owing to diminishing returns (e.g. because, given the same *FC*, the fixed input, say a factory, must be used more intensively). Overtime rates would be an example of such a disproportionate rise in variable costs.

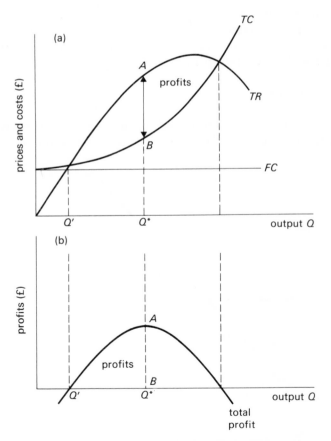

Figure 8.5 *Profit maximization and the profit-maximizing output*

As a consequence the economist is interested not so much in the break-even point Q' as in the profit-maximization point $Q*$ (figure 8.5). At $Q*$ the distance AB (i.e. $TR - TC$) is maximized (figure 8.5(a)). Figure 8.5(b) shows the profit information only, displayed in the form of a profit 'hill'. The profit-maximizing businessman will produce at output level $Q*$.

Sales maximization

Figure 8.6 shows that, for the conditions of figure 8.5, the sales-maximizing firm (as opposed to the profit maximizer) will produce at $\overline{Q}$, selling more (at a lower price), earning lower profits (CD) and achieving a higher TR.[2] D is the highest point on curve TR, whereas A was the highest point on the profit hill. Even sales maximizers may produce between A and D, however. If, for example, D is insufficiently high to satisfy shareholders, the firm may be sold and managers lose their positions if a take-over occurs. Consequently managers may still produce beyond $Q*$ but below $\overline{Q}$, in order to meet a minimum level of profits, or *profit constraint*, which, while not achieving maximum sales, will accomplish a trade-off between sales maximization and job security. In figure 8.7 this occurs at Q''.

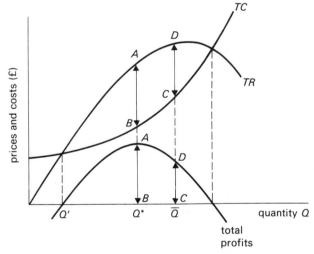

Figure 8.6 *Profit maximization and sales revenue maximization*

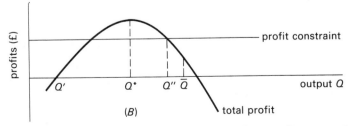

Figure 8.7 *Sales revenue maximization with a profit constraint*

Utility maximization

A more difficult alternative model of managerial behaviour is Oliver Williamson's theory of managers as utility maximizers.[3] He argues that managers attempt to maximize their utility, which has two main components:

1   Capital expenditure above that required for economic reasons. This discretionary investment is the firm's reported profits less two amounts: a profit constraint to ensure job security, and corporate taxation, since by law the government taxes profits before they can be used for purchasing plant, buildings, land or equipment.
2   Managerial, on-job perquisites (or perks) and the prestige associated with the number of staff the management group has reporting to it.

All of these things, it can be argued, provide satisfaction to the management in a way that straightforward profits (which belong to shareholders) do not.

Clearly managers will spend on discretionary investment, staff and perquisites until the profit constraint is attained. That much is similar to figure 8.7. Another similarity is that the output achieved, as in figure 8.7, will be higher than the profit-maximizing output. On this occasion the reason will be due less to a lower price and more to expenditure on staff and perquisites. This is so since staff and perquisites are assumed (in the model) to be equivalent in effect to sales promotion expenditure. That this is not implausible can be seen by considering the effect that high levels of personal staff attention will have on potential customers.

How will managers allocate their use of profit above the constraint between the two components of utility? The answer lies in two further assumptions:

(a)   Capital expenditure is not deductible from profits until after deduction of tax, expenditure on perks and salaries for personnel (this assumption is actually a legal fact).
(b)   For each additional pound spent on one or other component the extra or additional satisfaction (not the total satisfaction) obtained diminishes, and vice versa.

Given these assumptions the managers will allocate the surplus to each until the last pound spent on each produces identical additional (or marginal) satisfaction (*MS*). That is, where

$$MS_P = MS_I (1 - t)$$

where *P* and *I* are perquisites and staff expenditure, and discretionary capital expenditure, respectively, and *t* is the corporation tax rate. This requires a little amplification. For simplicity, first assume that *t* is zero and so can be disregarded. Then assume that managers can measure their satisfaction in numbers with some hypothetical unit, and that the following holds:

$$MS_P = 12$$
$$MS_I = 8.$$

It would now pay the managers to shift £1 from I to P because this would forfeit 8 units of satisfaction and gain 12, a net increase of 4. Because of assumption (b) this process will not continue indefinitely. MS_P will become less than 12 and MS_I more than 8. Ultimately the two will be equal ($MS_P = MS_I$), management utility will be optimized, and no incursion will have been made into the profit constraint, since all that has occurred is a transfer of supra-constraint resources from I to P.

Now let us reintroduce taxation into the picture. Assume that the corporation tax rate is 25 per cent; then the firm's profit and loss account could read as follows under (A):

	(A)		(B)	
Sales		200		200
less costs (excluding				
staff & perks)		100		100
actual profits		100		100
less staff & perks		40		20
reported profits		60		80
less tax @ 25%		15		20
		45		60
less minimum constraint				
(assumed)		30		30
available for discretionary				
capital expenditure		15		30

If the managers, in order to equate MS_P with MS_I, wish to transfer £15 from P to I, how much must they transfer? The question seems stupid until the difference in tax treatment is recalled. The answer is £20 and can be understood by comparing the profit and loss accounts (A) and (B). Thus if £15 is transferred to I the cost of the transfer is

$$£15/(1-t) = £15/(1-0.25) = £15/0.75 = £20.$$

So before tax, for every £1 spent on P, £1 must be earned, and for every £1 spent on I, $£1/(1-t)$ must be earned. Thus to transfer £1 from P to I results in a loss of MS_P per pound earned (before tax) and a gain of $MS_I(1-t)$ per pound earned (before tax). Since we are interested in the allocation by managers of reported profits which they must earn (less the constraint), and not the vagaries of the tax system, the required optimum is $MS_P = MS_I(1-t)$.

Maximization and environmental changes

It is interesting to compare the predictions of the three types of theory as to how managers will react to various environmental changes.

If demand falls, a lower price must be accepted at each output level. In figure 8.6, the *TR* curve pivots clockwise, generally by ever-increasing amounts. In figure 8.7, the profit hill consequently falls and shifts to the left. The profit maximizer will reduce output (to remain at the summit of the new hill). The sales maximizer reduces output also as the right-hand slope of the hill now hits the unchanged profit constraint at a lower output level. The utility maximizer will also reduce output. Because the reported profit hill falls, *I* decreases. Consequently $MS_I(1-t)$ rises. To restore $MS_I(1-t) = MS_P$ the available profits are reallocated away from staff and perks towards *I*, thus raising MS_P relative to $MS_I(1-t)$. A reduction in *P* causes a fall in output.

If fixed costs rise the profit hill will fall by the same amount all along its length. The summit will remain unchanged in position. In figure 8.6, the distance *AD* will be less but *Q** will still be the summit of the hill. In figure 8.7, the sales maximizer will reduce output, however, since the now lower profit hill will hit the profit constraint to the left of *Q″*. The utility maximizer will also reduce output. The reasons are analogous to the previous case except that the profit hill will fall because *TC* rises, not because *TR* falls.

If corporation tax rises the profit hill will again fall vertically, but will do so proportionately most at its summit and least, in fact not at all, where it cuts the quantity axis and profits are zero. Thus the profit maximizer will remain at *Q** (the position of the lower summit) and the sales maximizer will move to the left of *Q″*, again to meet the profit constraint. But since the hill is falling less at lower levels (there is less profit to tax) the movement to the left will be less than in the previous case. The utility maximizer will raise output. $MS_I(1-t)$ has become smaller since *t* is larger. Perks and staff become relatively cheaper and more attractive. Reallocation away from *I* towards *P* occurs until $MS_I(1-t)$ again equals MS_P. Since *P* affects output (by assumption) volume sales rise. This is consistent with casual observation. Many firms deliberately try to reduce their tax bills after a tax increase. Raising pre-tax expenses such as *P* is an easy way to reduce reported profits and so tax.

When variable costs rise *TC* is pivoted up and to the left by ever greater amounts. The profit hill shifts down and to the left. All three types of firm reduce output in this case, for reasons closely analogous to those given in the case of a rise in fixed cost or a fall in demand.

Table 8.2 *Reactions of maximizers to environmental changes*

	Profit maximizer	Sales maximizer	Utility maximizer
Demand fall	Output down	Output down	Output down
Fixed cost rise	No change	Output down	Output down
Corporation tax rise	No change	Output down	Output up
Variable cost rise	Output down	Output down	Output down

The reactions of the three types of maximizer to the four changes described are summarized in table 8.2.

These varying predictions are of particular value if (a) firms do have different motivations and (b) the government is contemplating the impact of a corporation tax or local rate (fixed cost) change. For example, if firms are mainly profit maximizers a corporation tax change will have no (short-term) effect on, say, employment (it will have an effect on long-term investment). If they are sales or utility maximizers this is just not so, even in the short run.

Clearly the ramifications are enormous. We have already suggested, and will do so again later, that firms probably are, by and large, profit maximizers. To the extent that they are not, our view is that they can be analysed as if they were with little or no loss in comprehension.

References

1 J. Dean, *Managerial Economics*, Prentice-Hall, 1952.
2 W.J. Baumol, *Economic Theory and Operations Analysis*, Prentice-Hall, 3rd edn, 1972; see also W.J. Baumol, 'On the theory of oligopoly', *Economica* 31 (1958), pp. 75–83.
3 O. Williamson, *The Economics of Discretionary Behaviour: Managerial Objectives in a Theory of the Firm*, Prentice-Hall, 1964.

9

Financial Decision-taking and Control

'Annual income twenty pounds, annual expenditure nineteen nineteen six, result happiness. Annual income twenty pounds, annual expenditure twenty pounds ought and six, result misery.' Micawber's words still ring true, but generations of economists and accountants have wrestled with this concept, which is simple but so maddeningly evasive. Profits, loosely defined as the difference between a firm's revenues and costs over a given period, have played a key role in economics since the writings of Adam Smith (1776) at least, yet they still remain the source of controversy. Value theory, the dissection of price into its constituent elements, payments to factors of production, rent, profits, etc., lay at the heart of classical economics. The issue of profits— whence they came and where they went—still occupies the foreground of both market and Marxian economics. For present purposes the ideology of profits will be neglected, and we shall concentrate on the problems of how we can measure them.

Consider the problems faced by accountants in the production and audit of a set of company accounts. It is obvious that all business forms, whether companies, partnerships or sole traders, should keep some set of books, if only for the purpose of recording and monitoring their financial position and performance. The legal obligations to maintain these records vary, but we shall defer consideration of the various business forms until the next chapter. Here we concentrate on the large public corporation with shares quoted on the Stock Exchange. In the drawing up of accounts, a major consideration must be the requirements of their users; these include shareholders, investment analysts, the City (the Stock Exchange etc.), creditors and lenders, other companies, employees, management, the government and official bodies, and the general public. Are all their various requirements reconcilable, uniform, and reasonably unchanging? If not, a question mark is raised over the utility of one unique set of accounts. Pressure for the production of information will come from various sources—company and tax legislation and Stock Exchange regulations, plus the statements of standard accounting practice issued by professional accountancy bodies, which determine the form and content of accounting statements and which reflect, to varying degree, the needs of users.

The information produced can be used externally to monitor and compare the efficiency with which companies are managed. We will consider *financial accounting*—the assembly and preparation of the financial information required for company shareholders. We will consider also *management accounting*, which is concerned with the provision of financial information about the organization to its own managers, to enable them to plan, control, monitor and generally measure the effectiveness of their own operations. Obviously there are close links between the two types of accounting and some of the information generated will be utilized for both.

A major consideration will be that of accounting for price changes (i.e. inflation), a thorny and controversial issue that has resulted in a number of different systems and rather grudging acceptance by accountants of current orthodoxy enshrined in SSAP 16 (Standard Statement of Accounting Practice 16, Accounting Standards Committee, 1980). The problem is still in search of a solution.

As accounting provides information about economic aspects of business activities, there are links between the two disciplines. Much empirical work in economics has its foundation in accounting data. Yet accountants and economists have been described as 'uncongenial twins'. This is partly because they have had different emphases. Accountants have tended to look backward and report results relating to a historical period, the accounting year. In contrast, economists have concentrated on decision-making at firm level—a forward-looking process which anticipates future events and the consequences of current actions. The controversy about *inflation accounting* and the move towards *value accounting* (more of which follows) have moved the two approaches closer. Both are obviously vital processes. If a business is to survive, grow and prosper it must assess past performance, monitor current progress and formulate policies concerning the optimum path(s) to follow in the future. The last is of key concern in company financial management. Decisions must be made about which new ventures and/or new production techniques should be adopted, and about the scale on which new developments should be made. Related decisions must be made about how to fund these activities. Should it be by debt or equity, or a judicious mix of the two? Do shareholders prefer the company to pay them a high proportion of current profits as dividends, or to retain those profits for reinvestment in projects which lead to even greater profits later? What are the objective criteria on which these decisions can be made? These issues will be considered below as we broach the problems of the investment decision, the capital structure problem and financial policy issues.

The Role of the Accountant

Accounting is as old as commercial activity itself. Any delegation of economic responsibilities, if it is to be effective, requires the keeping of records. Early accounting systems, concerned with the management of secular and religious estates, were maintained by the steward to safeguard his position and testify to his honesty, rather than to calculate a 'profit' made. There is evidence that the system of *double-entry bookkeeping* was practised in thirteenth century Italy.

The system involves a dual classification of all business transactions, applied so that every one appears as a debit on the left-hand side (LHS) and a credit on the right-hand side (RHS) in the ledger records. For example, if a business spends some cash (a RHS entry), either it will receive an asset in exchange, or it will have an expense or profit appropriation to record, or it will have removed a liability (all LHS entries). The system provides a check in that all entries appear twice, and so total debit balances should equal total credit balances. This check does not ensure an absence of errors, as, for example, compensating mistakes can be made. The system is neutral, and therefore unhelpful, with respect to the definitions adopted for classifying items (e.g. capital or revenue expenditure). As it is compatible with numerous systems of classification, and is designed for business generally, it does not ensure that the system meets the requirements of any unique user.

However, it has been universally adopted. A business's resources are termed its *assets*, and the claims of any parties against them are either liabilities or capital claims. *Capital claims* refer to the interests of members; these are the owners of the company, the *shareholders* whose capital claim represents the investment (including profits reinvested) that they have made in the company. *Liabilities* are the claims of external parties who have no direct say in the operation of the company but are its *creditors*; they have lent it money or provided it with goods or services on credit (the latter group are known as trade creditors). The fact that all assets are claimed by someone, either the shareholders or the creditors, means that certain basic accounting identities follow:

assets = capital + liabilities

capital = contributed capital + retained profits
(capital is known collectively as the *owner's interest*)

capital (net worth) = assets − liabilities.

This identity underlies the structure of the balance sheet, which is a list of components of the above items at a particular time, giving a 'snapshot' view of the financial condition of a company. Comparison of a series of balance sheets may give a better guide to developments within the company over time. The double-entry system applies in the production of all the accounts, but if we take the balance sheet as an example then any entry which affects one side must also affect the other. Suppose that the shareholders have just injected £250,000, which is still held by the company as cash (perhaps before expenditure on an asset). There will be an entry on the debit side (LHS) which will show the value of the cash, and an increase on the credit side (RHS) showing the injection of capital:

cash debits £250,000
capital credits £250,000.

At the time of the passage of the 1948 Companies Act balance sheets tended to conform to this (horizontal) pattern, with liabilities shown on the LHS and assets on the RHS. The form of balance sheets, though not their composition, now tends to vary. They often appear as lists, either with owner's interest and long-term loans at the top, followed by details of fixed and current assets, followed by current liabilities, or in reverse order, with the latter section at the top and capital employed at the bottom. (In a survey undertaken by the Institute of Chartered Accountants in England and Wales in 1979 of the published accounts of 300 major UK companies, only 13 used the horizontal form of balance sheet presentation.)

The *profit-and-loss account* shows the returns generated from the employment of the company's assets during the *accounting year*—the period between balance sheets. This account will include an indication of the profit or loss made over the period before the deduction of corporation tax. The *gross profit* figure is broadly the sales figure minus the costs of sales. From gross profits must be deducted administration and distribution costs, depreciation (the allowance for wear and tear on capital equipment), interest payments, hire charges and auditors' and directors' fees. The remaining balance will be the *net profit* before taxation; this will then be debited with the estimated corporation tax charge for the year. The final section, sometimes called the *appropriation account*, shows how net profit after taxation has been apportioned between dividend payments to the shareholders and transfers to various reserves.

In reality there are three stages in the calculation of profitability before the final figures emerge in the profit-and-loss account. A *manufacturing account* will provide a measure of the manufacturing costs over the trading period. In the *trading account* the various manufacturing costs will be deducted from sales revenue. The resultant gross profits figure will then be utilized in the profit-and-loss account, and together these three accounts lead up to the production of the company's *income statement*. These accounts could well be subsumed in a single account, but have been presented separately below for ease of interpretation. They are also of very limited use for management control purposes because they are presented as aggregates. They might make most sense in a single-product manufacturing enterprise. For simplicity we have chosen such an enterprise, but this is far from typical.

Accounting example

In tables 9.1, 9.2, 9.3 and 9.4 is presented a hypothetical set of accounts for company XYZ Ltd, a manufacturing group. In table 9.1 the manufacturing account gives details of the costs associated with the manufacturing process,

Table 9.1 *XYZ Company Ltd: manufacturing account for the year ended 31 December 1981*

	£m	£m
Opening inventory as of 1 January 1981		22.3
Purchases		210.0
		232.3
Less closing inventory on 31 December 1981		24.8
Cost of materials		207.5
Factory wages		60.5
Prime costs of manufacture		268.0
Factory overheads:		
Repairs	4.0	
Rates	6.0	
Factory gas, water and electricity	11.0	
Depreciation	25.0	
Portion of government grant for purchase of		
plant and equipment	(1.0)	45.0
		313.0
Less increase in work in progress		1.5
Factory cost of production		311.5
Less stocks of finished goods in factory		10.0
Cost of goods to warehouse: to trading account		301.5

Table 9.2 *XYZ Company Ltd: trading account for the year ended 31 December 1981*

	£m
Finished goods:	
Opening inventory 1 January 1981	35.0
Cost of manufactures transferred	301.5
	336.5
Less closing inventory 31 December 1981	30.0
Cost of sales	306.5
Gross profit: to profit-and-loss account	126.5
Sales	433.0

Table 9.3 *XYZ Company Ltd: consolidated profit-and-loss account for the year ended 31 December 1981*

	1981[a] £m
Group turnover (note 1)[b]	433.0
[Gross profit (note 2)	126.5]
Group profit before interest and tax (note 3)	75.5
Interest (note 4)	4.1
Group profit before tax	71.4
Taxation (note 5)	32.3
Group profit after tax	39.1
Minority interests (note 6)	0.9
Group profit available for dividends and retentions	38.2
Dividends (note 7)	13.6
Group retentions (note 8)	24.6
Earnings per ordinary share: 52.22 pence	
Movements in reserves:	
Reserves at the beginning of the year	119.5
Profit retained	24.6
Reserves at end of year	144.1

[a]Comparative figures from the previous year are required by law. These have been omitted for simplicity
[b]For explanatory notes see text

and includes: raw materials' costs; expenditures on wages, rates, heating and power; and the various expenses associated with running the factory and its contents, including depreciation charges, changes in the value of stocks, and work in progress. The result is a costing of the value of goods produced over the year, which is transferred to the trading account (table 9.2). In turn, the gross profits from the trading account are transferred to the profit-and-loss account and used in the calculation of profit before interest and tax (table 9.3). The accounts in tables 9.1 and 9.2 are not normally published, but information of the type presented in those accounts would be vital to the development of the published accounts. A traditional balance sheet for company XYZ is shown in table 9.4.

Accounting will change once the provisions of the 1981 Companies Bill

Table 9.4 *XYZ Company Ltd: consolidated balance sheet for the year ended 31 December 1981*

	1981 £m
Group capital employed	
Ordinary share capital (note 9)[a]	18.25
Reserves	144.1
	162.35
Minority interests (note 6)	3.25
Loans (note 10)	79.6
Deferred liabilities (note 11)	4.2
Deferred tax (note 12)	12.7
Capital grants (note 13)	2.25
	264.35
Employment of group capital	
Current assets:	
Stocks (note 14)	82.55
Debtors	79.9
Cash and liquid assets (note 15)	46.4
	208.85
Current liabilities:	
Short-term borrowings (note 16)	3.9
Creditors	61.8
Taxation (note 17)	22.2
Dividends (note 7)	7.35
	95.25
Net current assets	113.6
Fixed assets (note 18)	92.25
Goodwill (note 19)	58.5
	264.35

[a]For explanatory notes see pp. 131−6

become established practice. These reflect the movement towards the harmonization of accounting practice embodied in the EEC Fourth Directive. A further standardization of both the layout of company accounts and the information presented in the balance sheet and profit-and-loss account will result. An example of both a pro forma profit-and-loss account and a balance sheet conforming to the new requirements is shown in appendix 9.1.

Explanatory notes to accounts in tables 9.3 and 9.4

1 *Turnover.* Since the passage of the 1967 Companies Act, turnover figures must be provided (unless the business is exempted, as in the case of small companies with a turnover of less than £250,000). Companies have to indicate the method by which the figure is calculated; this differs from company to company, reducing the comparability of accounts.

2 *Gross profit.* Usually the figure following the turnover figure relates to operating profit after charging various expenses but before interest payments. In these specimen accounts an item has been added (in brackets [ ]) which indicates the level of profits before deduction of the expenses (see note 3).

3 *Selling and distribution cost plus administrative expenses.*

	£m
Salaries and wages	9.0
Advertising	14.5
R & D expenditure	13.0
Depreciation	7.0
General expenses	5.0
Hire of vehicles	1.0
Auditors' fees	1.0
Directors' fees	0.5
Total	51.0

The directors' fees will be shown in bands of £2500 in notes to the accounts, with the number of directors in each band indicated. Employees earning more than £10,000 p.a. will also be shown.

4 *Interest paid.* The company has a variety of loans with the following interest payments:

	£m
Loans wholly repayable within five years	1.1
Loans not wholly repayable within five years	4.2
Bank loans and short-term borrowings	2.45
Less interest received	(3.65)
Total interest	4.1

5 *Taxation.* Companies are liable for corporation tax at a normal rate of 52 per cent. The small-companies rate applicable on profits up to £90,000 is 40 per cent, and thereafter there is marginal relief available on profits up to £225,000. The figure in table 9.3 is made up as follows:

	£m
Corporation tax	22.7
Deferred tax	5.3
	28.0
Adjustments in respect of	
prior year	4.3
	32.3

There is now a very generous system of capital allowances in force as investment incentives (these are considered in detail later in this chapter). Companies can write off the full amount of industrial investment in the year in which it is made as a charge against their taxable profits. This would lead to wide swings in their tax bill if followed to the letter; most companies therefore create a deferred tax account which can be used to even out the charges over a number of years.

6 *Minority interests*. It is quite frequent for a holding company to acquire less than 100 per cent of the equity of a company taken over. In this situation, as it has control, it is usual to include the full amount of the assets and liabilities of the company taken over in its own accounts and to disclose the interests of the other shareholders as a distinct category in the balance sheet.

7 *Dividends*.

	Pence per share	£m
Interim	8.58	6.26
Final (recommended)	10.05	7.34
	18.65	13.6

8 *Retentions*. It would be unusual practice for directors to distribute all profits as dividends; hence revenue reserves are created from profits to be reinvested in the business. These should be distinguished from capital reserves which are non-distributable. The movements in the reserves are shown as the last section of table 9.3. Companies frequently have reserves under the heading 'share premium account'. This arises when shares are issued at a price above their nominal value. The premium account is itemized separately in the reserves and treated as a part of the company's paid-up capital; it cannot therefore be distributed as revenue. Specific reserves used to be created for this purpose under the title 'dividend equalization reserve', and companies still 'smooth out' dividend payments but do not tend to categorize individual reserves specifically for the purpose.

9 *Ordinary share capital*.

	Number of 25p shares	£m
Authorized	108,000,000	27.0
Issued and fully paid	73,000,000	18.25

10 *Loans.*

	£m
Loans wholly repayable within five years	8.95
Loans not wholly repayable within five years	58.4
Short- and medium-term bank loans	12.25
Total loans	79.6

11 *Deferred liabilities.* Certain funds have been put aside to meet unfunded retirement benefits in the subsidiary. The figure in the example is £4.2m.

12 *Deferred tax.* This account is created to even out the timing effects caused by the systems of capital allowances, stock appreciation relief, advance corporation tax (all considered later in this chapter) and any other factors which affect the timing of tax payments.

	£m
Amount deferred at the beginning of year	10.55
Movements during year	2.15
Amount deferred at end of year	12.7
Comprising:	
Accelerated capital allowances	16.45
Stock relief	8.8
Advance corporation tax	(3.15)
Other timing differences	(9.40)

13 *Capital grants.* The government provides grants towards capital expenditure as part of its industrial and regional development policies. The amounts involved are credited to the profit-and-loss account over the estimated useful life of the asset concerned. The amounts shown in the balance sheet represent the difference between the total grant received and the amount already credited to the profit-and-loss account. The figure in the example is £2.25m.

14 *Stocks.*

	£m
Finished and partly processed goods	57.75
Raw materials	24.8
Total	82.55

The problems involved in the valuation of stocks and the different methods available are considered later in this chapter.

15 *Cash and liquid assets.*

	£m
Certificates of tax deposit	6.0
Government securities	2.65
Short-term deposits	28.2
Cash and bank balances	9.55
Total	46.40

16 *Short-term borrowings.* These are made up of bank loans and overdrafts. The figure in the example is £3.9m.

17 *Taxation.* Note 5 was concerned with tax based on profit for the year. This note is concerned with tax planned to be paid this year.

	£m
Current taxation	19.8
Prior years	2.4
Total	22.2

The UK tax liability for the current year includes advance corporation tax (ACT) on the recommended final dividend. This is equivalent to the standard rate of income tax applied to the gross dividend. This rate currently stands at 30 per cent. The dividend after tax, the net final dividend recommended, has to be grossed up as follows:

$$\text{net dividend} = \text{gross dividend} (1 - \text{tax rate})$$

$$= \text{gross dividend} \left(1 - \frac{30}{100}\right)$$

$$\text{net dividend} \left(\frac{100}{70}\right) = \text{gross dividend}$$

$$\text{tax payable as ACT} = \text{net dividend} \left(\frac{30}{70}\right) = £7.35\text{m} \left(\frac{30}{70}\right) = £3.15\text{m}.$$

The above amount appears in the deferred tax account (note 12), as the whole of this amount can be carried forward to be set off against future corporate tax liabilities. For a fuller discussion of corporate taxation see later in this chapter.

18 *Fixed assets.*

	Cost	Aggregate depreciation	Net book value
	£m	£m	£m
Plant, equipment and vehicles	187.95	141.5	46.45
Land and buildings	45.8	—	45.8
Total			92.25

Assets are depreciated in order to ensure that, when they come to the end of their useful lives, sufficient funds will have been set aside to meet the cost of replacing them. If this were not done the business would be in danger of running itself down and paying profits out of capital. The calculation of depreciation charges is hedged round with difficulties; working life cannot be estimated with a great deal of accuracy since technological change can rapidly make assets redundant, and there is no agreed method of the amount of asset value to be written off in each year (see table 9.5).

Table 9.5 *Methods of depreciation*

	Number of companies		
	1978−79	1977−78	1968−69
Method adopted for all or most assets:			
Straight line	260	239	65
Reducing balance	5	5	3
	265	244	68
Mixture of methods	16	26	16
	281	270	84
Basis not disclosed	19	30	216
	300	300	300

Source: Survey of Published Accounts 1979, Institute of Chartered Accountants in England and
Wales, 1981

A popular method is the *straight-line* calculation in which equal
amounts are written off in every year of the asset's working life. The
reducing balance method would write off a constant percentage of the
net book value of the asset every year (i.e. the value of the asset after
deducting previous depreciation provisions). There are other methods
too, and obviously different amounts will be deducted from revenue
according to which particular method is chosen. Traditionally the original
or 'historic' cost has been the basis of the valuation of the asset. In
periods of inflation this cost will no longer be an accurate representation
of the cost of replacing the asset concerned, and if historic values are
utilized then depreciation provisions will be inadequate, profits will be
overstated, and businesses will be paying profits out of capital. This
problem will be returned to when we consider inflation accounting later
in this chapter.

The usual convention is to let land and buildings stand at cost rather
than depreciate them. Again, in times of inflation they may require
revaluing.

19   *Goodwill.* We will assume for the sake of our example that XYZ Ltd has
previously taken over a major distribution chain. The market values of
the shares it purchased in the subsidiary was well in excess of the fair
value of the net tangible assets of the subsidiary at the time of the take-
over. This excess value is termed 'goodwill' and only appears in accounts
on consolidation after a take-over or merger. The value of a thriving
business is typically greater than the sum of its parts. A number of
various factors may contribute to the development of goodwill—good
relationships with its workforce, its customers, special knowledge, the
benefits of advertising, secret processes, franchises, licences etc. This

will exist in all sound businesses to a varying degree but is only accounted for in the above case. Under the provisions of the EEC Fourth Directive, which entails a movement towards the harmonization of company accounts, goodwill has to be written off over five years or over the economic life of the asset concerned at the discretion of member states. This view was adopted in the 1981 Companies Act. At the moment it only applies to the treatment of goodwill in the purchase of assets, not subsidiaries, but it seems to represent EEC thinking on the matter; the forthcoming Seventh Directive, which will deal with goodwill on consolidation, will probably take a similar view. Once again this provides an example of a very arbitrary accounting convention. Goodwill is only accounted for in certain circumstances, even though it arises in all businesses (it could conceivably be negative), and when it does arise, why should it be written off? Presumably in a thriving business goodwill will be increasing over time?

Accounting Rules and Conventions

The 1948 Companies Act stated that company accounts should give 'a true and fair view' of the state of a company's affairs. Cynics might suggest that this is a statement of intent rather than an expression of reality. There are a number of reasons why it is difficult to provide an unequivocal statement describing a company's state of affairs. Accounting practices and conventions have evolved in a piecemeal fashion over a very long period. Some changes have been conditioned by successive additions to company law, which to a degree may have reflected the changing but still often conflicting requirements of users. Moreover, there has usually been initial resistance to requirements for greater disclosure of information on the grounds that it might assist competitors. Thus different standards can be in force simultaneously.

Accounting conventions still bear the imprint of times when businesses were owned as well as run by their managers and when the main providers of outside funds were the creditors, who required information about the stewardship of those funds. Traditional *historical cost accounting*, which involves the valuation of assets on the basis of their original costs as shown in our specimen set of accounts, has been built around the following conventions:

1 *Going concern.* This involves the assumption that the business will continue to operate in the foreseeable future. Our accounts did not attempt to represent the 'liquidation value' of the business.
2 *Accruals.* This involves the convention that revenue and costs are recognized or 'accrued' as they are earned and not when the actual payments are made. Accounts therefore do not directly refer to the underlying cash basis of the business. In association with this there is the next convention.

3 *Matching costs and revenues.* These are matched as far as their relationship can be established. The revenues and costs shown in the profit-and-loss account should arise out of transactions in the relevant period and any profit shown should be matched with the costs incurred in earning it.

4 *Prudence or conservatism.* This ensures that in cases of doubt profit figures and asset values are always conservatively valued and are recognized when realized, whereas losses or liabilities are given their maximum values. This too can distort the real economic picture.

5 *Consistency.* There should be a consistent treatment of similar accounting transactions both within and across time periods.

Normally, any assets other than money should be valued at the lesser of cost or net realizable value. In traditional historic cost accounts no attempt is made to ensure that the balance sheet gives a realistic statement of value or net worth (and for this reason the method is inadequate in times of inflation). Finally, the monetary unit is the unit of measurement, and therefore changes in purchasing power are ignored; the distortions caused by this are fully treated later in this chapter in a section on inflation accounting.

Accounting Problems in the Absence of Inflation

As can be seen from the previous section, there are a number of grey areas in which practice is largely a matter of adopted convention and where individual usage varies. Therefore the comparability of different sets of published accounts is greatly reduced. Some other factors have already been mentioned: the variety of calculations of depreciation provisions (note 18); the rather arbitrary treatment of goodwill (note 19); and the wide latitude available for the calculation of current tax liabilities (notes 5, 12 and 17). A number of other problems can be added to these.

The valuation of stocks

In the drawing up of accounts consideration has to be given to the valuation of current assets in the form of stocks of raw materials, work in progress, finished goods etc. in order to calculate profitability. Various methods are available for the valuation of stocks of raw materials. We will consider two extreme methods—*last in first out* (LIFO) and *first in first out* (FIFO). In times of changing prices the adoption of either of the two methods can lead to different closing stock valuations (table 9.6) and therefore profit levels (table 9.7). In LIFO, the last additions to the stock (in our example, 10 cwt at £20 per cwt) are considered to be the first issued; in general, stock is issued in the reverse order to receipt. In FIFO, on the other hand, stock is issued in the same order as receipt.

Yet another way of valuing stocks would be to value closing stock on the

Table 9.6 *Example of stock valuation*

Last in first out (LIFO)

	Receipts			Issues			Balance
	cwt	at £	value (£)	cwt	at	value (£)	(£)
June	15	10	= 150				150
July	20	15	= 300				450
August	10	20	= 200				650
September				20	(10 at £20)		
					(10 at £15) =	350	300
October				20	(10 at £15)		
					(10 at £10) =	250	50

First in first out (FIFO)

	Receipts			Issues			Balance
	cwt	at £	value (£)	cwt	at	value (£)	(£)
June	15	10	= 150				150
July	20	15	= 300				450
August	10	20	= 200				650
September				20	(15 at £10)		
					(5 at £15) =	225	425
October				20	(15 at £15)		
					(5 at £20) =	325	100

Table 9.7 *The effects of LIFO and FIFO on the calculation of profit*
for the example of table 9.6, ignoring production or any
other associated costs

	LIFO		FIFO	
	(£)	(£)	(£)	(£)
Sales		1200		1200
Less:				
Purchases	650		650	
Closing stocks	50		100	
		600		550
'Profit'		600		650

Table 9.8 *Disclosure of methods used to calculate the cost of stocks and work in progress*

	Number of instances		
	1978–79	1977–78	1976–77
FIFO method	41	43	41
Average cost	21	13	17
LIFO method, used by USA subsidiaries	4	11	11
Standard or unit cost	8	2	5
Retail prices less average sales margin, to derive approximate cost (used by retail stores)	5	4	9
Other methods using base stock valuation	4	5	4
Total[a]	83	78	77

[a]300 companies were surveyed but not all disclosed their method of stock valuation

Source: Survey of Published Accounts 1979, Institute of Chartered Accountants in England and Wales, 1981

basis of the *average costs* of raw materials bought in over the accounting period. Further complications arise from the necessity to allocate overhead costs associated with the storage of stocks as well as handling charges, and again methods vary. In practice, LIFO has found acceptance in the USA but in the UK the Inland Revenue requires FIFO for tax purposes. The range of typical practices is shown in table 9.8.

Extraordinary items

These represent a further adjustment which can have a major effect on the after-tax profit figure. They represent exceptional gains or losses, or those of a non-recurring nature not considered part of normal business activity. For example, an asset might be sold which had not been acquired with the original intention of resale, or part of the firm might be closed down with attendant losses, or there might be expropriation of foreign assets and so on. The difficulty arises from the wide grounds for discretion in deciding what exactly is an extraordinary item, and there may be a temptation to hide setbacks under this heading.

The Accountant's and the Economist's Definition of Profits

The foregoing discussion indicates that it is no easy matter to calculate exactly a business's profits, even in the absence of inflation. Professor Stamp was led to declare: 'The "income" of a corporation is an intellectual abstraction even more elusive than the electron. It is represented by nothing that can be seen or touched.'[1] Ideally, accounts should have the following, self-explanatory qualities: relevance, objectivity, reliability, timeliness, comparability, completeness and understandability.[2] This goal has yet to be achieved, but at least Sir John Hicks has provided a clear definition of what we are aiming at when we try to measure a company's profits. He suggested: 'Income ... must be defined as the maximum amount of money which the individual can spend this week, and still expect to be able to spend the same amount in real terms in each ensuing week.'[3] The crucial idea is that both the individual and the company have to maintain their capital stock. Hicks's maxim could be modified to apply to a company in the following manner: 'A company's profit is the maximum value which the company can distribute during the year, and still expect to be as well off at the end of the year as it was at the beginning'. Yet even if this end is achieved there are still considerable differences between the economist's and the accountant's view of profits.

The economist is not directly interested in past returns or profits; though not 'bunk', they are history, and only relevant to the extent that they aid predictions of their own future values. The economist stresses that the value of any asset, including that bundle of assets which makes up a company, is determined by the value of the stream of net future benefits which accrue from ownership. Thus the economic value of any asset is the sum of the present values of all those future benefits, and estimates of this should determine the values at which assets change hands in markets.

In his consideration of the role of business profits the economist typically forms hypotheses and uses them to build models which can be tested against empirical evidence via the utilization of their predictions. He assumes that the basic factors of production, land, labour and capital require recompense in the form of rent, wages and interest to entice their respective owners to involve them in productive processes. Thus the dividend paid to the owners of a company is not really part of 'profit' but a necessary reward to the owners of capital to entice them to risk their funds in business operations. The picture becomes even more clouded in the case of the single owner-manager. His reward will not be constituted solely by profits. It will consist in part of a wage for his entrepreneurship and labour, and in part of a return on the capital he has risked; only after these factors have been rewarded can the surplus be regarded as profit. In equilibrium, 'normal' profit consists merely of the required return to all factors of production including an appropriate payment to capital providers, and in disequilibrium, or situations of 'imperfect' competition, profits are the surplus above this.

In assessing profits over the historical accounting period, the accountant ignores the opportunity cost of capital provided by shareholders. He also suffers enforced myopia in that he must arbitrarily consider the accounting year, and use (by tradition) historical values when allocating costs and revenues. He is also constrained by the methods considered suitable in company law, which are acceptable to the revenue authorities and promoted by the profession. Yet the problems caused by accounting for inflation have narrowed the ground between the two views, as will be seen in the next section.

Accounting for Inflation

Even in periods where there is zero inflation it could be argued that accounts based upon historical costs do not provide a complete picture of the state of the business. The profit figure in the profit-and-loss account will not necessarily be a good guide to the company's liquidity position; nor is it intended to be. The depreciation charges deducted in arriving at this figure will be unlikely to bear any resemblance to expenditure during the period on fixed and current assets. An extra statement would be required—a statement of sources and uses of funds which would give an accurate indication of the cash position of the business (see the next section).

Apart from this, historical cost accounts are quite adequate given stable prices. However, in periods of a rapidly changing general price level they become woefully inadequate. In the balance sheet the value of assets shown at written-down historical cost will no longer reflect their value to the business, which could be variously defined as the cost of replacing them, or economic value, or net realizable value (see later in this section). The capital employed in the business will be understated, and depreciation provisions based on this original cost (as opposed to replacement cost) will be inadequate. Profit figures will be exaggerated, as will liability to tax.

Similar problems arise in the valuation of stocks. If they are valued on the FIFO basis and their cost has risen rapidly during the course of the year, then the value of stocks consumed in the productive process will be understated. To replace the stocks consumed would cost more than the charges in the profit-and-loss account. If the value of stocks bought in has increased, then there is a 'holding' gain on stock values. This is not truly part of the year's profits, because when the stocks are replaced the business will be put to greater expense to replace the original amount. This element of 'stock appreciation' will once again artificially inflate profits and lead to a greater tax liability. (This has been recognized by the authorities in their granting of tax relief on stock appreciation, first introduced in 1974; see later in this chapter. At that time it was estimated that stock appreciation accounted for nearly 50 per cent of the gross trading profits of companies.)

Similar distortions will take place in the value of other current assets and liabilities. Accounts drawn up in money units cannot directly reflect the decline in purchasing power of money in times of inflation. Yet current assets held in the form of cash will suffer declines in purchasing power, and the real value of liabilities fixed in money terms will decline. Hence there will be holding losses in the value of monetary assets and holding gains on monetary liabilities, but these will not be reflected in the accounts.

The problems seem quite apparent, but what is the best way of dealing with them? This question has occupied accountants for the last decade, and although a solution has emerged its acceptance has been grudging. At best it represents a compromise. A brief historical account is probably the simplest way of introducing the various arguments, and the disagreement and confusion is readily apparent from the number of reports and guidelines referred to in what follows.

Current purchasing power accounting[4]

The most radical change involved in current purchasing power (CPP) accounting was the replacement of the monetary unit by a unit of constant value—the purchasing power unit. Under this system the balance sheet would then reflect the amount of purchasing power represented by the company's net assets, and the profit-and-loss account would show the gain or loss of purchasing power over the accounting year.

Difficulties arose from the choice of the central price index to indicate changes in purchasing power. The use of the retail price index (RPI) would have been controversial, since this index refers to movements in the price of a basket of consumer goods rather than the rate of inflation as experienced by industrial and commercial companies. The suggestion was that CPP accounts should be presented as a supplement to historical cost accounts. Asset values in the CPP balance sheet would be adjusted by movements in the RPI over the accounting period. Depreciation provisions and the cost of stocks consumed would be based upon these revised values. Even more controversial was the inclusion of gains and losses on monetary items as part of CPP profits. This was an inevitable accompaniment of moving away from the use of money units. The value of monetary assets and liabilities would be adjusted for movements in the RPI and these adjustments would show directly in the profit figures. The upshot of this would be that relatively illiquid companies with large monetary liabilities would show a gain in profitability, and companies suffused with cash would show a relative loss of profitability.

The Sandilands Committee[5] decided that the gains in purchasing power should be shown in reserve movements rather than directly in the profits figure, and that the RPI was too crude a measure to accurately reflect a company's experience of inflation. They put forward an alternative recommendation: current cost accounting.

Current cost accounting

The Sandilands Committee recommended that current cost accounting (CCA) should revert to the use of money as the unit of measurement. Accounts drawn up under this system would be adjusted to neutralize the effects of inflation in a manner indicated below. They would replace historical cost accounts, though the net book value of assets on a historical cost basis, and associated depreciation provisions, would be shown in the notes to the accounts.

Under CCA, assets should be shown at their 'value to the business'. This is not necessarily equivalent to *net realizable value*, or what could be raised were the asset to be sold, but should approximate to the amount of loss suffered by the business should the asset be lost or destroyed. This reflects a movement towards the economist's concept of *economic value*. This value would be estimated by adjusting the values of fixed assets and stocks by movements in appropriate price indices—which would reflect changes in the prices of the assets concerned—rather than by the cruder movements of the RPI alone. The value of stocks consumed and depreciation provisions would be based on these revised values. These two adjustments—to reflect cost of sales and the value of assets consumed—were the sole modifications required to the profit-and-loss account to adjust for the effects of inflation. The intention was that the company's profit figure should indicate its *operating gains* (the difference between its sales revenue over the period and the value to the business of the various inputs used in generating its output in that time). *Holding gains*, such as stock appreciation, would not be shown in the profit figure but would be passed through adjustments to reserves in the balance sheet.

It will be noted that no mention has been made of gains and losses on monetary items. The movement back to the use of monetary units meant that such items would disappear from the accounts unless some express move was made to include them, and Sandilands chose to ignore them. This was one of the major causes of the subsequent controversy, but we will ignore the tedious details of this and move to consideration of the system adopted.

Current cost accounting as represented in ED 24[6] and SSAP 16[7]

The current view is that there are three major adjustments required to ensure that allowance is made for the impact of price changes on the funds required to maintain the value of the net operating assets of a business. These are:

Fixed assets: additional depreciation
Stocks: cost of sales adjustment (*COSA*)
Monetary working capital: monetary working capital adjustment (*MWCA*).

The main change is a movement back to the recognition of gains and losses on monetary items. The *depreciation adjustment* is based on the difference between the depreciation due on the current value of the assets and that based upon historical cost values. The Central Statistical Office (CSO) publishes sets of *Price Index Numbers for Current Cost Accounting*, which are used to revalue a company's assets (except in the case of land or buildings, where an independent valuation is required). For example, assume that a company buys an asset worth £10,000 at the beginning of the accounting year in January. If it has an estimated life of 10 years and depreciation is calculated on a straight-line basis, then in historical cost accounts £1000 would be written off in the accounts at the end of year. But now suppose that the relevant price index for this asset has gone up from 120 at the beginning of the year to 144 at the end, a 20 per cent increase. The revised value of the asset would be £10,000 × (144/120) = £12,000 and the relevant depreciation charge in CCA would have risen by a similar factor, to £1200.

The *cost of sales adjustment* (*COSA*) is made by applying the following formula:

$$COSA = (C - O) - I_a \left(\frac{C}{I_c} - \frac{O}{I_o} \right) \tag{9.1}$$

where C is the historical cost of closing stock, O is the historical cost of opening stock, I_a is the average stock index value for the period, I_c is the closing value of the stock index and I_o is the opening value of the stock index.

Suppose that the historical cost of closing stock is £10,000 and that of the opening stock £8000. Value is a function of quantity and price, and to disentangle the two effects we apply the formula above. From the overall change in the value of stocks, the first bracketed term, we deduct the difference between the average value of closing and opening stocks. Once this volume effect is deducted we have *COSA*, the cost of stock adjustment. Suppose that the index for stock values in January is 179.6 and in December 202.4; then the average is 191. Substituting these values in expression 9.1 we have:

$$
\begin{aligned}
COSA &= £10,000 - £8000 - 191 \left(\frac{£10,000}{202.4} - \frac{£8000}{179.6} \right) \\
&= £2000 - £930.2 \\
&= £1069.8.
\end{aligned}
$$

In the above example it has been assumed that the historical cost of stocks is calculated on a FIFO basis and that the change in stock levels occurs evenly over the year. The adjustment can then be applied to increase the historic cost of stock to the current cost of stock.

The *monetary working capital adjustment* (*MWCA*) is made as shown below, where we assume for simplicity that the monetary working capital (MWC) is made up solely of debtors and creditors. Debtors exceed creditors at both the beginning and the end of the period and the average age of both opening and closing MWC is assumed to be a month. In principle the adjustment is the same as for stocks, but the lag of a month between making payments to creditors and receiving payment from debtors means that the appropriate price index will relate to the previous month. Assume the relevant values for these indices are 178 and 201 for opening and closing MWC, giving an average value of 189.5; then:

	Debtors £000		Creditors £000		Balance £000
Opening MWC	10,000	–	6000	=	4000
Closing MWC	11,000	–	6500	=	4500

Applying a formula analogous to expression 9.1, we have:

$$MWCA = 4500 - 4000 - 189.5 \left(\frac{4500}{201} - \frac{4000}{178} \right) \text{ (£000)}$$
$$= 500 - 189.5(22.4 - 22.5) = 500 + 18.95 \text{ (£000)}$$
$$= £518,950.$$

In this case debtors exceed creditors and the *MWCA* is a charge against profits. Sales on credit are fixed in money terms, and with a positive rate of inflation the real value of those future payments is declining.

Finally, the same principle applies to any long- and short-term liabilities which are fixed in monetary terms. The real value of those commitments declines with every rise in prices. This is the basis of the *gearing adjustment*. Gearing can be defined as the proportion of a company's net operating assets financed by borrowing. (The various methods of measuring gearing will be fully discussed later in this chapter.) For the purposes of adjustment in inflation accounting it is defined as:

$$\text{gearing} = \frac{L}{L + S}$$

where *L* are liabilities (short and long) and *S* is equity capital plus reserves.

In this case gearing is defined as the proportion of net operating assets financed by borrowing. As a rough guide, averaged over the year, this would be equal to the value of long-term loans, plus deferred liabilities, deferred tax and bank loans, minus any positive cash balances, all divided by the sum of equity capital, reserves and the value of the borrowings used as the numerator.

The resultant gearing ratio will then be applied to the previous inflation adjustments—the revised depreciation charges, *COSA* and *MWCA*. The reason for this is that these three adjustments compensate for the impact of inflation on the value of the business as a 'whole' or in 'entity'. Yet in most cases the business as a whole will be financed not by equity alone but by a mixture of equity and debt. All borrowings, fixed in monetary repayment terms, are liabilities which decline in real value, given inflation. These are the holding gains on monetary liabilities which the Sandilands Committee chose to ignore. To reflect these gains, the three previous adjustments, which are additions to costs, are revised down proportionately by the gearing factor. The intention is to maintain the value of that 'portion' of the business which is owned and financed by the equity interest; this could be viewed as the application of the 'proprietorship' concept if it is the value of this interest which has to be protected.

The adoption of a system of inflation accounting should mean that companies' published results are much more realistic, and usually that their profits and rates of return on capital employed are much lower than under historical cost accounting. The effects of this are shown in table 10.6 which shows that companies' inflation-adjusted rates of return have dropped to very low levels in recent years.

Sources and uses of funds' statements

A clearer picture of the way in which funds have been raised and employed during the accounting year can be obtained from a statement of sources and uses of funds. This will distinguish between external and internal sources of funds, and between applications in fixed and working capital. An example of such a statement based on XYZ Ltd's historical cost accounts is shown in

Table 9.9 *XYZ Company Ltd: statement of sources and uses of group funds for the year ended 31 December 1981*

	£m
Source	
Group profit before tax	71.4
Adjustments for items not involving the use of funds:	
Depreciation	32.0
Deferred liabilities	1.0
Total from operations	104.4
Funds from other sources:	
Capital grants received	0.6
Loans	6.9
	111.9
Application	
Fixed assets	38.9
Taxation	32.3
Dividends	13.6
Repayment of loans	22.5
Increase/decrease in working capital:	
Increase in stocks	(0.5)
Increase in debtors	13.0
Increase in creditors	(6.7)
Net liquid funds	(1.2)
	111.9

table 9.9. Current cost accounting statements would reflect the revised depreciation charges and the cost of stock and monetary working capital adjustments, but it is debatable whether or not the gearing adjustment should be included, since it is not a cash flow item (see table 10.5 for details of the aggregated sources and uses of funds by industrial and commercial companies in recent years).

The Role of Management Accounting

Sizer defines management accounting as 'the application of accounting techniques to the provision of information designed to assist all levels of management in planning and controlling the activities of an organization'.[8] Accounting techniques are applied to generate information that will assist managements in their control of company operations, and which can be used as a basis for decision-making and planning. The management accountant will be involved not only in the analysis of historical performance, but also in looking to the future via development plans for investment and funding, the formulation of intermediate targets and budgets with the attainment of long-term objectives in mind, and the monitoring and analysis of current performance. These roles are indicated in table 9.10.

Table 9.10 *The role of management accounting*

Past performance	Current activities	Future objectives
Analysis of past performance	Monitoring current progress	
Measurement of deviations from planned performance, and assessment of likely reasons	Analysis of deviations from planned and budgeted positions	Development plans Investment plans Funding plans
Production of standardized costs—estimates based on past values	Motivation to achieve targets, decisions on corrective action where necessary	
	Pricing and costing decisions aimed at achievement of future objectives. Construction of budgets with similar purpose	

In the analysis of past performance and in the production of *standardized costs*, which can be used as a basis for assessing current operating performance, careful attention must be paid to the likely influence of inflation. Likewise, in the compilation of the various budgets for planning the course of the company's production, cash position etc. in the short- and medium-term, careful consideration must be given to the behavioural implications of the process. If the costs employed as standards are unrealistic, and if the budgeted positions are over-ambitious then the exercise may become dysfunctional and deter performance rather than spur it on.

As in all accounting decisions, there are a number of different ways in which costs can be assessed and overheads allocated. Likewise pricing decisions might be made on a marginal cost or on an average cost-plus mark-up basis, to mention but two possible methods. Neither time nor space permits full consideration of these various areas and we shall concentrate on break-even and contribution analysis. The consideration of long-term investment and funding decisions and the criteria on which these decisions may be made will be considered later in the chapter when attention is switched to financial management.

Break-even and contribution analysis

Break-even analysis (introduced in chapter 8) is concerned with the analysis of changes in the relationship between costs and revenue, and therefore profit, as a function of changes in output. In the break-even chart (figure 8.4 above, repeated here as figure 9.1), it is assumed that fixed costs are invariant and that variable costs are a constant multiple of output, whilst any output can

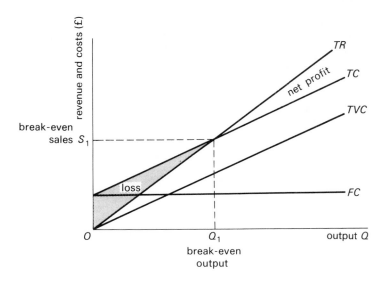

Figure 9.1 *The break-even chart*

be sold at a constant price. Output OQ_1 is the break-even level at which total revenue just covers total cost, and this is associated with a level of total sales revenue of S_1. Beyond this level of sales and output, profits start to appear. The relationships involved are shown below:

$$\begin{aligned}
\text{total revenue} &= PQ \quad (\text{price} \times \text{quantity}) \\
\text{fixed cost} &= F \\
\text{unit variable cost} &= V \\
\text{total variable cost} &= VQ \\
\text{total costs} &= F + VQ.
\end{aligned}$$

The break-even point occurs when total cost is equal to total revenue. This is where:

$$\begin{aligned}
PQ &= F + VQ \\
(P - V)Q &= F.
\end{aligned}$$

The assumptions in the above analysis are not very realistic in that constant unit variable costs imply constant marginal costs and therefore diminishing returns to scale never set in. This means that there is no unique profit-maximizing output and profit continues to rise as a function of output. The reason for this is the neglect of demand conditions in the assumption that any amount can be sold at a constant price. It might be necessary to increase expenditure on advertising and cut price before very large increases in sales can be achieved. Nevertheless, in the short term these assumptions might not be too gross a violation of reality.

In this period when many costs are fixed the contribution that additional sales may make towards fixed costs and profits can be assessed from a variant of the break-even chart which facilitates contribution analysis, shown in figure 9.2. *Total contribution* is defined as the difference between total sales revenue and total variable cost. It is from this contribution that a firm covers its fixed costs and makes a profit. If a firm has a number of product lines and

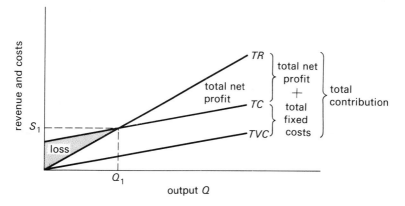

Figure 9.2 *Contribution analysis*

excess productive capacity in each, and at the same time a shortage of certain required inputs, perhaps raw materials or a particular type of skilled labour, then an analysis of the contribution made on each product line should give an indication of where to concentrate its activities if it wants to maximize its profits in the short-run.

Financial ratio analysis

We have considered the problems involved in the generation of financial information, including the wide areas in which discretion can be exercised and the difficulties posed by the existence of inflation. The broad areas of management accounting in which the information can be utilized by internal management has also been broached. We shall now examine briefly the interpretation and utilization of accounting information via the use of ratio analysis.

We will begin with the analysis of profitability. If a company is to grow and prosper it must make adequate profits to reward its shareholders and help finance future growth. If the company is not achieving a satisfactory return on the shareholders' equity base, then at worst they may become sufficiently dissatisfied to sell their shares and drive the share price down. If this happens on a large scale the company may be open to a take-over bid by a rival firm whose management are confident that they could make a higher return by managing the assets concerned themselves. At best a depressed share price may make the terms on which new capital can be raised from the market sufficiently unfavourable to deter expansion plans (see later in this chapter for a full discussion of the cost of capital).

The rate of return on the equity interest or shareholders' funds, expressed as a percentage, can be defined as:

$$\frac{\text{profit attributable to ordinary shareholders}}{\text{ordinary shareholders' interest}} \times 100.$$

The numerator in the ratio above will have had deducted tax, interest payments and any payments to preference shareholders and minority interests. The denominator is equal to ordinary share capital plus reserves. For simplicity we assume that there are no preference shareholders or minority interests. The rate of return achieved on the company's net operating assets will be a key determinant of the numerator, but this will be modified by the extent of the company's gearing (the proportion of its activities financed by borrowing) and the amount of tax paid as a proportion of pre-tax profits. The shareholders will also be interested in the various external financial ratios considered in chapter 10.

The management will acknowledge the importance of the above financial ratio, but they are more likely to be interested in the rate of return achieved on net operating assets since this gives a measure of how effectively a firm's overall resources are being employed. This ratio stands at the apex of a pyramid of ratios which reflect factors which govern the return on net operating assets and can be used as a basis for control and comparison within and across firms. Great care must be taken when using ratio analysis as a basis for inter-firm comparisons. Accounting ratios are subject to all the previously mentioned caveats concerning accounting processes, and different firms may use different conventions in drawing up their accounts. This problem is recognized by the Centre for Interfirm Comparison which tries to ensure that all firms subscribing to its service conform to a set of instructions concerning definition of terms, valuation principles etc. so that like is always compared with like.[9] The subscribers can then compare their general company performance with similar companies in the same industry and, if required, specific portions of their operations with that of rivals. It is very important that companies which are fairly homogeneous are compared, since the underlying logic behind ratio analysis is the assumption of constant proportionality. There are no underlying economic or logical grounds for assuming the prevalence of this relationship.[10] It may be particularly unrealistic if companies of vastly differing size and activities are compared. Given these reservations, ratio analysis can be a very useful means of analysing the components of a company's performance. Figure 9.3 shows the pyramid of ratios for a manufacturing concern.

If we start at the top of the pyramid, the following relationship emerges:

$$\frac{\text{net profit}}{\text{net operating assets}} = \frac{\text{net profit}}{\text{sales}} \times \frac{\text{sales}}{\text{net operating assets}}.$$

It follows that a relatively high or low rate of return on assets might be due either to a low profit margin, indicated by net profit/sales, or to a low rate of asset turnover, shown by sales/total assets. A low rate of asset turnover might be due either to excessive working capital or to poor use of fixed assets. These factors can be analysed by inspection of the third tier of ratios on the right-hand side of figure 9.3. On the other hand, low profit margins might be due to excessive production, selling or distribution costs, which can be examined via the second tier of ratios on the left-hand side of figure 9.3.

None of the ratios should be analysed in isolation, and there are obvious links between both sides of the pyramid. A company with relatively old, well-depreciated assets will probably have a low ratio of fixed assets/sales and a correspondingly high rate of asset turnover. But old plant will probably mean high production costs/sales and therefore net profit/sales will be correspondingly lower. A company in the same industry with new plant would probably show a lower rate of asset turnover but much higher profits/sales.

The study of a company's trend in ratios over time and appropriate inter-firm comparison should enable the management to pinpoint where things are going wrong, and they can then decide upon the appropriate remedial action. The relative performance between divisions of a firm can be analysed on similar lines so that the management can see where things need to be tightened up.

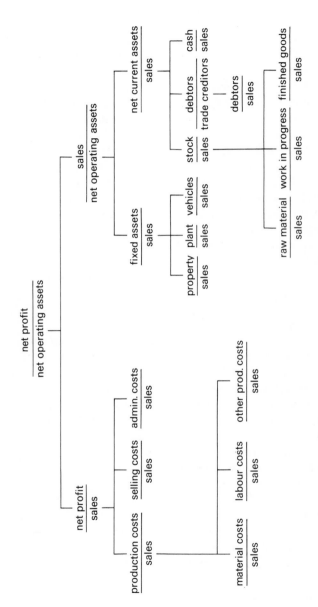

Figure 9.3 *Pyramid of ratios for a manufacturing concern*

The Tax System

In the course of this chapter we have already encountered numerous but scattered references to the tax system, and it seems sensible to draw these various threads together. A good starting-point is provided by the recommendations of the Meade Report, which in 1978 recommended a movement to an expenditure-based system of taxation.[11] A tax system could theoretically have an *income base* or an *expenditure base*. The main difference between the two is in the treatment of saving. As income can be used to finance consumption and saving, both are taxed in an income-based system. Under an expenditure-based system tax is only levied on expenditure on final consumption, and saving is therefore exempt. In an income-based system savings are made from taxed income, and are then invested to yield future income in the form of dividends, interest and capital gains, which are liable for more tax. The implication is that savings (or deferred consumption) are taxed twice under an income-based system and once under an expenditure-based system. One of the main aims of the Meade Committee's proposals was the removal of distortions and the encouragement of saving, for at the moment we do not have a purely income-based tax system but a muddled hybrid which contains elements of both income- and expenditure-based tax (as well as value-added tax (VAT), a direct tax on expenditure).

The current system of income tax in the UK involves a basic rate of 30 per cent, followed by graded increases in rate as taxable income is increased; the top threshold for taxable income is at present £27,750. The system for the tax year 1981–82 is shown in table 9.11; the rates and bands tend to be adjusted in every government budget.

Taxable income is equivalent to gross income minus the various allowances and expenses which can be set against income before tax; the single person's and married man's allowances stood at £1375 and £2145 respectively in the 1981–82 tax year.

Inflation poses an obvious problem. If nominal wages rise roughly in step

Table 9.11 *Personal income tax rates 1981–82*

Rate (%)	Band of taxable income (£)
30	1–11,250
40	11,251–13,250
45	13,251–16,750
50	16,751–22,250
55	22,251–27,750
60	over 27,750

with inflation, but the bands and allowances are not adjusted in line, then people who previously did not pay tax will begin to pay it, and previous tax-payers will gradually be pushed into higher bands. This phenomenon is termed *fiscal drag*.

Another serious anomaly arises from the lack of synchronization of the overlap between the tax system and the welfare benefit system. A wage earner in a low-income family with children may well find that there is little incentive to work overtime or achieve pay increases over a'broad range of income. This is because increases in income will lead to loss of income-related benefits, and a liability to tax, with the effect that net income will remain roughly constant.

Further anomalies arise from the hotchpotch of items which can be set off against pre-tax income. Relief is available on interest payments on loans to acquire property and on loans to invest in a partnership or co-operative, and, under the 'business start-up' scheme, on the cost of any 'outside' investor's equity investment in new trading companies, in qualifying trades, up to a maximum of £10,000 in ordinary shares in any one year. This form of saving is thus favourably treated in that it is only taxed once—when the gains from the investment are realized and available for consumption—and is thus equivalent to a tax system based upon expenditure. The same principle applies to the treatment of saving via an approved pension scheme; contributions are deductible from pre-tax income, but the pensions when paid are subject to tax.

Certain types of investment in government stocks receive favourable treatment. Income arising from savings certificates is not liable to tax; this is an incentive to hold the so-called 'granny bonds', which have been made available to all, and in the process ease the difficulties governments face in raising funds. Indeed, if income from investments in 'normal' securities exceeds £5500 in any one year, the excess is liable to an investment income surcharge of 15 per cent on top of the recipient's income tax rate.

Similarly most capital gains are liable to capital gains tax of 30 per cent, but if an investor holds a government gilt-edged stock for more than a year, and the change in interest rates is such that a capital gain is produced, he will not be liable for capital gains tax.

Thus it is argued that there are serious distortions in the capital markets which result from the favoured treatment of investment in government stocks and housing, and which therefore inhibit the free flow of capital. The system of company taxation is in even greater confusion.

The corporate tax system

In recent years there have been two major changes in the system of taxation of corporate profits; the introduction of corporation tax in 1965 and the movement to the imputation corporation tax system in 1973. The 'classical system' of corporation tax introduced in 1965 embodies the principle that the tax liability of the company should be completely independent of that of its shareholders. The company has to pay a flat rate of corporation tax on its taxable profits, and the shareholders must pay income tax on their dividends and capital gains tax on any gains made when they sell their shares. If the company chooses to pay dividends from its post-tax profits then those dividends are taxed at the marginal income tax rate of the recipient; any distributions to shareholders are therefore taxed twice. The system discriminates against dividend payments and favours debt funding, since interest payments are a charge against profits when assessing liability to corporation tax.

The discrimination against dividend payments was removed by the *imputation tax system*. This involves crediting the shareholders for corporation tax paid by the company; if they receive dividend payments, a tax credit equal to the standard rate of income tax due on the dividend is imputed to them and offset against the company's mainstream corporation tax. This means that the shareholders are not liable for income tax at the standard rate on their dividends, although higher-rate taxpayers must pay the appropriate marginal adjustments. From the company's point of view the only difference comes from the timing of some of its tax payments. To the extent that it has to pay advance corporation tax (ACT) at a rate equal to the standard rate of income tax on the gross dividend at the time it makes payments, it is marginally disadvantaged in that the timing of some of its tax payments has been brought forward. Its overall liability to tax remains the same in that any ACT payments are a credit against its mainstream corporation tax payments when they become due. The essentials of the two systems are shown in table 9.12.

It can be seen from table 9.12 that the result of the change to the imputation

Table 9.12 *The classical and imputation corporation tax systems*

	Classical (£)		Imputation (£)
Pre-tax profit	12,000		12,000
Interest payments	(2,000)		(2,000)
Taxable profits	10,000		10,000
Corporation tax (52%)	(5,200)		(5,200)
Available for distribution or retention	4,800		4,800
Ordinary dividend (gross)	2,100		3,000
Income tax (30%)	(630)	ACT[a] (30%)	(900)
Ordinary dividend (net)	1,470		2,100
Retentions	2,700		2,700
Tax due at year end	(5,200)		(4,300)

[a]ACT: advance corporation tax

system is that the shareholders have gained at the expense of the Inland Revenue.

Stock appreciation relief

This was first introduced in 1974 and has since undergone various modifications, though its calculation still seems a bit arbitrary. Under the latest system relief is given on the opening value of stocks and work in progress minus £2000; the net figure is then multiplied by the increase in the index of prices of all stocks to give the relief against taxable profits, as shown in the following example:

Movements in stocks index: December 1980, 180; December 1981, 189.

$$\text{increase} = \frac{189 - 180}{180} = 5\%.$$

	£
Stocks at 1 January 1981	500,000
Stocks at 1 December 1981	800,000
Taxable trading income	1,000,000

Stock appreciation relief = (opening stock − £2000) × increase in index
= £(500,000 − 2000)0.05
= £2400.

Taxable trading income becomes:

	£
Original figure	1,000,000
Less stock appreciation	2,400
Taxable trading income	997,600

It has been estimated that in 1978−79 companies' corporation tax payments were reduced by around £1.4 billion as a result of stock appreciation relief.[12]

Capital allowances

Allowances are given on a national basis without any regional discrimination. Since March 1972 up to 100 per cent of any expenditure on industrial plant and machinery can be set off against tax on profits in the year in which it is incurred, and if there are not sufficient taxable profits available it can be carried forward indefinitely. Alternatively the company can claim only part of its allowances in the first year and carry the balance forward, writing it off at 25 per cent on the reducing balance basis. It was estimated that in 1978−79 the first-year investment allowances due on investment in accounts totalled nearly £10 billion.[13]

Similarly, there are allowances on industrial building at an initial rate of

50 per cent of the cost and a subsequent writing-down allowance of 4 per cent per annum, which becomes operative once the building is in use. Estimations for the period 1978–79 suggest that roughly £700 million of allowances were due on industrial buildings.[14]

The resultant confusion and the need for reform

The result of all these measures has been that many companies are in a situation of *tax exhaustion*. They simply do not have sufficient taxable profits to enable them to utilize the various allowances. This is one of the major stimuli to the growth in leasing considered in chapter 10. In theory there is a high nominal rate of corporation tax of 52 per cent, yet in practice companies pay nowhere near this rate and have so much discretion in the timing of their use of allowances that the rate they actually pay is almost voluntarily determined by the companies themselves.

A further wide range of direct taxes have to be considered: social security contributions by individuals and employers; customs and excise duties; value-added tax; capital transfer tax; stamp duty; etc. The effect of all these measures is that in the United Kingdom roughly 40 per cent of taxation is based on expenditure rather than on income (see table 9.13).

Table 9.13 *Taxation as a proportion of GNP, and the proportion of taxation based on expenditure (1978)*

	Taxation and social security contributions as a percentage of GNP at factor cost	Percentage of total taxation (including social security contributions) derived from taxes on expenditure
Sweden	60	28
Norway	56	36
Netherlands	52	27
Belgium	47	28
German Federal Republic	45	32
France	44	36
United Kingdom	39	40
Italy	36	32
Canada	35	40
United States	33	27
Switzerland	32	23
Japan	25	29

Source: Central Statistical Office, *Economic Trends* (December 1980)

Obviously there is a need for reform, perhaps along the lines suggested by the Meade Committee.[15] If savings were exempt from taxation, most of the previously mentioned distortions would be removed. There are various ways in which an expenditure-based system could be applied—none would be more complicated than the existing system—and it could be planned so that it would be equally progressive.

Financial Management Decisions

Financial management policy and decisions are concerned with seeking answers to the following questions:

1 What projects or investments should the firm undertake?
2 How much should the firm invest?
3 By what methods of funding should the firm finance its investments?
4 How much of the firm's revenue should it distribute and in what form? Alternatively, what should be the firm's policy on retentions?

In seeking an answer to these questions, the management must have a clearly defined set of objectives in mind. Despite the existence of a number of possible objectives of varying plausibility, the custom in the literature has been to assume that the management take decisions on behalf of the owners (the shareholders in the case of a limited company) with the welfare of the owners in mind. It is assumed that maximizing the value of their interest will serve them best. This is not the same as maximizing profitability, though it is closely related to it since profitability is a one-dimensional measure (see chapter 2). It is assumed that investors in capital markets are concerned with three dimensions; returns or profitability, timing and risk. All these factors must be considered.

Time and discounting

Suppose that you have £100 cash. You have the choice of either spending it now or investing it in a risk-free bank account at an interest rate of 10 per cent per annum. If you leave it there for a year you will have the original amount of £100 plus the interest. The interest is £100 × 10 per cent = £10; this could be written as $£100(1 + r)$ where r is equal to 0.10 or 10 per cent in this case. The choice is depicted in figure 9.4.

£100 invested at 10 per cent for a year will be worth £110 in one year's time, as shown above. The line linking the two amounts is a present value line with a slope equal to the rate of interest. The slope is negative; its magnitude can be seen to be 1.1 since the length of the vertical side of the triangle in the diagram over that of the horizontal is 110/100 = 1.1.

The terminal value of $£X$ invested for a year at a rate of interest r is determined by $£X(1 + r)$. Similarly the present value of £110 in a year's time,

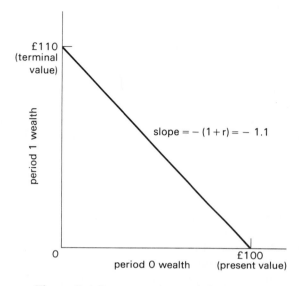

Figure 9.4 *Present value and discounting*

given an interest rate of 10 per cent, is £100. This can be calculated generally as $£X/(1+r)$. Thus as long as the rate of interest is positive we have to adjust amounts received in different periods by an appropriate discount factor to make them equivalent. Even in the complete absence of risk, the discount rate would be positive since people in general prefer to consume now rather than later. If they are to forgo present consumption and channel the value of it into investment, they must be rewarded for so doing.

If the investment in the above example had been at a rate of 10 per cent for three years it would have grown as follows:

present value   = £100
value at end of year 1   = $£100(1+r)$ = £110
value at end of year 2   = $£100(1+r)^2$ = £121
value at end of year 3   = $£100(1+r)^3$ = £133.

In general a sum $£X$ invested at a rate r for N years will grow in the following fashion:

$$\text{terminal value of } £X = £X(1+r)^N. \tag{9.2}$$

On the other hand, the present value of a sum $£X$ received N years in the future is given by:

$$\text{present value} = \frac{£X}{(1+r)^N}. \tag{9.3}$$

The present value of a series of different sums $X_1, X_2, \ldots, X_n$ received annually for N years at the end of each year is given by:

$$\text{present value} \quad = \frac{X_1}{(1+r)} + \frac{X_2}{(1+r)^2} + \frac{X_3}{(1+r)^3} + \dots + \frac{X_N}{(1+r)^N}$$

$$\text{present value} \quad = \sum_{i=1}^{N} \frac{X_i}{(1+r)^i}. \tag{9.4}$$

The principle of discounting is of vital importance in any investment decision involving multiperiod returns; different amounts at different times have to be transformed on to a common base before they can be evaluated. This is the rationale behind the use of discounting techniques for determining investment decisions.

Risk

Financial management decisions have to be made on the basis of imperfect information, and their consequences can never be predicted with complete certainty since the future cannot be known. One way of trying to assess uncertainty is to make a *subjective probability estimation* of the possible outcomes. This involves using a 0 to 1 scale to assign probabilities to future events. A zero probability would mean that the event is ruled out of consideration, and a probability of 1 would indicate that it will happen with certainty. Probabilities in between measure degrees of uncertainty. Suppose that you are intending to sell an asset in the near future and that you are not sure about the price you will receive. You estimate that the outcomes in table 9.14 are possible.

If it is assumed that the resultant probability distribution is normal, then it can be completely described by its mean $(\bar{b})$ and its standard deviation σ_b. The mean of a probability distribution is calculated by weighting all the possible outcomes by their probabilities and summing the resultant products, as shown in column 3 of table 9.14. The standard deviation, which can be used as a proxy measure of risk, is calculated by taking the deviation of each possible outcome from the mean, squaring it, weighting the product by the probability of the outcome concerned, summing all such products, and then taking the square root of the resultant sum. The calculation of the standard deviation σ_b is shown in the last three columns of table 9.14.

The mean of the distribution is used as a measure of expected value and the standard deviation as a measure of risk. If two investments have the same mean but different standard deviations, then it is assumed that investors would prefer the one with the smaller standard deviation or lesser risk. This choice is shown in figure 9.5.

The assumption is that investment A would be preferred to investment B. Both have the same expected value but there is a much higher probability of extreme deviations from the mean in the case of investment B. The level of return could be either much lower or much higher than that of A. It is assumed that typical investors are risk-averse when risking significant amounts of

Table 9.14 *Subjective probability estimations of the sale value of an asset,
and the calculation of the mean and the standard deviation*

Subjective probability	Sale price (£)				
a	b	ab	$b - \bar{b}$	$(b - \bar{b})^2$	$a(b - \bar{b})^2$
0.1	70	7	-20	400	40
0.2	80	16	-10	100	20
0.4	90	36	0	0	0
0.2	100	20	10	100	20
0.1	110	11	20	400	40
$\Sigma a = 1.0$		$\bar{b} = \Sigma ab = 90$			$\Sigma a(b - \bar{b})^2 = 120$
					$\sigma^2 b \qquad = 120$
					$\sigma b \qquad = 10.95$

money. They prefer to avoid risk and will only bear it if they are compensated
for doing so. They will put much greater weight on possible deviations below
the mean of *B* than those above it, and will therefore prefer *A* to it.

This means that investments of high risk will have to offer relatively high
returns or they will not be undertaken, and that high profits at high levels of
risk will not necessarily be preferred to lower profits at lower levels of risk.
The key factor will be whether the riskier profits are sufficiently larger to
compensate for their risk. This is the idea behind *certainty equivalents*; these

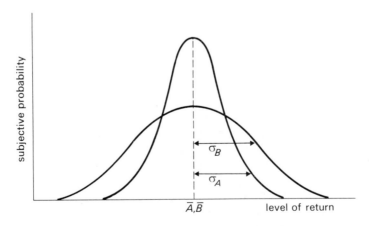

Figure 9.5 *Two investments with the same expected value but
different risk*

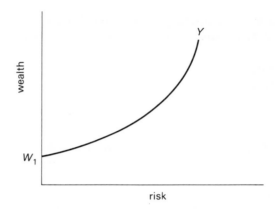

Figure 9.6 *Certainty equivalents*

equate higher levels of risky wealth with lower levels of certain wealth, and are shown in figure 9.6.

To an individual investor all points along the line W_1Y in figure 9.6 might be regarded as being equivalent. A high but risky level of potential wealth at point Y is regarded as being equivalent to an absolutely certain but much lower level of wealth at W_1.

The Investment Decision

Investment decisions are obviously of crucial importance to individual companies and to the economy as a whole, playing a key role in determining future growth and productivity. It is vitally important that they are made on a 'correct' basis. There are a number of traditional investment appraisal methods. One of the most popular is the *payback method*; this provides a means of ranking alternative investment projects by the time it takes them to repay their capital cost.

A simple illustration of the method is given in table 9.15. Two projects involve an initial outlay of £200; their year-end receipts are as shown above. Project A recoups its capital cost in three years and has a three-year payback period; project B has a four-year payback period. Project A would be preferred to project B, despite the fact that B nets an undiscounted surplus over costs of £220 [(7 × £60) − £200] whereas A nets only £40. This follows from the fact that only the payback period is considered and not the project's entire working life. The cash flows are undiscounted, so that like is not being compared with like. If the method was used on a universal basis it would lead to serious under-investment since many perfectly good projects would be rejected on the basis of an arbitrarily determined payback period.

Another very popular traditional method is the *return on capital method*,

Table 9.15 *The payback method of investment appraisal*

Period (years)	0	1	2	3	4	5	6	7
Project *A*	− £200	£70	£70	£60	£40	£0	£0	£0
Project *B*	− £200	£60	£60	£60	£60	£60	£60	£60

Table 9.16 *The average rate of return method of investment appraisal*[a]

Period (years)	0	1	2	3	4	5	6	average profit (after tax and depreciation)	Capital outlay	average rate of return
Project *A*	− £100	£50	£40	£30	£30	£20	£10	£30	£100	30%
Project *B*	− £100	£10	£20	£30	£40	£55	—	£31	£100	31%

[a]Assume a straight line method of depreciation is used (i.e. project *A* had £16.66 deducted from profits each year to recoup the capital outlay, while *B* had £20 deducted annually)

of which there are a number of variations. It could be defined as;

$$\text{average rate of return} = \frac{\text{average profit after tax and depreciation}}{\text{capital outlay}}$$

This method is popular because the data required are often available in similar form in accounting statements, but it has many defects. It once again ignores the time value of money. It cannot distinguish between projects with different lengths of life. It is also biased by the method of depreciation used.

Some of these problems are illustrated by the example of table 9.16. Two projects require an initial outlay of £100, but project *A* yields returns for six years as opposed to *B*'s five-year life. The method suggests that *B* is to be preferred since its rate of return is slightly higher. However, *A* yields much higher returns in early years; these are particularly valuable since they can be reinvested elsewhere at a positive rate of interest. *A* also offers six years of returns, with an average of £30, rather than five. The method is clearly misleading, and it is because of distortions mentioned above that *discounted cash flow methods* are to be preferred.

The net present value method

The net present value (*NPV*) method of investment appraisal involves discounting all the after-tax cash flows from a project at the company's marginal cost of capital. This rate, sometimes termed the required rate of return, is the cost to the company of raising the required funds to finance the project (see later in this chapter). No account is taken of depreciation provisions since the cost of the investment is automatically accounted for in the calculations.

The calculation is as follows:

$$NPV = NCF_0 + \frac{NCF_1}{(1+r)} + \frac{NCF_2}{(1+r)^2} + \ldots + \frac{NCF_N}{(1+r)^N}$$

$$= \sum_{i=0}^{N} \frac{NCF_i}{(1+r)^i} \tag{9.5}$$

where NCF_i is the net cash flow after tax in period i (in period 0 it will usually have a negative value equal to the cost of the investment, after adjustment for capital allowances), and r is the required rate of return (the firm's marginal cost of capital or MCC).

An example of the use of the NPV method is shown in table 9.17.

Table 9.17 *The use of the net present value method*

Period (years)	0	1	2	3	4
Net cash flows	− £100	£70	£80	£60	£50
Discount factors $r = 10\%$	1	1.1	1.21	1.331	1.4641
Net discounted cash flows	− £100	£63.64	£66.12	£45.08	£34.15

$$NPV = \Sigma \text{ net discounted cash flows } = \pounds 109$$

The decision rule is simple. If the NPV of the sum of the discounted after-tax cash flows is positive, then the project is valuable and should be accepted. To do so will add to the firm's value. This is because it offers a rate of return higher than that required by the providers of the firm's capital—the test discount rate or marginal cost of capital.

The internal rate of return method

An alternative investment appraisal technique based on the use of discounting is the internal rate of return (IRR) method. The condition for calculating IRR is:

$$NCF_0 + \frac{NCF_1}{(1+r^*)} + \frac{NCF_2}{(1+r^*)^2} + \ldots + \frac{NCF_N}{(1+r^*)^N} = 0$$

$$\sum_{i=0}^{N} \frac{NCF_i}{(1+r^*)^i} = 0 \tag{9.6}$$

where NCF_i is the net cash flow in period i, and r^* is the solution discount rate or IRR that satisfies condition 9.6.

The IRR method involves adjusting the discount rate r^* until the net present

Table 9.18 *The use of the internal rate of return method*

Period (years)	0	1	2	3	4
Net cash flows	− £100	£70	£80	£60	£50
Discount factors					
$r = 61\%$	1	1.61	2.89	4.17	6.72
Net discounted					
cash flows	− £100	£43.48	£30.88	£14.39	£11.9

Σ net discounted cash flows ≈ 0

value of the sum of all the inflows and outflows of cash associated with the project is equal to zero. This solution discount rate is the project's internal rate of return, which can be compared with the firm's marginal cost of capital. If the *IRR* is greater than the marginal cost of capital (*IRR* > *MCC*) then the project is profitable and should be undertaken. The calculation of the *IRR* for the same project as in table 9.17 is given in table 9.18. It can be seen that the project in the example above has an *IRR* of approximately 61 per cent.

The equivalence of the two methods for the example chosen is shown in figure 9.7. The two methods give the same answers in a straightforward accept/reject investment decision. If the firm's *MCC* is 10 per cent the project has a positive *NPV* and should be accepted. Its *IRR* is much greater than 10 per cent and the project should be accepted according to that decision criterion

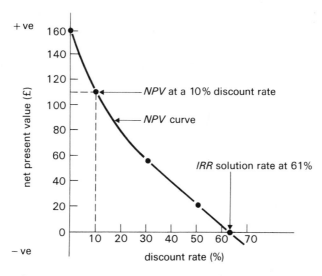

Figure 9.7 *The NPV and IRR methods compared*

too. In the use of both *NPV* and *IRR* the project becomes marginal with an *MCC* of 61 per cent. Although both methods are preferable to non-discounting techniques, there are some problems in their application.

Difficulties involved in the application of NPV and IRR

The *IRR* method is probably more problematic. Some projects may involve negative cash outflows in more than one period over the project's life. If this is the case multiple solution discount rates may emerge and it can be difficult to interpret them. There are adjustments which get round the problem but they are rather *ad hoc*. More seriously, as the *IRR* is a rate of return it cannot distinguish between the relative size and length of life of two different projects (admittedly this criticism applies to some extent to *NPV* as well). One way round this problem is to use the *NPV* approach to construct a *profitability index*:

$$\text{profitability index} = \frac{\text{present value of inflows}}{\text{present value of outflows}}.$$

This will give the management an idea of the relative desirability of projects. However, if there exist limited financial resources or some sort of constraint on funds which necessitates choosing some profitable projects at the expense of others, neither *NPV* nor *IRR* can cope, and resort has to be made to mathematical programming techniques.

Risk and inflation

Both methods can be adapted quite readily to cope with both risk and inflation. The certainty equivalent method considered earlier suggests that there are two ways in which future cash flows can be adjusted to allow for risk; either the numerator or the denominator in the discount rate can be altered. The adjustment to the numerator is given by αNCF_i, where α is a positive constant and $0 < \alpha < 1$. Future risky cash flow estimates will be revised downwards to reflect risk. (If this is done the discount rate used must be the riskless rate of interest reflecting the time value of money alone, since risk has been accounted for in the numerator.) Alternatively the discount rate can be inflation above the pure interest rate to allow for risk. This is probably the more useful approach since the firm's marginal cost of capital (considered later in this chapter) usually reflects the capital market's perception of the riskiness of the company's operations. Indeed, the firm's marginal cost of capital could be viewed as being made up of the following components;

discount rate = pure interest rate + risk premium + inflation premium.

A market-determined cost of capital automatically takes into account both risk and likely inflation. This leads to another potential source of bias. If the *MCC* has an inflation adjustment built in, care must be taken that estimates of a project's future cash flows are not in terms of today's prices but are adjusted upwards for likely inflation; otherwise a project's profitability will be biased downwards.

Portfolio considerations

The risk premium required by a shareholder will reflect his estimation of the firm's operating risk—the risk associated with its day-to-day operations, plus, where appropriate, an additional component for the company's financial risk if it has a lot of borrowings (see the next section for a full treatment of gearing). The shareholder's perception of relevant risk will change if he holds a collection or portfolio of investments in the shares of a number of different companies. In this context an individual share will be important in terms of the marginal contribution it makes, in the form of additional risk and expected return, to his overall portfolio. Following the original contribution by Markowitz, portfolio theory has been extended to the point where it underlies most of the theoretical work on financial markets and provides a means of pricing risky assets.[16] Although the theory involves a considerable amount of mathematics its gist can be conveyed on a common-sense basis.

When an investor purchases a share he cannot be sure of the return he will obtain; dividends are paid out of after-tax profits, and whether or not a company pays a dividend, and how large it is, are at the discretion of the board of directors. The investor could summarize his expectations by drawing up a subjective probability distribution along the lines considered earlier. The mean of the distribution will indicate the return he expects over his investment holding period (made up of dividends and capital gains or losses via changes in the share price). The standard deviation will indicate the risk or uncertainty he attaches to his estimates (assuming the distribution is symmetric and normal).

So far we have not considered the benefits of *diversification*. Investors typically spread their risks by investing in a number of different securities rather than by putting all their money into one. The benefits of diversification can be measured by the extent to which the returns on two securities (i.e. shares) vary together (as measured by their covariance). Let us suppose that one company (A) produces ice-cream and the other (B) umbrellas, and therefore bad weather for one means good business for the other. The hypothetical returns on their shares are shown in figure 9.8.

If the investor put all his funds in either company A or company B his return would vary between X and Z, although over time it would average out at Y. By investing in both companies he is guaranteed a return of Y at all times; diversification has significantly reduced his exposure to risk. Practical illustration of diversification is given by the investment holdings of the financial institutions shown in tables 10.15–10.18. Investments are spread over a number of different types of security and in home and overseas markets.

The *capital asset pricing* model uses this principle to price risky assets. If it

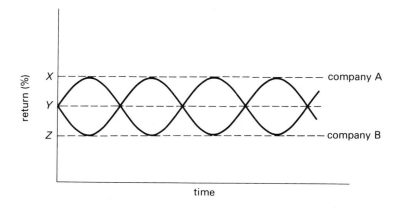

Figure 9.8 *The benefits of diversification*

is assumed that all investors hold an effectively diversified 'market' portfolio, then part of a security's risk—the 'unsystematic' component—will have been diversified away. Only the undiversifiable 'systematic' risk will remain, as measured by the covariance between the returns on the security and those on the market portfolio, which by definition cannot be diversified away. Thus securities will be priced, in equilibrium, according to their non-diversifiable systematic risk (normally termed their *beta* (β) *coefficient*). A risk-free security earns a return equal to the risk-free rate, and a risky security earns an additional premium in proportion to its beta coefficient. This may sound rather frightening, but the reader can comprehend what is meant by examining figure 9.9. This shows a simple linear relationship (equation 9.7), which may be expressed (as for equation 7.1) in an ordinary least-squares (OLS) equation (equation 9.8).

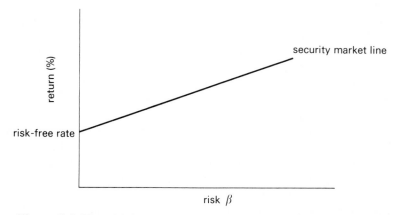

Figure 9.9 *The risk/return relationship according to the capital asset pricing model*

The basic linear relationship is:

$$Er_j = RF + \beta_j(ER_M - RF) \qquad (9.7)$$

where Er_j is the expected return on security j, RF is the risk-free rate, β_j is the covariability of returns on security j and those of the market portfolio divided by the variance of the market portfolio, and ER_M is the expected return on the market portfolio.

The basic assumptions behind the formal mathematics which lead to the derivation of the above relationship are unrealistic. They run as follows. All investors invest for the same period and have the same expectations about the future returns and the risk of the securities in the market. There are no tax effects. There is only one risk-free borrowing rate. All investors are rational and averse to risk (they dislike risk and will only bear it if compensated by higher returns). All investors hold the fully diversified market portfolio. There is no inflation. Despite its unrealistic assumptions, this model has yielded valuable insights into the market pricing process, and it has some novel implications for capital budgeting. For a start, if a company's shareholders hold its shares as part of a diversified portfolio then, from their point of view, there is no point in the company choosing projects which have offsetting risks or merging with other firms to reduce risk. These risk reduction effects have already been achieved in the portfolios of the shareholders at much lower cost. If the assumptions of the capital asset pricing model are not too gross a violation of reality, an approximate estimation of a company's cost of capital can be obtained by running the following regression:

$$r_j = \alpha_j + B_j RI + e_j \qquad (9.8)$$

r_j is the return on company j's shares, defined as $(p_t + d_t - p_{t-1})/p_{t-1}$, where p_t and p_{t-1} are the share prices in periods t and $t-1$, and d_t is the dividend received during period t. α_j and B_j are constants estimated by running an ordinary least-squares regression, RI is the return on a stock market index $[(RI_t - RI_{t-1})/RI_{t-1}]$ used as a proxy for the return on the market portfolio, and e_j is a random error term.

The regression line can be fitted by using the required data over some historical period, and if the project is not going to be financed by a new 'mix' of debt and equity, and does not involve risks different from those of the company's existing operations, then it should provide an estimate of the firm's MCC. In practice it is very difficult to estimate a company's cost of capital, since the above approach requires a number of strong assumptions and financial mix is very important. The difficulties are considered in the next section.

Capital budgeting in practice

During the past couple of decades increasing use has been made of discounting techniques, though traditional non-discounting methods remain popular.

Table 9.19 *Capital budgeting techniques employed by major European companies*[a]

	Substantial usage (%)	Some usage (%)	Total (%)
Payback period	61	33	94
Internal rate of return	70	13	83
Net present value	41	22	63
Accounting rate of return	20	19	39
Profitability index	15	9	24

[a]57 companies in sample from *Financial Times* largest 200 West European companies ranked by sales
Source: J.C. Baker, 'Capital budgeting in West European companies', *Management Decision* 19 (1981)

Table 9.19 shows the results of a survey of the investment appraisal techniques of 57 of the largest European corporations. Many combine the use of a number of different methods.

Capital Structure and Cost of Capital

A company's financial structure is determined by the way in which it is financed; traditionally this is shown on the left-hand side of its balance sheet. On the other hand, a company's capital structure could be defined as the structure of the permanent financing of the company—in other words, the relative proportions of debt, preference and equity share capital plus reserves. There are various ways in which this relatively simple concept can be defined and measured. Valuations could be on the basis of nominal or market values. The treatment of preference capital is a moot point; should it be placed with debt as a fixed payment commitment, or with equity on the grounds that payment can be waived? Yet another approach would be to measure the proportion of profits accounted for by fixed interest commitments, though this would be a move towards measuring financial structure since short-term liabilities would be included. We shall simply define capital gearing as the ratio of the market value of a company's long-term debt and the market value of its equity capital plus reserves:

$$\text{capital gearing} = \frac{\text{market value of loan capital}}{\text{market value of equity capital plus reserves}}$$

Financial risk

It is obvious that an increase in gearing involves an increase in financial risk, particularly from the shareholder's point of view. Debenture interest payments are prior charges against profits which have to be paid if the company is to avoid being forced into liquidation; therefore the greater the size of these prior commitments, the greater the probability that, in a bad year, profits will not be sufficient to cover them. The moral is that companies with very stable profits and valuable assets against which debenture issues can be secured (hotel and brewery chains are usually highly geared) can risk gearing up. Speculative companies with wildly fluctuating profits should stick to equity finance.

On the other hand there are positive benefits associated with gearing up. In the absence of inflation, debenture finance is usually cheaper than equity finance in that the yield demanded by investors is not as high (for further consideration of yields see chapter 10). If the interest payment demanded by a debenture holder is not as high as the dividend per share expected by a shareholder, then financing a portion of a company's asset by relatively cheaper debentures will benefit the shareholders of a company; this is further emphasized by the tax deductibility of interest payments. Table 9.20 shows this effect.

Gearing up can benefit the shareholder; in year 1, the shareholder in Hi-gear Corporation receives 7.6 per cent compared to a yield of only 4.8 per

Table 9.20 *The return to the equity interest and gearing effects*

Equity Corporation			Hi-gear Corporation		
Capital structure:					
1000 £1 ordinary			500 £1 ordinary		
shares	1000		shares	500	
			500 4% debentures	500	
Capital employed	1000			1000	
	Year 1	Year 2		Year 1	Year 2
Gross profits	100	50		100	50
Interest payments	0	0		20	20
	100	50		80	30
Corporation tax					
(52%)	52	26		42	16
Net dividend	48	24		38	14
Net dividend yield	4.8%	2.4%		7.6%	2.8%

cent in Equity Corporation, yet both companies are the same size and making the same return on capital employed. The danger is shown in year 2 when there is a 50 per cent reduction in return on capital employed. This halves the yield to the shareholders in Equity Corporation but reduces that to shareholders in Hi-gear Corporation by 67 per cent. The financial risk involved in high gearing involves increased variability of returns to the shareholders. The crucial question is whether judicial use of gearing can benefit a company's shareholders and lower its cost of capital.

The level of gearing varies both within and across industries in the UK, and on an even greater scale internationally. In part, international variations are a reflection of the lack of developed equity markets on the scale of those of the UK and USA, plus other social, institutional and historical factors. The wide variations are indicated in table 9.21.

Table 9.21 *An international comparison of capital gearing*[a] *(percentages)*

	1970	1972	1974	1977
UK	56	55	59	49
USA	57	60	57	55
Japan	299	325	339	352
Germany	—	97	95	—
France	111	126	140	156
Italy	208	293	265	363
Sweden	141	176	173	—

[a]Capital gearing is defined here as the ratio of long- and short-term debt to shareholder's interest

Source: *Report of the Committee to Review the Functioning of the Financial Institutions* (Wilson Committee), Cmnd 7937, HMSO, 1980

Gearing and the cost of capital

It was demonstrated previously that the economic value of a project is made up of the sum of the discounted values of the future net benefits that accrue to the owners. The value of a financial asset such as a share or a debenture is determined similarly. The value of a share is made up of the sum of all discounted values of the future dividend payments which are likely to accrue to the owner. To keep things simple assume that these are constant and known with certainty:

$$\text{share price} = \frac{D}{(1+r)} + \frac{D}{(1+r)^2} + \ldots + \frac{D}{(1+r)^N} \qquad (9.9)$$

where D is the constant dividend payment and r is the appropriate discount factor, in this case the risk-free rate. If this is assumed to be a perpetual stream of payments the sum above simplifies as follows. First multiply the share value by $(1 + r)$:

$$\text{share price} \times (1 + r) = D + \frac{D}{(1 + r)} + \frac{D}{(1 + r)^2} + \ldots + \frac{D}{(1 + r)^{N-1}}. \quad (9.10)$$

If we subtract equation 9.9 from equation 9.10 we have:

$$\text{share price} \times (1 + r) - \text{share price} = D - \frac{D}{(1 + r)^N}$$

$$\text{share price} \times r = D - \frac{D}{(1 + r)^N}.$$

If we then assume that D is a perpetual stream of payments which goes on to infinity the second term will disappear; the result as

$$\text{share price} = \frac{D}{r}. \quad (9.11)$$

This is an important result, but the assumptions of a constant level of risk and a constant dividend payment must be borne in mind. This result can be applied to the valuation of any stream of perpetual payments. Perusal of equation 9.11 will give rise to the following observations. If the company is investing in positive projects which are going to increase the size of future profits and the future size of D, the share value should increase. On the other hand, any increase in the company's risk will increase the discount rate r and therefore reduce the share price. Increases in risk could come either from branching out into risky operations with increased operating risk, or from increased financial risk from higher gearing.

We wish to examine the effects of gearing, and so we are concerned purely with the effects of financial risk. Therefore operating risk, investment policy, and the possibility of increased future earnings are effects which have to be neutralized by assuming them constant.

As an example, take two companies, A and B. Suppose that company A is financed by equity S and debt B. Let Y stand for the income accruing to the shareholders and let I be the interest payments to the debtholders. Assume that two companies of the same size and operating risk make the same rate of return on their assets, which we shall term net operating income; for simplicity assume that this is expected to be constant in perpetuity. Company B is financed entirely by equity. In the example shown in table 9.22 we ignore the influence of taxation.

The example in table 9.22 shows the effects of one extreme of gearing on cost of capital and company value, termed the *net income approach*. This suggests that the use of gearing can increase a company's value as shown in the example. The crucial assumption is that the equity capitalization rate does not increase despite the fact that company A has geared up; in the

Table 9.22 *Gearing and the cost of capital*

	Company A (geared)		Company B (no gearing)	
Net operating income	Y	£1000	Y	£1000
Interest payments on debt I (pure rate of interest r × face value of the debt B)	rB	5% of £4000 = £200	0	
Value of debt is perpetual stream of payments to debt holders capitalized at the pure interest rate r	$\dfrac{rB}{r}$ $= B$	$\dfrac{£200}{0.05}$ £4000	0	
Net income	$Y - rB$	£1000 − £200	Y	£1000
Value of equity S is the perpetual stream of payments to the equity holders capitalized at the equity capitalization rate k_e	$\dfrac{Y - rB}{k_e}$	$\dfrac{£800}{0.10}$	$\dfrac{Y}{k_e}$	$\dfrac{£1000}{0.10}$
Value of company	$S_A + B$	£8000 + £4000 = £12,000	S_B	£10,000

example it remains at 10 per cent. True, the net income payable to the share-holders in A has been reduced by the interest payments on debt; $Y - rB$ is payed to shareholders, but the interest payments to the debtholders have also to be taken into account in that they are capitalized at the pure interest rate r (5%). The value of the geared company is made up of the values of its debt and its equity. But the value of the geared company must be greater if the equity capitalization rate k_e is the same for both, since company A differs from company B by a factor equal to $[(-rB/k_e) + (rB/r)]$; since $k_e > r$ this must always be positive.

It could be argued that this approach is unrealistic in that gearing up involves increased financial risk to both debt and equity holders. A large

amount of fixed prior claims against operating earnings increases the probability, in a bad year, of there being insufficient earnings to pay any dividends
to the shareholders or, at worst, of bankruptcy. This problem was assumed
away in our simplified example, but in practice it suggests that k_e should rise
with increases in gearing. The *net operating income approach* to the valuation
of geared companies suggests that k_e will rise just sufficiently with increases
in gearing to offset any gain from cheaper debt financing, so that the net
effect is to leave the value of a geared company unchanged. It can be shown
that this will be the case if the equity capitalization rate of the geared company
is as follows:

$$k_g = k_e + (k_e - r)\frac{B}{S} \tag{9.12}$$

where k_e is the equity capitalization rate of a company with the same operating
risk but no gearing, k_g is the equity capitalization rate of the geared company,
B is the market value of the debt issued and S is the market value of the equity
assuming that gearing has no effect on valuation.

If we apply the figures from the example in table 9.22 to expression 9.12 (S
is £6000, the sum needing to be added to the debt value of company A, £4000,
to bring the total to the value of company B where no gearing has taken
place, £10,000) we have:

$$k_g = 0.10 + (0.10 - 0.05)\frac{£4000}{£6000}$$

$$= 0.133.$$

If the £800 of annual income accruing to shareholders in A were capitalized
at this rate the equity in A would be worth £6000 and the combined value of
the debt and equity would be equal to £10,000, the same value as company B.

We could define the company's average cost of capital as the rate at which
net operating income is capitalized, indicated by the ratio of net operating
income to market valuation. In the above example, we would have:

$$k_o = \frac{Y}{B + S} = \frac{£1000}{£10,000} = 10 \text{ per cent.}$$

In the case of a company using a number of different sources of funds the
rate could be viewed as a weighted average of the costs of the sources of
funds employed.

$$k_o = W_1 k_e = W_2 k_d \tag{9.13}$$

where W_1 is the proportion of equity in the capital structure [$S/(B + S)$],
W_2 is the proportion of debt in the capital structure [$B/(S + B)$], k_e is the
cost of equity and k_d is the cost of debt.

It is obvious that the net income and the net operating income approaches

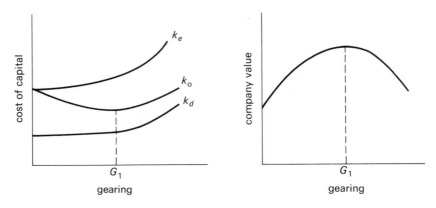

Figure 9.10 *Gearing and cost of capital: the traditional view*

to company valuation are extreme views. It is true that Modigliani and Miller have provided theoretical justification for the net operating income approach, but their proof requires perfect market assumptions which do not hold in practice.[17] The 'traditional view' of the effect of gearing upon capital cost is something of a compromise.

The traditional view of the effect of gearing on cost of capital

The 'traditionalists' suggest that judicious use of gearing can lower a company's cost of capital. At relatively low levels of gearing the financing of a portion of the company's assets with relatively cheap debt (assuming no inflation), and the favourable tax treatment of debt interest, mean that the equity capitalization rate does not increase much; therefore the combined effect is to lower the cost of capital and increase the value of the company until the optimum point is reached at a gearing level of G_1 in figure 9.10. At this point the cost of capital is minimized and the value of the company is maximized. Movement beyond this point increases financial risk and the probability of bankruptcy to a degree that motivates both the debt and equity holders to start demanding higher returns to compensate them for higher risk.

The analysis also implies that if a company is geared up to the optimum level then any new finance must be in those optimal proportions, otherwise the cost of capital will start to rise. There are *spill-over effects* on the costs of existing debt and equity from a new issue of purely debt or equity; such an issue does not maintain the optimal capital mix. For this reason the appropriate hurdle rate or test discount rate for appraising new investment projects is the marginal cost of funding them, which would take into account any spill-over effects, as shown in figure 9.11.

In a given period if X_1 volume of funds is raised in a manner which involves an increase in the average cost of capital, the appropriate discount rate for

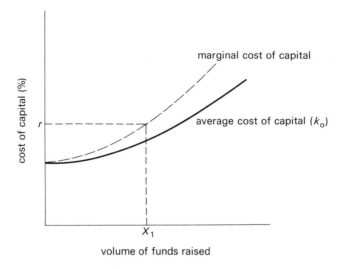

Figure 9.11 *The marginal cost of capital*

the projects which the funds are being used to finance is the marginal cost of raising those funds, r. The calculation of the cost of capital is far from simple. If equity or retained earnings are to be used the cost is not necessarily the opportunity cost or yield on the company's equity, and likewise the cost of debt issued is not just the tax-adjusted cost of debt. These potential effects on the costs of existing sources must be considered.

Dividend policy and retentions

A company's dividend policy and its retention policy are two sides of the same coin, since by definition what a company does not distribute is retained. Miller and Modigliani have demonstrated that, in a perfect market, given an investment policy not subject to change, dividend policy does not matter.[18] Shareholders can either enjoy extra dividends now at the expense of the dilution of future returns necessitated by a new issue to finance investment, or forgo dividends now and have offsetting increased returns in the future. Yet markets are not perfect and both companies and governments behave as if dividend policy is important.

In various periods the government has introduced tax measures which discriminate against dividend payments as a means of encouraging reinvestment of profits via retentions, and between 1973 and 1979 dividend increases were restricted as part of counter-inflation policies. The argument was that if other sources of income were restrained, dividend income should have like treatment.

There are various factors that could make the dividend decision extremely important. Capital gains are typically taxed at a lower rate than dividend income. Higher-rate taxpayers could well prefer a policy of low dividends and high retentions so that they can take most of their return via a capital gain. Although the opportunity cost of a new share issue should be the same as financing by retentions, the various transactions and issue expenses make finance by retentions more attractive. On the other hand, uncertainty about future income could lead shareholders to put a premium on dividend payments now rather than uncertain capital gains later. This is popularly termed the 'bird-in-the-hand' argument. Companies seem to be extremely reluctant to change their dividend policy in response to every movement of earnings. Lintner produced evidence of a 'target payout' ratio and a lagged response of dividend policy alterations to changes in earnings.[19] It is argued that there is an 'information content' to dividend policy, and that any change in policy conveys a change in management's expectations of future earnings prospects; they are thus unwilling to alter policy unless they are fairly sure that the company's circumstances have changed.

Financial Management—the Puzzles Remain

Despite considerable advances in our understanding of financial decisions many of the central areas of financial management are puzzles which still await satisfactory resolution. There are many different theories but no clear evidence about how a company should choose its capital structure or dividend policy—or, indeed, about whether the choice really matters. There is no clear evidence or agreement about the conditions required to make companies invest. There is clear evidence of a lack of investment and decline in profitability, as will be seen in chapter 10.[20] These factors, together with the variety of funding methods available to various types of enterprise, the patterns of funding activity in recent years, and the financial markets which govern the allocation of savings and investments, are considered in the next chapter.

References

1 E. Stamp, 'Accounting standards and the conceptual framework: a plan for their evolution', *Accountants' Magazine* (July 1981), pp. 216–22.
2 Accounting Standards Steering Committee, *The Corporate Report*, July 1975.
3 Sir John Hicks, *Value and Capital*, Oxford University Press, 2nd edn, 1968, p. 174.
4 Accounting Standards Steering Committee, *Provisional Statement of Standard Accounting Practice 7* (PSSAP 7), Institute of Chartered Accountants in England and Wales (ICAEW), 1974, discussed in the text as current purchasing power (CPP) accounting.
5 *Report of the Inflation Accounting Committee* (Sandilands Committee), Cmnd 6225, HMSO, Sept. 1975.
6 Accounting Standards Committee (ASC, formerly ASSC), *Current Cost Accounting*. Exposure Draft 24, ICAEW, 1979 produced further modifications on the CCA theme.

7 *ASC Standard Statement of Accounting Practice 16*, ICAEW, 1980, the 'final' 'received' version of CCA.

8 J. Sizer, *An Insight into Management Accounting*, Penguin, 2nd edn, 1979, p. 15.

9 H. Ingham and L. Taylor Harrington, *Interfirm Comparison*, Heinemann, 1980.

10 G. Whittington, 'Some basic properties of accounting ratios', *Journal of Business Finance and Accounting* 7 (1980), pp. 219–32.

11 Institute of Fiscal Studies, *The Structure and Reform of Direct Taxation*, Report of a committee chaired by Professor J.E. Meade, Allen & Unwin, 1978.

12 *Committee to Review the Functioning of the Financial Institutions*, Report, Cmnd 7937, HMSO, 1980, appendix 6.

13 *Ibid.*

14 *Ibid.*

15 For further discussion of the Meade Committee findings, see P.W.J.N. Bird, 'An expenditure tax for the United Kingdom', *National Westminster Bank Quarterly Review* (August 1979).

J.A. Kay and M.A. King, *The British Tax System*, Oxford University Press, 1978.

16 H.M. Markowitz, *Portfolio Selection*, Wiley, 1959.

W.F. Sharpe, 'Capital asset prices: a theory of market equilibrium under conditions of risk', *Journal of Finance* (1964), pp. 425–42.

17 F. Modigliani and M.H. Miller, 'The cost of capital, corporation finance, and the theory of investment', *American Economic Review* (1958), pp. 261–97.

18 M.H. Miller and F. Modigliani, 'Dividend policy, growth, and the valuation of shares', *Journal of Business* (1961), pp. 411–33.

19 J. Lintner, 'Distribution of incomes of corporations among dividends, retained earnings and taxes', *American Economic Review*, papers and proceedings, 1956, pp. 97–113.

20 For a discussion of this and related problems, see W.E. Martin (ed.), *The Economics of the Profits Crisis*, HMSO, 1981.

APPENDIX 9.1
Pro forma **Profit-and-Loss Account**

	£
Turnover	x
Cost of sales	(x)
Gross profit or loss	x
Distribution costs	(x)
Administrative expenses	(x)
Other operating income	x
Income from shares in group companies	x
Income from shares in related companies	x
Income from other fixed asset investments	x
Other interest receivable and similar income	x
Amounts written off investments	(x)
Interest payable and similar charges	(x)
Tax on profit or loss on ordinary activities	(x)
Profit or loss on ordinary activities after tax	x

Extraordinary income	x	
Extraordinary charges	(x)	
Extraordinary profit or loss		x
Tax on extraordinary profit or loss		(x)
Other taxes not shown under the above items		(x)
Profit or loss for the financial year		$£x$

his own name and has personal liability for his business debts. This involves considerable risk since personal assets can be put at the disposal of creditors should the business run into debt. Profits from the business are taxed at the owner's marginal rate of income tax. This complete identity of ownership and control means the owner has total (financial) freedom to run his business as he sees fit. There is a minimum obligation to maintain financial records but not beyond the requirements of income tax, value-added tax (VAT) and social welfare regulations. Small businesses, indeed, do not have to register for VAT until their taxable turnover is in excess of £15,000 per annum.

This relative freedom and simplicity has its disadvantages. The fact that the sole trader is unlikely to produce detailed financial information means that potential external sources of finance will lack sufficient information to judge the business. This means in turn that the equity or risk capital to fund the business is likely to be restricted to the owner's own savings or those of close friends and family. Outsiders would be unwilling to provide risk funds since they have little information and no control regarding the operation of the business. The only other long-term external source of funds will be borrowing. If the owner of the business has sufficient assets to offer as security, perhaps his house, then he will be able to raise funds by a mortgage loan. The asset cover, and the regular interest and capital repayments involved in a loan, guard the interests of the creditors and compensate for the lack of detailed knowledge of the business operations, since the loan is secured against the asset rather than the business. (Such creditors will not, of course, be totally unconcerned with the viability of the business.)

The only financial institution likely to have the requisite knowledge of the sole trader's business soundness will be his bankers. His overdraft facility, and any secured loans he is able to arrange with the bankers, are likely to be his major external sources of finance. He may obtain limited short-term funds by receiving credit from suppliers, and medium-term funds by leasing or hiring equipment, but his financial alternatives remain strictly limited. If he remains a sole trader any continuous expansion of operations is thus likely to be funded from ploughed-back income.

Partnerships

A partnership is an association of two or more people, working together in a profit-oriented business, jointly providing the finance, sharing control and participating in the profits, as required by the 1890 Partnership Act and subject to any overriding clause in the partnership agreement. Partnerships are very common amongst the professions. Indeed, certain professional bodies (e.g. solicitors and accountants) require that their members adopt this business form. The upper limit on the numbers involved in a partnership was 20 but this restriction was removed by the 1967 Companies Act in the cases of accountants, stockbrokers and solicitors. The advantage of the partnership over the sole trader is that there can be a pooling of both funds and personal expertise. But there are still considerable disadvantages.

Partners remain liable for debts. But here exposure to risk is greater than that involved in a sole tradership in that all ill-conceived judgement or breach of faith on the part of one partner could (legally) endanger the personal assets of all the others. The partnership is an unwieldy legal form. It can be dissolved by mutual consent or on the death or bankruptcy of a partner. If one partner owes the business money it is difficult to sue him on behalf of the business since he is part of it. It is difficult to transfer ownership since a partner cannot transfer his interest unless the other existing partners agree to accept the new partner(s). Profits are taxed at the personal income tax rate of the recipient partner, which may mean exposure to high marginal rates.

Sometimes a so-called 'sleeping' partner will put up funds, whilst taking no part in day-to-day business operations; these will be undertaken by other partner(s) with the necessary expertise. There are also provisions for the creation of limited partnerships; these extend the benefits of limited liability to those partners who are prepared to refrain from taking an active part in the business, while the remaining active partners remain fully and personally liable. For this reason limited partnerships are uncommon.

The partnership, therefore, has few advantages over the sole tradership. It facilitates the pooling of capital but can increase the individual exposure to risk. The other external sources of funds available are much the same as those at the disposal of the sole trader.

The limited liability company

The concept of the joint stock company evolved during the seventeenth and eighteenth centuries. These were originally temporary groupings of individuals banding together to finance 'one-off' merchant trading ventures. At the completion of a successful trading voyage each individual financier would share in the proceeds in proportion to his ventured 'stake'. When the idea of permanently subscribing risk capital became established the culmination was the notorious (and fraudulent) episode of the South Sea Company. The 1720 Bubble Act, passed to protect ill-informed share dealing of the type which occurred with South Sea stock, effectively outlawed joint stock companies unless set up with parliamentary permission. This hindered the progress of incorporation, but the Industrial Revolution and the development of capital-intensive industries spurred the demand for industrial capital and so for the joint stock company as an appropriate fund-raising vehicle. In 1825 the Bubble Act was repealed. The passage of the Joint Stock Companies Act of 1844 and the Limited Liability Act of 1856 then paved the way for the development of the modern corporation and industrial capital markets as we know them today.

Types of company

The 1948 Companies Act defines three types of company which can be registered: those limited by shares, by guarantee, and unlimited companies. The second and third categories are relatively rare. In *companies limited by guarantee*, in the event of the company being unable to meet its debts, the members are liable for a certain specified sum. This form is usually adopted by companies whose activities are not primarily profit-oriented, such as those engaged in promoting charitable causes. *Unlimited companies* are extremely rare and are usually set up to manage family estates.

The normal company is one in which the owners' liability is *limited by shares*. Shareholders participate in ownership by agreeing to purchase shares, and by so doing commit funds up to the nominal or *par value* of the shares concerned. Should the company go bankrupt, through lack of sufficient funds to pay creditors, then the creditors will only receive payment from those funds which can be raised by selling or 'liquidating' those assets (stocks of finished goods, equipment, property, etc.) which remain in possession of the company. The shareholders lose (at most) their original stake, but they are not liable for any further money to meet the company's debts, and their personal assets are secure. This is not the case with the sole trader or the normal form of partnership. Clearly 'limited liability' cuts down the risk involved in putting up money to fund business activities enormously. Risk obviously remains, in that any money ventured may be lost, but that is its total extent. The advent of limited liability provided a tremendous stimulus to the growth of industrial capital markets.

Setting up a Private Limited Company

A private company can have between two and fifty members, who have to file the following main documents with the Registrar of Companies.

Memorandum of association

A firm's legal remit is set out within the memorandum of association, which also contains the following details: the name of the company; the situation of its registered office; and the objectives of the company (broadly defined so that they include everything that the company is likely to undertake). These give indications, to both prospective members (i.e. shareholders) and persons dealing with the company, of the nature of its activities, the size of its authorized share capital, information about its division amongst the subscribers, plus the subscribers' signatures.

Articles of association

These document the rights of company members and define the manner in which the company shall regulate its activities according to Table A of the 1948 Companies Act. Included in the articles are: regulations concerning the rights, and variations thereof, to share capital; the provisions for calls on, transfer, transmission, and forfeiture of shares, and the alteration of capital; the procedure to be followed at meetings and the voting rights of members; the appointment, powers, and process for the retirement of directors; and provisions relating to the annual accounts, profits and dividends, and to the winding-up of the company. The articles can be altered by special resolution at a meeting of the shareholders.

The distinction between a private and a public company

The main distinctions between a private and a public company follow from the restriction on the membership of a private company to a maximum of 50 whereas a public company has a minimum of seven members but no upper limit. There are further restrictions on the right to transfer shares and a prohibition of the offering of its shares or debentures to the general public. This confers the benefit of not having to divulge the information included in a prospectus, which is required when offering shares to the general public.

Private companies controlled by five or fewer 'interests' are defined as 'close companies' following the introduction of Corporation Tax in 1965. They are required to distribute a certain proportion of their profits or are deemed by the authorities to have done so. The intention is to discourage the use of companies as tax avoidance mechanisms, a considerable attraction given the disparity between corporate and personal tax rates.

The advantages of incorporation

Apart from the previously mentioned benefits of limited liability there are a number of other attractions to incorporation. Companies have a separate legal personality, and enjoy perpetual existence until wound up. Company property is distinct from that of the members, and the company can enter into contracts in its own right and sue or be sued. There is not necessarily an identity between the owners and the managers of a company. Should a former owner/manager wish to retire, he could simply do so and maintain his shareholding, or if he wished to realize his interest and use the proceeds to go on a round-the-world cruise, he could arrange for the transfer of his shares. The situation, as we shall see, is even more straightforward for a shareholder in a publically quoted company.

Sources of finance available to a private company

The private company is better placed to raise finance than the two previously considered business forms. Appropriation of profits to reserves escapes income tax, and hence the company is more likely to be able to finance growth via the retention of profits. The company can issue *debentures* (loan finance) and offer security to the holders by means of a floating charge against the company's assets. Private companies vary enormously in size up to businesses that are very large with turnovers of millions of pounds. For the larger private company a number of financing alternatives will be available.

In the short term (periods up to a year) it will probably take *credit* from suppliers (in the form of delaying payment for consignments of raw materials and components) as well as give it to customers. *Bank overdrafts* will be a major source of short-term funds, as they are for all forms of business. (There is some disagreement about the status of overdrafts in that many companies have persistent overdrafts, but as these facilities can be withdrawn by banks with minimal notice and since the terms can be subject to frequent alteration, they are regarded as being short-term funds.) The company may also be able to arrange medium-term loans (of a period from two to seven years) from its bank.

Table 10.1 shows the total volume of bank advances (loans) to UK enterprises outstanding in early 1981. The firms are classified according to their activities in manufacturing, other production, finance and services. The service sector shown does not include advances to central and local government and the public utilities. The figures are aggregated and therefore include loans to all types of business, including private and public companies. The London clearing banks provide the lion's share (in the region of 44 per cent). The accepting houses are made up of the major merchant banks, whose activities, together with those of the money and currency markets, are discussed at greater length below. Foreign banks, particularly American ones, are providing an increasing share. Traditionally, they have been more willing to offer *term loans* (fixed term loans of a medium period, 2–7 years) than have the British banks, who prefer lending on overdraft. However, foreign competition and government exhortation have led to an expansion of term lending. Indeed, in the April 1981 budget the Government introduced a pilot loan guarantee scheme to benefit small companies in which it would insure the banks against defaulters on term loans to a value of 80 per cent of the loan.

In evidence submitted to the Wilson Committee the banks were criticized as being too cautious and restrictive in their lending policies to small businesses.[2] Certainly, the terms and conditions are more onerous, but this is largely a reflection of the increased risk and administrative cost of lending relatively small amounts to small businesses. The banks, however, are a major source (in relative and absolute terms) of external funds to small businesses.

Invoice discounting and *factoring* have become increasingly popular

Table 10.1 *Bank advances to UK enterprises: amounts outstanding 18 February 1981 (in sterling and foreign currencies)*

	Manufacturing	Other production	Financial	Services[a]
	(£m)	(£m)	(£m)	(£m)
London clearing banks	7,407	3,959	2,002	7,668
Scottish and N. Ireland clearing banks	947	1,099	351	241
Accepting houses	389	73	857	597
Other British banks	2,459	585	2,019	3,027
American banks	2,876	826	1,723	1,144
Japanese banks	302	53	167	896
Other overseas banks	1,445	333	1,497	1,041
Consortium banks	109	27	168	206
All banks	15,936	6,955	8,784	15,820

[a]Excluding Public Utilities, National and Local Government
Source: CSO, Financial Statistics (April 1981), table 6.8

methods of raising short-term finance. If a company has sold items and delayed the receipt of payment by extending credit terms, it can approach a finance company engaged in invoice discounting which might offer to advance funds up to 75 per cent of the value of the invoices outstanding. The company benefits from the immediate injection of funds; at a later date, when payment has been received, it repays the finance company together with an interest and service charge.

Alternatively the company can sell its debts to a factor, probably a subsidiary of one of the clearing banks. Factors offer three basic services; debt collection and credit management, insurance against bad debts, and the provision of finance on the security of the debt. As the services are more extensive the cost is proportionately more, but a credit management and debt collection service can be very valuable to a rapidly growing small company, which has neither the time nor resources to expend on this activity.

Deferred tax payments form another useful source of short-term business funds. The extent of the delay depends on the company's accounting dates, but there is typically a year's lag between the generation of profits and the payment of tax on that accounting year's profits. Similarly, any situation in which there is a deferment of expenses due adds to a company's liquidity.

Additions to medium-term funds are likely to come from the *leasing and hiring* of equipment, and from term loans (if available). The availability of long-term funds will be discussed in more detail in the next section, when we consider the transition from private company to public company status.

Table 10.2 gives some indication of the way in which small companies have financed themselves. It is derived from a sample survey undertaken by the Wilson Committee of nearly 300 small companies. The companies are categorized according to the size of their capital employed (defined as total capital and reserves and minority shareholders' interests, plus deferred tax, plus bank loans and overdrafts, long-term and short-term loans, plus net amount due to other group members). 'Smaller' companies are defined as those having a capital employed of less than £250,000, and 'medium small' as those having £250,000 to £4m. (Inevitably the definition of 'small' is somewhat arbitrary. The Bolton[3] and Wilson Committees were considerably exercised by these problems of definition.)

From table 10.2, the prominent features of smaller and medium small companies' balance sheets compared with those of larger companies are as follows:

(a) A greater proportion of funds is tied up in short term assets and liabilities.
(b) A large amount of trade credit is both taken and given.
(c) The importance of bank overdrafts, as already mentioned, is apparent.
(d) There is a slightly smaller shareholder's interest but a marked reliance on loans from directors, perhaps to make up for the deficiency of loans from other sources, which are employed to a greater extent by large companies.
(e) There seems to be a more cautious attitude towards liquidity on the part of the smaller companies, who have a higher proportion of assets in the form of cash and short-term deposits.

The small companies are probably wise in this caution indicated in (e). However, some family-controlled businesses have such a fierce desire to maintain their independence, and to avoid any diminution of control or security, that they would prefer to forgo growth opportunities rather than raise further external finance. This is a matter for the companies concerned, but in recent years there has been a growth of 'half-way houses' which considerably ease the transition from private to public company status. For even with a membership of 50 the time is likely to arrive when the combined resources of those concerned are not sufficient to meet the financing requirements for expansion.

Table 10.2 *Balance sheet structure, 1975: percentages of total assets/liabilities*

	Manufacturing			Non-manufacturing			All small companies			Large companies
	Smaller	Medium small	Total	Smaller	Medium small	Total	Smaller	Medium small	Total	
Fixed assets:										
Tangible fixed assets, net	29.4	26.6	27.4	33.0	34.0	33.5	32.0	30.3	31.1	36.2
Goodwill	0.4	0.6	0.5	0.1	1.7	0.9	0.2	1.2	0.7	3.2
Investment in unconsolidated subsidiaries	—	1.9	1.3	0.2	0.9	0.5	0.1	1.4	0.8	0.3
Total fixed assets, net	29.8	29.0	29.2	33.3	36.7	34.9	32.4	32.8	32.7	39.7
Current assets:										
Stocks and work in progress	21.5	32.6	29.4	25.7	27.9	26.7	24.6	30.2	27.8	27.5
Trade and other debtors, etc.	34.8	34.5	34.6	28.7	28.2	28.4	30.3	31.3	30.9	23.3
Investments	3.5	0.8	1.6	1.5	1.9	1.7	2.0	1.4	1.6	4.5
Cash and short-term deposits	10.4	3.1	5.2	10.9	5.4	8.3	10.7	4.2	7.1	5.0
Total current assets and investments	70.2	71.0	70.8	66.7	63.3	65.1	67.6	67.2	67.3	60.3
Total fixed and current assets	100.0	100.0	100.0	100.0	100.0	100.0	100.0	100.0	100.0	100.0
Current liabilities:										
Bank overdrafts and loans	6.8	10.4	9.4	12.7	16.5	14.5	11.1	13.4	12.4	9.7
Short-term loans	2.6	0.6	1.2	2.9	2.6	2.8	2.8	1.6	2.1	3.0
Trade and other creditors	35.7	29.5	31.3	34.6	29.7	32.3	34.9	29.6	31.9	25.2
Dividends and interest due	0.5	0.9	0.7	0.8	0.6	0.7	0.7	0.7	0.7	1.0
Current taxation	3.8	3.4	3.5	2.3	3.3	2.8	2.7	3.4	3.1	2.3
Total current liabilities	49.4	44.7	46.1	53.3	52.7	53.0	52.3	48.7	50.3	41.1

Net current assets	20.8	26.2	24.7	13.4	10.6	12.1	15.3	18.4	17.1	19.2
Total net assets	50.6	55.3	53.9	46.7	47.3	47.0	47.7	51.3	49.7	58.9
Capital and reserves:										
Shareholder's interest:										
Ordinary shares	5.8	10.7	9.3	6.3	9.1	7.6	6.1	9.9	8.3	11.6
Preference, etc. shares	0.6	0.9	0.8	0.3	0.4	0.4	0.4	0.7	0.5	0.7
Capital and revenue reserves	28.8	27.6	28.0	20.9	23.5	22.1	23.0	25.5	24.4	26.8
Total shareholders' interest	35.1	39.2	38.0	27.4	33.1	30.1	29.5	36.1	33.3	39.1
Loans from directors	8.3	0.8	3.0	12.3	0.6	6.8	11.2	0.7	5.3	—
Other long-term loans	1.1	6.8	5.1	3.7	6.4	5.0	3.0	6.6	5.0	10.3
Deferred taxation	6.1	8.1	7.5	3.3	7.1	5.1	4.0	7.6	6.0	7.4
Minority interests in subsidiaries	—	0.4	0.3	—	0.1	0.1	—	0.2	0.1	2.1
Total capital and reserves	50.6	55.3	53.9	46.7	47.3	47.0	47.7	51.3	49.7	58.9
Total capital and liabilities	100.0	100.0	100.0	100.0	100.0	100.0	100.0	100.0	100.0	100.0
£ billion	3.0	7.4	10.5	8.4	7.4	15.8	11.4	14.9	26.3	79.2

Source: The Financing of Small Firms, Interim Report of the Committee to Review the Functioning of Financial Institutions (Wilson Committee), Cmnd 7503, HMSO, March 1979, appendix 3

The transition from private to public company

If a private company wishes to 'go public' then the issuing houses and merchant banks are sometimes willing to place its shares with their own private clients. Private company shares are unattractive in their limited marketability, but the knowledge that a listing is likely in the near future, with the likelihood of an appreciation in value stemming purely from increased marketability, is a considerable sweetener.

For the private company about to go public there are basically three options. First, it can go public but refrain from immediately asking the public to subscribe for its shares. In this circumstance it has to lodge a statement in lieu of a prospectus (issued when making a share issue) with the Registrar of Companies, and by so doing loses most of the privacy of information attached to private status. Second, it can invite the public to subscribe for shares without having them quoted on the Stock Exchange. Third, it can seek a full listing. The second and third alternatives require the issue of a *prospectus*, a fairly detailed financial document whose contents will be reviewed later in this chapter.

Companies not yet ready to seek a full quotation can have their shares dealt in the 'over-the-counter' market. M.J.H. Nightingale have successfully operated such a market and in 1979 were arranging deals in the securities of 16 unlisted companies. Stock Exchange rule 163(2) allows brokers to deal in unlisted securities and its use is being encouraged. In the five-year period up to October 1977 the securities of some 850 companies had been traded in this market. The main advantage over a full listing is that it avoids having to place 25 per cent of total share capital on the market, which is the minimum requirement for a full listing. The reduced marketability and resultant discount can make the unlisted market an expensive place for raising new capital.

Raising new equity (share) capital for the private company can be a considerable problem. The minimum *market capitalization* (number of issued securities × their price) required to make a quotation realistic is around £5 million plus, equivalent to pre-tax profits of a £1 million plus. This is not a new problem; in 1931 the Macmillan Committee identified the 'Macmillan Gap',[4] defined as the difficulty encountered by small to medium companies raising external finance up to an amount in the region of £200,000, which would be equivalent to £2 million today. Admittedly there are a number of specialist institutions which help to fill the gap (these are reviewed in appendix 10.1). Many companies are not in a position to go public. The total number of companies on the Register in Great Britain at 31 December 1978 was 692,182, of which 676,357 were private companies and only 15,825 were public ones.

Types of Company Security

The various types of security available to a public company wishing to raise long-term funds are shown in figure 10.1. The share capital is the company's risk capital and is held by the members of the company. Together with the shareholder's reserves it represents their total interest. As the risk bearers, the shareholders receive payment last, after all interest payments to creditors (the right-hand side of figure 10.1). The payments to creditors are a tax-deductible expense paid out of pre-tax income, whereas the shareholders are

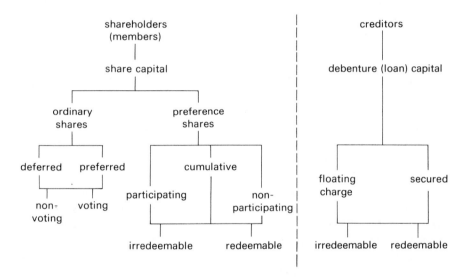

Figure 10.1 *The raising of long-term funds*

paid from after-tax income (i.e. after corporation tax). In the event of the company failing and being put into liquidation the creditors receive capital repayment first.

The basic division in the share capital is between the ordinary and preference shares. The *preference shares* rank first behind creditors for payment of dividends and repayment of capital on liquidation. Usually the dividend is of fixed rate but some preference shares have a right to participate in profits to a further limited extent in good years. In a bad year the dividend may be passed (not paid), but cumulative preference shares have a right to make up for previous passed dividends. Redeemable preference shares raise funds for a fixed period and the nominal value of the money raised is repaid to the holder at the redemption date. Irredeemable preference shares have no such provisions and if the holder wants to recoup his funds he will sell the shares on the Stock Exchange at the going rate. Since the passage of the Finance Act in 1965, which introduced the tax deductibility of interest payments, very few preference shares have been issued. If a company wants to raise fixed interest finance it makes more sense to issue debentures (the interest on which can be charged against tax payments) rather than preference shares (whose fixed dividends are paid out of after-tax income).

Ordinary shareholders have security of neither dividend nor capital repayment. The holder's right of ownership, manifest in their voting right, entitles them to appoint and dismiss directors. (However, shareholders are typically a diverse and geographically scattered body with a tradition of apathy, which probably stems from the fact that it is easier to register disapproval by selling the shares than by taking the trouble to attend a company annual general meeting.) The shareholders receive a variable return, and the size of each year's dividend is left to the discretion of the directors. In a bad year the dividend might be cut (reduced) or not paid at all. The shareholders have no recompense, as the risk bearers, and have to hope that trading conditions will improve in the next year, with an accompanying restoration of dividend payments, or else sell their shares. Companies sometimes issue different classes of ordinary shares and the deferred shares rank last for the payment of a dividend. A few companies have issued shares with either restricted or no voting rights. This can be a considerable disadvantage to their holders, particularly in a take-over bid where voting rights are crucial. To compensate, such shares are generally traded at a lower price than voting shares but suffer no dividend reduction.

The holders of a company's loan capital (debentures) remain outside creditors and have an entirely different relationship to the company from that of the shareholders (as indicated by the dotted line dividing figure 10.1). Loan capital represents the company's long-term borrowings and the principal or sum involved is a liability to the company, as are the annual interest payments. These must be paid at the stipulated times in the agreed amounts. If interest payments are not made, the trustees, appointed on behalf of the debenture holders, can force the company into liquidation in order to secure repayments due. Debentures might be secured against a specific piece of property (mortgage debenture) or asset, or else by a floating charge against the general assets of the company.

If they are redeemable the company has agreed to repay the principal of the loan at some specified future date, as well as making the regular interest payments (usually biannual) on the loan. An irredeemable debenture holder is in a similar position to an irredeemable preference shareholder, and will liquidate his holding by selling it via the Stock Exchange.

In theory the debenture holders bear less risk than the shareholders, as their interest payments are guaranteed and fixed in amount, and the principal of their loan is secured and ranks first in the event of liquidation. In terms of figure 10.1 the shareholders on the left-hand side bear the most risk, followed by the preference shareholders, and then the debenture holders on the right-hand side. It is normally assumed, and the evidence seems to support it, that investors are averse to risk. They do not like bearing risk for the sake of it and will only do so if compensated by the prospect of higher returns. Thus, all other things being equal, the return or yield on a share should be higher than the return on a debenture. The converse of this is the company's position, since the yield on its securities is a cost to the company. The servicing cost of debt should be less than that of equity (the cost of capital was considered in more detail in chapter 9).

Other factors which play a part in the decision to issue debentures are the tax advantage mentioned previously—the tax deductibility of interest payments—and the fact that payments are fixed in nominal terms and will decline in real value with any inflation. If investors have not fully anticipated the likely effect of inflation in setting the desired nominal rate (see expression 10.7) then there will be an additional bonus to the company. Furthermore debentures do not confer voting rights and do not involve dilution of control. On the other hand, it will be remembered from the discussion in the previous chapter that they do increase financial risk. Thus there are a number of issues to be considered apart from the straight yield or cost of servicing. With regard to this, an understanding of the nature of yields and returns hinges on the concepts of the time value of money and discounting, introduced in chapter nine.

Present values and discounting: yields and returns

It will be recalled from expression 9.2 that the terminal value of a sum S invested for n periods at a rate of interest r is given by:

$$\text{terminal value } (TV) = S(1 + r)^n. \tag{10.1}$$

Likewise, the present value of a terminal sum TS received n periods into the future, given an interest rate r, is given by:

$$\text{present value} = \frac{TS}{(1 + r)^n}. \tag{10.2}$$

We can now apply these concepts to the returns on securities. The return on a share held for n periods is made up of the dividend payments over those n periods plus the price for which the share is sold at the end of the n periods, all discounted back to give their present value. In effect we are saying;

$$\text{gross return} = d_0 + \frac{d_1}{(1+r)} + \frac{d_2}{(1+r)^2} + \ldots + \frac{d_n}{(1+r)^n} + \frac{S_n}{(1+r)^n}$$

where d_t is the dividend received in each period, $(1+r)$ is the appropriate discount factor and S_n is the terminal sale price of the share.

We could write this as:

$$\text{gross return} = \sum_{t=0}^{t=n} \frac{d_t}{(1+r)^t} + \frac{S_n}{(1+r)^n}. \tag{10.3}$$

To get the net return we would have to deduct the original price paid for the share, S_0, from the gross return. An alternative way of looking at the problem is to view the yield as being the discount rate that will equate the value of future dividend payments plus terminal share value with the current share price:

$$S_0 = \sum_{t=0}^{t=n} \frac{d_t}{(1+k)^t} + \frac{S_n}{(1+k)^n}. \tag{10.4}$$

where all symbols are as before and k is the yield on the share which equates the value of future payments with the current share price. The yield on a debenture is determined similarly:

$$D_0 = \sum_{t=0}^{t=n} \frac{CP}{(1+R)^t} + \frac{RD}{(1+R)^n}. \tag{10.5}$$

where D_0 is the current market price of the debenture, CP are the fixed 'coupon' or interest payments on the debenture, RD are the redemption provisions equal to the repayment of the nominal or par value of the debenture in period n, and R is the yield on the debenture which equates the value of future payments with the current market price of the debenture.

We have suggested that the yield on an ordinary share (k) would typically be greater than the yield on a debenture (R). This follows from the fact that there is more uncertainty about the value of the future dividend payments (strictly speaking the values in equation 10.4 are expected values since a dividend does not have to be paid) than there is about the coupon payments on debentures, which are fixed in money terms.

Now consider the *effects of inflation*. If there is a persistent and 'high' level of inflation, as has been the case in the UK, then the value of future payments will have to be further discounted to allow for the effects of inflation. If there is inflation the apparent nominal yield will have to be discounted by the rate of inflation given the true yield:

$$(1+r) = \frac{(1+R)}{(1+PI)} \tag{10.6}$$

where r is the true real yield, R is the apparent nominal yield, and PI is the rate of inflation as measured by a price index.

Cross-multiplying equation 10.6 we obtain:

$$\begin{aligned} 1 + R &= (1+r)(1+PI) \\ &= 1 + r + PI + rPI. \end{aligned}$$

We can ignore the small quantity of rPI, and we then obtain:

$$R \approx r + PI. \tag{10.7}$$

Equation 10.7 shows that the nominal rate is approximately equal to the real rate plus a premium to reflect the rate of inflation. This is known as the

Table 10.3 *The yields on securities*

January	Gross redemption yield on 20-year government securities (%)	Gross redemption yield on 20-year company debentures (%)	Dividend yield (all shares) (%)	*Financial Times* actuaries share index: 10 April 1962 = 100 (all shares)
1974	14.77	16.44	7.68	106.75
1975	14.39	15.95	6.43	133.11
1976	14.43	15.19	6.10	153.04
1977	12.73	13.41	5.52	191.91
1978	12.47	12.75	5.54	216.68
1979	12.99	13.23	5.75	245.52
1980	13.79	14.16	6.32	271.32

Source: CSO, Financial Statistics (April 1981), tables 13.6 and 13.8

Fisher effect. The effect of inflationary expectations is likely to be an increase in the discount rate used to value the returns on shares and debentures. This should, on its own, lead to a fall in the present or market values of both. Both the interest payments and the redemption provisions on debentures are fixed, and therefore a debenture is ill placed to deal with inflation. Dividends on a share are not fixed, and if the company can pass on the inflated value of its costs, in its product prices, then profits and dividends could increase in line with inflation. Hence equity (ordinary shares) are a better inflation hedge than debentures and in this sense debentures are more risky. This has been reflected in yields. Since 1959 fixed interest security holders have demanded a higher yield on debentures than the dividend yield on ordinary shares—a phenomenon called the *reverse yield gap*, which can be seen in table 10.3.

It can be seen from this table that the yield on 20-year company debentures is higher than that on the correspondingly dated government stocks, a reflection of the higher risk attached to company borrowings. On the other hand, the yield on company shares is much lower—the reverse yield gap. This yield represents the average cost of servicing company shares but it does not represent the total return to the shareholder, since he may well obtain a capital gain if he sells his share for a greater price than he originally paid for it (as represented by the value of term S_n in expression 10.4). Share prices fluctuate considerably and have not kept pace with inflation. In periods of stock market depression they have had very low values, as in 1974, but they have also had remarkable periods of recovery, as can be seen from the last column of table 10.3, and there is scope for a much greater capital gain on a share than on a fixed interest stock.

The Bond Market

If governments spend more than they collect in taxes then like any private citizen or firm they must make up the deficit by borrowing. This they do by printing IOUs or *government bonds* (*gilts*), which are sold to the general public (households, firms, commercial banks or overseas equivalents) or to the Bank of England (which in effect means selling them to itself). Here our discussion will be restricted to sales to the public.

What is the effect on aggregate demand of financing budgets in this way? Bonds are simply certificates of debt. They have a face or par value which states in pounds what the borrower will pay back on pay-off or maturity day. They also have a coupon interest rate which merely states the amount in pounds that the government will pay each year to the holder of the bond. (When the coupon rate is expressed as a percentage it refers to the interest paid on bonds with a face or par value of £100.)

The actual rate of interest (before adjustment from nominal to real for purposes of inflation) depends on the price the owner had to pay for the bond. This, in turn, is determined in the stock market and is unconnected with the par value. Figures 10.2 and 10.3 are two ways of illustrating these statements.

In the bond market (figure 10.2) demand slopes down because lenders receive a fixed payment (the coupon) no matter what price they pay for the bond. The lower the price of the bond, the more attractive this fixed payment becomes. Supply slopes up because issuers of bonds will be more willing to make a promise to provide the fixed coupon payment the higher the price they get for the bond in the first place.

Suppose that, on a given trading day in the bond market, supply and demand intersect to provide a market price of P_1. The government now

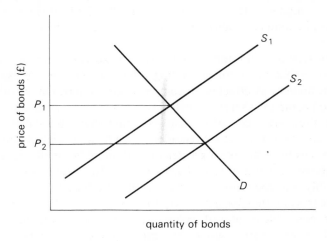

Figure 10.2 *The supply of bonds*

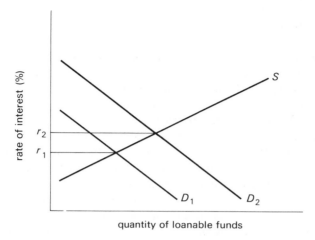

Figure 10.3 *The demand for loanable funds*

decides to issue additional bonds to finance a deficit. Supply increases from S_1 to S_2 by this new issue of bonds at each and every price, and to clear this increase in supply the bond price must fall to P_2. However, although coupon rates are unchanged, the actual rate of interest earned by bond holders rises. Consider a bond with a face value of £100. Assume that the market price is £50 and that the coupon rate is 5 per cent. The government has an obligation to pay £5 per year to the holder of that bond. £5 as a percentage of £50 is 10 per cent, the actual rate of interest. If the market price now fell to £45, the actual rate would rise to £5 expressed as a percentage of £45, namely 11 per cent. Only when bonds sell for their face values are coupon and actual rates identical.

On the other hand, the bond market can be examined (as in figure 10.3) as the market for loanable funds. Here the government is viewed, not as supplying bonds to the public, but as demanding loans from the public. The public are suppliers of the loans. The higher the actual rate of interest, the more willing are the public to supply loans. The lower the rate of interest, the more willing is the government (and others) to borrow.

If the government wishes to fund its deficit it increases its demand for loanable funds at each interest rate. It issues more bonds. Demand rises from D_1 to D_2 and the previous equilibrium interest rate moves up from r_1 to r_2. The rise in interest rate is equivalent to the fall in bond price in figure 10.2. The two are inversely related.

To some extent then, government borrowing to finance a deficit is likely to affect the equilibrium structure of interest rates. It has been further suggested that this could raise the cost of company borrowing in the debenture market and thus deter some companies from approaching the market—the *crowding out* thesis. (For further discussion of this see later in this chapter.)

Quoted Company Financing

It can be seen from table 10.4 that equity issues have been predominant in the company new issue market. There are substantial fluctuations from year to year which reflect both the state of company balance sheets and market conditions. The rapid rise in inflation following the OPEC oil price increases and the synchronized movement into recession in 1973–74, plus the depressed state of the stock market, meant that companies had to ease the inflationary pressures on their funding by borrowing at the short end of the market. As soon as the stock market recovered in 1975 there was a flood of equity rights issues (i.e. at the long-term end of the market) to restore balance sheets to a semblance of 'equilibrium' and ease the amount of borrowing.

There have been extreme strains on company funding during the 1970s which are the result of a number of factors. Foremost amongst these have been persistently high levels of inflation, high levels of interest rates, and a continuing decline in real levels of profitability. The corporate debt market was an extremely important source of funds in the 1960s but has dwindled rapidly in recent years (see table 10.5).[5] High interest rates and uncertainty about the future have made companies reluctant to commit themselves to borrowing long term at fixed rates. It makes more sense to borrow short or medium term at variable rates. The strains on company funding and the

Table 10.4 *New issues by company by type of security*

	Debt		Preference		Ordinary		
	Total (£m)	% of total issues	Total (£m)	% of total issues	Total (£m)	% of total issues	Total issues (£m)
1970	284.3	80.4	17.2	4.9	51.9	14.7	353.4
1971	340.4	51.3	12.8	1.9	310.4	46.8	663.6
1972	295.6	30.9	10.9	1.1	649.9	68.0	956.4
1973	42.9	20.4	14.0	6.7	153.6	73.0	210.5
1974	42.8	26.4	—	—	119.3	73.6	162.1
1975	212.8	13.5	44.9	2.8	1320.7	83.7	1578.4
1976	92.5	8.0	44.5	3.8	1023.9	88.2	1160.9
1977	93.8	9.9	33.9	3.6	819.6	86.5	947.3
1978	8.8	1.3	41.3	6.2	612.5	92.5	662.5
1979	61.4	6.9	34.6	3.9	789.2	89.2	885.1
1980	217.2	19.6	37.1	3.3	853.6	77.1	1107.9
1981	440.4	16.5	113.1	4.2	2110.8	79.2	2664.3

Source: Midland Bank Review (Spring 1982)

methods of financing adopted in recent years are shown in table 10.5, which shows company sources and uses of funds.

Companies need finance to function; they need working capital to finance stocks of goods, raw materials and components, work in progress, and trade debtors. The money value of all of these increases with inflation and hence additional money is required to replace them as they are used. Furthermore, firms also need to replace (again at higher money prices) plant, equipment, vehicles, etc. as they wear out. These extra funds are required merely to maintain the business in inflationary times and even more will be required to finance expansion.

Traditionally, the major source of company funds has been those which are internally generated. These are composed of trading profits, including depreciation (see below) minus any payments of interest, tax, and dividends, plus any capital transfers (investment grants). Since the early 1960s internal funds have usually accounted for about 70 per cent of total funds, but their contribution has declined in recent years. External sources have made up the difference, the major component being supplied by bank borrowing, whilst equity issues have remained a sporadic but important source of long-term funds (see table 10.5).

Around 60 per cent of the uses of funds is made up of fixed investment. Other important requirements include additions to stocks and work in progress, the purchase of subsidiaries and trade investments for cash, acquisitions of foreign assets and additions to liquid assets. In 1973 and 1974 the funding of inflationary increases in the value of stocks was a major problem, exacerbated by the fact that companies were taxed on these notional increases in value. Legislation was first introduced in November 1974 to alleviate this problem. Since 1976 tax relief has been granted, calculated on the basis that should the value of closing stocks exceed the value of opening stocks (the difference between stock value at the beginning and end of the accounting period) then this excess, if greater than 15 per cent of trading profits (after deducting capital allowances), is an allowable, tax-deductible expense. This particular method of calculation has now been superseded (see chapter 9) and is currently under review, but the principle of granting stock appreciation relief now seems well established.

Company funding difficulties have been accentuated by the continuing decline in real post-tax profitability experienced in recent years. Companies should not pay income from capital resources, whose value they should maintain intact. They do this by depreciating or writing off the value of an asset as a charge against profits over its economic life, so that they have sufficient funds set aside to replace it. If there is no inflation, writing off a value equal to the original historic cost is quite sufficient. When measured on this basis, companies' pre-tax returns have appeared quite adequate (see table 10.6). Given the existence of inflation, asset values increase, and depreciation provisions should be inflated to represent replacement cost rather than historic cost. If this is done and the effects of stock appreciation are

Table 10.5 Sources and uses of funds of industrial and commercial companies, 1958–79 (percentages of total sources or uses)

	1958–62	1963–67	1968–72	1973–77	1973	1974	1975	1976	1977	1978	1979
Sources											
Undistributed income[a]	72	67	52	49	44	32	53	51	62	67	59
of which depreciation[b]	(28)	(30)	(28)	(34)	(19)	(30)	(47)	(38)	(38)	(39)	(42)
Capital transfers (net)	—	2	8	3	3	3	5	3	2	2	2
Bank borrowing	10	12	19	24	34	41	6	18	18	15	23
Other loans and mortgages	4	3	4	3	6	1	5	4	1	2	3
Import and other credit received	—	—	3	5	4	7	3	7	4	3	7
UK capital issues:											
Ordinary shares	11	3	3	5	1	1	12	6	4	4	4
Debentures and preference shares	—	9	5	—	—	—	2	—	-1	—	—
Overseas[c]	3	4	6	11	7	15	14	11	10	7	2
Total sources	100	100	100	100	100	100	100	100	100	100	100

Uses

Gross domestic fixed capital formation	58	61	53	57	37	57	77	61	60	59	56
Value of physical increase in stocks and work in progress	7	9	4	4	10	12	−20	2	8	4	12
Acquisition of financial assets:											
Liquid assets[d]	4	4	13	15	20	1	21	14	18	15	4
Cash purchases of subsidiaries and trade investments	8	8	6	5	7	3	4	6	4	4	5
Investment overseas[e]	7	6	5	6	7	8	2	6	4	9	9
Export and other credit given	2	3	2	6	4	9	4	10	4	5	7
Other identified assets[f]	—	1	2	4	11	−1	8	5	6	—	−2
Unidentified (residual)	14	8	15	3	4	11	4	−4	−4	4	9
Total uses	100	100	100	100	100	100	100	100	100	100	100
£ billion (annual averages)	2.9	3.8	6.2	12.4	13.3	10.7	8.8	13.2	16.2	18.8	21.4

[a] Including increases in tax balances after deducting stock appreciation, but before providing for depreciation and additions to reserves; excluding unremitted profits of overseas subsidiaries of UK companies, but including unremitted profits of UK subsidiaries of overseas companies.

[b] Capital consumption at current replacement cost.

[c] Capital issues overseas; overseas direct investment in securities; intra-company investment by overseas companies (adjusted for unremitted profits).

[d] Bank deposits, notes and coin; British government securities; other liquid assets.

[e] Investment in overseas securities; intra-company investment by UK companies overseas (adjusted for unremitted profits).

[f] Other accruals adjustments; other identified domestic and overseas assets.

Source: Financial Statistics, reproduced in the Report of the Committee to Review the Functioning of Financial Institutions (Wilson Committee), Cmnd 7937, HMSO, 1980, chapter 10

Table 10.6 *Rates of return on trading assets of industrial and commercial companies (excluding their North Sea activities) (percentages)*

Year	Pre-tax historic cost	Pre-tax historic cost, net of stock appreciation	Pre-tax real	Post-tax real[a]
1963	16.1	15.6	11.6	6.5
1964	16.9	16.1	12.1	6.8
1965	16.0	15.2	11.4	6.3
1966	14.3	13.5	10.1	4.3
1967	13.7	13.5	10.2	4.6
1968	15.0	13.5	10.3	5.0
1969	15.0	13.4	10.0	5.2
1970	14.5	12.2	8.7	4.4
1971	15.3	13.3	8.9	5.1
1972	16.8	14.5	9.3	4.9
1973	19.6	15.0	8.8	6.1
1974	19.1	10.9	5.2	4.3
1975	17.7	11.2	4.7	3.6
1976	19.6	12.8	5.1	3.8
1977	18.8	14.4	5.8	4.2
1978	18.0	14.9	5.9	4.5
1979	17.8	11.6	4.1	3.5

[a] Backward looking (in the sense that it takes into account the system of investment allowances in force when units of investment were undertaken)

Source: 'Profitability and company finance: a supplementary note', *Bank of England Quarterly Bulletin* (January 1980)

deducted, then real pre-tax rates of return have declined to around 4–5 per cent and post-tax rates of return are even lower.[6] Although very low, they are higher than one might expect (given pre-tax returns) because of the effects of stock appreciation relief and the system of 100 per cent investment allowances on plant, machinery, ships and aircraft. (As we have seen, a company investing in these items can currently write off the whole cost as an allowable expense against taxable profits in the year in which the expenditure is made if it so chooses.) The effect of these measures combined with relatively low levels of profitability in the industrial sector has meant that many companies are paying virtually no mainstream corporation tax, and this has been a major incentive to the growth of leasing.

Leasing

In recent years there has been a high and continued rise in the use of leasing. It is estimated that it currently accounts for about 10 per cent of all new capital investment and provides up to 25 per cent of company external funding.[7] The stimulus to its growth has come from the generous system of investment allowances coupled with the fact that many companies are suffering from 'tax exhaustion'. They do not have sufficient tax liabilities to absorb the capital allowances available on new investment.

Rather than buy the asset themselves they lease it from a leasing company, usually a subsidiary of a bank or financial institution with substantial taxable profits. The leasing company retains the ownership of the asset and can therefore claim the investment allowances. The lessee company, the user, has full use of the asset over its economic life but never actually owns it. The lessor, or owner company, will pass on some of the benefits of being able to claim the investment allowances in the form of reduced lease charges to the lessee. Thus, both parties gain from the operation.

Leasing is essentially of two types; financial leasing or operating leasing. A *financial lease* involves a commitment to make obligatory payments over a specified period (usually medium term) sufficient to amortize the capital outlay of the owner company and provide some profit. (Amortization is the process of reducing a debt through a sinking fund.) *Operating leases* are cancellable, do not fully amortize the cost of the asset, and often include maintenance clauses. They are very popular in circumstances where equipment might rapidly become obsolete, and computers are often leased under these terms.

Financial leasing involves a liability indistinguishable from that of medium-term debt, but its accounting treatment is different and it is not recorded as a liability on the balance sheet. This had led to suggestions that it misleadingly increases a company's credit-worthiness for borrowing purposes. However, no professional analyst would be misled in this way. Nevertheless it remains a very convenient way of arranging for the finance of an asset.

Sale and lease-back

If a company owns a valuable asset, usually property, and wants to convert it into an injection of funds, yet retain its use, it can arrange for its sale and lease-back from the new owner. A number of companies owning high street stores have engaged in this operation, and there are ready buyers amongst the financial institutions who are usually keen to add to their property portfolios.

Bills of exchange and the inter-company market

There are a number of additional means by which large companies can raise short-term finance. A bill of exchange could be viewed as a postdated cheque. When a supplier arranges a sale to a buyer, the buyer might sign an agreement to pay in three months' time. The supplier could then either wait for the full period or sell the bill to a bank or discount house to obtain funds immediately. In the case of a commercial bill the supplier draws up the document and the buyer agrees to pay on the due date. The bills are usually used to finance foreign trade and are secured by documents of title to the goods in transit. Once a bill is accepted by a banking house which thereby accepts responsibility for repayment, the bill can be sold in the discount market at a higher price (thereby obtaining funds on better terms). As a means of providing further security the exporter can insure the credit with the ECGD (Export Credit Guarantee Department), and thereby protect the bank against the possibility of the buyer defaulting.

Another variant on this is buyer credit, which is usually supported by ECGD and involves the finance being provided directly to the foreign buyer by a UK bank. Companies sometimes obtain finance directly from other companies, often with a bank acting as its agent.

Project finance

Sometimes a company may be involved in a project, such as North Sea oil exploration, which has a high risk and demands very large funding in relation to the company's resources. In these circumstances, although the company's credit standing is of some importance, the key factor is the commercial viability of the project. Syndicates of banks have been prepared to fund suitable projects. To recompense them for providing medium- to long-term, relatively high-risk, finance, the banks have received higher rates and perhaps royalties as well as interest payments.

Table 10.7 summarizes the major forms of financing available to public companies. Since they tend to be larger, can offer better security, and provide

Table 10.7 *Sources of funds available to public companies*

Long term	Medium term	Short term
Ordinary share capital	Term loans	Bank overdraft
Preference share capital	Hire purchase	Bills of exchange
Debentures	Leasing	Invoice discounting and factoring
Sale and lease-back		Deferred expenses and taxes due
Project finance		Trade credit
Capital grants		Inter-company loans

more detailed information about their activities, their choice of funding is much greater than that available to smaller businesses. Details of capital grants and assistance via regional policy will be covered in chapter 15.

The Stock Exchange

The Stock Exchange developed in response to two major stimuli; the growth of permanent government funding and the growth of company funding. By the late seventeenth and early eighteenth centuries both were fairly well established. If an individual has lent funds for a lengthy period of time to the government, or permanently subscribed to the share capital of a company, then he requires a market where he can liquidate his holding, by selling it to some one else, should he require to do so. Thus, the Stock Exchange and any capital market has a number of functions. It provides a primary market where new money can be raised by the issue of securities—government debt, company debt and equity—plus a secondary market in which existing securities can be bought and sold so that their original holders are not locked in. These two functions are very closely related and the existence of such a market is a major factor in encouraging the channelling of savings into productive investment.

In the channelling of savings the market plays an important allocatory role. The market should be competitive and well informed or 'efficient'. In this context 'efficiency' means that prices should fully reflect all available information, and there is considerable empirical evidence that this is the case.[8] This means that investors should get a fair level of return for the risk of their investment, and that companies should face a realistic cost of capital that can be used as a yardstick in appraising their investment expenditure. The Stock Market capitalization or valuation of a company's securities is an important indicator of corporate value, based not on historical results but upon investors' expectations of future returns. These expectations can be quite volatile, as economic circumstances and company prospects can change quite rapidly with the unfolding of events. The Stock Exchange seeks to ensure that the interests of investors are safeguarded and that they are well informed. Brokers expend a vast amount of time and effort in analysing company prospects and producing information for the benefit of their clients.

Brief reconsideration of the share and debenture pricing formulas given in expressions 10.4 and 10.5 remind us that a very wide range of factors are likely to influence stock market prices. The appearance of new information at any level—company, industry, or even general economy—might have the effect of causing investors to revise their expectations of a company's future levels of earnings and dividend payments. This would cause revisions to the numerators in expression 10.4. Similarly, such information could change perceptions of the company's risk, causing revisions of the discount factor applied in the denominator in expression 10.4. In the case of fixed interest stocks, changing expectations could also cause revisions in the discount factor. Thus share prices can be very volatile and can change rapidly to reflect alterations in the market's mood, even though the payments on debt are usually fixed, at least in nominal terms. The price of debt will also change in response to changed views of company risk and movements in the general structure of interest rates.

Originally the market was very informal and was conducted in coffee houses (to this day Stock Exchange messengers are termed waiters). In 1812 the Stock Exchange first published rules, by which time it had its own premises and operated on lines very similar to those of today.

Table 10.8 *Members of the Stock Exchange*[a] *1957–79*

At 25 March	Members re-elected	Jobbing firms	Broking firms
1957	3493	117	318
1962	3422	83	294
1967	3208	45	225
1972	3457	26	168
1977	3907	20(14)	260(110)
1979	4026	20(14)	245(107)

[a] London Stock Exchange only until 1973. Numbers of jobbing and broking firms in London are shown in brackets in 1977 and 1979

Source: The Stock Exchange Fact Book, as reported by the Committee to Review the Functioning of Financial Institutions (Wilson Committee), 1980

The Stock Exchange is an independent association of stockjobbers and stockbrokers, centred on London, and since 1973 amalgamated to include the former regional trading floors. The 'single-capacity' system comprises (a) *jobbers* who act as principals, making a market by dealing in securities for a profit, and (b) *brokers* who cannot deal directly but act as agents for their clients who wish to buy or sell securities. In theory the jobbers compete in their activities and earn their living from their 'turn', the difference between the price at which they will buy and sell securities and the capital appreciation in the value of their holdings of securities. The brokers charge a fixed commission rate on their dealings which is tapered according to the value of the transaction.

The large amounts of capital required to maintain the jobber's 'book' of securities has led to mergers and a decline in the number of jobbing firms, as shown in table 10.8. This has led to worries about the possible decline in competition.

The Stock Exchange rule book, including the fixed commission system, has been referred by the Director General of Fair Trading to the Restrictive Practices Court, where an investigation is still under way.

The Stock Exchange prides itself on its system of self-regulation, which is administered by the Council of the Stock Exchange, a body of 46 elected members. As the spirit if not the letter of its code is sometimes flouted there have been worries about its relative lack of sanction over company, rather than member, activities. The legal framework is provided by the various Companies Acts and the 1958 Prevention of Fraud (Investments) Act. Overall supervision of the securities markets is under the ambit of the Council for the Securities Industry (set up in 1978), which oversees the activities of the Council of the Stock Exchange and the Panel on Take-overs and Mergers.

The market for government stocks

This market, known as the 'gilt-edged' market, has consistently provided the largest proportion of the Stock Exchange's turnover in securities. It is made up of British government and government-guaranteed stocks, plus those issued by local authorities, public boards, and Commonwealth governments.

Table 10.9 *The public sector borrowing requirement (£m)*

	Central government	Local authorities	Public corporations	Total public sector
1975	5017	2818	2645	10,480
1976	4695	1615	2818	9,128
1977	2607	1592	1796	5,995
1978	6171	1021	1139	8,331
1979	6594	2339	3661	12,594
1980	6567	3101	2633	12,301

Source: CSO, Financial Statistics (April 1981), table 2.5

Operations in these markets are part of the government's policy for controlling the money supply and managing the national debt. The need to fund a persistently large public sector borrowing requirement (see table 10.9; see also the section on the bond market earlier in this chapter) has led to suggestions that the required movement in yields and general government manipulation of the market has 'crowded out' the company sector. The high interest rates required to persuade investors to hold government stock arguably force up company costs, deter companies from borrowing and inflate their cost of capital. There is no doubt that companies have successfully obtained funds (as will be seen in the next section), but whether the costs have been desirable at a macro-economic level is a moot point.

The market for company securities

Obtaining a quotation

A company seeking a quotation must agree to conform to the Exchange's regulations, which require the annual disclosure of certain information and additional disclosure when new capital is raised. In the latter circumstance the company must issue a prospectus. This will furnish potential investors with detailed information about the company's recent performance and current standing and will help them make an informed judgement about the attractiveness of the company as an investment proposition. The contents of the prospectus will be fully analysed and reported in the financial press. An indication of the contents, drawn up to conform with the 1948 Companies Act, is given in table 10.10.

In the case of a company obtaining a quotation the Stock Exchange rules

Table 10.10 *An outline of the information disclosed in a prospectus*

Details of the names, addresses, and interests and remuneration of the directors.

The minimum subscription required in a share issue to purchase property, pay expenses and commissions, repay borrowings and provide for working capital.

Details of the timing and amounts payable on allotment of shares.

Details of any options (rights to purchase at a prefixed price) held on the company's shares or debentures.

If property is to be purchased by the issue proceeds, then full details of the purchase consideration, its form (whether shares, cash, etc.) and information about the vendors.

Full disclosure of the issue expenses and to whom payable.

Full disclosure of any contracts made outside the 'normal course' of the company's business during the previous two years.

The names and addresses of the company's auditors.

The nature and extent of any director's interest in property to be purchased.

The voting, dividend and capital rights of all classes of the company's shares.

A full report from the auditors giving details of profits and losses for the previous five years and of assets and liabilities at the last accounting date; also an indication of dividends paid on each class of share for the previous five years.

If the company has any subsidiaries, then similar disclosure of their accounting details.

If the issue's proceeds are to be spent on acquiring another business, then a full auditor's report on that business.

Pro forma **Balance Sheet**

	£	£
Called-up share capital not paid		x
Fixed assets:		
Intangible assets	x	
Tangible assets	x	
Investments	x	$\dfrac{x}{x}$
Current assets:		
Stocks	x	
Debtors	x	
Investments	x	
Cash at bank and in hand	$\dfrac{x}{x}$	
Less:		
Creditors: amounts becoming due and payable within one year	(x)	
Net current assets/liabilities		$\dfrac{x}{\,}$
Total assets less current liabilities		x
Creditors: amounts becoming due and payable after more than one year		(x)
Provisions for liabilities and charges		(x)
Accruals and deferred income		$\dfrac{(x)}{£x}$
Capital and reserves:		
Called-up share capital		x
Share premium account		x
Revaluation reserve		x
Other reserves		x
Profit and loss account		$\dfrac{x}{£x}$

This is an abbreviated version of the new format and full details of the composition of the items listed above would have to be given in notes to the accounts.

10

Financing British Industry

Financial decisions can be analysed in various ways. As a topic finance can be viewed as a question of income and/or risk apportionment and, of course, business control. Alternatively, it has been suggested that financial managers seek an answer to three basic questions:

(a) What is the optimum size of an enterprise and how quickly should it grow?
(b) What type of assets should it hold?
(c) What should be the structure of its liabilities?[1]

We have already encountered questions (a) and (b) and possible answers to them in chapters 6 and 9. This chapter is concerned with reviewing some of the various alternative responses to question (c), which determine the demand for funds, and related issues affecting the supply of funds. To start with, from the point of view of demand, it has to be borne in mind that the range of financing alternatives open to a business are a function of its legal form.

Business Forms and Financing Alternatives

Throughout this book the public company with its shares quoted and traded on the Stock Exchange is referred to as the 'typical' organization, but other forms of enterprise are more important numerically if not in terms of the value of assets controlled. Indeed, the type of legal entity an organization assumes is normally a function of its size and the amount of finance required. We consider successively sole traderships, partnerships, private limited liability companies and public limited companies.

The sole trader

The sole trader is the most common business form. It is adopted by most shopkeepers, tradesmen and farmers. There is no distinction between the identity of the business and that of the person who runs it. He trades under

also apply. These, in addition, require disclosure of the financial results for the previous ten years and a forecast of trading prospects. A private company going 'public' will have to alter the relevant sections in its articles of association which prevent the public from subscribing for its shares. If it ensures that at least 25 per cent of its share capital is held by the public it can avoid 'close company' status.

Methods of issue

1 *Introduction.* This does not involve the raising of new money but secures a market and a listing for existing shares. The public are not invited to subscribe for shares.
2 *Placing.* This involves the shares being placed by the issuing house with its clients, usually the institutional investors (insurance companies, pension funds). In the case of a public placing at least 25 per cent of the shares must be made available to the public. It is an attractive and inexpensive method of issuing shares but is normally only permitted for the use of smaller companies.
3 *Offer for sale.* The company sells its shares to an issuing house which then advertises a prospectus and resells them to the public. The method can be used to either obtain a quotation for existing shares or to issue new shares. The issuing house could either sell them at the original price and charge a fee, or gain its remuneration by selling them at a higher price.
4 *Issue by tender.* A minimum price is set in the prospectus and the public are invited to submit tenders stating the price and number of shares they would be prepared to take up. The issue is then allocated at a price which will clear it. This method cuts down the profits taken by *stags*. These speculators subscribe to new issues, confident in the knowledge that the issue price (to ensure success) is usually at a discount on the subsequent market price, affording the possibility of a quick profit by subscribing and immediately reselling.
5 *Public issue by prospectus.* The company directly offers the public the right to subscribe for shares at a fixed price, with the full details from the prospectus being advertised. The issuing house acts as an agent for the company and advises on the terms of the issue and arranges the underwriting (see next section) to ensure its success. This method is relatively expensive and only suited to a large, well-known company.
6 *Rights issue.* A company which already has a quotation will usually use this method to raise new share capital. It offers the existing shareholders the right to subscribe to new share capital in a fixed proportion to the number of shares they already hold (1 for 2 etc.). The shareholders can either take up the rights or sell them. Either way it ensures that their interests are served, as they can avoid dilution of control or the penalty of having new shareholders participate in the company on more favour-

Table 10.11 Gross capital issues[a] on UK market by UK listed companies, by method of issue, 1961–79: annual averages (£m)

Method of issue	1961–62	1963–67	1968–72	1973–77	1973	1974	1975	1976	1977	1978	1979
Public issues and offers for sale	49	75	114	77	93	23	103	103	61	18	22
Tenders	6	6	23	24	8	15	36	31	28	14	22
Placings	106	296	211	113	90	31	71	101	275	106	81
Offers to shareholders (rights issues):											
Ordinary shares	321	114	224	650	71	115	1226	1025	812	920	946
Preference and loan capital	46	66	116	34	27	1	104	32	7	9	33
Total	528	557	688	897	289	185	1539	1291	1183	1067	1103

[a] Estimates relate to new money raised, and so exclude issues in which the cash raised accrues not to the borrowing company but to its existing shareholders.

Source: Bank of England, reproduced in the report of the Committee to Review the Functioning of Financial Institutions (Wilson Committee), 1980, appendix 14

able terms. Rights issues are relatively inexpensive, merely requiring the issue of a circular to existing shareholders rather than the production and advertising of a prospectus, and are consequently the most popular method of raising further capital (see table 10.11).

Underwriting

The company cannot be sure when offering shares to the public that the issue will be a success. The process of issue takes time and conditions can change very rapidly in financial markets. To guarantee that the required funds will be raised the issuing house will arrange the underwriting of the issue. A number of financial institutions—investment trusts, insurance companies, pension funds, etc.—will undertake to take up the issue should it not be fully subscribed by the public. They are paid an underwriting fee (usually 1.25 per cent) whether or not their services are required, and should they have to take up any shares there is the additional attraction that they are usually relatively 'cheap'.

The Stock Exchange indices

The *Financial Times* ordinary index, familiar in the press and news, is a useful indicator of the general state of stock market trends and sentiment. It is an equally weighted index of 30 leading company shares which are representative of their market sector. It is calculated hourly, and the base date is 1935. The *Financial Times* actuaries index is a much more detailed value-weighted index, published daily and broken down into detailed market sectors; it is useful for the purpose of investment analysis, since a company's performance can be seen against that of its market sector.

External financial ratios

There are a number of financial ratios, published in the financial press, which provide useful tools for the assessment of company performance and the selection of securities. Their use has been complicated by the move to the imputation corporation tax system in 1973, and this will be considered next.

Tax complications

The change in the tax system in 1973 has led to complications in the definitions of what exactly constitute a company's earnings per share. Tax considerations can alter this figure, particularly where a company has substantial foreign earnings, and cannot completely set its advance corporation tax, paid to the revenue authorities in the UK when it paid dividends to its UK shareholders, against its foreign tax (table 10.12 illustrates this problem). (A fuller account of the tax system has been given in chapter 9.)

Table 10.12 *Different definitions of earnings per share*

	£	£
Profit before tax	100	100.00
Less tax (overseas) (52%)	52	52.00
Profit after tax	48[a]	48.00
Less unrelieved ACT	12	20.57
	36[b]	27.43[c]
Dividend gross	40	68.57
Less tax (30%) (ACT)	12	20.57
Dividend net	28	48.00
Retentions	8	0.00

[a] Earnings on 'nil' distributions
[b] Earnings on 'net distribution'
[c] Earnings on 'maximum' distribution

The imputation system involves shareholders receiving a net dividend plus a tax credit equal to the standard rate of income tax on the gross (pre-tax) dividend. (If the income tax rate is 30 per cent this can be estimated by 'grossing up' the net dividend by 30/70.) The shareholder does not, therefore, have to pay any standard rate income tax on the dividend, as the company has already done it for him in the form of advanced corporation tax (ACT); however, he may have to pay the difference required to adjust the tax to his marginal rate if he is in a higher tax band. The company pays part of its corporation tax early when it pays a dividend to shareholders as an ACT payment to the revenue authorities, but it can offset these payments against its mainstream corporation tax when this becomes due. This is where the difficulties arise. If the company cannot completely offset ACT payments against foreign tax, as in table 10.12 (which represents an extreme case where the entire earnings are derived overseas and none of the ACT payments can be offset against foreign tax), or if it is in a situation of tax exhaustion and does not pay sufficient mainstream tax to match ACT payments, then the mere fact that the company has paid dividends, and with them ACT, will alter the earnings per share figures.

It can be seen in table 10.12 that if the company pays no dividends—i.e. there is 'nil' distribution—there is no problem and the earnings are the after-tax profits. However, if the company pays a dividend, and with it ACT, then there may be complications. This is shown in our example where the earnings figure is reduced by the amount of unrelieved ACT to give the 'net' distribution definition of earnings, which takes account of this. If all available earnings are paid out as dividends we have the third definition of earnings, the 'maximum' distribution, which has the greatest effect in altering the earnings figures in our example.

Earnings per share

The earnings per share are simply the earnings available in a given year divided by the number of shares. Earnings figures are usually calculated on a net, nil, or maximum distribution basis as shown in table 10.12.

Dividend yield

The dividend yield is given by:

$$\text{dividend yield} = \frac{\text{dividend per share}}{\text{market share price}} \times 100.$$

It shows the percentage return received by a shareholder in dividends, and could be calculated net or gross of tax; the gross yield might be regarded as preferable in that it is not distorted by the shareholder's marginal tax positions.

Dividend cover

The dividend cover gives an indication of the extent to which earnings available for distribution exceed or 'cover' the dividends paid:

$$\text{dividend cover} = \frac{\text{earnings available for distribution to ordinary shareholders}}{\text{dividends paid to shareholders}}.$$

It is more realistic if earnings net of taxation and prior charges are compared with net dividends.

Earnings yield

The earnings yield is given by:

$$\text{earnings yield} = \frac{\text{earnings per share}}{\text{market share price}} \times 100.$$

The question then arises over which definition of earnings per share is appropriate. The *Financial Times* has adopted the figure based on 'maximum' distribution (as shown in table 10.12).

The price/earnings ratio

The price/earnings (P/E) ratio indicates how long, given the current figures, the share would take to earn its cost. It is given by:

$$\text{price/earnings ratio} = \frac{\text{market share price}}{\text{earnings per share}}.$$

Before the tax complications introduced by the imputation system it used to be the reciprocal of the earnings yield, but different definitions of earnings per share are now adopted. The *Financial Times* calculates this ratio using both the 'net' and 'nil' distribution figures.

The above yields can be used for the relative evaluation of company shares, though they have to be used with caution. Earnings and dividends are 'historic' figures, whereas the share price reflects market expectations about the level of future earnings. Companies with low dividend and earnings yields and high P/E ratios may well have 'growth' stocks about which the market may be *bullish* (expects the future earnings and price to rise). On the other hand, companies with high yields and low P/E ratios may well be spent forces of which the market takes a *bearish* view (expects the future earnings and price to fall). These sentiments are already reflected in the current share price.

The Supply of Funds

Up to now we have considered the different types of securities that companies or the government issue and the motives and considerations which may influence the demand for them. However, we have not considered where the funds to purchase them originate, and that is the purpose of this section.

The analysis which follows is best understood when considered in terms of

Table 10.13 *Financial surplus or deficit: analysis by sector*[a] *(£ million)*

Year	Public	Financial institutions	Industrial & commercial	Personal	Overseas[b]	Residual error[c]
1976	− 8,428	− 36	− 154	5,687	1060	1871
1977	− 5,876	130	− 755	5,190	206	1105
1978	− 8,060	− 590	− 58	8,731	− 707	684
1979	− 8,306	− 109	− 4391	11,599	1630	− 423
1980	− 11,045	928	− 2772	16,605	− 2737	− 979

[a] This balance is equal to saving, plus capital transfers, less gross domestic fixed capital formation, less increase in book value of stocks and work in progress. The sum of the sectors for each year is zero

[b] Equals, apart from the change in sign, the current balance in the balance of payments accounts, plus capital transfers

[c] The residual error in the national income accounts

Source: CSO, *Financial Statistics* (April 1981)

the flow of funds. Any individual, company, institution or even government, when considered over a period of time, will exhibit a financial surplus, deficit or balance. Whichever state pertains will depend on the relationship between the body's savings and investment undertaken, on the one hand, and its purchases or sales of financial assets on the other. If a company is in financial surplus it can either purchase additional financial assets or repay debt. If it is in deficit it must either reduce its holdings of financial assets or borrow more. This means that the following identity holds:

financial surplus = savings − investment
= increase in financial assets − increase in financial liabilities
= net acquisition of financial assets.

This analysis can be applied to both individual economic agents or to whole sectors of the economy, as is the case in the national accounts shown in table 10.13. The supply of funds comes from savings made by the personal sector, companies, public corporations and central and local government, plus transfers from overseas. These funds can be channelled into investment, either directly, as tends to happen in every category except personal savings, or indirectly via the acquisition of financial assets. In total, savings and gross investment have remained stable over the last 20 years, accounting for roughly 20 per cent of GDP, but within these overall figures there have been marked sectoral changes. Personal savings have shown a steady growth (see table 10.14), whereas the other sectors, particularly the public sector, have tended to move into deficit in recent years.

The increase in personal savings has been remarkable and it currently

Table 10.14 *Personal income and saving (£ million)*

Year	Total personal disposable income[a]	Personal saving[b]	Saving ratio[c]
1970	35,018	3,240	9.3
1972	44,507	4,324	9.7
1974	60,694	8,205	13.5
1976	84,799	10,048	11.9
1978	112,746	14,370	12.7
1980	158,725	24,243	15.3

[a] Equals total personal income before tax, less payment of taxes on income, national insurance etc. contributions and net transfers abroad. Before providing for depreciation, stock appreciation and additions to tax reserves

[b] Before providing for depreciation, stock appreciation and additions to tax reserves

[c] Personal saving as a percentage of total personal disposable income

Source: CSO Financial Statistics (April 1981)

stands at a record relative level of 15 per cent of total disposable personal income (see table 10.14). The exact reasons behind this growth remain obscure, but there are a number of obvious contributory factors. Increased uncertainty about the future course of the economy and inflation may have led to a desire to add to nest-eggs. A positive stimulus has been provided by the growth of contractual savings to meet the requirements of pension provisions and life insurance commitments, reinforced by the tax advantages of these forms of savings. (This sector accounts for roughly 50 per cent of personal savings in recent years.) Another large portion has gone into savings lodged with the building societies. In theory depositors are given preferential treatment when applying for mortgage loans, and house purchase is a particularly tax-efficient form of investment (interest payments on loans up to £25,000 to finance house purchase are tax deductible and there is no capital gains tax liability on the sale of a 'principal' residence). Deposits with building societies have accounted for roughly one-third of personal savings in recent years.

The remaining personal sector savings tend to be lodged in liquid assets such as deposits with the banks, other financial institutions, national savings, or in government debt of various maturity. It has not been placed in company securities. Indeed, the personal sector has been a net seller of its direct holdings of company securities since 1957. There are a number of factors at work behind this trend. The combined effects of income and capital taxes have led to the demise of the 'aunt Agatha' type of investor. The tax incentive to invest indirectly via pension and life assurance funds has already been noted. The structure of transactions and dealing costs penalize the small investor, and this, plus the benefits of diversification, suggests that it is wiser to invest indirectly via unit trusts or investment trust companies than directly in company securities. The personal sector provides the lion's share of the funds coming onto the capital market but this share tends to arrive indirectly, via the financial institutions, who are therefore responsible for deciding where they will be placed.

The Financial Institutions

The financial institutions can be grouped roughly into the banks, discount houses, merchant banks, finance houses, building societies, unit trust and investment trust companies, insurance companies, and pension funds. The activities of each and the markets they serve will be briefly reviewed in turn.

The banks

The banks are a heterogeneous group of institutions whose common characteristic is the acceptance of deposits of a short-term nature (table 10.15). They then perform the classic role of the financial intermediary and transform

Table 10.15 *Banks in the United Kingdom: summary of their position 18 March 1981. £ million (percentages in parentheses)*

Sterling liabilities

| Notes outstanding | Total deposits 90,371 (83.5) made up of: | | | Items in suspense and transmission | Capital and other funds |
	Sight deposits	Time deposits	Certificates of deposit		
560	26,710	58,453	5208	3665	13,576
(0.5)	(24.7)	(54.0)	(4.8)	(3.4)	(12.6)

Other currency liabilities

| Total deposits 219,893 (99.1) made up of: | | Items in suspense and transmission | Capital and other funds | Total liabilities/assets |
Sight and time deposits	Certificates of deposit			
195,316	24,577	477	1625	330,138
(88.0)	(11.1)	(0.2)	(7.3)	

Figures in brackets denote individual sterling liabilities as a percentage of total sterling liabilities, and individual foreign currency liabilities as a percentage of total foreign currency liabilities

Source: CSO, *Financial Statistics* (April 1981), table 6.5

them into advances and loans of longer duration. The Banking Act of 1979 requires deposit-taking institutions to apply to the Bank of England for formal recognition of 'bank' status. The major banks are the London and Scottish clearing banks, plus the Northern Ireland banks, accepting houses, and a growing number of branches of overseas banks. They are supervised by the Bank of England, which ensures the observance of certain solvency and liquidity requirements consistent with prudent operation, and also implements the official credit control policy. At the moment the banks are required to maintain a 'reserve asset' ratio of 12.5 per cent of 'eligible liabilities' (sterling deposits plus any foreign currency deposits switched into sterling). Reserve assets are largely made up of government stocks with a year or less to maturity, Treasury bills, money at call with the discount market, certain other short-term bills, and balances with the Bank of England (excluding special deposits). As a further reinforcement of controls the banks may be required to lodge 'special deposits' or 'supplementary special deposits' with the Bank of England. As these are relatively unprofitable they provide a very strong lever for the authorities to apply to the bank's deposit-taking activities. However, there has been a good deal of controversy about the effectiveness of the system and moves are afoot to change it to a cash-based system.

Banking activities can be broadly divided into retail and wholesale banking. The clearing banks' widespread branch network facilitates retail banking and they attract funds via interest-bearing deposit accounts and non-interest-bearing current accounts. Their customers are provided with a broad range of services apart from their money transmission and cash distribution services. Sterling and foreign currency deposits typically make up in excess of 90 per cent of the bank's liabilities, and of the sterling deposits nearly one-third are sight deposits theoretically payable on demand.

Wholesale deposits involve large amounts, usually in excess of £50,000, and bear higher interest rates. These funds are frequently provided by other banks with surplus funds, other financial institutions, and large companies. A popular instrument is the certificate of deposit which states that a deposit has been made with a bank which will be repayable to the holder on maturity. These are negotiable instruments so the bank has the advantage of a fixed term deposit and the holder can always sell the certificate if he wants immediate liquidity. The foreign and merchant banks (the accepting houses) tend to concentrate their banking activities in the wholesale markets.

Clearing bank lending varies greatly in size and nature, from overdrafts to individual customers up to syndicated multi-million-pound loans to multinational companies. Although traditionally favouring overdraft lending, the banks have been increasingly providing term loan facilities to companies as well as their leasing, factoring, and instalment credit facilities. The banks also accept bills for customers (traditionally the role of the merchant banks and reviewed with their activities) and maintain their traditional financial advisory role. (A breakdown of bank advances to UK enterprises is given in table 10.1.)

The discount houses

The discount houses make a market in short-term financial instruments. The banks deposit money at call with them and thereby earn interest on surplus cash. The market includes bank and trade bills—indeed, the houses revived the commercial bill market—plus certificates of deposit, Treasury bills, and local authority bills. The discount houses have an agreement to cover the whole of each week's Treasury bill issue, which they then pass on to other institutions, in particular the deposit banks. The discount houses are guaranteed that the Bank of England will always accommodate them as a lender of last resort. However, the Bank can intervene in the market when there is a shortage of surplus of cash in a number of ways. Shortages are relieved by its purchasing bills, but if it wishes to create a shortage and raise interest rates it can sell bills to the houses and provide them with the necessary cash by lending them funds at an appropriate lending rate.

Merchant banks

The traditional business of the merchant banks lies in the acceptance of bills and thus the 17 members of the Accepting Houses Committee are major merchant banks. However, although this remains an important part of their business they have an extremely wide and diverse range of activities. On the one hand there are their wholesale banking activities; in these they compete with all the other banks but their advances only account for about 4 per cent of total advances. On the other they provide industry and personal clients with the whole gamut of financial services which do not involve them in lending their own funds. Amongst these activities could be included financial counselling, guidance in take-overs and mergers, investment management, and the issuing and acceptance business. They play a major role in facilitating the procurement of funds, both via their acceptance business and through the arrangement of syndicated credit. All are members of the less exclusive Issuing Houses Association and are active in arranging and underwriting UK capital issues and in managing Eurobond issues (bonds denominated in Eurocurrencies). Some of them have a number of other activities, including leasing and factoring, property development, foreign exchange, commodity and bullion dealing, etc.

Finance houses

The finance houses' traditional business has been instalment credit; most of their activities have been tied up with hire purchase or credit sale. Their main sources of funds are either borrowings, particularly from the banking sector, or deposits from banks and companies. Many are owned by banks or other institutions. Some offer banking facilities with deposit accounts and cheque issue. Their activities have branched out into leasing and factoring, credit granting, and the provision of various types of personal loans. They have branch networks but their facilities are frequently offered directly by the retailer who will have an agreement with a finance house for the provision of credit to his customers.

Building societies

The building societies are mutual organizations (i.e. owned by their members) which attract personal savings on a short-term basis (in the form of share or deposit accounts which are practically withdrawable on demand), and relend them long term in the form of mortgage advances for funding house purchase. These advances account for about 80 per cent of the societies' assets. They are required to observe a minimum liquidity ratio of 7.5 per cent in the form of cash and liquid investments but the average ratio actually maintained has been well above this, just below 20 per cent in recent years. Their activities are regulated by the Chief Registrar of Friendly Societies in accordance with the Building Societies Act 1962. Their mortgage rate is related to the rate paid to their investors after allowance for expenses. As there are high administrative costs associated with the adjustment of rates they do not follow every movement in short-term interest rates and have more stable 'sticky' rates.

Unit trusts and investment trust companies

Unit trusts are trusts subject to trust law and are authorized by the Department of Trade, according to the Prevention of Fraud (Investments) Act 1958. The interests of unit holders are safeguarded by their trustees and until 1979 the determination of trust management expenses was also governed by the Department of Trade. They are 'open-ended' funds, through which individuals can invest to obtain the benefits of economies of scale in dealing expenses plus access to professionally managed, diversified portfolios. When someone buys a unit he obtains an interest in the trust's assets and investment income. The actual size of the fund will depend on the balance of net purchases and sales of units.

A trust's investment policy is limited both by legislation and by its stated objectives; it may have general, overseas or specialized interests. Authorized trusts can only invest in government securities or shares and debentures. They are further limited to holding no more than 5 per cent of their total fund in unlisted securities. They are further limited by the fact that they

Table 10.16 *Investments of unit trusts: amounts outstanding, market values at year end 1980*

	£m	%
Net short-term assets	162	3.8
Foreign currency loans	− 12	− 0.3
British government securities	55	1.3
Local authority securities	2	0.0
UK company securities:		
Loan and preference	56	1.3
Ordinary	2977	70.2
Other	25	0.6
Overseas:		
Company loan and preference	12	0.3
Ordinary	954	22.5
Other	9	0.2
Total	4240	100.0

Source: CSO, *Financial Statistics* (April 1981), table 8.11

cannot build up reserves and time their investments but must sell or buy according to the balance unit purchase/sales.

Investment trusts are companies in their own right and are not subject to the same restrictions. They are 'closed-ended' funds with their capital subscribed by their share and debenture holders. Thus they can gear up their investments by fixed interest borrowings, build up reserves, and time their entry and exit from the market. A shareholder who sells thus simply transfers his ownership to another individual. The trust does not redeem in cash as does a unit trust; therefore the managers can be relatively unconcerned about day-to-day fluctuation in demand for shares. Despite these advantages, in recent years there has been a persistent considerable 'discount' or difference between the market value of investment trust company shares and the value of the securities in their portfolios, going well beyond the costs of the interposition of a layer of management expenses. They offer advantages to the small investor similar to those of the unit trusts, and some, like the unit trusts, have general portfolios whereas others concentrate on sectors or geographical areas and seek to maximize either income or capital growth.

The investment holdings of unit and investment trusts are shown in tables 10.16 and 10.17 respectively, where it can be seen that in excess of 90 per cent of their holdings are in UK and overseas companies.

Table 10.17 *Investments of investment trusts: market values of holdings at year end 1980*

	£m	%
British government securities	234	3.2
Listed UK company securities:		
Loan and preference	69	0.9
Ordinary	3758	51.7
Unlisted UK company securities:		
Loan and preference	41	0.6
Ordinary	250	3.4
Public corporation securities	2	0.0
Unit trust units	10	0.1
Other financial assets	78	1.1
Property	17	0.2
Other real assets	6	0.1
Overseas:		
Government	19	0.3
Company loan and preference	86	1.2
Ordinary shares	2696	37.1
Total	7270	100.0

Source: CSO, *Financial Statistics* (April 1981), table 8.12

Insurance companies

Insurance company business can be conveniently divided into two categories; general (fire, accident, life and marine insurance) and long term (mainly life assurance). Most of the liabilities of general insurance companies are short term and thus a greater proportion of their funds will be placed in short-term securities than is the case with life funds. On the other hand they need to build up reserves and maintain solvency margins, so they also have very substantial long-term investments.

Table 10.18 *Insurance companies: market values of holdings of assets by long-term and general funds at year end 1979*

	General funds		Long-term funds	
	(£m)	(%)	(£m)	(%)
Cash and other short-term assets (net)	1448	13.8	1805	4.3
British government securities	2388	22.8	11,129	26.3
UK local authority securities	185	1.8	553	1.3
UK company securities:				
Loan and preference	437	4.2	1865	4.4
Ordinary shares	1983	18.9	10,588	25.0
Overseas government and company securities	832	7.9	1243	2.9
Unit trust units	11	0.1	1097	2.6
Loans and mortgages	313	2.3	3104	7.3
Land, property and ground rents	1056	10.1	10,225	24.2
Agents' balances	1733	16.5	542	1.3
Other	98	0.9	162	0.4
Total	10,486	100.0	42,311	100.0

Life assurance involves long-term liabilities and therefore assets tend to be correspondingly long term. The wide variety of policies, including 'with profits' schemes which offer some participation in profits from investments in return for higher premiums, and endowment policies with an emphasis on saving, mean that the companies have to be very conscious of investment returns. An increased awareness of the ravages of inflation has led them to place a greater proportion of their funds in property and equity as possible inflation hedges. They are exceedingly important channellers of funds into the capital markets and the structure of their holdings is indicated in table 10.18.

Pension funds

The pension funds have grown tremendously in scope and importance since
1945 as increased demand and legislation for better pension provision has
boosted contributions. However, not all schemes involve the building up of
investment funds, and some are paid directly out of revenue, as is the case
with the state pension scheme. The majority, however, including those
operated by the public sector, local authorities, and private companies,

Table 10.19 *Superannuation funds; holdings in market values at year
end 1979*

	£m	%
Short-term assets	1639	4.8
Long-term borrowing	− 280	− 0.8
British government securities	7482	21.8
UK local authority securities	182	0.5
UK company securities:		
Ordinary shares	14,543	42.3
Loan and preference	615	1.8
Overseas securities:		
Ordinary shares	1789	5.2
Loan and preference	61	0.2
Government	43	0.1
Unit trust units	107	0.3
Local authority mutual investment trust	108	0.3
Property unit trusts	853	2.5
Loans and mortgages	769	2.2
Land, property and ground rents	5798	16.9
Other	663	1.9
Total	34,374	100.0

Source: CSO, *Financial Statistics* (April 1981), table 8.14

involve advance funding, in which both employee and employer make
contributions over the period of employment, and these funds, together with
investment income, are accumulated to meet future pension liabilities.

    Funded schemes could be divided between insured schemes, in which the
management of funds and actuarial risk is undertaken by a life assurance
office, and self-administered schemes, in which the funds are directly invested,
although the management of investment funds is usually contracted out to
an appropriate specialist financial institution.

The liabilities of the funds are their commitments to present and future pensioners; hence contributors cannot use their pension rights as collateral for raising money, and the liabilities are completely distinct from those of the company or body involved with the scheme on behalf of its employees.

The growth in importance (in terms of the market value of their holdings) of the pension funds continues apace and they are still far from the plateau where accruals will just match liabilities. Indeed, in 1978 it was estimated that net contributions plus investment income were running at a rate of surplus of £3.7 billion (self-administered schemes); this figure is being added to invested funds each year and is likely to remain at this level for a good many years to come. They therefore have a tremendous influence and significance within the capital market. An indication of the scope and nature of their investment holdings is given in table 10.19. The major change in their holdings in recent years has been a much greater commitment to equity and property, again prompted largely by the influence of inflation.

Controversies and Conclusions

The financial institutions are active in a number of different markets. These include the 'parallel' money markets in which inter-bank unsecured deposits, certificates of deposit, and local authority bills are the primary instruments. There is the Eurocurrency market in which foreign currency borrowing is undertaken between banks on a short-term basis, plus the trading of certificates of deposit denominated in foreign currency. There is also the Eurobond market in which bond issues denominated in foreign currency can be floated. British companies do play a part in these markets, but from the point of view of raising long-term external finance the Stock Exchange provides the most important market.

Security holdings on the Stock Exchange are being increasingly dominated by the financial institutions—in particular, the insurance companies, pension funds, unit trusts and investment trust companies. By 1978 these groups of institutions held 47 per cent of all outstanding UK company equity issues and 46 per cent of British government securities. This has led to a number of controversies.

It has been suggested that the desire to deal in bulk has led to a built-in bias towards the larger companies at the expense of the smaller ones. Trading in large blocks of securities is relatively cheaper and buying a given amount in a large company is less likely to push the price against the buyer than the purchase of a holding of equal value in a smaller company; in addition there are statutory limitations on the size of interest permissible. As the holdings are managed by a small group of professionals it has been suggested that the market decision base has been narrowed, which could lead to the emergence of a herd instinct and greater price volatility. However, there seems little evidence of either as yet. Further criticism is made on the grounds that institutional investors are a passive body of shareholders who do not want to attract government attention by interfering in company activities, although in a number of recent cases they have been playing an increasingly active role in making the shareholder view felt. Fears of this nature were part of the stimulus towards the setting up of the Committee to Review the Functioning of the Financial Institutions which reported in June 1980 and provided the first major report on the working of the financial system since the Radcliffe Report in 1959.[9] In the recent report there seemed to be an agreement that the real rate of company profitability in the UK was far too low, and that this, coupled with the cost of capital they faced, was unlikely to provide any stimulus to investment. Yet there was no agreement on how adequately the financial system had coped. A majority felt that all that was required were a number of piecemeal measures to meet particular needs, whilst a minority favoured the creation of a major new investment bank, funded partly by institutional capital and partly by North Sea oil and gas revenue, which would provide funds to restructure and modernize British industry. It seems to the author that the supply of funds is not the problem and that the UK financial system has proven itself to be remarkably robust and innovative. The problem lies in the lack of demand for funds, and this will only return when companies show higher real profitability.

References

1 E. Solomon, *The Theory of Financial Management*, Columbia University Press, 1963, p. 9.

2 Committee to Review the Functioning of Financial Institutions (Wilson Committee), *Interim Report—The Financing of Small Firms*, Cmnd 7503, HMSO, March 1979, p. 23.

3 *Report of the Committee of Inquiry on Small Firms* (Bolton Committee), Cmnd 4811, HMSO, Nov. 1971.

4 *Report of the Committee on Finance and Industry* (MacMillan Committee), Cmnd 3897, HMSO, June 1931.

5 See 'The UK corporate bond market', *Bank of England Quarterly Bulletin* (March 1981).

6 See 'Financing British industry', *Bank of England Quarterly Bulletin* (Sept. 1980); 'Profitability and company finance: a supplementary note', *Bank of England Quarterly Bulletin* (Jan. 1980).

7 J.R. Franks and S.D. Hodges, 'The role of leasing in capital investment', *National Westminster Bank Quarterly Review* (August 1979).

8 A.W. Henfrey, B. Albrecht and P. Richards, 'The UK stock market and the efficient market model', *Investment Analyst* (Sept. 1977).

9 *Report of the Committee to Review the Functioning of Financial Institutions* (Wilson Committee), Cmnd 7937, HMSO, June 1980.
   Report of the Committee on the Working of the Monetary System (Radcliffe Committee), Cmnd 827, HMSO, 1959.

APPENDIX 10.1
Special Financial Institutions

Most of the financial institutions in the UK have evolved from the initiatives of groups of individuals in the private sector. They perceived an opportunity within the financial sector and pursued it for reasons of personal gain or in some cases, as with the friendly societies, for collective benefit.

However, other specialist institutions have been set up by the government to meet specific requirements and to combat perceived inadequacies or weaknesses in certain sections of the markets. The identification of the Macmillan Gap led to the setting up of the Industrial and Commercial Finance Association (ICFC) in 1945; it had the specific function of providing long- and medium-term finance for small- and medium-sized companies. Loans are normally repayable over the period of the loan, typically fifteen to twenty years, at fixed rates determined by ICFC's costs of raising funds. In particularly risky circumstances, equity stakes may be taken as part of a funding package; moreover, the ICFC has the right, rarely exercised, to place a non-executive director on the board of companies in which it invests. Its commitment may vary between £5000 and £2m. It is jointly owned by the Bank of England and the London and Scottish clearing banks.

Finance Corporation for Industry was also set up in 1945, by the same interests to provide longer-term finance for larger companies. Finance For Industry (FFI) was set up in 1973 to act as a holding company for both ICFC, FCI and a number of other more specialized subsidiaries. These include Estate Duties Investment Trust (EDITH), which was set up to assist small companies with estate duties and has most of its funds in unlisted shares, and Technical Development Capital (TDC) which provides medium-term loan finance for technologically innovative businesses.

The British Technology Group was formed in 1982 to take over the roles and functions of two previously separate bodies, the National Research and Development Corporation (NRDC) and the National Enterprise Board (NEB). NRDC was originally established in 1948. It assisted the development or exploitation of inventions and provided finance for industry and trade where adequate finance was not available from other sources. This was done either through joint venture projects or via the provision of equity and loan finance. NEB had been set up in November 1975 under the Industry Act with a view to the provision of equity and loan finance to industry, in particular manufacturing industry. It also provided finance and advisory services to promote industrial restructuring. It acted as a holding company for various companies which have been acquired in the course of its activities, or transferred to it by government (British Leyland, for example).

Equity Capital for Industry (ECI) was set up in 1976 with a view to meeting an 'equity gap' in the supply of equity funds to smaller and medium listed companies. It had an initial capital of £46 million provided by a consortium of financial institutions.

There are also a number of government agencies which provide local assistance to industry. For example in 1975 the Scottish and Welsh Development Agencies (SDA) and (WDA) were set up in their respective areas. They have a brief to further economic activity, safeguard employment, assist in environmental improvement and promote industry in their respective areas. They have a wide range of financial and other powers. They can make loan and equity investments, form companies or enter into partnerships, build and make available factories, and give guarantees.

11

British Industry and its Changing Pattern

This chapter examines the structure of British industry as it is, as it has developed and as it is evolving. Study of industrial structure is interesting, not only for its own sake, but because many economists believe that theoretical linkages between perfect competition and price, and monopoly and price, are reflected in reality in company behaviour. As a consequence public policy recommendations are sometimes made to government, to nationalized industries or to government agencies such as the Monopolies and Mergers Commission which are based on inferences drawn about industrial behaviour, which in turn depend on the view that market structure affects behaviour. Although we noted in chapter 5 that a more meaningful distinction might be made between open and closed markets, and price takers and searchers, than between perfect competition and monopoly, such a distinction is less easy to apply as a generalism (even if more accurate). Consequently here and in chapter 12 we tend to use the more traditional means of measurement and analysis contained in the industrial economist's tool-kit. The first section of this chapter examines the organization of British industry. The second discusses the validity and meaningfulness of some of the measurement tools used in the descriptive section.

Industrial Structure and Morphology

When considering changes in employment, output and contribution to GDP by Standard Industrial Classification (see chapter 2) care should be exercised for at least six reasons:

1   The output growth figures are measured by a range of incompatible indices varying largely with data availability (e.g. sales, volume, and employment may be used as proxies for net output).
2   The aggregated SIC orders may disguise contrary movements within the MLHs which go to make up the orders.
3   Output variations are not traced within any two points in time studied.

Thus while mining has been in almost continuous decline for over three decades, oil has only rapidly risen since 1975.

4 Quality changes are largely, if not totally, ignored by the indices.
5 Employment data do not allow for changes in labour type or in quantity of hours worked.

Table 11.1 *Relative importance: sectors of the UK economy, 1980*

	% GDP	% employment
Agriculture, forestry and fishing	2.2	1.6
Mining and quarrying	5.6	1.5
Manufacturing	24.8	30.2
Construction	6.7	5.5
Gas, electricity and water	3.0	1.5
Transport and communication	7.9	6.6
Distributive trades	10.0	12.0
All other services	39.8	41.1
Total	100.0	100.0

Source: *Annual Abstract of Statistics*, 1982, pp. 352 and 152

Table 11.2 *Relative importance of manufacturing sector by employment: UK, 1980 (percentages)*

Food, drink and tobacco	10.0
Coal and petroleum products	0.6
Chemicals and allied industries	6.3
Metal manufacture	5.9
Mechanical engineering	12.7
Instrument engineering	2.1
Electrical engineering	10.7
Shipbuilding and marine engineering	2.3
Vehicles	10.6
Other metal goods	7.5
Textiles	6.2
Leather, leather goods and fur	0.5
Clothing and footwear	5.2
Bricks, pottery, glass, cement, etc.	3.6
Timber, furniture, etc.	3.6
Paper, printing and publishing	7.8
Other	4.4
Total	100.0

Source: *Annual Abstract of Statistics*, 1982, p. 152

6 Interdependencies between MLHs and/or SICs are ignored. Thus if
   vehicles (SIC XI) change one would expect metal manufacture (SIC VI)
   to alter in a similar direction since vehicle producers purchase large
   quantities of inputs from SIC VI.

Table 11.1 summarizes the industrial structure of the UK by net output
and by employment in 1980. Again this emphasizes the importance of the
secondary and tertiary sectors of the economy. Table 11.2 further subdivides
the manufacturing labour force by its sectoral occupation.

Table 11.3 highlights even more clearly than did the highly aggregated
figures of table 2.3 that production growth and decline are not necessarily
linked to employment changes. Technology can improve, thus dramatically
changing labour productivity for the better. Alternatively, industries may be
contracting; firms may wish to avoid declaring workers redundant (itself
costly in the short run, given statutory redundancy payments only partially
subsidized by government) to minimize the risk that if any trading downturn
is temporary then costly labour upheavals, sackings and subsequent recruit-

Table 11.3 *Relative growth rates of certain sectors of UK manufacturing
industry 1975–80 (percentage leads and lags: base 100 in 1975)*

	Production	Employment
Pharmaceutical chemicals and preparations (MLH 272)	+ 12.9	− 2.7
Synthetic resins and plastics etc. (MLH 276)	+ 22.7[a]	− 3.6
Radio and electronic components (MLH 364)	+ 49.8	− 6.9
Electronic computers (MLH 366)	+ 151.9	0
Plastic products (MLH 496)	+ 27.1	− 4.0
Bread, cakes and flour confectionery (MLH 212)	− 5.1	− 8.0
Iron castings (MLH 313)	− 37.4	− 10.1
Telegraph and telephone equipment (MLH 363)	− 15.2	+ 2.8
Electrical appliances (domestic) (MLH 368)	− 14.8	− 6.2
Motor vehicle (MLH 381)	− 14.1	− 7.9

[a] 1979

Source: Annual Abstract of Statistics, 1982, pp. 152, 153, 202 and 203

Table 11.4 *Distribution of employment by sector, 1931–80*

	1931	1951	1971	1980
Primary (agriculture, forestry and fishing; mining and quarrying)	12	9	4	3
Secondary (manufacturing, construction, gas, electricity and water)	37	44	43	37
Tertiary (transport and communication; distributive trades; other services)	51	47	53	60
Total	100	100	100	100

Source: Department of Employment Gazette, October 1975 and table 11.1 above

ment and retraining can be avoided. If this decision is taken then, of course, labour productivity falls and employment declines less rapidly than production. In the period covered by the table, however, factors such as these seem to have been less important than the shedding of labour which, by inference, was surplus to requirements.

Table 11.4, which relates to a much longer time span (1931–80), shows how dramatic has been the broad employment shift in the last 50 years. Manufacturing has remained fairly static as an employer of labour (albeit there have been significant movements within that sector). But the major shift has been from agriculture, mining, and other primary industries (1 in 8 of the employed labour force in 1931 to 1 in 33 in 1981) towards the service sector.

This is not necessarily a matter for condemnation. It is a typical pattern in most advanced economies that the tertiary sector should grow in relative importance. Sometimes it is bewailed that this is 'eroding the country's industrial base' but services can be just as important as tangible goods. Without the intangibles of distribution and insurance, many tangible manufactures would never reach the consumer. Without the intangible of advertising, many consumers would never learn of new technologies in consumer hardware such as microwave ovens or video cassette recorders. As material wealth rises people also often tend to prefer the intangible satisfaction of a holiday abroad, a symphony concert, better health care, a football match or even pop music. From the viewpoint of the consumer, social value lies in what the consumer believes the goods or the services are worth. A singer may produce a sound which vanishes the instant it is produced, but if the consumer values it sufficiently highly to pay to listen to that sound then the tertiary sector increases and is valued as productive by those members of society who pay for its use.

Table 11.5 *Share of 100 largest non-nationalized firms in manufacturing net output*

	%		%
1949	22	1963	37
1953	27	1975	40
1958	32	1977	39

Source: S.J. Prais, *The Evolution of Giant Firms in Britain*, Cambridge University Press, 1976, table 1.1; and Business Statistics Office, *Reports on the Units of Production*

Concentration in Manufacturing Industry

Not only has British industry changed significantly over the years in terms of sectoral or subsectoral importance, but so also has its organization and structure. Table 11.5 shows how in manufacturing industry (distribution is treated separately in chapter 13) the share of net output accounted for by the 100 largest firms has increased from 22 per cent after World War II to around 40 per cent in the 1970s, with the main rise occurring in the late 1950s and 1960s.

It would appear that this increase in the importance of the top 100 firms is not due to growth in the average size of plant or manufacturing establishment, however. Plants, on average, are bigger than they were, but this is not the causal feature underlying table 11.5. In table 11.6 the first column, using a method derived by Sargent Florence, shows that the median worker was employed in a plant of 480 people in 1968 (i.e. 50 per cent of all workers were in plants smaller than the 480 employees size, and 50 per cent in larger plants). The second column, using a measure evolved by S.J. Prais, indicates that 25 per cent of all workers were employed in plants of under 130 persons in 1968, and 25 per cent in plants of over 1600 employees.

Prais points out that despite this (admittedly non-spectacular plant size increase) the share of the 100 largest plants in net output only rose from 9 per cent in 1948 to 10.8 per cent in 1968. Thus the increase in net output attributed

Table 11.6 *Plant size changes in manufacturing measured by employees*

	Florence median	Prais central range
1948	340	100–1220
1958	440	120–1650
1968	480	130–1600

Source: Prais, *The Evolution of Giant Firms in Britain*, 1976, table 3.2

to the largest firms in table 11.5 probably owes far more to an increase in multiplant ownership by individual firms than to an increase in establishment size as such.

Measures of aggregate concentration must, of course, be treated with care. First, they do not necessarily reflect what is happening at the level of the individual industry. Second, the yardstick used may alter the picture somewhat (e.g. net output, employees and capital assets could all be chosen and each could give different implications as to the level of concentration). Third, the number 100 is arbitrary. The top 50 or the top 200 firms, say, may or may not have changed in importance as did the top 100. Further, no indication is given, no matter what the number chosen, to what extent the firms examined are the same firms. Some of the top 100 firms in earlier years may now be extinct as a consequence of bankruptcy or take-over, others may have shrunk and so fallen in ranking out of the top 100. Some of today's top 100, however, may not even have been in existence in earlier years; or, if they were, may have been tiny. The effect such corporate mobility has for aggregate concentration is concealed, its implications are unclear and the inferences which could or should be drawn are indefinite. And, of course, no attempt is made here to ascertain which industries are or are not subject to overseas import competition or ownership.

Tables 11.7 and 11.8 attempt to shed some more light on British industrial organization, albeit they also introduce yet additional difficulties. They show the five-firm concentration ratios for employment and net output for a range of MLH manufacturing industries and for the SIC orders respectively. *Concentration ratios* show the percentage of whatever variable is being measured which is controlled by the top few firms (in this instance five). The number of firms chosen will itself obviously influence the results.

Table 11.7 *Five-firm concentration ratios, 1975, for 118 MLH industries*

Five-firm concentration ratio (%)	Employment		Net output	
	Number of industries	Percentage of employment	Number of industries	Percentage of net output
0–19	11	14.24	11	13.69
20–39	33	25.91	29	20.28
40–59	39	30.51	38	31.40
60–79	20	22.32	23	25.05
80–100	15	7.02	17	9.59
Total	118	100.00	118	100.00

Source: M.C. Sawyer, *The Economics of Industries and Firms*, Croom Helm, 1981, table 3.2

Table 11.7 shows that neither net output nor employment is heavily concentrated in those 17 and 15 industries respectively where the top five firms control more than 80 per cent of net output and employment. Rather both net output and employment is fairly evenly spread across the middle groupings of industries, peaking where the top five firms control between 40 and 59 per cent of the relevant variables. In these industries (39 and 38) the percentage of total employment provided and of net output emanating is 30.51 and 31.4 respectively. Interestingly the groups of industries with the lowest levels of concentration have both substantially higher employment and higher net output figures than the most concentrated groupings. Although table 11.7 shows that something like 60 per cent of all employees and 66 per cent of all net output is produced in industries with five-firm concentration ratios of 40 per cent and above, it does not guide us as to which industries

Table 11.8 *Average five-firm MLH concentration levels analysed by SIC order, 1975*

Order	Industry	Number of MLH industries	Concentration ratios	
			Employment	Net output
III	Food, drink and tobacco	17	63.1	59.1
IV	Coal and petroleum products	3	61.6	66.6
V	Chemicals and allied industries	17	64.2	62.4
VI	Metal manufacturing	6	58.7	56.2
VII	Mechanical engineering	20	44.7	44.0
VIII	Instrument engineering	4	53.4	54.0
IX	Electrical engineering	12	67.6	66.5
X	Shipbuilding and marine engineering	1	50.8	49.2
XI	Vehicles	6	69.7	68.8
XII	Other metal goods	11	38.8	36.3
XIII	Textiles	16	48.6	46.8
XIV	Leather, leather goods and fur	3	20.4	20.5
XV	Clothing and footwear	9	28.7	26.1
XVI	Bricks, pottery, glass, cement, etc.	7	62.1	58.4
XVII	Timber, furniture, etc.	6	15.4	14.0
XVIII	Paper, printing and publishing	8	40.2	37.4

Source: Sawyer, *The Economics of Industries and Firms*, 1981, table 3.3

these are. Table 11.8 provides this information by SIC, and although this is much more aggregated than table 11.7 it does show the very few industries which have only low concentration levels.

Only a minority of the SIC industries have five-firm concentration ratios below 40 per cent. If the average figures in table 11.8 were adjusted or weighted for the relative importance of the MLHs, then again the results would be little altered from the crude data of the table. The industries with low levels of concentration are those particularly suited to small-scale production (e.g. SICs XIV and XVII); conversely, where mass production and heavy capital equipment are likely to favour scale economies, high concentration levels appear (e.g. SICs XI and V). In other cases high concentration is apparent where, at least at first glance, scale economies would not appear to be vitally important (e.g. SIC III).

Several comments should be made about all of these data on industrial structure. First, international statistics suggest that the UK has a more highly concentrated structure than most other countries (table 11.9 refers to comparably sized economies; the comparison with a large country like the USA would be even more extreme). Second, table 11.10 shows 30 individual industries in descending importance of market share represented by their *minimum* optimum or *efficient scale* (the MES, or where the long-run average cost curve bottoms out in relation to the quantity axis as a percentage of total market). The 'market' in the MES column is the UK home *and* export market except where indicated. A number, but by no means all, of the industries have appreciable economies of scale. However the penalty for operating at half MES is also small in many cases.

In short, in a number of cases firms may be larger, or as we saw earlier, have more plants than are apparently required to reap the benefits of scale economies (or conversely be possibly unnecessarily large to avoid the often small costs of failing to operate at MES). This emphasizes a third point: the continuing importance of small firms in the economy.

Table 11.11 shows that although compared to pre-World War II figures small firms are becoming less important, this decline ceased in the 1960s and 1970s.

Table 11.9 *Four-firm employment concentration ratios in EEC countries*

	Weighted average concentration ratio (%)			
	UK	West Germany	France	Italy
41 industries	30	19	22	19
All manufacturing industries	32	22	24	20

Source: K.D. George and T.S. Ward, *The Structure of Industry in the EEC*, Cambridge University Press, 1975, table 3.2

Table 11.10 *MES as percentage of UK market, in relation to percentage increase in total cost per unit at 50 per cent MES*

Product, etc.[a]	MES as % of market	% increase in total costs at 50% MES
Aircraft	>100	>20
Diesel engines	>100	>4
Machine tools	>100	5
Newspapers	100	20
Dyes	100	22
Turbogenerators	100	5
Computers, etc.	100	8
Steel rolling: plant	80	8
Polymer manufacture	66	5
Electric motors	60	15
Cars	50	6
Refrigerators, etc.	50	8
Oil refineries: plant	40	5
Cement: plant[b]	40	9
Bulk steel production: plant	33	5−10
Bread: plant[b]	33	15
Polymer extrusion: plant	33	7
Sulphuric acid: plant	30	1
Cylinder blocks: plant	30	10
Ethylene: plant	25	9
Detergents: plant	20	2.5
Bicycles	10	(small)
Beer: plant[b]	6	9
Bricks: plant[b]	5	25
Warp knitting: plant	3	(small)
Cotton textile: plant	2	(small)
Book printing: plant	2	(small)
Plastics: plant	1	(small)
Engineering castings: plant	0.2	5
Footwear: plant	0.2	2

[a] Unless a plant is specified, 'product' refers to one type, model or range of models
[b] Serving regional submarket

Source: A. Silberston, 'Economics of scale in theory and practice', *Economic Journal*, 82 (1972), pp. 369–91

Table 11.11 *Small firms in manufacturing*

Year	Number (% of total)	Net output (% of total)	Employment (% of total)
1935	97	35	38
1958	94	20	24
1963	94	16	20
1968	94	16	19
1970	95.1	21.2	18.4
1971	95.3	20.9	17.8
1972	95.3	21.5	18.7

The figures above and below the line are not computed on comparable bases
A 'small firm' is defined as one employing under 200 people

Source: P.S. Johnson, 'Policies towards small firms: time for caution', *Lloyds Bank Review* (1978), pp. 1−11

Table 11.12 stresses even more than tables 11.6−11.11 just how important the small plant (if not the small firm) continues to be in UK industry. In 9 industries out of 16, small establishments are responsible for over 40 per cent of total employment (on average the figure is 36.5 per cent). In some industries, where technical scale economies are obviously unimportant, the figure exceeds 60 per cent. Conversely, in only 5 of the 16 industries do large units account for more than 40 per cent of total employment, and in only 2, shipbuilding and marine engineering and vehicles, do the large units account for more than 60 per cent of industry employment. Thus again our initial view that British industry appears to be concentrated at the firm rather than the plant level is substantiated. When large plants exist they appear to do so in industries where technical scale economies would be important. Large firms, therefore, must exist either to facilitate reconciliation of the optima of the five Robinsonian criteria (see chapter 6), or for reasons not yet fully discussed, such as the wish to acquire monopoly power, or to obtain as yet unrealized scale economy benefits at plant level. Given international comparisons, such as those of table 11.9, and the evidence of table 11.10, the last reason may be less likely than variants of the other two.

Industrial Structure: its Measurement and Meaning

There are several problems involved in the measurement of aspects of industrial structure, and indeed a range of different variables to measure in any

Table 11.12 *Small establishments in manufacturing, 1976: relative importance to total employment (%)*

	Total	Small units (under 200 employees)	Large units (1000 or more employees)
All manufacturing industry	100.0	36.5	29.0
Food, drink and tobacco	10.2	29.4	27.8
Coal and petroleum products	0.5	19.2	42.0
Chemicals and allied industries	5.3	25.4	34.8
Metal manufacture	6.7	21.4	47.6
Mechanical engineering	12.8	40.4	23.3
Instrument engineering	2.1	40.7	21.1
Electrical engineering	9.6	20.6	42.8
Shipbuilding and marine engineering	2.5	16.9	67.2
Vehicles	10.4	5.3	69.6
Other metal goods	7.2	56.4	9.8
Textiles	7.0	43.2	12.4
Leather, leather goods and fur	0.6	82.2	0.0
Clothing, footwear	5.6	63.4	2.6
Bricks, pottery, glass, cement, etc.	3.4	41.6	16.4
Timber, furniture, etc.	3.7	76.8	1.4
Paper, printing and publishing	7.6	46.4	16.0

Source: Annual Abstract of Statistics, 1980, p. 166

case. We will discuss the following: costs; monopoly power; competition; vertical integration; and diversification.

Costs

In the discussion above we inferred that an industry's minimum efficient scale on MES was important. Figure 11.1 illustrates how even if unit costs are the same, the level of MES and the way in which it is achieved can have considerable impact on an industry or firm. Minimum unit costs in each of industries X, Y and Z are C_1, but whereas eight firms could operate in X after achieving full scale economies, only two could in Y and Z. If the firms in Y and Z were only large enough to produce output Q_1, those in Y would operate at a unit cost of C_2, only slightly above C_1; yet the firms in Z would incur a much greater cost penalty in having to operate at C_3.

Clearly bodies such as the Monopolies and Mergers Commission are interested in how estimates of MES can be arrived at. There are three main

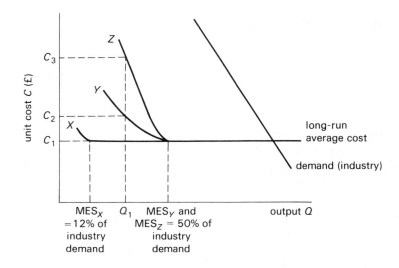

Figure 11.1 *Costs and minimum efficient scale*

methods of arriving at the data underlying a firm's or industry's long-run average cost (*LRAC*) curve.

First, there is *statistical cost analysis* whereby differing sizes of plants are compared at any one time. A number of problems must be overcome, however, if the results are to have credibility. The financial accounts of the firms to be compared must be uniform. Depreciation policies, for example, must be similar. Factor prices should be identical, a difficult requirement if a plant in Scotland is being compared with one in the South-East. Labour costs in Scotland may be lower but fuel prices may be higher. Each firm should be operating with the most efficient known methods. Perhaps most important of all, each firm should be operating in an equilibrium position on their short-run average cost curves, not on their long-run ones. Short-run costs will be confused with long in the analysis. The statistician cannot even assume that, given a sufficiently large sample, at any one output level short-run costs will be evenly distributed round the long run and so the error will be averaged out. Short-run costs can exceed, but cannot possibly be less than, long-run average costs at any one output level (see figure 6.1).

Second, long-run costs can be estimated by the *engineering technique*. This is based on hypothetical estimations made by those with a knowledge of the production technology involved. Optimal input combinations are estimated for given quantities and the cost curve is found by applying to these data the relevant input prices. The technique is none the worse for being based on hypothetical data. Its accuracy may be questioned, however. Often scale economies or diseconomies cannot be envisaged until a given scale of operations is empirically operated. The subsequent 'scaling-up' problems chemical engineers have when moving from pilot plant to full-scale factory operation are ample testimony of this assertion.

Both of these techniques are further complicated by the presence of multi-product firms. The problem of apportioning joint costs must too often be solved in an arbitrary fashion.

Finally, there is the *survivor technique* developed by George Stigler. In essence this involves classifying the firms in an industry by size and calculating the share of industry output or capacity provided by each class over time. Size classes whose share increases over time are deemed to be more efficient and to have lower average costs, and vice versa. This technique does not give the precise level of money costs, it shows only the shape of the long-run average cost curve. It presupposes that all size classes of firms face the same economic environment; that they have the same objectives; and, unless technology has been constant over time, that they have been equally adept at introducing and assimilating new techniques. Since the survivor technique is used over time the LRAC inferred does comply with the unchanging technology assumption of cost theory.

Monopoly power

When governments examine industrial firms they like to know to what extent the firms have monopoly or market power. We will now examine some common indices of this; none of them is flawless.

Lerner Index

Under traditional perfect competition the Lerner index, or price:cost ratio, equals zero. It is calculated as $(P - MC)/P$ (P is price, MC is marginal cost). In conditions of monopoly it is positive, and the larger the index, it is presumed, the larger is the firm's degree of monopoly power. However, the index depends partly on price elasticity which, although determined in turn partially by industry structure, is also dependent on the nature of the good sold. Second, the index also depends on the level of costs. High marginal costs could give a low index even if monopoly power was great. Third, the index ignores market size. The index might be low for Sainsbury and high for the corner grocer in a suburban housing estate, yet the market power of each is very different. Fourth, it depends on traditional perfect competition theory yet, as we saw, if entry is free and if demand is downward sloping, price can equal average cost and be well above marginal cost, and no monopoly power need be present.

Cross-elasticity of demand

Cross-elasticity of demand is high in conditions of perfect competition and very low in conditions of monopoly. The more acceptable are substitutes, the higher is the index. Note that this measure depends on the acceptability of substitutes to consumers, not on their numbers. But again it rests on traditional theory. If markets are closed rather than open, even if they are 'near-perfect' by other traditional measures, then monopoly power can be high if all suppliers can take or get a price high relative to costs. Regulation-protected industries such as taxi-drivers or chartered accountants could fall into this category.

Ratio of profit rates to interest rates

This index rests on the assumption that, under perfectly competitive conditions, accounting profits are merely the normal return on interest rate on the capital employed in the business. In such circumstances the ratio would equal zero and would become increasingly large as the firm approached monopoly with larger and larger monopoly profits. It ignores the implications of X-inefficiency (that is, operating at less than lowest technological and managerial costs), and it ignores the possibility that supra-normal profits can arise for reasons, such as risk bearing or innovation, other than monopoly.

Concentration ratios

There are a variety of different methods of measuring concentration. One of the commonest is to measure the percentage of some index of industry size (e.g. sales, assets, employment) which is in the hands of the three (or five) largest firms (see earlier in this chapter). The larger the ratio the more monopolistic is the industry. An alternative is to measure the number of the industry's largest firms which account for a given percentage of industry size. The smaller is this number the more concentrated is the industry.

Such measures fail to indicate the differences in industrial behaviour which can occur as a result of differences in the remaining number of firms in an industry. They do not indicate whether the 'tail' of firms is composed of a few medium-sized firms or a plethora of small ones. In like manner, they do not indicate whether the top three firms themselves are of similar size or are composed of one giant and two small firms. These problems can be partially overcome with the use of more information, such as *cumulative share curves*.

Table 11.13 shows the approximate standards given by Bain for concentration in manufacturing industries. The zone of moderate concentration is shown in figure 11.2, together with three hypothetical cumulative share curves. The curves enable comparisons to be made between industries (A, B or C) or between different points in time for one industry (where A, B and C are points in time). They show the concentration ratios firm by firm from one through to the total number of firms in the industry. The firms are ranked along the horizontal axis from the largest to the smallest, cumulatively, until the share of all firms (namely 100 per cent) is reached. Clearly B and C are more highly concentrated than A. C is more concentrated than B only at certain levels of numbers of firms (e.g. at the 5- or 10-firm concentration ratios). After 14 firms the situation is reversed; in B the smaller firms have a

Table 11.13 *Concentration standards for manufacturing industries*

Percentage of market occupied by the first four firms	Percentage of market occupied by the first eight firms	Degree of concentration
75% or more	90% or more	Very high
65–75%	85–90%	High
50–65%	70–85%	Moderately high
35–50%	45–70%	Moderately low
under 35%	under 45%	Low

Source: J.S. Bain, *Industrial Organisation*, Wiley, 1967, pp. 137–44

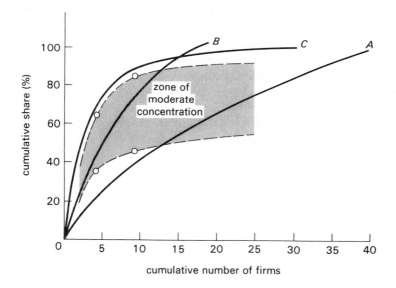

Figure 11.2 *Concentration: cumulative shares*

larger share than in *C* and there are fewer of them. *A* would not be regarded as a highly concentrated industry whereas *C* would; *B* is moderately concentrated, at least up to the 12-firm level.

An alternative measure of concentration which takes account of the total number of firms in an industry (and hence is called a summary concentration index) is the *Herfindahl concentration ratio*. It focuses on the inequality of firm sizes, or relative concentration, as opposed to the absolute concentration ratios we have looked at so far. It is equal to $(c^2 + 1)/n$, where c is the coefficient of variation of firm sizes and n the number of firms in the industry. When all firms in an industry are of equal size the standard deviation of firm sizes equals zero and so the index equals $1/n$. If there is only one firm in an industry, the standard deviation is again zero and the index reaches a maximum value of unity.

The same (numerical) result can be obtained for the Herfindahl index by summing the squares of the (decimal) values of the market shares of each firm. The Herfindahl index, however, although attempting to account for differences in firm size, is still heavily weighted towards larger firms. (The square of the market share of a firm with 1 per cent of the market is $0.01^2 = 0.0001$.) Adding this to the overall value of the index will make very little difference. In fact, because of this the Herfindahl index is often inverted to obtain the so-called *number equivalent* index: that is, the hypothetical number of firms of equal size which could produce the industry's output and have the same Herfindahl index as the actual number of firms. Thus if a Herfindahl index of 0.2 is calculated, the numbers equivalent is five, since five firms, with 20 per cent of the market each, would also result in a Herfindahl index of this value ($0.2^2 \times 5 = 0.04 \times 5 = 0.2$).

A more obvious way to obtain a relative measure of concentration (also graphical but less ambiguous than cumulative share curves) is to use a *Lorenz curve* as in figure 11.3. Unlike cumulative share curves the Lorenz curve for one industry will not intersect with that for another. This is because of the difference in method of construction of the two curves. The vertical axis is identical, but the horizontal axis is the cumulative proportion of firms in the industry, not the absolute numbers.

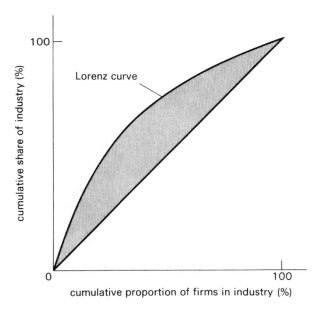

Figure 11.3 *Concentration: Lorenz curves*

Thus curves *B* and *C* in figure 11.2 would have common starting and finishing points; their curvature might differ but they would not cross. If all firms are of equal size then the Lorenz curve is the straight diagonal running from bottom left to top right in figure 11.3. The greater the curvature the greater the inequality in firm sizes. The shaded area can be measured by the *Gini coefficient*; this ranges from zero in cases of complete equality to unity when firms are completely unequal in size (i.e. a single-seller monopoly with only one firm plotted in the group in the extreme top left-hand corner). The Gini coefficient is the ratio of the shaded area to the total triangle above the diagonal. Clearly it takes no account of firm numbers. Thus 2 firms of equal size and 100 firms of equal size could all be plotted on the diagonal and the coefficient in both cases would be zero.

Competition

We have already noted that while monopoly and perfect competition are regarded as opposites, the use of the words themselves is misleading. Moreover, since the measures of monopoly described earlier are imperfect, their use as measures of rivalry (as opposed to perfect competition) will also be misleading, possibly more so. Two measures of firm rivalry are the rank correlation coefficient and the Hymer–Pashigian index. Again both of those have faults, but they do shed further light on industrial structure, particularly inter-firm rivalry from a dynamic viewpoint.

A measure of firm turnover (such as the *rank correlation coefficient*) looks at an industry at two points in time. All the firms in the industry are ranked by size in descending order (something like a sports league table) at the opening of the period and again at the close. They are awarded numbers 1, 2, 3 and so on from the leader downwards. The rank correlation coefficient is then calculated.

If the ranking positions of the firms are unchanged a coefficient of $+1.0$ would be obtained (the implication is that the industry is uncompetitive). The more movement there is in the positioning of the firms the lower is the calculated coefficient and the more competitive the market is deemed to be (the possible values range from -1.0 to $+1.0$). However, while changes in the rank of a firm can be meaningful in economic terms, they need not be. Certainly if a change in rank implies a substantial change in firm size or market share then it may well have meaning. But if there is any tendency for firms in a market to bunch together in size then rank change measures are meaningless. Alternatively, a market can undergo changes of great economic importance but experience no change in firm ranking. For example, a two-firm industry (a duopoly) composed of firms *A* and *B*, where *A* had 51 per cent of the market and *B* 49 per cent, would produce a rank correlation coefficient of unity even if *A*'s share rose to 99 per cent and *B*'s fell to 1 per cent. Another defect of the index is that it ignores differences in economic importance between the leading and lagging firms. The 'tail' of small firms may influence the calculated coefficient, but it is what is happening between the large firms (or to them if small ones are growing) which matters.

The *Hymer–Pashigian* or *instability index* takes account of all firms, even the smallest, but is only affected by them if they grow substantially. Equally it is only sensitive to the presence of large firms if they experience significant size changes. It is calculated between two points in time by subtracting each firm's share of the industry from its corresponding share at the later or earlier period (whichever is the larger). The differences are then summed. The higher the value of the index the more unstable and hence the more competitive is the market. To illustrate, consider again a duopoly where *A* and *B* exchanged ranking but simply moved from a 51:49 to a 49:51 relationship. The rank correlation coefficient would register unity (negatively), the most 'competitive' value. The instability index would register 4. Conversely, had the market shares changed instead from 51:49 to 99:1 the rank correlation coefficient would be + 1.0, implying no ranking change, while the instability index would have a value of 96 (as against 4) implying a very high degree of economic change.

Finally, irrespective of the measure of monopoly or competition, what are the factors to be borne in mind when selecting the variable to measure firm size? Absolute concentration ratios measured by fixed assets are often higher than ratios measured by sales, for the same industries. This reflects the fact that larger firms tend to be more capital intensive than smaller.

The ratio of assets (and employment) to sales will be higher the more vertically integrated is the firm examined. Thus, unless all firms in an industry are equally vertically integrated, asset, employment and value-added concentration ratios will differ from the sales concentration ratios, and will reflect vertical aspects of firm size as well as horizontal aspects. These two concepts of size are best kept separate. Similarly, when a firm is diversified, sales or value-added concentration ratios are preferable to employment or asset measures. The latter inputs would require to be arbitrarily allocated in some way between industries.

Vertical integration

The degree to which an industry is vertically integrated can be measured in at least three ways.

Ratio of value added to sales

Value added (i.e. sales less expenditures for raw materials, fuel and power) to sales will be higher the greater the number of productive stages carried out by the firm. However, input and output price changes will alter the value of the index. Second, other things being equal, a more profitable firm will have a higher ratio than a less profitable one. The index will also be lower, other things being equal, at later stages of production than at earlier, since sales figures will be higher at each successive stage. It is really only of value when comparing firms in the same industry, at the same stage of the productive process, facing the same input and output prices.

Ratio of inventory values to sales

The rationale for this index is that the greater the number of successive stages performed by a firm the greater will be the value of stocks carried. This assumption is not altogether realistic if vertical integration permits economizing on stockholding. Also it is dependent on the levels of both input and output prices.

Degree of dependence on input and output markets

An example of this index as a measure of backward integration is the ratio of interfirm purchases or transfers at a particular stage to total inputs used at that stage. To gauge forward integration total interfirm transfers of output at a particular stage would be expressed as a proportion of total output at that stage. These ratios will be invariant with input and output price changes since both numerator and denominator involve the use of the same price. Alternatively, volume rather than value data could be used. The main problems will arise around the definition of a 'stage' in the productive process.

Diversification

Here two main methods are in common use.

Ratio of non-primary output to total output

The higher is this ratio the more diversified is the firm. The drawback with it as an index is that no indication is given as to whether non-primary output is divided between several industries or confined to only one.

Straight count of industries in which the firm operates

This overcomes the objection to the previous measure but may give undue weight to many activities which account for only a small proportion of the firm's total business. An alternative or additional measure is to use a composite index, such as the arithmetic product of the non-primary output ratio and the straight count. The danger with composite indices, at least if used in isolation, is that they may conceal more than they reveal. For example, a composite index of 3 would be obtained for a firm with a ratio of non-primary to total output of 1:10 and a straight count of 30 industries, as well as for a firm with a ratio of 1:2 and a straight count of 6 industries.

Conclusion

This chapter has given a broad brush picture of the structure of industry in Britain. In addition to the statistical description, measurement tools which can be used to probe further into the nature of industrial organization have been detailed. The next two chapters leave this broad canvas to concentrate on government-owned industries and on retail and distribution industries respectively.

12

The Public Sector

In the previous chapter we studied British industry in general and measures of its monopoly power or lack of it. However, the public sector was not explicitly examined; this omission is now rectified.

There are two main reasons for treating the public sector separately. First, it occupies a large portion of the economy but does not always have to adhere to the pressures of the investor or the consumer in the market-place as does the private sector. Second, nationalized industries are frequently monopolies. As a consequence governments can and do resort to economic theory to derive controls for them. Some of the problems this inevitably raises are discussed in the following pages.

The Public Sector

The government-owned sector of British industry is a somewhat heterogeneous collection of operations. The state owns shares (directly or indirectly) in the Bank of England, British Petroleum, Cable and Wireless Ltd, Leyland, British Aerospace and others. Share ownership in these operations is due variously: to a *de jure* formalization of a *de facto* situation (as with the Bank of England's nationalization); to Sir Winston Churchill's desire to secure strategic oil supplies in the inter-war years (in the case of BP); to a government 'rescue' of a near-bankrupt concern (Leyland); and to the Labour Party's constitutional view (clause 4) that all the means of production should be state owned (British Aerospace). In all of these cases return of ownership to members of the public as individuals requires no more upheaval (for the consumer's management and workers of the industry) than the sale of the shares. Indeed both a Labour and a Conservative government have sold off shares in BP, and a Conservative one shares in British Aerospace and Cable and Wireless.

More traditionally, the government also 'owns' the British Broadcasting Corporation (BBC), the Post Office, British Telecommunications, the National Coal Board, the gas, electricity and railway industries and British Airways.

The BBC received a Royal Charter in 1925 and became financed out of licence fees. Its first Director General was J.C.W. (later Lord) Reith. Reith was a strong advocate of the BBC's monopoly of broadcasting, which he argued (to the Crawford Committee which recommended the BBC's establishment) was 'essential ethically' in order 'to give the public what we think they need (since) few know what they want and very few what they need'. The monopoly remained unchallenged until the advent of commercial television three decades later. The reason for the monopoly was one of history rather than of any malicious intent to centrally control a propaganda machine. Communication (i.e. the postal service) was a traditional government monopoly. Cable communications, telephones and wireless, as competitors to letter post were immediately seen as a threat by the General Post Office (GPO). Licences for transmitting private wireless messages had consequently to be obtained. The first general broadcasts in Britain were made in 1922 and were transmitted by private enterprise firms (e.g. General Electric, British Thomson–Houston, Metropolitan–Vickers, Western Electric Radio Communications, and Marconi, the last having initiated broadcasting in this country in 1920 by transmitting Dame Nellie Melba's voice). The infant industry was referred to the Imperial Communications Commission; the Postmaster General complained about 'wavelength shortages' and 'interference with major communications' and with 'genuine work'. All of this sounds reminiscent of the debates over commercial TV, commercial radio in the 1970s, citizens' band radio and cable TV in the early 1980s. The Commission never reported to the public but the Postmaster General informed the House of Commons that he accepted its recommendations. The Crawford Committee's recommendations three years later presumably fulfilled all the Post Office's aspirations.

The Post Office itself developed out of Henry VIII's appointment of a Master of the Posts in 1516. This established a regular service along the main roads for official purposes (the Royal Mail). Inevitably unofficial correspondence was also carried, and in 1627 the system was laid open to the public for payment of an appropriate fee. Private and municipal posts were suppressed along the royal routes and a monopoly established. Although private carriers were still permitted on the highways not covered by the royal system, they too are now prohibited under the Post Office's statutory monopoly. That they would not reappear is, puzzlingly, an argument used by the Post Office for the continuance of this monopoly; why they would not, or why some more modern form of personal communications such as teletext machines would not emerge if unimpeded, is left unexplained.

The most overtly state-owned industries are the nationalized industries of coal, gas, steel, the railways, some road transport and the state airline. Here the industries were all radically restructured after nationalization (separate private or municipal firms were merged and reorganized internally, and control tended to be vested in central, unitary boards of management). The ownership is not simply one of holding shares in one or more firms in an industry (as with BP) and so being able to buy or sell such shares with minimal disturbance to the firm or industry in question. Rather, as long as ownership (generally vested in a statutory corporation) persists, there is a presumption that all final policy decisions will be taken by Her Majesty's Government and that the government has the expertise to so take. In practice the government has been closely involved not only with the nationalized industries' strategy but on occasion with their tactics as well. In addition their organizational structure was determined by the act of nationalization, or subsequent amendment, and the form of legal ownership makes it considerably more difficult for the government to withdraw. For example, the National Freight Corporation, comprising Pickfords, British Road Services, and other divisions had first to be turned into a public limited company; arrangements had to be made with banks for part loans to purchasers of the new shares before it could be sold in 1982 to individual citizens (in this case the managers and employees of the firm itself). Similar complicated legal manoeuvres were required for the partial sale of British Aerospace shares in 1981, and of the Gleneagles Hotel Group Ltd (formerly part of British Rail) in the same year. In these cases bank loans were not required since the shares were floated in the normal manner, but in the latter case the hotels in question had to be organizationally disentangled from the remaining railway hotels.

So much for the difficulties of denationalization relative to buying and selling existing shares. But why does nationalization occur? As mentioned above, nationalization is a political matter. Of the four main national UK political parties, Conservative, Labour, Liberal and Social Democrat, one, the Labour Party, is committed to nationalization in its official constitution. The late Hugh Gaitskell, leader of the Labour Party, wrote in a Fabian Tract in 1956 that nationalization has four main objectives: to encourage social equality; to ensure that the means of production are fully used to the best advantage; to promote industrial democracy through community ownership of capital and the power that allegedly goes with it; and to encourage co-operation in society. On the first point, Gaitskell argued that equality is promoted, although not greatly, by personal ownership of government stocks rather than company shares. The interest gained is presumably smaller than dividends received from profits (but larger than no dividends from losses). Taxation, not nationalization, makes it more difficult to make large fortunes. Similarly large capital gains are less probable. At the employer level top salaries can be held down, but again Gaitskell did not feel that this was particularly efficacious in achieving the goal of equality. (The cynical view is now held in most nationalized industries that if you pay peanuts to managers you get monkeys.) On the second point, Gaitskell argued that macro-economic management had reached such a level of sophistication that while nationalization might facilitate full employment, other tools might accomplish it also and possibly more effectively. On the third issue, Gaitskell, while approving of a diffusion of decision-making, argues that 'nobody can say that the decisions (so taken) must always be better.' Finally, Gaitskell conceded that 'no very noticeable general change among employees to a less materialistic outlook' has yet emerged.

Gaitskell's reasons for being lukewarm about the traditional arguments for nationalization may have been strengthened or weakened by the experiences of the thirty years since he made his analysis. But the arguments, with or without the benefit of hindsight, are largely political in nature; we will leave them to the reader's own judgement. More importantly, when the activity of nationalization was at its height (1945–50) Labour Party spokesmen relied less on socialist rhetoric and more on economic persuasion. They asserted that nationalization was the best way to achieve bigger production, greater efficiency and protection against the harm of monopoly. Whether or not this is the case is something which should, in principle, be economically measurable.

Unfortunately most of the industries nationalized were immediately reorganized on a more or less monolithic basis, and certainly as monopolies (albeit state owned and not owned by members of the public). But this raises the problem of judging whether consumers are getting the goods and services they want at the prices they are willing to pay. Since there are no alternative sources of supply for customers to transfer their patronage to if they are dissatisfied, the question remains unanswered. So too does the question about production efficiency. If a monopoly is not subdivided in some way it is difficult if not impossible to tell whether costs are or are not being minimized. There is no standard of comparison. In short the economic arguments for nationalization can only be tested against the market criteria of competition and consumer choice. This implies decentralization. It does not, of course, require denationalization.

The same arguments apply in the market for capital loans as in the market for goods and services. How does one decide whether an industry or firm should be deprived of investment funds or supplied with additional capital? The answer lies in how satisfactorily it satisfies the lender (i.e. in the provision of profits, interest or dividends: the nomenclature is unimportant). This in turn depends on the ability to satisfy the concern's ultimate consumers of its goods and services. When the lender is government, however, return on capital is only one of many criteria to be satisfied. Voters' preferences (not overall but in particular sections of society) must be satisfied. Public opinion and trades unions must be heeded (again not overall but sectionally). These sectional pressures may well exert more influence on decisions affecting dispersal of government investment funds than return on capital reflecting consumer wants. This is so since consumers have low-intensity, short-lived interests in everything, whereas sectional groups have deep and vociferous concern about one or a small number of issues. Such groups can then exert an influence disproportionate to their number and do so on explicit issues. Although in aggregate the population at large may disagree with them there is little it can do. Examples of such groups are the managers and trade unions in the nationalized industries themselves. Thus a given industry may well be expanded (and as a corollary, in a non-growth market some other sections of the economy must be contracted) if, say, one such group can persuade the relevant bureaucrats and politicians to grant their wishes. The civil servants and politicians themselves, of course, are not wholly altruistic but have as goals the expansion and security of their own careers, which again need not reflect the desire of consumers.

Why then do economists still tend to favour nationalization (or in America regulation) in certain industries? The answer lies in that fact that some industries are *natural monopolies*. As a consequence no one firm could be large enough to exhaust all the scale economies available from expansion. The industry tends, therefore, to be monopolized and governments can then instruct nationalized (or regulated) industries to behave 'as if' they were perfectly competitive by setting prices equal to marginal costs and appraising investments according to a required rate of return. Examples of this type of government-required behaviour are provided in recent White Papers.[1,2]

Littlechild argues that the approach has failed since it assumes that outputs and technologies are 'given'. There is no incentive to change, and the 'perfect competitive' framework is thus inapposite.[3] Second, as pointed out above, managers, civil servants, politicians and trade unions have their own objectives including smooth (not necessarily efficient) running of their industry, avoidance of bad publicity and so on. Instructions to price at marginal costs on investment appraisal then become either irrelevant or are ignored.

We will look first at the theory of natural monopoly and then at the outcome in some UK nationalized industries.

Natural Monopoly and Pricing Policy

We have already used the term price searchers (chapter 5). One reason for their existence was economies of scale, i.e. (up to a point) a larger firm can produce goods at a lower unit cost than a smaller. When a single firm can do this and do so at a lower unit cost than any larger number of firms the situation is called natural monopoly. Consequently only one firm will survive. Two problems occur. Entry to the industry is extremely unlikely and there is only one seller. If left to its own devices the firm would be in the situation of figure 12.1(a), where its demand curve and the industry demand curve coincide and where it would choose the profit-maximizing price and output of P' and Q' at marginal revenue equal to marginal cost ($MR = MC$).

This has two unattractive results. In contrast with price takers (but in common with other price searchers) price exceeds marginal cost. When this is so, too little of the good is being produced in the sense that the value consumers place on having one more unit is greater than the additional cost of producing more. Whatever price is set, consumers adjust their purchases so that the marginal value they place on the last unit they buy is just equal to the price they pay for it. Since that is above marginal cost, the marginal value

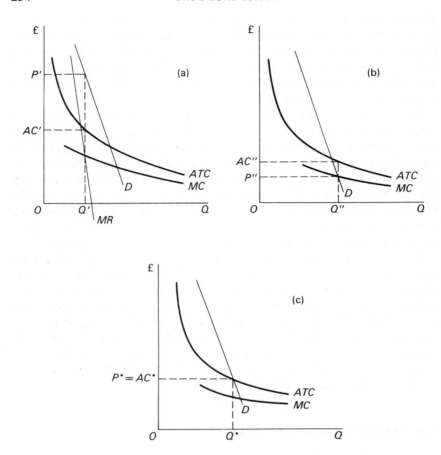

Figure 12.1 *(a) Profit maximization of a natural monopolist*
(b) Price equals marginal cost 'solution'
(c) Price equals average cost 'solution'

placed on the good by consumers is greater than the marginal values they
place on goods they buy instead and which would be forgone and not bought
if more of the good were produced (i.e. the marginal cost). Resources are not
going to their highest-valued uses.

The second result with an unnationalized or unregulated natural monopoly
is that the firm is making economic or supra-normal profits (rectangle
$(P' - AC') \times (Q' - O)$ in figure 12.1(a)). In both price-taker and price-
searcher cases, when there is free entry, these are eliminated. But in the
extreme case of natural monopoly, entry would only occur if the potential
entrant expected to drive the incumbent out of business; the cycle would then
recommence.

To cope with those problems, economists have proposed two alternatives.
The first held its greatest sway in the nationalized industries from 1967 to

1978. To solve the problem of price above marginal cost, the industry was forced to charge price equal to marginal cost (figure 12.1(b)). The problems with this approach are several. First, average total cost (*ATC*) is falling and so the firm must operate at a loss since by definition *MC* will be less than *ATC*. (The loss is the rectangle (*AC″* − *P″*) × (*Q″* − *O*).) Taxes must therefore be levied in order to subsidize the industry. But the taxes will rarely, if ever, be raised on the industry's consumers but rather on society as a whole. This leads to inequity. The subsidies themselves encourage managerial and worker inefficiency since neither the carrot of profit nor the stick of losses will be present, and no yardstick is available to assess what the minimum-loss, lowest-level *ATC* is. Second, and a related point, since the *ATCs* of comparable well-run firms are unknown, the *MC* is even harder to determine, and so the objective of setting price equal to *MC* is rarely attained and was, not surprisingly, also rarely attempted.

Alternatively, the firm could be instructed to earn zero economic profit and set price equal to *ATC* (figure 12.1(c)). This means that the industry will then be earning an accounting profit equal to but no more than that which it would earn in a non-monopolistic setting. Before 1967, and since 1978, government White Papers have leant towards this approach to the regulation of the nationalized industries. The problems are that price is now above *MC*, although by no means as much as in figure 12.1(a), and that it is again difficult to ensure that managers are diligent and innovative and have an incentive to cut costs.

Efficiency in the Nationalized Industries[4]

Tests of efficiency are many and varied when the normal profit criteria are lacking. Indeed by normal accounting standards the performance of the nationalized industries has been abysmal in most instances.[5] Losses are the order of the day.

Have they been able to meet demand at a price the consumer is prepared to pay? This question is only meaningful where the industry does not have a monopoly. Otherwise the price chosen by the industry may be so low that waiting lists arise because people value the product more highly than it costs to produce. On the other hand, the price may be so high that the waiting lists disappear but consumers would buy the product if the price was lower (figure 12.1(a)). Table 12.1 suggests that the nationalized industries have not achieved the target of meeting consumer wants.

Thus nationalized industries are unequivocally less preferred by consumers when there are alternative sources of supply available. But do they use the least possible quantity of resources to produce what they do produce? In table 12.2 labour productivity changes are shown to be below those of all manufacturing industry except for the 'expected' industries of gas (the advent of natural gas), airways (wide-bodied jets), telecommunications (advancing electronic technology permitting direct subscriber trunk dialling

Table 12.1 *Market share changes by non-monopolistic nationalized industries*

	1968	1976
British Steel Corporation (BSC) (sales as % of domestic market deliveries)	106	87
Volume of traffic carried by: The National Freight Corporation Private hauliers (1968 = 100)	100 100	90 125
Sales and installation of electrical appliances by: Electricity boards' showrooms Other electrical goods shops (1968 = 100)	100 100	139 181
Sales revenue of BR shipping division	100	100
Sales revenue of European Ferries and the B & I line (BR = 100)	58	124

Source: R. Pryke, 'Public enterprise in practice', pp. 216–17, in W.J. Baumol (ed.), *Public and Private Enterprise in a Mixed Economy*, International Economic Association, 1981

Table 12.2 *Percentage growth per annum in productivity per worker*

	1968–73	1971–76
British Airways	7.8	8.7
British Gas	10.9	8.1
Telecommunications	7.8	6.8
BR	2.6	−1.7
Electricity boards	8.8	3.2
BSC	2.5	−1.6
NCB: deep-mined coal	—	−1.3
National Freight Corporation	4.0	2.3
Postal services	−1.4	−1.8
National and Scottish bus groups	2.2	1.5
Manufacturing	4.3	2.9

Source: Pryke, 'Public enterprise in practice', p. 218

(STD)) and electricity generation (the bringing on stream of highly capital-intensive generating systems). Indeed, in the later period railways, steel, coal and the postal services have not only lower labour efficiency than the private sector, but also a declining rate of productivity.

Pryke argues that over-manning (brought about by a combination of trade union stubbornness and/or managerial inefficiency) is responsible for much of the decline. (Only British Airways did not suffer a productivity decline in the periods examined in table 12.2, and by comparison with British Caledonian and overseas carriers it is itself notoriously overstaffed.)

For example, since 1968 the NCB have been introducing more and more mechanical tunnelling and retreat mining (i.e. instead of leaving in artificial props or pillars of coal to hold the roof up, all the coal is removed by mechanized cutters, which retreat, and the roof is allowed to collapse). Despite this, productivity has declined. A study in 1976 showed that miners spent only 1.75 hours at work, one-third of an available shift. Pryke blames this on lack of motivation following the abolition of piece-work from 1966. Between 1971 and 1977 the NCB eventually renegotiated productivity payments in the face of stiff union opposition.

BR likewise is seen by Pryke as highly inefficient. 'Firemen' are carried on diesel and electric trains. Guards are present on passenger trains with power-operated doors and, until recently, on automatic braking trains. Where they are essential (goods trains with loose coupled wagons and so with no automatic brake) comparison with European railways shows that such trains disappeared from Europe in the 1930s. Likewise Pryke sees ticket collectors as unnecessary. Guards could do the job on Inter-City routes, and automatic ticket barriers on suburban ones (as is the practice on the railways of other countries). Indeed, the 1982 rail strike with the firemen's union (ASLEF) took place over issues of manning flexibility.

BSC produces less steel per man-shift than foreign steel works of comparable size and technology. According to Pryke, 'one important reason is that demarcation lines' imposed by trade unions are far stricter. Similarly in the Post Office, although improved methods of sorting mail were devised in the 1960s, management has been unable to implement them owing to union opposition (this includes even such simple devices as the employment of part-time staff at particular 'peak' times of day).

As a consequence of low and declining inefficiency the industries have raised their prices more rapidly than the private manufacturing industry average in an attempt to meet their statutory requirements. Only gas (the advent of natural gas), the airways (outside competition) and telecommunications (reduced labour inputs owing to direct dialling and associated advances) were able to or had to buck this trend. Electricity generation price increases were almost identical with the average inflation rate. For the electricity generation industry, partly because labour is a small part of generation costs, capital costs are dominant; however, this benefit was offset by the dramatic increase in the price of coal, which the generating boards are

Table 12.3 *Prices and earnings: percentage changes 1968–76*

	Prices	Average weekly earnings of manual workers
NCB: deep-mined coal	295.5	226.9
BSC: iron and steel	227.1	229.1
British Gas	51.9	220.4
British electricity boards	142.5	241.9
BR	160.3	197.6
National and Scottish bus groups	193.6	213.2
National Freight Corporation	182.6	—
BA	78.6	172.3
Postal services	276.6 ⎱	
Telecommunications	125.0 ⎰	200.8
Manufacturing	144.3	187.2

Source: Pryke, 'Public enterprise in practice', p. 223

compelled to buy from the NCB irrespective of whether cheaper fuels are available elsewhere, including overseas.

Table 12.3 highlights not only how prices rose in nationalized industries faster than the norm as one consequence of declining labour productivity, but also how the pressure on management to raise prices was exacerbated by the fact that earnings per man rose more rapidly there than in the private sector. The upsurge in union militancy after the Labour Government's ill-fated attempt to curb union power in 1968 (the White Paper *In Place of Strife*) was most especially felt in the nationalized industries. As Pryke puts it: 'In 1971, 1972 and 1974 the nationalized industries with 7 per cent of all employment accounted for 40–50 per cent of days lost in strikes. The extent to which the (state) sector has contributed to wage and price inflation requires detailed investigation, but there is little doubt that during the period 1968–76 it was significant.'

Because of the large price increases shown in table 12.3, the conventional accounts of the nationalized industries are healthier than they were in the 1970s. None the less, as a rule the only two enterprises which typically earn enough to cover their replacement cost depreciation are telecommunications and the Gas Corporation (the latter largely because of an agreement to buy North Sea gas from the exploration companies at a price well below the ruling world market rate). As a consequence exploration for gas in the North Sea is no longer attractive and the companies have moved to the northern sectors to explore for oil, which they can sell on the mainland at a higher profit than they can sell gas to the only permitted buyer, British Gas. The folly of this is demonstrated by the German market's willingness in winter 1982 to buy considerable amounts of gas from Norwegian gas fields at the world market price. British gas explorers are (a) not permitted to sell in this way and (b) are unable to supply sufficient quantities even if they were, since British domestic consumption has risen because of the artificially low price while supplies are lower than they would be in the presence of a higher price. This is a textbook example of shortages caused by a price ceiling.

The accounts of all the nationalized industries are viewed with suspicion by outsiders because of government or ministerial interference, resulting in subsidies, capital debt write-offs, price controls and the like. Lapsley[6] lists several of these. British Airways (as BOAC) received £25 million in 1968–69 to cover the additional cost of purchasing British aircraft which were not its original choice. British Gas received £74.9 million over the three years to 1973–74 for price restraint. The Electricity Council received £41 million over the period 1974–75 for accelerated capital expenditure and carrying excess levels of coal stocks, and £26 million for price restraint in the period 1970–75. The National Coal Board received £230.7 million to cover the cost of industrial disputes and lesser amounts for pneumoconiosis compensation (£60 million) and special redundancy payments (£38 million).

Table 12.4 provides profit-and-loss figures for the nationalized sector. They should be treated with scepticism for the reasons outlined. In addition, the poor profitability is highlighted by contrasting certain of the industries with private equivalents, where possible.

The consensus view now seems to be that the nationalized industries do

Table 12.4 *Profits as a percentage of turnover prior to depreciation and trading surplus after depreciation at replacement cost, 1976*

	% sales	£m
NCB: deep-mined coal	8.4	− 25
BSC: iron and steel	4.5	− 239
British Gas	35.7	365
Electricity boards	25.9	− 26
Electricity showrooms (Curry Ltd)	0.7 (8.0)	—
BR	− 22.0	− 430
BR shipping (European Ferries and B & I)	− 2.5 (6.5)	—
Bus groups	− 3.5	− 56
NFC (two large private road hauliers)	4.2 (9.7)	− 13
BA	14.1	66
Postal services	11.0	110
Telecommunications	52.0	804
Manufacturing industry	—	4009

Source: Pryke, 'Public enterprise in practice', pp. 223–5

'fail the nation'. They are inefficient and monolithic, and because of government policies may even perform less well than they otherwise might. Open-ended subsidies sap the incentive of management, and encourage workers to resist industrial change. Industrial relations conflicts are intensified and most of the objectives identified by the late Hugh Gaitskell have become more difficult rather than easier to achieve.

Even the argument that the nationalized industries have 'social obligations' to meet which others do not, and that therefore losses are inevitable, is beginning to look threadbare. Nove has argued that transport industries (e.g. BR) are the externality industries *par excellence*—that is, they provide benefits to society which cannot be wholly recouped through the sales revenue arising from their services. Otherwise, 'what conceivable reason can there be for putting transport under public ownership? Who has ever doubted that transport, of all things, has external effects?'[7] This view rests on social aspects of mobility. Certain sectors of the population—the young, female and elderly from less affluent regions—may not have access to private cars in the way others do.[8] Similarly manufacturers located in sparsely populated regions may be unable to afford economic freight rates.

However, to subsidize railways (for example) for these reasons ignore:

(a) The necessary resulting taxation already mentioned.
(b) Cost–benefit studies suggesting that many rural rail routes impose net social costs on the community once the open-ended subsidy has been received to maintain them (the benefits are trivial: the subsidy enormous).
(c) Even with a subsidized rail price most regular travellers will not switch their mode of travel unless the subsidy is very high indeed, since most private car travellers already perceive that they are reaping large benefits over costs when they use their car and not rail.
(d) If people switched to rail, to the extent that they are commuters, rail congestion would increase.
(e) If a subsidized price results in a journey which would not otherwise be made, is this a social benefit? At worst it is not since the traveller previously did not value the journey highly enough to pay for it. At best it is debatable whether it is since someone has to be taxed to pay for the subsidy and so be deprived of satisfaction to provide the journey (which was not highly valued in the first place).
(f) Any freight switching to rail will still involve road collection and delivery, plus lift-on and lift-off costs at each end of the journey.
(g) The question is further begged as to whether the 'social equalization' will, in fact, occur. Taxing inner city dwellers to subsidize middle and upper income inhabitants of pleasant rural surroundings may achieve the reverse effect, compounding rather than alleviating the problem.

In the high unemployment of the 1980s the most attractive reason for subsidizing the nationalized industries, that 'it will preserve jobs', is also specious. Surely, it is argued, it is better to subsidize a job than to provide unemployment benefit? First, as in the case of BR's firemen, many such workers are wholly unproductive and no output will be sacrificed if they are made redundant. Second, since overall economic prospects and employment depend on productivity relative to international competitors, then improving the labour productivity of British industry, state or private, increases our trading capacity and increases our total employment. Thus false short-term palliatives to reduce unemployment, which also reduce productivity, only serve to increase unemployment in the whole economy in the long term. In 1982, with 3 million unemployed, Britain is reaping the bitter harvest of just such a policy carried out by both political parties, when in office, for over two decades.

Similar considerations apply in steel and coal, where either the government, the NCB or BSC have retracted on decisions (as recently as 1981 in coal) to cancel or defer plant and pit closures. Again the only outcome is managerial indifference, demotivation and still further worker resistance to future change.

This chapter has concentrated on government-owned industry as such. The problems that managing state enterprises presents to government have been detailed. Government also has a role in the regulation of private enterprise. This role is discussed in detail in chapter 15.

References

1 *Nationalized Industries: a Review of Economic and Social Objectives*, Cmnd 3437, HMSO, 1967.
2 *The Nationalized Industries*, Cmnd 7131, HMSO, 1978.
3 S.C. Littlechild, *What Should Government Do?*, in *The Taming of Government*, IEA Readings no. 21, Institute of Economic Affairs 1979, pp. 9–10.
4 This section draws heavily on Richard Pryke, 'Public enterprise in practice', in W.J. Baumol (ed.), *Public and Private Enterprise in a Mixed Economy*, International Economic Association, 1981.
5 G. Polanyi and P. Polanyi, *Failing the Nation: The Record of the Nationalized Industries*, Fraser and Ansbacher, 1974.
6 I. Lapsley, 'Income measurement at a state railway corporation: the "social profit" illusion?', *Journal of Business Finance and Accounting* (1981), p. 543.
7 A. Nove, *Efficiency Criteria for Nationalized Industries*, Allen & Unwin, 1973, p. 15.
8 J. Hibbs, *Transport without Politics?* Hobart Paper no. 95, Institute of Economic Affairs, 1982.

13

Markets and Distribution Channels

The Development of the Mass Market

The Industrial Revolution and the techniques of mass production which developed from it reached full flower in the manufacture of Henry Ford's Model T. The Model T was the epitome of the success of the Industrial Revolution. Ford's achievement was due to one main selling point, lowness of price, coupled with a lack of similar, inexpensive products in the past. Before the advent of the Model T, the individual seeking a cheap, personal transportation system had to invest in a horse and buggy, a product which could hardly be called the most satisfactory of substitutes, and one which, in any event, would be manufactured on a custom-built, one-off, high-cost basis at the local coachbuilders. The poor were thus precluded from owning their own personal transport, and only the very rich could contract out of the disadvantages associated with horse-drawn vehicles by buying the very costly products of Benz and Royce.

Ford's low price depended on standardization of product and uniformity of assembly technique. These are the basic components of mass production technology. Mass production depends in turn on a mass market to absorb the output. In Ford's case the mass market was made possible by mass communication about the product and by its attractively low price. So the circle was completed and marketing's place in it defined.

The Development of the Marketing Concept

Scope for further change in the nature and extent of marketing as we now know it had to wait until later in the twentieth century. The days when lowness of price and uniformity of product were sufficient to sell a product ended. ('You can have any colour you want, so long as it's black', growled Old Henry.) Incomes were rising, people no longer had to buy the cheapest, black car as a form of transport. They could afford to exercise their preferences for something different, or defer purchase till a satisfactory product

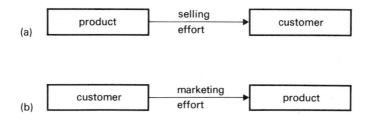

Figure 13.1 *Change in selling from (a) a product-oriented firm to (b) a market-oriented firm*

became available. In the automobile trade, General Motors willingly obliged by producing coloured Chevrolets. By 1946, Ford was turning in losses of $10 million each month.

So the marketing concept was born. Firms became aware that to stay in business it was not sufficient to produce a well-engineered product, then try to sell it. The market had to be studied, its varying wants assessed, and then a product, or products, tailored to meet them. Figure 13.1 conceptualizes this change from product orientation to market orientation: the firm's entire way of thinking is reversed.

When firms operate according to the marketing concept they must ask

1 Who are our potential customers?
2 Where are they?
3 What demographic features do they have (age, sex, marital status, etc.)?
4 What other socio-economic features do they possess which will affect their market behaviour?
5 What channel of distribution should we use to reach them?

The first four questions can be quickly answered, at least at the national level. The British population is rising and is forecast to continue to do so. Moreover, it is probable that this growth will continue to be predominantly in the South-East as the population moves from less prosperous areas (table 13.1).

Changes by age grouping in the last decade give guidance as to market

Table 13.1 *United Kingdom population*

	UK (millions)	(%)	England (millions)	(%)	Wales (millions)	(%)	Scotland (millions)	(%)	N. Ireland (millions)	(%)
1951	50.3	100	41.4	82.3	2.6	5.2	5.1	10.1	1.4	2.8
1981	55.9	100	46.2	83.0	2.8	5.0	5.1	9.1	1.5	2.7
1991 (forecast)	57.1	100	47.5	83.3	2.9	5.1	5.1	8.9	1.6	2.8
2001 (forecast)	58.4	100	48.6	83.2	3.0	5.1	5.1	8.7	1.7	2.9

Source: Annual Abstracts of Statistics

Table 13.2 *UK population age changes (selected age groups)*

	1970 (million)	1980 (million)	% change
Total	55.4	55.9	+ 0.9
Under 21 yrs	18.0	17.3	− 3.9
45−64 yrs	13.4	12.5	− 6.7
65 and over	7.2	8.3	+ 15.3

Source: Annual Abstracts of Statistics

trends in the future. Thus as table 13.2 indicates, the elderly segment is growing more rapidly than the population as a whole; thus 'retirement' goods such as gardening and other leisure-related activities could see an upswing in demand. People born in the post-war baby boom are now about thirty years of age—the point in the life cycle when homes are being set up, furniture bought and, in turn young families established with implications for industries such as toys and infant foods. By inference the teenage and early-twenty market is also growing relatively fast with positive implications for firms in leisure-related or electronic hardware industries. The middle-aged are declining in number both absolutely and relatively; in turn, this implies a decline in tomorrow's numbers of elderly and, in the nearer future, a weaker demand for replacement furniture, private cars and other durables purchased when children leave home.

All of these examples are, of course, subject to the caveat of 'other things equal'. Other things, however, are rarely equal. One very important demographic change has been the increase in the numbers of married women who have jobs and who therefore have increased the disposable income of households. The impetus for this has continued through two decades. Table 13.3 provides the figures supporting this statement.

This implies that not only will consumers' expenditure grow as disposable

Table 13.3 *Working population, Great Britain*

	Male (million)	(% change)	Female (million)	(% change)	Total (million)	(% change)
1959	14.2		7.6		21.8	
1969	16.1	+ 7.0	8.7	+ 14.5	24.8	+ 13.8
1980	15.7	− 0.2	10.1	+ 16.1	25.7	+ 3.6

Source: Ministry of Labour and Department of Employment Gazettes; Annual Abstracts of Statistics

Table 13.4 *Consumers' expenditure, United Kingdom, 1970 and 1980: selected items, constant (1975) prices*

	1970 (£m)	1980 (£m)	% change
Total	89.3	110.4	23.6
Food	12.0	12.7	5.8
Alcohol	3.7	5.4	45.9
Tobacco	2.7	2.7	0
Motor cars and motor cycles	1.8	2.4	33.3
Furniture and floor coverings	1.3	1.8	38.5
Radio, electrical and other durables	0.9	2.2	144.4
Miscellaneous recreational goods	1.3	2.1	61.5
Entertainment and recreational services	0.8	1.5	87.5

Source: Annual Abstract of Statistics 1982, pp. 354–5

incomes rise, but also, as households with two or more incomes grow in number, so consumers' expenditure will be diverted, at least in relative terms, away from necessities towards luxuries. Table 13.4 confirms this hypothesis. In addition, with more and more women at work, the conventional distribution channels have had to adapt to this sociological change.

Marketing Channels and Middlemen

The traditional distribution channel is conceptualized in figure 13.2(a). Goods are 'pushed' through from manufacturer to consumer via several intermediaries. The manufacturer's salesmen would approach a wholesaler, whose sales force in turn sold to retailers, who, in their turn, recommended purchase to (often personally known) individual customers. Now, the selling effort is primarily directed at the final consumer (figure 13.2(b)). The mass media are often used for this purpose; face-to-face recommendation has no place in the increasing number of self-service stores, and the goods are 'pulled' by consumers through the channel. The alert retailer must stock the items which consumers have chosen from those listed in advertisements that they, the consumers, have seen.

At first glance the presence of wholesaling intermediaries in distribution channels may appear to be inefficient. This was not and is not necessarily the case. Middlemen perform services to both manufacturers and retailers. Only

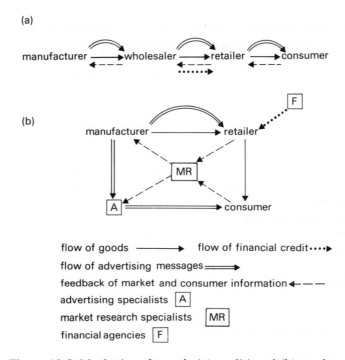

Figure 13.2 *Marketing channels (a) traditional (b) modern*

when this service is either no longer wanted, or is performed by the manufacturer or retailer himself, does the wholesaler become redundant. In short the wholesaling function always exists, but it need not be performed by an independent entity known as a wholesaler.

The wholesaler reduces the number of trading relationships between buyers and sellers and by so doing he achieves *economies of intervention*. For example, if three retailers deal independently with three manufacturers there is a total of nine trading relationships. If they deal indirectly through a wholesaler, however, the number of these relationships is reduced to six. Figure 13.3 illustrates this. The number of trading relationships (depicted as lines) is reduced from the product of the number of traders to their sum (from 3 × 3 to 3 + 3). The savings become progressively greater the larger the number of traders.

The wholesaler serves the retailer by assembling goods from a wide variety of suppliers. The retailer now needs to purchase from only one source instead of several. He can rely on the wholesaler's purchasing expertise and knowledge, and concentrate his own resources on selling. Similarly, since the wholesaler sorts out the range of goods into each retailer's desired assortment, the retailer need now have only one large drop-off of stock instead of many arriving at his warehouse. In addition, wholesalers often extend credit to retailers (figure 13.2(a)) and they also assume a stock holding risk. If each

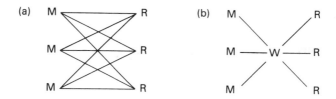

Figure 13.3 *Manufacturers and retailers trading (a) directly (b) through a wholesaler*

retailer had to carry sufficient stock to guard against the risk of running out of supplies during a busy period then the aggregate stock held would have to be very much greater than that which a central wholesaler would have to carry to meet the variations in demand from the total trade. This has already been referred to as the economies of massed reserves (chapter 6), a variant of *the fire insurance principle*.

The other side of the coin is the wholesaler's service to manufacturers. He eliminates the need for the manufacturer to make a plethora of small drops. Transportation and shipment costs are thus reduced. Similarly the manufacturer's selling costs are reduced in that he now need only visit a relatively small number of wholesalers and not a plethora of retailers. The wholesaler is also closer to the market and presumably therefore can pass back to the manufacturer market information which is more reliable for production scheduling than the manufacturer's own estimates.

The rationale for the existence of a middleman can also be explained in terms of the discussion on trade and exchange of chapter 2. Consider figure 13.4(a) in which the demand and supply curves of figures 2.2 and 2.3 are reproduced. Joe and Fred, it will be recalled, originally had 20 packs of butter each but each could be made better off (in his own eyes) if he traded beer for butter until Joe had 16 and Fred had 24 packs. However, for such a trade to occur Fred and Joe must incur transactions costs. They must advertise and inform each other of their wishes. They must transport the exchanged goods and negotiate and seal the bargain.

Assume that the agreed trading price is again 8 pints of beer but that this time there are, in addition, transaction costs of 3 pints of beer per butter unit (irrespective of whether either or both individuals incur that cost). Then Fred will increase his butter holding to 22 packs, and Joe reduce his to 18. (Beer will also change hands.) Assume Fred and Joe incur the costs in a 2:1 ratio. To acquire one unit of butter Fred will willingly part (initially) with 12 pints of beer while Joe will require (initially) 6 pints. From the difference (12 − 6) of 6 pints, 3 pints of beer must be deducted in transactions costs. Thus equilibrium will only be reached in the presence of such costs when the difference in net receipts and expenditures is 3 pints of beer (in figure 13.4(a), at a buying price of 10 and a selling price of 7 respectively). The rectangle between the two shaded areas represents the transaction costs, and less trading is done

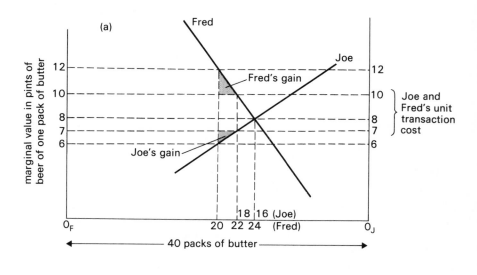

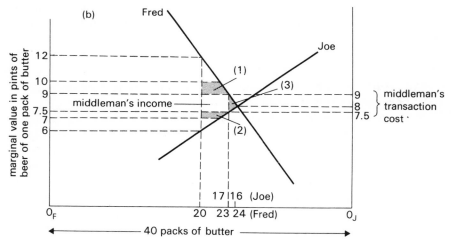

Figure 13.4 *(a) Transaction costs in trade of figure 2.3*
        (b) middleman costs in same trade. Key to (b):
        (1) Fred's additional gain from use of wholesaler
        (2) Joe's additional gain from use of wholesaler
        (3) further gains possible if transaction costs
        were zero

than would have been in their absence. The trade point of figure 2.3 is only
worth while reaching if transaction costs are zero.

Suppose, however, that a specialist wholesaler can undertake the costs of
trading more efficiently than Joe or Fred could on their own. Suppose he can
do it for half the cost. Then trading will continue until the spread between

Joe's and Fred's net transaction costs prices is only 1.5, not 3 (for example, at 9 and 7.5). Both Fred and Joe are better off as a result of the middleman's intervention (see figure 13.4(b)). The middleman receives an income which covers his normal costs. But again, of course, the original zero transaction cost point of 16 and 24 packs is still, and always will be, unattainable.

Evolution of Marketing Channels

If a case can be made out for the presence of a middleman or wholesaler, why have distribution channels tended to move away from the situation illustrated in figure 13.2(a) to that of figure 13.2(b)? There are three groups of mutually reinforcing reasons; those relevant to the retailer, consumer and product respectively.

Changes at the retail level

In the 1970s the number of shops, of any kind, in Britain fell from 510,000 in 1971 to 388,000 in 1978. The biggest decline was in single-outlet independent retailers who, in the same period, decreased in number from 338,000 to 231,000. Large multiple retailers began the decade with 88,000 outlets (1386 firms) and by 1977 had 78,000 shops (1374 firms). Table 13.5 compares the share of total retail sales held by different types of outlet. In 1971 the retail trade employed over 2.8 million persons. By 1977 this had shrunk to 2.4 million and all this despite real increases in the volume of goods sold.

Table 13.5 *All retail trade: percentage of turnover held, by retailer classification*

	1950	1961	1971	1978
Independents	59.4	56.4	49.8	43.2
Multiples	23.0	27.6	37.9	44.3
Co-operatives	12.0	10.8	7.2	7.2
Department Stores	5.5	5.3	5.0	5.2

Sources: Board of Trade Journals; Annual Abstracts of Statistics

Independent retailer

The independent retailer is ubiquitous by both location and trade type. One hundred years ago most shops were of this type. They required skilled crafts-men to make shoes, compound medicines, cure bacon or whatever tasks were appropriate to the trade. Breaking bulk and repacking (e.g. for tea and cheese) was common. These functions have now been taken over by the wholesaler and/or manufacturer. The skilled craftsman has been replaced by (often unskilled) salesmen.

The strength of the independents lies in their flexibility of pricing, product range, opening hours, close knowledge of customer requirements and convenient locations. They also often have the apparent advantage of low labour and rent costs if family members are willing to work uncongenial or longer hours, and if the store is part of a domestic residence. These are misleading 'advantages', of course, since the full opportunity costs of the self-employed should be charged against the firm's profits.

The disadvantages of the independents lie in their limited buying power, their limited access to capital to improve premises, and their lack of management skills. The independent retailer has to be his own staff trainer, accountant, buyer, stock controller, salesman, supervisor and window display specialist. Clearly it is impossible for one individual to aspire to such a range of skills.

Department stores

Department stores, unlike the independent retailer, have on the whole retained their market share of all retail sales. Historically (along with the co-operatives) they were the first large-scale retailers. Their basic principles were: entrance was free of any obligation to buy; customer complaints were dealt with by a generous returns policy; merchandise was arranged departmentally; prices were clearly marked; personal service (credit, delivery, etc.) was of a high order; and departments existed explicitly to encourage custom (rest rooms, restaurants, generally pleasant environment, etc.). This formula was successful towards the end of the last century and early decades of this century as town population grew; suburban areas were also growing but improved personal transport of all kinds ensured that they were included in the catchment area of the stores; the development of lifts and escalators made the marketing concept of the stores a practical possibility in a multistorey building on one site.

Co-operatives

The co-operative societies have seen their share of total retail turnover drop from 12.0 per cent in 1950 to 7.2 per cent in 1978. Co-operatives are worth examining as an entity distinct from department stores and multiple retailers, because they differ not in their trading practices but in their means of ownership and the distribution of their trading surplus. They are owned by their members, some of whom may have provided capital which earns a fixed rate of interest. But any profits are distributed not in proportion to capital provided but in relation to purchases made in the trading period. Members' meetings are run on a one-person, one-vote principle and votes are weighted neither by capital nor by purchases.

Co-operatives have access to many of the advantages of multiples (see next section). However, they have additional and unique disadvantages. Their membership tends to be concentrated in specific geographic areas (generally economically depressed areas with an emphasis on heavy and/or declining industries) and within lower-income groups. Consequently they tend to suffer more than the average of UK retailing in times of economic downturn. In addition they tend to jealously guard their local autonomy and independence which means that several smaller societies fail to achieve the scale economies available to retailers. This situation is compounded by the fact that boards of directors tend to be elected laymen who, as customers in their own right, are often protective of sectional customer interests rather than concerned with the society's overall welfare. (This manifests itself in an unwillingness to close down uneconomic branches or discontinue slow-moving lines, which in turn implies that other parts of the society must cross-subsidize them out of their profits. As a consequence, there is a reduction in the ability of the society to compete in price or other terms with other retail types, particularly multiples.) Lay board members can also fail to see the need to spend heavily on staff training, shop fittings, higher salaries for managerial staff and the like. Internal promotion is also prevalent, thus reducing the pool of managerial talent from which to draw. Certainly some of the above are changing as societies merge and individual board members are less able to influence policy in such short-sighted ways. Table 13.6 shows how the fall in numbers of societies, owing to mergers, has been quite dramatic in the last two decades.

Table 13.6 *Number of co-operative societies*

1960	875	1977	206
1971	313	1979	195
1975	227		

Source: Annual Abstracts of Statistics; Nielsen Researcher

In turn, individual societies have become larger, gained more purchasing muscle, engaged more professional management, and become more loyal to the Co-operative Wholesaling Society (CWS) which they own. The CWS, in turn, has established eight major distribution centres in the UK. These supply 30 per cent of the warehousing and distribution needs of the retail societies for packaged groceries. A further 30 per cent of these products are bought by the societies via the CWS as purchasing agent. The CWS thus acts as a central buyer and also a national advertiser for retail co-operatives. All of this rationalization activity has halted the relative decline of the co-operative movement. In the process even the previously sacrosanct dividend has been subject to radical alteration. In some outlet types, particularly groceries, it has been abandoned altogether—a somewhat ironical state of affairs since multiples regularly equal or better any price in co-operatives, yet still pay a dividend to their shareholders. In others it has been reduced to minimal level, and elsewhere it has been replaced by trading stamps which can be accumulated by the consumer until sufficient are held to be traded in for either goods or cash. Certainly dividend abandonment had an underlying rationale. When dividends were pitched at a high level, this discouraged the setting of low prices, the ploughing back of profits to improve shops and equipment and the stocking of items with low margins. As an undifferentiated price reduction over a wide range of goods and outlets, it encouraged cross-subsidization and discouraged efficient decision-taking.

Multiples

The story of the multiple retailers since 1950 has been one of major success. They can achieve the economies of large-scale retailing (as can the co-operative and department stores) as well as other benefits. Definitions of multiples vary but a working description is a situation of ten or more shops operating under one management/ownership structure. Because of their scale they can afford to employ (and fully utilize) specialists in accounting purchasing, advertising, co-ordination and control. Their size enables them to spread overheads such as advertising, rent and staff training over a larger volume of business. Their buying power is large, enabling them to obtain large discounts on list price. In turn this facilitates provision of either a low-service/low-price marketing mix or a high-price/sophisticated service mix, neither of which an independent could compete with on equal terms.

By integrating backwards and carrying out many of the functions of the wholesaler they can capture several economies of integration. Central buying can be practised. Stocks held in a central warehouse can be minimized. Advertising, promotion and pricing policies can be co-ordinated with each other and with the firm's stock position. Test marketing can be undertaken in selected branches. Risks of stock holding such as deterioration and demand changes are also minimized because of the close interaction between the seller and buyer in the multiple organization. Multiples also generally have access to the capital markets, and the cost of finance to the integrated firm may therefore be much less than the use of extended credit by retailers from independent wholesalers. Delivery, order assembly, and transport costs are lowered because days of drop-off from the central warehouse can be scheduled smoothly over the week instead of peaking, as with an independent wholesaler, towards the weekend.

These advantages are offset, although only partially, by disadvantages. The multiple may assume overheads that the small independent store never would (e.g. advertising, high-rent sites, elaborate services and the employment of specialists). Moreover, the multiple may well not provide the individual personalized attention to customers that the independent does. In addition, the local management may not have the authority to alter company

Table 13.7 *Number of self-service grocers, UK*

1961	7,700	1967	24,300
1963	12,900	1969	28,062
1965	17,500		

Source: Nielsen Researcher

policy on pricing and selection of stock in order to enable him to adapt to localized consumer preferences and competitors' activities.

All of this has meant that the multiple retailer has in general increased his share of retail sales. Nowhere is this more true than in grocery retailing. One of the first overt consequences of this was the move to self-service selling. Table 13.7 depicts their growth in numbers. The series stops in 1969 when two-thirds of all grocery turnover passed through self-service selling stores; the data collectors felt that although the trend would continue the basic economic interest in it had ceased. Self-service was stimulated in Britain, at least initially, by high labour costs not by a desire to cut prices (as in the USA). Partly this was due to the existence of Resale Price Maintenance on many goods prior to 1964 and partly to a general staff shortage. Self-service had the major attribute of catering for both traditional shoppers and working wives. Shopping could be a leisurely activity with plenty of time for comparison, or it could be hurried into a compressed period. This, plus bright, attractive atmospheres, coupled with well-filled shelves and clearly marked prices, ensured the success of self-service outlets.

Not only did self-service stores grow in number; they also took an increasing amount of business. In 1965 they accounted for 45 per cent of grocery turnover; by 1969, just four years later, this had risen to 64 per cent. This new method of retailing was more efficient in its use of staff resources; moreover, since the store was in part a warehouse, it resulted in stocks held being minimized. As a consequence, less capital was tied up in stocks and savings were made in working capital. Table 13.8 illustrates the impact of this on the grocery trade as a whole.

Supermarkets, and more recently, hypermarkets also increased in number

Table 13.8 *Grocery stocks and sales in UK (1964−65 = 100, current prices)*

	Sales	Stocks
1964−65	100	100
1966−67	107	98
1968−69	122	94

Source: Nielsen Researcher

over the years. (Definitions vary; for example, a supermarket may be defined as a store with over 4000 square feet of selling space and a hypermarket or superstore as one with over 25,000 square feet of selling space.) These three developments were particularly suited to the multiple retailer with large capital resources and access to managerial expertise. As a consequence of all of these advantages the multiples have taken an increasingly large share of the retail grocery trade in the country. This is illustrated in table 13.9.

Table 13.9 *Turnover share by types of grocer, UK (%)*

	Co-operatives	Multiples	Independents
1939	23	23	54
1959	22	26	52
1963	19	32	49
1967	15	38	47
1971	15	43	42
1975	14	49	37
1979	15	59	26
1981	14	63	23

Source: Nielsen Researcher

The co-operative movement appears to have slowed its decline by the process of rationalization referred to earlier. The multiples, however, continue their inexorable advance. This has considerable implications for manufacturers and wholesalers. Table 13.10 shows how heavily concentrated is the buying power in groceries in Britain.

Changes at the wholesale level

Clearly the futures of the wholesaler and the independent retailer are closely linked. Recognizing this, many wholesalers and retailers clubbed together

Table 13.10 *Number of outlet types and proportion of grocers' business controlled or influenced in UK, 1979*

	No.	% of turnover
Co-operative societies	195	15
Major multiple head offices	6	41
Other multiple head offices	44	18
Major symbol wholesalers	40	7
Total	297	81

Source: Nielsen Researcher

into voluntary chains or symbol groups such as Spar and VG. In essence the retail members of a *symbol group* retain their independence of ownership but agree to purchase the major part of their merchandise from the whole-saler; to take delivery on specified days; to display prominently given items which may be subject to special promotion by the wholesaler; to pay promptly; and to display the chain symbol. In return supplies are cheaper because of the wholesaler's cost savings; merchandising assistance and large-scale promotion will be provided; and other centralized services such as insurance, shop-fitting advice and market research information may be provided. Table 13.11 shows how the practice of small retailers buying directly from manu-facturers has virtually disappeared. Symbol groups have been growing in importance, and although not directly evident from the figures, the traditional wholesaler is becoming more and more of a cash-and-carry outlet for his retail customers.

One interesting feature of table 13.11 is the inferred greater selectivity of the symbol groups. Only significant independents, not 'lost causes', will now be admitted to the groups. An alternative or simultaneous explanation is that cash-and-carry wholesaling has become of more importance and convenience to the retailer.

Table 13.11 *Trend of purchasing by independent grocers (%)*

	Directly	Symbol groups	Traditional wholesalers and cash-and-carry outlets
1960	32	10	58
1968	9	42	49
1979	0	28	72

Source: Nielsen Researcher

Changes at the consumer level

The changes in distribution channels outlined in figure 13.2 have been due not only to wholesaler and retailer changes but also to consumer changes. Increasing car ownership has increased consumer mobility and choice ability. Rising numbers of working wives have preferred the speed and convenience of shopping epitomised by self-service. Rising levels of ownership of deep freezers and refrigerators have permitted and encouraged large unit purchases.

Changes at the level of the producer

There are two principal reasons for the active entry of the producer and manufacturer into distribution in the last few decades. First, the growth of large-scale production units necessitated long, unbroken production runs.

This in turn required a steady flow of orders which independent wholesalers and retailers might not be prepared to give (or, if they could be encouraged to give them, the transaction costs of dealing with large numbers of customers might be too great; recall the discussion of figures 13.2 and 13.3). Second, manufacturers realized that sales and profits could probably be increased if they concentrated on promoting their own products to final consumers (pulling goods through the channel), rather than leaving it to a third party or parties to push them through when such wholesalers and retailers were under no obligation to devote special attention to any one manufacturer.

The methods adopted by manufacturers were of three types. First, formal *forward integration*, as practised by some flour millers, petrol companies and brewers where they own their own retail bakeries, filling stations and public houses.

Second, brewers, car manufacturers and petrol companies have also adopted *tied outlets* as forms of retail control. Here the ownership remains with the original retailer but he is contractually obliged to take a given percentage (often 100 per cent) of his supplies from the manufacturer. Other conditions may also be imposed. For example, a car dealer may have to carry minimum levels of stocks and spares, be able to provide a given level of mechanical servicing to customers, and so on. In return the tied outlet would often have exclusive trading rights to a particular geographic region.

Both of these forms of distribution channel control are practised in trades where traditionally the retailer has offered only a restricted range of products. They tend not to be found, for example, in the grocery trade or in the variety chain stores such as Woolworths. The reason is obvious. Only an extremely diversified manufacturer could supply his owned or tied outlets in these fields. Producers are rarely diversified to this extent; their skills lie in the manufacture of a given product, and their knowledge of the retailing problems involved with alien products is slight or non-existent. Hence the cost disadvantages (e.g. errors, learning time) of forward integration would outweigh the benefits. (One exception to this is the Asda hypermarket chain which evolved from the original Associated Dairies. The link with grocery retailing, however, is obvious. Moreover, as the firm has expanded it has become more of a grocery retailer with a self-owned dairy division and less of a dairy producer with a self-owned chain of grocery retailers. Indeed as a hyper-market chain the quantity of non-foods sold by this firm in its stores takes up a large percentage of both turnover and floor space.)

Third, and most common, manufacturers attempt to pull goods through the channel indirectly by *branding and advertising* reinforced with market research.

The Role of Advertising

Implicit control of distribution channels through the use of advertising and market research is outlined in figure 13.2. The intention is to operate primarily through consumer demand, and ideally (from the producer's viewpoint) consumers will refuse to accept another firm's brand and go to another retailer who does stock the advertised product. The original retailer will be encouraged to purchase the product for fear of losing further trade.

Thus although some manufacturers' advertising and promotion is still directed at the retailer (via salesmen, trade journals, trade exhibitions, etc.) the bulk of it goes via specialized advertising agents and mass media such as TV and the press to the final consumer. The product-handling middleman is bypassed. The consumer information on which the manufacturer bases his production and promotion decisions comes to him by way of specialized market research agencies. They can obtain data on sales rates by type and location of retailer, and on consumption patterns by household and the demographic features of households (family size, income, region, education level, newspaper taken, etc.). This information is fed at frequent intervals to manufacturers, advertising agents and the advertising media themselves.

When information flows backwards in this way it is both speedier and more accurate than consumer feedback via word of mouth or order level changes in the distribution channel of figure 13.2(a). Traditionally, such backward information flows were either too slow or too distorted to enable the producer to quickly adjust his output to meet consumer demands. Faulty assumptions can distort facts by escalation, quite apart from any distortion caused simply by repeated transmission of a message. For example, consider a retailer with normal monthly stocks, and sales of commodity X of 100 cases per month. His policy is to retain stocks at the level of anticipated sales. If sales fall 20 per cent, 20 cases are left in stock. The retailer then assumes only 80 cases are going to be sold in future; he thus orders 60, a 40 per cent fall in the normal order to the wholesaler. If the wholesaler services 10 retailers, each of whom suffer the same experience, then his sales will drop by 400 cases. If he also works on a policy of stocks equalling anticipated sales then, having 400 cases left in stock, he may assume sales will now only be 600 monthly rather than 1000; he will thus order only 200 cases from the manufacturer. Thus a 20 per cent fall in sales has escalated to an 80 per cent reduction in orders from the manufacturer.

Market research at the level of the retailer, or better still the household, will show far more accurately and quickly what is actually happening in the market-place at consumer level. (For example, *audits* of household consumption on a fortnightly basis, given a sample of households, show what is really being consumed, where products are being bought, and by whom. Such audits are often carried out by visual inspection of the sample members' kitchens or even by physical collection of empty containers. The latter may sound rather unhygienic—it is called the 'dustbin audit'—but it does overcome problems of memory default. It highlights frequency of consumption by household types and container size.)

Market research, in short, reinforces the producer's attempt to pull goods through the channel. It enables the producer to tailor his product, his brand image and his advertising to what the consumer wants. In short, he can apply the marketing concept (figure 13.1). He can choose the appropriate media for reaching the customers who do not but might buy the product. He can adjust the product and the packaging according to consumer wants and to the requirements of the retailer that these consumers visit (rather than to the requirements of retailers little frequented by the consumers the manufacturer is primarily interested in).

Advertising itself has two main effects. First, it reduces long-run demand elasticity through its association with branding. Second, it increases short-run price sensitivity. This may sound contradictory; let us examine the statements in turn. Figure 13.5 shows how demand can be made less elastic. D is the long-run demand curve prior to advertising. D' is the curve after advertising; it is placed up and to the right of D. The original price/quantity combination of P', Q' is thus altered to P', Q'', or, if the firm wishes to raise price, to P_1, Q_1. Note that the elasticity of D' is less than that of D. For a similar price rise (P' to P_1) the decreased quantity demanded is less (Q'' to Q_1 as against Q' to Q_2).

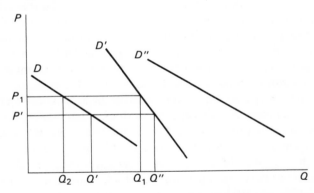

Figure 13.5 *Advertising reduces long-run demand elasticity*

The reason for this is embodied in *brand loyalty*. Branding depends on advertising. As Professor Sir Dennis Robertson put it: 'There is a real spiritual comfort in buying a packet of a known and trusted brand of cocoa rather than a shovelful of brown powder of uncertain origin.' A brand gives the customer assurance that the commodity will be constant in quality, appearance and taste wherever it is purchased. An unidentified commodity may vary from day to day and shop to shop. If the consumer likes it the consumer can continue to buy. Alternatively, if the product is not preferred, the brand identifies it and it can be avoided. A poor brand will go to the wall more quickly than an unidentified, low-quality product. There is thus a strong economic motivation for the manufacturer to produce and maintain a product of acceptable and consistent characteristics.

Branding, of course, depends not only on advertising but also on *prepackaging*—that is, packaging by the manufacturer rather than the retailer. Modern packaging technology has removed the bulk breaking function away from the 'back shop' to the factory. It permits branding, facilitates stacking on open shelves, and encourages self-service retailing. Thus medicines, cheeses, tea, bacon and chickens are now all produced and packaged at a much earlier stage than previously. The large and modern machines which made this possible perform the operations more efficiently and encourage in turn the more productive forms of retailing that we have already examined.

How does branding and advertising increase short-run price sensitivity? In essence, the answer is simple. Long-run price elasticity is always greater than short-run because people have time to both learn about and react to changes in product price (the second law of demand). If it is possible to reduce the learning period by making consumers more aware either of product price itself or of changes in price, then the long-run elasticity moves closer (in time terms) to the current or short-run period. Advertising and branding by making goods more identifiable and by making more information (including price) available about them thus increases short-run demand elasticity. Consumer reaction to price levels and changes is speedier and so price sensitivity is increased. In brief, the demand curve in the short period is shifted (in figure 13.5) from D' (a possible original position) to D''.

Whether the effect of advertising in both periods together is to raise or lower price elasticity is, of course, an empirical question. Whether price itself is higher or lower is also open to debate. The price the firm will select will depend not only on the demand curve but also on the cost curve (including advertising). Figure 13.6 illustrates this dilemma.

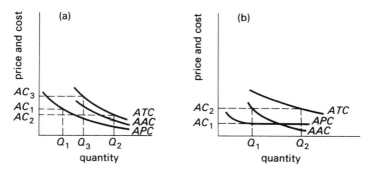

Figure 13.6 *Advertising and overall price selection*

Average total cost (ATC) can only be reduced by advertising where average advertising cost (AAC) is less than the savings per unit obtained in average production cost (APC) when the scale of production is increased. If APC is constant or rising, then any advertising must raise ATC, since advertising itself adds to the costs. The two alternatives are illustrated in figure 13.6(a) and (b). In both diagrams, Q_1 represents output before advertising, Q_2 output after advertising. Even figure 13.6(a) does not give an unambiguous answer, of course. Had output only been raised to Q_3, then ATC would have *risen* from AC_1 to AC_3.

Nothing can be deduced a priori about the influence of advertising on total unit costs. Whether cost differences due to advertising will or will not lead to corresponding price differences cannot be determined merely by examining the direction in which costs have moved. If advertising has resulted in lower costs then the new equilibrium price will depend upon what has happened to marginal receipts as well as to marginal costs. The outcome may, but need not necessarily, be a lower price.

14

Industrial Relations and the Market for Labour

In this chapter we shall be concerned with the pricing and allocation of a major factor of production; labour. We can employ the tools of supply and demand to analyse this market, just as we can in any other. Certain major caveats must be borne in mind, however. The market for labour can be segmented on an industrial, geographical, and even on a firm-specific basis. Any general principles operate within a complex legal and institutional framework and each individual sector of the market may vary according to the degree of unionization and the relative strengths of sellers and purchasers of labour. Labour mobility and the elasticity of supply of labour might be further governed by local conditions, availability of housing, schools, and other factors in the social infrastructure of the locality. In addition the demand and supply of labour are affected by inducements under the government's regional policy and by sociological willingness or unwillingness to move from traditional areas of residence. In addition, one major preoccupation of successive administrations has been the containment of inflation and this has on occasion manifested itself in measures aimed at controlling wage increases. The market for labour is thus influenced by a very complicated pot-pourri of factors.

We shall proceed by considering how economic analysis can be applied to the study of the labour market, and then consider in turn some of the other various factors and issues mentioned above.

Economic Analysis and the Labour Market

Adam Smith suggested that: 'The whole of the advantages and disadvantages of the different employments of labour and stock must, in the same neighbourhood, be either perfectly equal or continually tending to equality.'[1] The idea is that factors of production will pursue the most advantageous opportunities of employment, and as long as there are no restrictions and liberty to change occupations the pressure of the pursuit of individual advantage would enforce equality of returns for similar occupations. But the supply of labour is only half the story, and consideration must be given to the demand for labour. This is necessarily a derived demand, since employers demand labour not for its own sake but for the contribution it can make when combined with other factors of production to produce goods and services. In practice it is very difficult to disentangle the contributions made by the different factors of production. Smith was aware of some of the difficulties, but it was Marx who developed them fully, turned them around and argued that the process of production in a capitalist system involved the appropriation by the capitalist interest of surplus value produced by labour.[2] The Marxian approach reaches one of its culminations in the work of Sraffa.[3] A simplistic version of the Marxian view would run as follows; if a man and an oven make a pie the value of that pie belongs to the man only. Smith had pondered the problem and failed to ascertain how much of the pie value belonged to the man and how much to the owners of the oven. The issue is even more complex, however. The man may put as much effort and sweat into producing a mince pie as he would a mud pie. What reward should he and the oven owner receive then? Clearly the mud pie will sell for zero; it has no value, despite the labour input. The meat pie does have a value; this is the price consumers will willingly pay for it. But how is this apportioned? The pie could not be baked without the oven, and the oven could not bake without the man. Let us consider the work of Marshall.

If it is assumed that producers seek to maximize profitability they will apply the familiar marginal conditions developed in chapter 5. They should employ each factor of production up to the point where its marginal contribution to revenue is equal to the marginal cost of employing the last unit of it. Marshall employed the homely analogy of the farmer determining how many shepherds to employ.[4] The demand for labour will be determined by the value of the marginal product of labour in the particular employment concerned. The farmer will be moved to hire another shepherd if he thinks that the man's contribution will be, say, to increase his output of good quality sheep by 20 per annum, and the cost of a shepherd's annual subsistence is less than or equal to the value of 20 sheep. This is shown in table 14.1. It can be seen from the table that the farmer should hire up to 11 shepherds and no more. The value of the marginal product of the eleventh shepherd is equal to 20 sheep and, as a shepherd's wage is the equivalent of 20 sheep, we have marginal equivalency. At this point profits or the surplus are maximized, and to hire any more shepherds would be counter-productive. Marshall went on to argue that in every occupation labour would be hired until its wage was equal to the value of its marginal product; however, he was careful to add that this in itself was not a theory of wages, since to value the marginal product of labour we have to take for granted all the other costs of the productive process. It remains, nevertheless, an important element in a neoclassical theory of wage determination.

Table 14.1 *The farmer's demand for shepherds as determined by the value of their marginal product (all values in terms of the number of sheep produced)*

Number of shepherds	Annual output of sheep	Marginal product due to last shepherd	Average product	Wages bill	Surplus (output − wages)
8	580	—	$72\frac{1}{2}$	160	420
9	615	35	$68\frac{1}{3}$	180	435
10	640	25	64	200	440
11	660	20	60	220	440
12	676	16	$56\frac{1}{3}$	240	436

Source: Alfred Marshall, *Principles of Economics* (1890), Macmillan, 9th edn, 1961, book 6, chapter 1

We can extend the analysis further by consideration of the nature of the firm's production function in the short run on the lines introduced in chapter 4. In the short run it is assumed that a factor input, usually capital machinery, is fixed. Given this it follows that the law of diminishing returns will ensure that successively greater labour inputs will add less and less to total output. The total physical product will behave, as a function of labour inputs, in the manner shown in figure 14.1. Marginal physical product will be zero at a labour input of L_1 in the figure; this corresponds to the maximum point on the total physical product curve. We are now in a position to derive the firm's demand curve for labour in the short run.

If it is assumed that the firm's objective is to maximize profits, it will be interested in the marginal revenue product associated with the use of extra units of labour (as shown previously in the example of the farmer hiring shepherds). Furthermore if the firm is operating under conditions of perfect competition, which we shall assume for simplicity of argument, then the marginal revenue associated with selling extra units of output will be a constant equal to the price of the goods sold. In these circumstances, multiplying the previous marginal physical product curve by the good's price (the firm's marginal revenue) will give us a marginal revenue product curve which is the firm's demand curve for labour, as shown in figure 14.2.

If the firm hires labour in a competitive labour market with a wage rate fixed at W_1, it will pay the firm to hire L_1 units of labour so as to maximize profits. The downward-sloping portion of the firm's marginal revenue product curve is its short-run demand curve for labour. By equating this with the marginal cost of labour, in this case the wage rate W_1, the firm maximizes its profits.

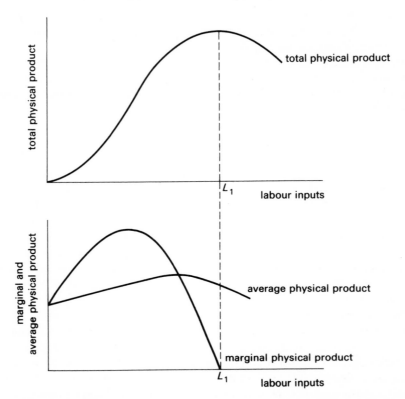

Figure 14.1 *The behaviour of total, average and marginal physical product in the short run, given fixed capital and variable labour inputs*

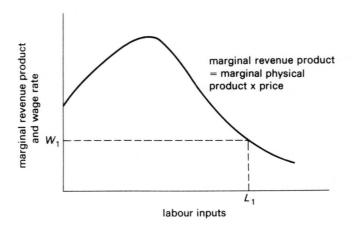

Figure 14.2 *The marginal revenue product curve: the firm's short-run demand for labour*

It can be shown that in the case of a firm selling its product in an imperfect market, which implies a downward-sloping demand curve for its product, the firm will demand less labour than under perfect market conditions. This follows since the marginal revenue curve is below the demand curve, and therefore the marginal revenue product curve is derived by multiplying marginal physical product by the lower figure of marginal revenue, rather than price as used in the perfectly competitive case.

The industry demand for labour in terms of marginal productivity theory

The industry demand for labour in the short run under conditions of perfect competition cannot be derived by simply summing the marginal revenue product curves of all its constituent firms. Consider the effect of a lowering of the wage rate. Each firm would react by hiring more labour and by expanding its output. This means that the industry's output as a whole will increase and therefore the equilibrium price will fall. Yet remember that the individual firm's demand curve for labour was derived by multiplying labour's marginal physical product by the constant equilibrium price, which has now changed to a lower value. Thus the marginal revenue product curve must have shifted bodily to the left, and would have shifted in the opposite direction had there been an increase in the wage rate. This is shown in figure 14.3.

In this figure it can be seen that when the wage rate falls from W_1 to W_2 the firm's demand for labour increases from L_1 to L_2, the two points of intersection of the wage rate with the two marginal revenue product curves MRP_1 and MRP_2. The firm's short-run demand curve for labour is therefore the locus of all the points of contact of the various wage rates with the various marginal revenue product curves associated with those differing wage rates.

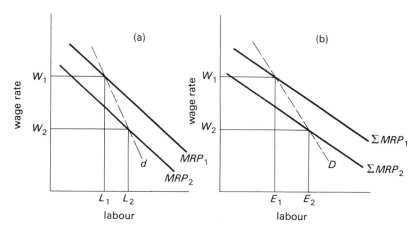

Figure 14.3 *The demand for labour in the short run (a) the firm
(b) the industry*

The firm's short-run demand curve is marked *d* in the diagram. The sum of all the individual firms' demand curves for labour produces the industry demand curve for labour *D*. If the industry is the sole employer of this type of labour then this would be the market demand curve for that labour, but if more than one industry uses the labour then a similar exercise involving all firms across the relevant industries would produce the overall demand curve for that type of labour.

A similar type of analysis will establish the firm's long-run demand curve for labour. There are additional complications in that changes in the utilization of labour, following a fall in the wage rate, will alter the marginal productivity of capital. It follows that capital inputs will be altered too, but as soon as this happens there are changes in the marginal productivity of labour. The net result of this chain of interactions is that in the long run the demand for labour is likely to be more elastic than in the short run. Marshall enumerated the factors which affect the elasticity of demand for labour but Hicks subsequently modified one of them.[5] We shall also follow Hicks in citing Pigou's more succinct account of Marshall's rules governing the elasticity of derived demand.[6] Pigou's version of the rules are:

1 'The demand for anything is likely to be more elastic, the more readily substitutes for that thing can be obtained.
2 The demand for anything is likely to be less elastic, the less important is the part played by the cost of that thing in the total cost of some other thing, in the production of which it is employed.
3 The demand for anything is likely to be more elastic, the more elastic is the supply of co-operant agents of production.
4 The demand for anything is likely to be more elastic, the more elastic is the demand for any further thing which it contributes to produce.'[7]

The above rules normally hold good and the only problem, Hicks suggests, is with rule 2 in extreme circumstances. It holds as long as purchasers of the final product can substitute other goods more easily than the entrepreneur can factors, and we would normally expect this to be the case.

The determination of the supply of labour

We have considered the determinants of the demand for labour; we shall now look at the factors which affect its supply. The basic choice facing an individual is about whether to work or not and about how much time to devote to work. This can be viewed as a question of the allocation of time between work and non-labour market activities usually subsumed under the title leisure. The choice is shown in figure 14.4.

This figure is drawn up under the assumption that the individual concerned receives a constant remuneration per number of hours worked. If he chose not to work at all he would draw the state-guaranteed social security minimum and have 24 hours/day leisure. As soon as he begins to work his income

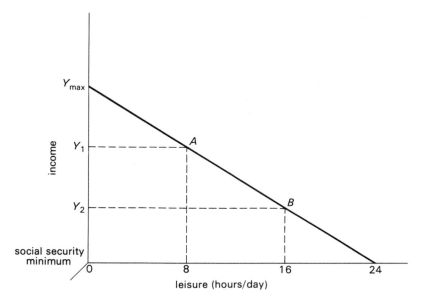

Figure 14.4 *The income/leisure choice*

begins to rise and his leisure time falls (ignoring taxation and factors like the 'poverty trap'). So he starts moving up the line in the diagram, and at its other end, representing a theoretical but impractical extreme, he could work 24 hours/day, have no leisure but an income of Y_{max}. The question is, where on the line will he locate himself? Will it be at point A, which involves having only 8 hours leisure but an income of Y_1, or at point B, where he has 16 hours of leisure but an income of Y_2?

We can approach the problem from the point of view of marginal utility theory considered in chapter 3. The person concerned will work up to the point where the utility of the income derived from the last hour's labour just equals the utility of the hour's leisure sacrificed to earn the income. We have

$$\frac{\text{marginal utility of income}}{\text{hourly wage rate}} = \frac{\text{marginal utility of leisure}}{\text{price of leisure (hourly wage rate)}}$$

It is assumed that successive additions to a person's income will yield smaller increments of satisfaction, and that successive losses of hours of leisure time will lead to progressively greater loss of satisfaction as leisure time becomes ever more scarce. This will determine whether our individual places himself at A or B in figure 14.4.

This conveys the essence of the problem but in reality the circumstances will be far more complicated. The choice would realistically involve either working a few hours at a relatively low part-time rate, or switching to a full-time job with a higher rate but a minimum eight-hour day, or, finally, working a few hours overtime at an even higher rate.

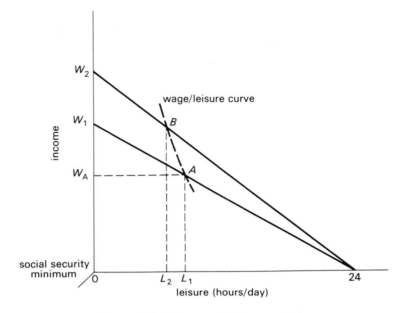

Figure 14.5 *The wage/leisure curve*

The next obvious question concerns the effect of an increase in the wage rate. If this were to happen, would our individual choose to work more or less? The analysis of this question is shown in figure 14.5. In this figure the original wage rate gives a maximum hypothetical wage of W_1 if no leisure is taken. Our individual chooses to locate himself at point A where he has an income of W_A and a leisure time of L_1 hours/day. Then the wage rate is increased giving a maximum attainable wage of W_2. His new preferred position is at B, where it happens that he has an income of W_1, equal to the maximum attainable under the old wage rate, but still has leisure of L_2 hours/day. The effect of the wage rate increase has been to increase the number of hours that he works to $24 - L_2$, and to reduce the amount of leisure taken to L_2. The movement from point A to point B in the figure could be viewed as involving an income and a substitution effect, as considered previously in chapter 3.

An increase in the wage rate means that the relative price of leisure has increased; it is more expensive than previously. The response we would expect via the substitution effect is a reduction in the consumption of leisure as a result of its increased price. But there is also the income effect to consider.

The fact that the wage rate has increased means that at all levels of work the individual will be better off than previously; he has gained an increase in income. The 'normal' effect of an increase in income is to increase expenditure on 'normal' goods. The income effect of the wage increase, if leisure is a normal good, will be to increase the consumption of leisure. The net results

Figure 14.6 *An individual's short-run labour supply curve*

will depend upon the balance of these two opposing effects. In the case of the individual in figure 14.5 the substitution effect dominates and the net effect is a reduction in the amount of leisure taken.

The wage/leisure curve in figure 14.5 traces out the relationship between leisure taken (or hours worked) and alterations in the wage rate. It is a short step from this to the derivation of an individual's labour supply curve, which shows the relationship between hours worked and the wage rate. It would probably look something like figure 14.6.

This figure shows that the number of hours an individual is prepared to work is likely to be positively related to the wage rate. There is some controversy about the top section of the curve. Whether an individual chooses to work more or less in response to a wage increase depends on the relative magnitudes of the income and substitution effects. If the income effect outweighs the substitution effect he might well respond by taking more leisure hours. This would produce a backward-bending labour supply curve at high wage rates, as shown in figure 14.6 by the dotted section of the curve. There is not much empirical evidence on this point, and hours actually worked are a function of both supply and demand factors, but it has been traditionally argued that in certain industries increased absenteeism and 'unofficial' days off might suggest that the labour supply curve behaves in this fashion.

The long-run supply of labour is a function of a number of complex demographic, sociological and educational and other factors. Before we proceed to consider these it might be wise to have a closer look at the labour market in practice. We can begin by looking at the working population.

The Labour Force

The supply of labour will be governed by the overall size of the labour force and by *economic activity rates*; that is, by the proportions of the various sex and age groups which make up the population and who are working or actively looking for work. The labour force in Great Britain increased by over 2 million between 1961 and 1979 with the bulk of this growth taking place in the 1960s (see table 14.2).

Table 14.2 *The size of the labour force in Great Britain*[a] *(millions) (estimates)*

	Females			Males	All persons
	Married	Non-married	All females		
1961[b]	3.9	3.9	7.7	16.1	23.8
1971[b]	5.8	3.4	9.2	15.9	25.1
1981	6.6	3.7	10.3	15.7	26.0

[a] Excluding students in full-time education. From 1973, 15 year olds are excluded as a result of raising the school leaving age

[b] Estimates for 1961 and 1971 are taken directly from the Census of Population. Data for later years are based on the EEC Labour Force Survey

Source: Social Trends 13 (1983), p. 52

The major changes involve a large increase in the female labour force combined with a slight reduction in the male labour force. The increase in the male population has been offset by the raising of the school leaving age and a decline in activity rates; this decline is most evident amongst older men, who have recently shown a tendency to retire earlier. Details of activity rates are given in table 14.3.

The large increase in the female labour force over the period considered has largely been the result of the growth in the proportion of married women wanting to work plus an increase in demand for part-time workers. The increase in female activity rates is evident from the table. The pattern for males has shown more stability, and during the 1970s about 92 per cent of men in the 16−64 age group were economically active.

There are a number of ways in which the economic analysis developed previously can be applied in the analysis of activity rates. But first and foremost it could be argued that most of the labour force is in households and that it is therefore household rather than individual income which is the most important factor. A distinction is often made between primary workers, such as married men who are likely to be the family breadwinners, and

Table 14.3 *Economic activity rates in Great Britain:*[a] *by age and sex (percentages)*

	15–19[b]	20–24	25–44	45–59/64[c]	60/65 +[d]	All ages
All females						
1961[e]	71.1	61.8	40.3	41.4	10.0	37.3
1971[e]	55.9	60.1	50.6	57.4	12.4	42.7
1981	64.2	68.9	61.4	63.6	6.5	46.6
All males						
1961[e]	74.6	91.9	98.5	96.8	25.0	86.0
1971[e]	60.9	89.9	97.9	94.5	19.4	81.4
1981	70.9	88.9	97.0	88.4	8.0	77.3

[a] Excluding students in full-time education
[b] From 1973, 15 year olds are excluded as a result of the raising of the school leaving age
[c] 45–59 for females, 45–64 for males
[d] 60 + for females, 65 + for males
[e] Estimates for 1961 and 1971 are taken directly from the Census of Population. Data for 1981 are based on the EEC Labour Force Survey

Source: Social Trends 13 (1983), p. 52

secondary workers, such as their wives, who are more likely to move in and out of the workforce, depending on family circumstances, incidence of childbirth, and so on. Indeed, the activity rates for primary workers are much higher. The fact that activity rates have risen in a period in which real incomes have risen would suggest that the income effects of increases in income have not outweighed the substitution effects, but this is a complex field in which there have been many factors which have altered. There have been alterations in the number of hours worked and in the availability of holidays, as shown in table 14.4.

Average normal weekly hours were 39.8 at the end of 1980 as compared with 40.2 hours at the end of 1970. The labour force is defined as all those in employment; employees, employers, self-employed, Her Majesty's forces, and those identified by censuses and surveys as seeking work (including those both registered and unregistered as unemployed, but excluding students in full-time education. It is difficult to predict changes in this force with any degree of accuracy. It is estimated that between 1981 and 1986 the total population of working age should rise by 762,000, but activity rates will be affected by, for example, changes in the birth-rate and by the level of unemployment, since it is argued that in periods of high unemployment some potential workers are discouraged from seeking work by the difficulty of finding suitable work.[8]

Table 14.4 *Holidays with pay*

End year	Percentage of manual workers with basic holidays of					Percentage with extra service holiday entitlement
	2 weeks	between 2 and 3 weeks	3 weeks	between 3 and 4 weeks	4 weeks and over	
1971	28	5	63	4	—	17
1975	1	1	17	51	30	26
1980	—	—	2	24	74	40

Source: Employment Gazette, Department of Employment (April 1981), p. 184

The labour force in terms of type of occupation

The industrial sector of the economy, defined to include manufacturing, gas, electricity, water and construction industries, has been in decline in recent years, with a shrinkage of employees of almost 2 million between 1961 and 1979. This was partly offset by an increase of 0.5 million men working in service industries. Female employees in the industrial sector declined by about 0.75 million against a background of a rise in female employees of 1.5 million between 1961 and 1979. There was also a large increase in part-time working, much of it female and the bulk of it concentrated in service industries. Table 14.5 gives a breakdown of employment by sector.

Notable features of this table are the continuing decline of the manufacturing sector, no doubt exaggerated by the recession, but with relative employment down 6 per cent since 1973. The other side of the coin is the continuing advance of the service sector; insurance, banking and finance now account for 12.4 per cent and professional and scientific services for 17.4 per cent of total employment. On an international comparative basis with other developed countries, the proportion in the service sector is not unduly large, and we still have a relatively large industrial sector, as can be seen from table 14.6.

However, the relative advance and decline of the different sectors is symptomatic of major structural changes and dislocations within the UK economy, and is the root of much of the disparity in regional unemployment rates considered in the next section.

Unemployment and the Regional Problem

Those members of the workforce who are actively seeking employment and

Table 14.5 *Employees in employment in UK, broken down by industrial sector. Dated at June. Industries analysed according to the SIC 1968. Thousands (percentages in parentheses)*

	1973	1977	1981[a]
Total employees in employment[b]	22,663 (100.0)	22,619 (100.0)	21,205 (100.0)
Total, production industries[c]	9,917 (43.8)	9,259 (40.9)	7,847 (37.0)
Agriculture, forestry and fishing[d]	432 (1.9)	388 (1.7)	360 (1.7)
Mining and quarrying	363 (1.6)	350 (1.5)	332 (1.6)
Manufacturing industries	7,830 (34.5)	7,292 (32.2)	6,041 (28.5)
Construction	1,380 (6.1)	1,270 (5.6)	1,134 (5.3)
Gas, electricity and water	344 (1.5)	347 (1.5)	340 (1.6)
Transport and communication	1,524 (6.7)	1,468 (6.5)	1,440 (6.8)
Distributive trades	2,744 (12.1)	2,753 (12.2)	2,636 (12.4)
Insurance, banking, finance and business services	1,058 (4.7)	1,145 (5.1)	1,233 (5.8)
Professional and scientific services	3,250 (14.3)	3,646 (16.1)	3,695 (17.4)
Catering, hotels, etc.	794 (3.5)	863 (3.8)	872 (4.1)
Miscellaneous services[b] (excluding catering, hotels, etc.)	1,359 (6.0)	1,480 (6.5)	1,542 (7.3)
National government service[e]	608 (2.7)	650 (2.9)	615 (2.9)
Local government service	977 (4.3)	964 (4.3)	964 (4.5)

[a] Provisional
[b] Excluding private domestic service
[c] The industries included in the index of production are orders II–XXI of the SIC 1968
[d] The estimates for agriculture are taken from the censuses of agriculture and exclude a small number of employees of agricultural machinery contractors
[e] Excluding members of Her Majesty's forces

Source: Monthly Digest of Statistics (Oct. 1981)

are unable to find it are said to be unemployed. The distinction is normally made between this type of unemployment, which is involuntary, and voluntary unemployment, which describes those potential members of the workforce who have withdrawn their labour, perhaps because they think the inducement to work at the prevailing rate they command is inadequate.

Table 14.6 *An international comparison of civilian employment by sector,
1979 (percentages)*

	Agriculture[a]	Industry	Services	Total
United Kingdom	3	39	58	100
Canada	6	29	65	100
France	9	36	55	100
German Federal Republic	6	45	49	100
Italy	15	38	47	100
Japan	11	35	54	100
USA	4	31	65	100

[a] Includes hunting, forestry and fishing

Source: Department of Employment; and *Social Trends*, 11 (1981)

Unemployment is categorized into various types. People changing jobs are unlikely to move between one job and another instantaneously, and so there will always be a certain amount of what is termed *frictional unemployment*. Vacancies will vary with the seasons; hotels, the building industry and agriculture will have varying demands for labour according to the time of year, and so there will be seasonally related unemployment. Both national economies and the collective international economy display cycles of economic activity with periods of boom and slump. If demand is depressed and the authorities are pursuing 'tight' monetary policies with regimes of high interest rates there will be *cyclical unemployment* (the relationship between the rate of unemployment and the rate of inflation will be considered later in this chapter). Finally, and particularly important in the UK context, there is *structural unemployment*. This is caused by changes in the structure and relative importance of different sectors of the economy. The run-down of some of the more traditional industries such as iron and steel, cotton and textiles, shipbuilding etc. means that in the localities where these industries are concentrated—Scotland, Northern England and South Wales—there are likely to be higher and more persistent unemployment rates (these problems are considered more fully in chapter 15).

The fact that the world is currently experiencing a synchronized recession, owing to the transfer of oil revenues to the OPEC countries and the fact that most authorities are pursuing fairly tight monetary policies means that unemployment in the UK currently stands at record levels in terms of absolute figures for the post-war period. The dismal situation is shown in table 14.7.

There has been criticism of the unemployment statistics, which are based upon the number of workers actually registered as unemployed. It is argued that some potential workers, particularly married women, do not bother to

Table 14.7 *United Kingdom unemployment rates: estimates on a Census of Employment basis, seasonally adjusted (thousands)*

	Working population	Unemployed, excluding adult students	Percentage unemployed
1970	25,344	555	2.2
1974 June	25,652	542	2.1
1977	26,299	1,450	5.5
1979	26,493	1,402	5.3
1980 March	26,362[a]	1,478	5.6
1981	26,168	2,485	9.5
1982 June	25,754	2,911	12.2

[a] The figures are affected by the introduction in Great Britain of fortnightly payment of unemployment benefit. In arriving at the seasonally adjusted working population figures, a deduction of 20,000 has been made to allow for the effects of the new arrangements

Source: Monthly Digest of Statistics (Oct. 1982), table 3.1

register, even though this could mean the forfeit of possible unemployment or supplementary benefits. On the other hand it is also argued that some people register with the attainment of these benefits in mind without having a real desire to find work. It is difficult to be sure of the numbers involved in these effects, but there can be little argument about the magnitude of the regional disparities in unemployment rates shown in table 14.8.

The gravity of the current regional unemployment rates is self-evident. Even the traditionally prosperous South-East now has a 9 per cent unemployment rate. The Northern regions, Scotland, Northern Ireland and Wales have had persistent problems in the post-war years. Even more dramatic is the change in fortune of the West Midlands; this region, traditionally prosperous, though heavily reliant on the motor industry, light engineering, and textiles, now has the fourth highest rate of unemployment.

Serious though these figures are, it could be argued that the important statistic is not the number of unemployed at any one time, but the length of time or duration that people are unemployed. Since 1961 unemployment at all durations has increased, but it is particularly marked in the case of those unemployed for a year or more. In 1971 this group accounted for about one-sixth of the unemployed but it had risen to one-quarter by 1979. The composition of the group varies; the young, the old and the unskilled are particularly at risk. There is a greater demand for skilled labour, and consequently the duration of its unemployment is likely to be less.

We have now considered the supply of labour in terms of the composition of the labour force and the distribution of unemployment. We can now look

Table 14.8 *Regional unemployment numbers and rates: analysis by standard regions (thousands)*

	North	Yorkshire & Humberside	East Midlands	East Anglia	South-East	South-West	West Midlands	North-West
1976	101.3	114.0	73.6	33.9	316.3	102.9	133.1	197.0
1980	147.5	163.6	104.0	41.4	363.1	113.1	181.6	264.5
1981 (8 Oct.)	216.2	277.4	177.0	70.1	686.5	179.8	349.7	424.2
Unemployment rate 8 Oct. 1981[a]	15.9	13.2	10.9	9.7	9.0	10.7	15.1	14.9

	Wales	Scotland	Northern Ireland
1976	78.1	154.4	54.9
1980	111.3	225.7	78.8
1981 (8 Oct.)	170.1	325.4	112.2
Unemployment rate 8 Oct. 1981[a]	15.7	14.4	19.5

[a] Percentage rates have been calculated by expressing the total numbers unemployed as percentages of the numbers of employees (employed and unemployed) at the appropriate mid-year

Source: Monthly Digest of Statistics (Oct. 1981), table 3.11

more closely at more detailed aspects of the labour market. We shall begin by looking at pay differentials and then examine some of the factors behind them such as trade union activity, government regulation, strike activity and the like.

Pay Differentials

One of the striking features of changes in pay differentials in both Britain and Western Europe in recent years is the narrowing of pay differentials between manual and non-manual workers. It is also true that the bulk of these changes were concentrated in the early 1970s and that the recent picture has been much more static. The broad picture is given in table 14.9.

Although the relative position of management in Britain has deteriorated there are compensatory factors in the form of the various management perquisites which are not taken into account in the figures; though, admittedly, management make up a small proportion of non-manual workers.

Pay differentials are likely to be influenced by a great many factors, amongst which might be included: general economic factors; excess demand or supply of various types of labour in particular industries; union activity and collective bargaining agreements; government policy; and the various 'skill' differentials between occupations. A brief snapshot of the more extreme differentials for manual workers between industries is given in table 14.10. In the other Western European countries similar patterns are displayed, with energy industries and printing being in the top ranks and clothing, footwear, wool and leather being generally well represented at the bottom of the league. Competition with Third World producers is probably a major factor here,

Table 14.9 *Manual/non-manual differentials in average gross monthly earnings in industry, October 1972 and 1979: men and women combined (non-manual as percentage of manual monthly earnings)*

	Great Britain[a]	West Germany	France	Italy
1972	120.7	129.2	167.4	175.3
1979	112.2	137.6	155.9	144.8[b]
If no change in manual worker's weekly hours:				
	112.7	124.1	142.4	134.8[b]

[a] April to April
[b] April 1979

Source: *Employment Gazette* (July 1981); D. Marsden, '*Vive la différence*: pay differentials in Britain, West Germany, France and Italy'

Table 14.10 *The five highest- and the five lowest-paid UK industries:*
manual men, October 1979 (average hourly earnings as a
percentage of average for all of industry)

Five highest-paid industries		Five lowest-paid industries	
Coal mining (deep)	136.9	Knitting mills	90.3
Printing	126.9	Cotton	87.0
Tobacco	126.9	Wool	82.9
Oil refining	122.7	Leather	81.9
Iron and steel	114.4	Clothing	78.2

Source: Employment Gazette (July 1981); Marsden, *'Vive la différence'*

but these industries tend to employ a large number of women and younger
people. Although differences in occupation 'accounted' for about one-
quarter of the dispersion in overall monthly earnings, age, sex, and length of
service were also important factors. Economic factors are also important; in
1972 the car industry was at the top of the league in the UK, but the combined
effects of the oil crisis, the recession and import penetration pushed it well
down the league in 1979. By contrast, the West German car industry remains
in the top five in that country.

It is no accident, however, that in coal mining and printing the unions are
particularly strong. This is, therefore, an appropriate point to consider the
role of trade unions and the systems of collective bargaining (a term coined
by Beatrice Webb to describe an agreement concerning pay and conditions
of work settled between trade unions on the one side and employers or
employers' associations on the other) practised in Britain.[9]

The Role of Trade Unions

The Donovan Commission defined a trade union as 'any combination of
employees the principal activity of which is the regulation of relations between
employees and employers'.[10] The aggregate membership of trade unions in
the United Kingdom at the end of 1979 was 13,498,000, an increase of 386,000
on the 1978 figure. At the same time the number of trade unions was 454
compared with 462 the year previously. Over the last ten years, trade union
membership has increased by 28.8 per cent whilst the number of unions,
frequently through amalgamations, has declined by 24.4 per cent.[11] This has
meant an increase in the average membership of unions to 30,000. The
overall numbers break down into roughly 9 million male and 4 million
female members with the latter category showing the most rapid rate of
increase in recent years. The largest unions ranked by membership for the

1978–79 period are shown in table 14.11 together with the largest employers' associations ranked by subscription income.

The great majority of unions in the United Kingdom are affiliated to the Trades Union Congress (TUC), which has its headquarters in London. The craft unions of skilled workers were the first to emerge and in the nineteenth century membership was confined to this small group. Their initial aim was to maintain standards and to control the rate of entry to the craft via the apprentice system. This was the product of the development of an industrial system which required a set of craftsmen who were destined to remain employees for their entire working life rather than own their own workshops.

If we return to the consideration of Marshall's four rules, which determine the elasticity of derived demand for a factor, we see that the craft unions are particularly well placed to make use of rule 2; the demand for their labour is likely to be inelastic, as they normally only account for a small proportion of total production costs. By their control of entry to the craft they were able to control the supply of labour and shift it to the left. This reduction in supply meant that their wages would be high relative to non-craft union labour, with only a slight diminishment in the employment of craft labour. Craft unions will have a membership which spans industries, depending upon where specific skills are required.

In the last decade of the nineteenth and the early decades of the twentieth century, there was a growth of general unions which recruited from a wide variety of workers, mainly unskilled, and from a wide variety of industries. This type of union labour faces a relatively elastic demand, since it is relatively easy to substitute non-union for union labour, and in the earlier years of the century there was usually a substantial pool of unemployed labour. General unions therefore aimed at organizing all sellers of labour so that they could minimize the substitution of non-union labour.

In America and Europe industrial unions which seek to organize all workers in a particular industry, regardless of their level of skill, are quite common, but they have not taken hold in Britain. The nearest parallel is the National Union of Mineworkers which represents the interests of the vast majority of workers in the mining industry.

Apart from a continuing tendency to amalgamation, the most notable feature of unionism in the post-war period has been the growth of white-collar unionism—a natural concomitant of the continued growth of the service sector and the relative decline of the manufacturing sector. White-collar unions are now well represented in both the public and private sectors, as evidenced by the growth of the various teaching unions, such as the National Union of Teachers (NUT), and by the representation of local government officers by the National Association of Local Government Officers (NALGO) and of management in the private sector by unions such as the Association of Scientific, Technical and Managerial Staffs (ASTMS).

Unions in the United Kingdom are usually governed by an executive council elected by the membership, and the majority have a full-time staff supervised

Table 14.11 *The largest unions and employers' associations 1978–79*

Trade unions

Rank	Name	Year ended	Number of members
1	Transport and General Workers' Union	31–12–79	2,086,281
2	Amalgamated Union of Engineering Workers[a]	31–12–78	1,494,382
3	National Union of General and Municipal Workers	29–12–79	967,153
4	National and Local Government Officers' Association	31–12–79	753,226
5	National Union of Public Employees	31–12–79	691,770
6	Association of Scientific, Technical and Managerial Staffs	31–12–79	491,000
7	Union of Shop Distributive and Allied Workers	31–12–79	470,017
8	Electrical, Electronic, Telecommunication and Plumbing Union	31–12–79	443,621
9	National Union of Mineworkers[b]	31–12–78	371,740
10	Union of Construction, Allied Trades and Technicians	31–12–78	325,245

[a] Comprising four constituent branches: Construction (35,235 members); Engineering (1,199,465); Foundry (58,728); Technical, Administrative and Supervisory (200,954)

[b] Includes 29 areas and other constituents of the union which submit separate figures

by a general secretary. The larger unions have full-time officials at local level as well as local and regional organizations of lay members. At the level of the individual plant the workforce usually elects a shop steward who acts as their spokesman and representative in negotiations with management.

The economic analysis of union activities

It is undoubtedly true that both political and economic factors are inextricably linked in the activities of trade unions, but does this mean that economic analysis has to be discarded as a means of analysing their behaviour? This was the basis of the celebrated Ross/Dunlop debate.[12] Ross suggested that union activity could not be analysed along the traditional utility-maximizing lines of economic theory. This followed from the fact that a union is typically made up of a heterogeneous group of people with a heterogeneous set of objectives. At any point in time political compromise within the union would

Table 14.11 *cont.*

Employers' associations

Rank	Name	Year ended	Subscription income (£000)
1	National Farmers' Union	31−10−79	4869
2	Engineering Employers' Federation	31−12−78	4631
3	National Federation of Building Trades' Employers[c]	31−12−78	3199
4	General Council of British Shipping/ British Shipping Federation	31−12−79	2725
5	British Printing Industries' Federation[d]	31−3−79	1419
6	Chemical Industries Association	30−6−79	1225
7	British Paper and Board Industry Federation	31−12−79	865
8	Federation of Civil Engineering Contractors	31−12−79	764
9	Road Haulage Association	31−12−79	694
10	Newspaper Society	31−12−79	692

[c] Comprising 17 separate engineering employers' associations
[d] Comprising 12 constituent associations

Source: The Times 1000, Times Books, 1980

balance these conflicting interests and place greater emphasis on the attainment of certain objectives at the expense of others. Dunlop countered with the view that although political factors may be important in the short run, in the long run economic forces are of prime importance and the behaviour of wages and conditions of employment will be determined by market forces. The latter view is adopted in this text.

However, there are difficulties involved; a major one is concerned with the specification of union objectives. Two obvious ones concern the level of wage rates and the volume of employment within a market, and they cannot be simultaneously pursued, as can be seen in figure 14.7.

D is the demand curve for labour and MS_1 is the supply curve of labour in the absence of union activity. Once the labour market is unionized the union establishes a higher wage for its members than the previous competitive wage OW_1. The new unionized labour supply curve is MS_2 and the equilibrium wage rate is now OW_2, but this is established at the expense of a drop in

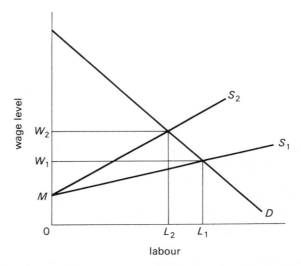

Figure 14.7 *The trade-off between setting the wage level and the volume of employment*

employment from OL_1 to OL_2. Given a downward-sloping demand curve and an upward-sloping labour supply curve it is inevitable that there must be a trade-off between the level of employment and the wage rate established. The extent of the trade-off depends upon the previously considered elasticity of demand for labour, and hence the craft unions are better placed facing a relatively inelastic demand.

It has been suggested that a compromise between these two objectives can be effected by assuming that unions seek to maximize the wage bill, given by the area of the rectangle $OW_2 - OL_2$ in figure 14.7 if W_2 is the equilibrium wage. This can cause difficulties. Suppose a wage rate at W_2 does maximize the wage bill. This implies that if supply conditions had been different and a higher equilibrium wage had been established, then the union would have taken a wage cut. This behaviour is not commonly observed.

It is quite possible that a union will place differing emphasis on the wage rate and the level of employment depending upon the relative magnitudes of the two. The compromise adopted is revealed in the *wage preference path* shown in figure 14.8. The steeper the slope of this line the greater the emphasis being placed upon increases in the wage rate rather than on the level of employment. The kink at the current equilibrium wage rate suggests that the union is loth to accept a cut in wages and is prepared to accept relatively rapid drops in the level of employment in order to maintain its wage levels; however, its response to an increase in demand is to switch to placing greater emphasis upon the wage rate than on the level of employment. The union's preferred response to shifts in the demand for labour is shown by the wage preference path. Downward shifts in demand will cause rapid reductions in employment but upward shifts in demand increase the wage rate.

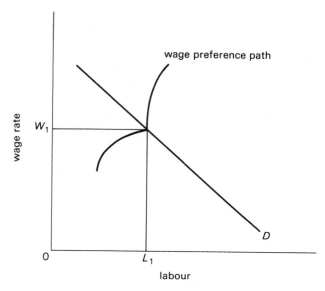

Figure 14.8 *The wage preference path*

The term *wage rate* as employed above covers a multitude of aspects of pay bargaining, including overtime and shift rates, sick pay, holiday pay, pensions provision, arrangements to pay laid-off workers, and so on. However, it could be argued that the components of this 'package' are regarded by the labour force as being close substitutes, though the emphasis in negotiations will vary with time and circumstance, and from the company's viewpoint they are all labour costs. So the analysis holds good.

Theories of Bargaining

We shall begin by considering two models which set limits on the wage rates considered in the bargaining process between employers and unions, but leave the actual solution indeterminate, and then proceed to some more direct theories of the actual bargaining process. In figure 14.9 we utilize the wage preference path again. The initial equilibrium position is at point A with a wage rate set at W_1 and an employment level of OL_1. Then the demand for labour increases from D to D_1. If the employer could attract all the extra workers he required at the existing wage rate (i.e. there is a perfectly elastic supply of labour), then he would employ OL_3 units of labour in total at a wage rate W_1. By so doing he is equating the marginal revenue product of labour with its marginal cost, and therefore seeking to maximize his profits. Suppose the union steps in. Its wage preference path indicates that it is prepared to accept lower employment in order to obtain a higher wage rate for its members. Its preferred position is at point C with a wage rate of W_2

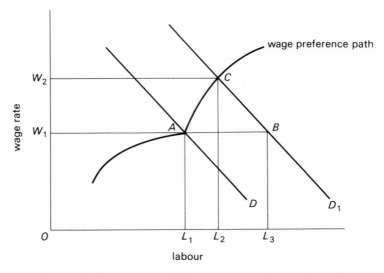

Figure 14.9 *The wage preference path and wage bargaining*

and an employment level of OL_2. The points C and B set boundaries to the wage bargaining positions, and the eventual outcome will be somewhere between these two points, depending on the relative bargaining skills and strengths of the two parties.

A similar result is obtained from the neoclassical model of *bilateral monopoly* which assumes that a monopsonistic employer faces a union with a monopoly of the labour supply, as shown in figure 14.10. The employer seeks to maximize his profits by following the familiar marginal conditions; he equates the marginal cost of labour *MC LS* with his marginal revenue product curve—the demand curve D, as shown at A. He therefore employs OL_1 units of labour and seeks to pay them a wage rate of W_3, since the labour supply curve *LS* shows that at this wage rate the required labour force would be forthcoming. The union as a monopolist, on the other hand, will seek to maximize the collective rents of its employed members. This will be effected by equating the marginal revenue curve associated with the demand curve for labour, *MD* (lying below the demand curve, since every unit increase in employment requires a wage rate cut), with the labour supply curve *LS*, as shown at C. In the figure this also produces the same level of employment OL_1. The union will then try to maximize the economic rent of the employed labour force, indicated by the area EW_1AC, by charging the maximum wage rate that the market will bear: W_1: Thus there is an area of indeterminacy between the two extreme wage rates W_1 and W_3. This encompasses the competitive wage rate of W_2, indicated by the intersection of the labour supply and demand curve at point B. But the actual wage rate determined will depend on the outcome of the bargaining process and could lie anywhere between the two extremes.

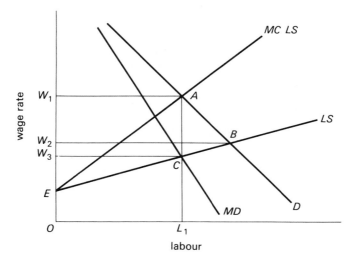

Figure 14.10 *The bilateral monopoly model of employer/trade union bargaining*

This approach has been criticized on the grounds that the analogy between a monopoly producer and a union is a rather strained one. A company producing goods experiences costs, whereas those experienced by a union are of a rather different nature and not directly related to changes in the supply of labour. The union is merely an agent which represents its members in the bargaining process, and is unlikely to have an appreciation of the marginal cost or supply price of its members.

Sir John Hicks was one of the first to produce a direct theory explaining the bargaining process.[13] He directly included the threat and potential cost of industrial action in the form of a strike as a means by which a union can compel an employer to pay higher wages. The bargaining process is analysed by means of an *employer's concession curve* and a *union resistance curve*. In figure 14.11 W_1 is the wage rate that the employer is prepared to pay in the absence of a strike and W_2 is the union's maximum wage demand. The employer faces a trade-off between the expected cost of a strike, in terms of loss of production and customer goodwill, and the cost of conceding a higher wage. If he is faced with the probability of a very long and costly strike he will be prepared to pay a higher rate to buy industrial peace. Hence his employer's curve rises as a function of expected strike length, but it rises at a diminishing rate and there comes a time when he would rather go out of business than pay excessively high wage demands.

The union resistance curve falls as a function of the expected length of strike since there is a limit to both the union's ability to fund a strike and the sacrifices its members are prepared to make. The curve shows the minimum wage the union will accept rather than strike for a given time. Ultimately it

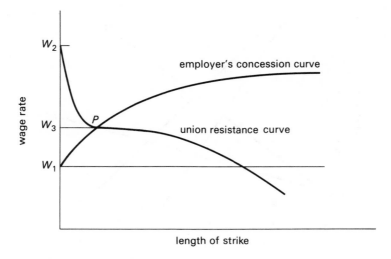

Figure 14.11 *Hicks's analysis of the bargaining process*

intersects the minimum wage offered by the employer since there is a limit to the period for which the union is prepared to strike. The curve is relatively flat over a portion of its length, since there is a level of wages to which the men think they are entitled; they will hold out for a relatively long time to achieve this, though they will not be very concerned to raise wages above it.

The two curves intersect at P and the corresponding wage rate W_3 represents the highest wage that skilful negotiation can expect to extract from the employer. If the union sets a wage demand below W_3 the employer will be fairly ready to concede but the union negotiators have not done particularly well. It is assumed that in the negotiating process each side has a clear idea of its own, but has to estimate that of the other. If the mutual perceptions are fairly accurate both parties will be fairly ready to settle for wage W_3. But if perceptions are inaccurate, or the curves shift over time, there is a likelihood of a strike.

A similar and straightforward approach resting on the perceptions of relative costs by both sides of the bargaining process was suggested by Chamberlain.[14] If both parties are rational economic agents and wish to produce a solution which minimizes costs, then the following rules hold;

$$\text{employer's bargaining power} = \frac{\text{cost to union of disagreeing with employer}}{\text{cost to union of agreeing with employer}}$$

$$\text{union's bargaining power} = \frac{\text{cost to employer of disagreeing with union}}{\text{cost to employer of agreeing with union}}$$

The simple rule which follows from this approach is that if the cost ratio is less than 1 the party concerned will refuse the other's terms, but if it is greater than 1 it will agree. Neither can be sure of the other's cost position and the successful bargaining ploy will be to ensure that the other party's ratio is pushed above unity whilst one's own remains below.

UK Industrial Relations in Practice

The Donovan Commission suggested in 1968 that at that time Britain had two systems of industrial relations; a formal system embodied in official institutions and an informal one created by the actual behaviour of the parties and individuals involved. The centre-piece of the formal system was the industry-wide collective agreement, which the Royal Commission on Labour of 1891 compared with a 'regular and well thought out treaty'. A broad distinction can be made between 'multi-employer' agreements which involve a coalition or association of employers acting in common, and 'single-employer' bargaining in which an individual employer independently nego-tiates agreements with his own labour force. Multi-employer bargaining, spanning industries at a local or national level, developed in Britain in the nineteenth century and further advanced after World War I. National Joint Industrial Councils fostered negotiations between unions and employers' associations which set pay and conditions of work for individual industries.

For many years successive governments tried to encourage industry-wide bargaining agreements via the creation of wages councils in those industries where trade unionism was weak. The balance of power on these was held by representatives held to be independent of management and unions, and their awards were given statutory force via a wages inspectorate. In Europe industry-wide bargaining has reigned supreme but this has not been the case in Britain. Post-war full employment undermined these agreements and pressure from the labour market led employers to supplement industry-wide wage rates with payments by results, overtime and other supplements.

The trend towards single-employer bargaining was noted by the Donovan Commission, which referred to the remarkable transfer of authority in collective bargaining associated with the market decline, over the previous thirty years, in the extent to which industry-wide agreements determined actual pay. This trend has been further confirmed by a recent major survey of British industrial relations undertaken at Warwick University.[15] This involved a survey of practices at 970 manufacturing establishments during 1977–78. It was found that industry-wide agreements (including wages council awards) were regarded as the most important factor in pay deter-mination by only 33 per cent of establishments surveyed. Single-employer bargaining is now the most important factor for two-thirds of manual workers, and amongst non-manual workers its significance is even greater. The incidence of single-employer bargaining is more strongly associated with large, multiplant enterprises. Industry-wide agreements are now regarded as providing a 'floor' which affects the earnings of only the lowest-paid workers.

This change has had a major effect on the role of employers' associations. In the years up to 1914 they were important innovators of industrial relations practice—for example, in the coal and iron industry they introduced collective regulation of pay before stable unions were formed—but, in the years since, this role has been inherited by the unions and government. Even so, membership of the associations has not declined, though their emphasis has changed from being primarily concerned with negotiating industry-wide agreements to one of operating procedures for the resolution of disputes and providing advisory services. Advising on labour law and government legislation now seems to be a major function.

The Donovan Commission considered that disorder in factory and workshop relations and pay structures was due in no small measure to the conflict between the formal and the informal system of industrial relations. Greater order had to be reintroduced but it could not be done via employers' associations and trade unions working at industry level. It required effective and orderly collective bargaining over issues such as the regulation of hours worked, incentive schemes, work practices, facilities for shop stewards, disciplinary rules etc., and this was likely to be done most effectively at the level of the factory. The desired shift in focus could best be achieved by individual companies' boards of directors.

This view does seem to have been taken on board. The Warwick survey found that there had been a marked increase of specialist industrial relations management at the board of director level and this again appeared to be linked with firm size. In the companies surveyed with more than 5000 employees, 81 per cent had a director with industrial relations as his sole responsibility. There was a further link with establishment practice and the presence of a specialist at board level increased the likelihood of there being a parallel specialist at establishment level.

Following the promptings of the Donovan Commission there has been a tightening up of procedural practice and much government legislation has been to this end. This has included: *In Place of Strife* (1979); the *Industrial Relations Code of Practice* (1971), in which employers were encouraged to formalize negotiating procedures; and the setting up of the Commission on Industrial Relations (CIR) to encourage the process. A new branch of the High Court, the National Industrial Relations Court (NIRC) was set up and empowered to sit in judgement over cases of 'unfair industrial practices'. Amongst its powers was the facility to impose a full ballot of union members and to recommend 'cooling off' periods to delay industrial action. Subsequent controversy and opposition led to the abolishment of NIRC and CIR. In 1971 statutory protection was introduced against unfair dismissal which covered the manner as well as the reasons for dismissal.

Various other pieces of legislation have focused management attention on industrial relations practice. The Equal Pay Act was passed in 1970 and came into force in 1975. The 1975 Sex Discrimination Act outlaws discrimination on grounds of sex or marriage, and the Employment Protection Act of 1975 has further extended the rights of employees in cases of unfair dismissal. The Advisory, Conciliation and Arbitration Service (ACAS) was set up in 1974 to provide mediation in industrial disputes on a voluntary basis, though it can offer independent advice to the parties concerned. Its position was confirmed by statute in the following year. Further impetus has been given by a series of counter-inflation measures and attempts to control the increase of incomes by a variety of measures including 'incomes policies' (see later in this chapter).

The trends towards single-employer bargaining, greater professionalism of industrial relations management, and the reform of disputes procedures have provided a major impetus to the enhancement of the role of the shop steward. The existence of shop stewards is strongly associated with the size of the workforce and a very large proportion are now appointed on a full-time basis.

Another prominent recent trend has been the growth of the closed shop. The Warwick survey estimated that about 46 per cent of manual workers in manufacturing industry are members of a closed shop. In general, company management appears to be strongly in favour of it, frequently on the grounds that it ensures that unions and shop stewards represent all employees, thereby imparting greater stability to collective bargaining. Multi-unionism, on the other hand, can make collective agreements more difficult to attain and maintain. Management support for union activity is further underlined by the widespread use of the 'check-off' facility by which the management collects union dues by deducting them at source from wages. Consultative meetings between management and unions are now more prevalent; this has been stimulated by Acts such as the Health and Safety of Work Act of 1974 which required joint consultation on these matters. The shop steward frequently plays a key role in the negotiation of factory procedures and agreements and now stands in the foreground of British industrial relations practice.

Strikes

There are a large number of forms of industrial action including overtime bans, go-slows, working to rules and threatened strikes, as well as strike activity itself. Concentration on strike activity gives only a partial picture; it could be argued that the statistics provided by the Department of Employment understate strike activity in that they exclude stoppages involving fewer than ten workers or those which lasted for less than a day, unless the total number of days lost in aggregate exceeds 100.

It is frequently suggested that Britain has a poor industrial relations record in terms of the frequency of strike activity, but table 14.12 shows that in terms of other OECD countries our record is not particularly bad, though there is room for improvement.

Table 14.12 *Measures of the level of strike activity. Annual average 1969 to 1978, all industries and services*

	Number involved per 1000 employees	Rank	Working days lost per 1000 employees	Rank
Australia	287	19	638	16
Austria	6	5	13	2
Belgium[a]	25	7	255	9
Canada[a]	60	12	927	18
Denmark	43	9	255	10
Finland	205	17	609	15
France[a,b]	113	15	205	8
Germany (FR)[a]	9	6	53	6
Iceland[a,c]	275	18	1605	19
Irish Republic	51	11	731	15
Italy[a]	604	20	1625	20
Japan[a]	51	10	133	7
Netherlands	6	4	36	3
New Zealand	113	14	293	11
Norway	4	2	46	4
Spain	137	16	560	14
Sweden	5	3	48	5
Switzerland	0.3	1	2	1
United Kingdom[d]	60	13	472	12
United States	32	8	533	13

[a] Data on workers involved cover only those directly involved in stoppage
[b] France does not collect statistics for stoppages in agriculture and public administration
[c] No data available on number of stoppages or workers involved for 1978
[d] Number of workers directly involved in UK for the period averaged 45 workers directly involved per 1000 employees

Sources: ILO Yearbook, OECD Labour Force Statistics, as quoted in *Employment Gazette* (Nov. 1980)

There are a number of caveats about the comparability of the statistics shown in this table. Definitions of stoppages vary; some countries include only those directly involved, whereas others include indirect involvement (i.e. workers laid off because of a dispute elsewhere in the plant); and finally the method of compilation and source of statistical returns varies. The figures are shown in relative rather than absolute terms to adjust for differences in the size of the labour force of the countries shown. In terms of the average number of working days lost per 1000 employees, Britain is ranked 12th out

Table 14.13 *Stoppages in years 1960–1980 (at four-yearly intervals) (thousands)*

Year	Stoppages beginning in year	Workers[a] involved in stoppages in progress in year[b]	Working days lost in stoppages in progress in year
1960	2832	819	3024
1964	2524	883	2277
1968	2378	2258	4690
1972	2497	1734	23,909
1976	2016	668	3284
1980	1330	834	11,964

[a] Workers involved in more than one stoppage in any year are counted more than once in a year's total

[b] Figures exclude workers becoming involved after the end of the year in which the stoppage began

Source: Employment Gazette (July 1981)

of 20. Our record is better than that of Italy, Canada, Australia and the USA, though we fare worse than Japan, France and Germany.

Not surprisingly, the industrial relations systems in these various countries vary considerably. In Canada and the USA collective agreements are legally binding, so contravention is illegal. Hence disputes tend to arise over new agreements and can be protracted, as the terms are binding once agreed. In Sweden and West Germany agreements are also legally binding and yet there are far fewer strikes, perhaps because of the existence of more comprehensive grievance procedures. However, before we consider the various possible causes of strike activity we will look in more detail at the British record.

In 1980 in the UK there were 12.0 million working days lost through stoppages compared with 29.5 million in 1979. Disputes over pay caused 48 per cent of the stoppages in 1980 and 89 per cent of working days lost. The annual average of working days lost over the period 1970–79 was 12.9 million. The pattern varies markedly from year to year as can be seen in table 14.13.

The major cause of the considerable fluctuations shown in this table is the change in incidence of large strikes, which we shall arbitrarily define as those which involve the loss of 200,000 working days or more.[16] Over the past 20 years there have only been 64 such strikes, but they accounted for 46 per cent of the total number of working days lost. The industrial distribution of large stoppages is shown in table 14.14.

The more notable of the large strikes in the 1960s included: three one-day stoppages in the engineering industries, five in 1962 and one in 1968; the seamen's strike in 1966; the car workers' strike in 1969; and the miners'

Table 14.14 *The industrial distribution of large[a] stoppages 1960–79*

SIC order (1968)	Industry group[b]	Stoppages beginning in period	Working days lost in stoppages in progress (thousands)
II	Mining & quarrying	6	18,944
III	Food, drink & tobacco	2	670
VI	Metal manufacture	4	1050
VII–X	Engineering & shipbuilding	13	23,602
XI	Vehicles	13	7981
XVI	Bricks, pottery, glass, cement, etc.	1	346
XVIII	Paper, printing & publishing	2	792
XIX	Other manufacturing industries	1	240
XX	Construction	2	4137
XXI	Gas, electricity & water	1	305
XXII	Transport & communication	11	10,585
XXIV	Insurance, banking, finance & business services	1	267
XXV	Professional & scientific services	1	285
XXVI	Miscellaneous services	1	600
XXVII	Public administration & defence	5	6483
	All industries	64	76,286

[a] Those involving 200,000 or more working days lost
[b] Particular stoppages are allocated to their SIC order group according to the principal industry involved in the dispute

Source: *Employment Gazette* (Sept. 1980)

strike for a 40-hour week in the same year. In the 1970s the miners struck three times, in 1970, 1972 and 1974; the dockworkers twice in 1970 and 1972; the postal workers in 1971; and local government, health workers, firemen, and other public service staffs in 1970, 1978 and 1979. The construction industry struck in 1972; the car workers and print workers in 1978; the lorry drivers in 1979; and—the largest in terms of working days lost—the engineering workers in 1979.

Of the 64 large strikes in the period, 40 were known to be official, and although table 14.14 shows that large disputes occur over most sectors of the economy, strike activity is concentrated in certain sectors. Of the working days lost by large stoppages, 80 per cent were accounted for by strike activity in four broad industrial sectors; engineering and shipbuilding, mining, transport and communications, and vehicle manufacture. However, in engineering 16 million working days were lost in one dispute alone, and this probably distorts the picture.

What are the contributory causes of strike activity? Clegg has put forward a theory of strikes which suggests that plant bargaining leads to a relatively large number of official strikes whereas industry or regional bargaining leads to a smaller number of larger official strikes.[17] Comprehensive and efficient disputes procedures cut down the number of unofficial strikes, whereas disputes are more likely where the distinction between official and unofficial action is ill-defined. Yet Clegg concedes that this theory does not explain the incidence of major strikes, which he suggests are due to changing economic circumstances and relationships between unions and government.

In a pioneering paper, Prais has shown that the frequency of strikes in manufacturing industry plants is closely correlated with plant size and that the burden of strikes on larger plants is greater in three respects; the chance of having a strike-free year is lower, the expected number of strikes per year is greater, and the number of days lost per employee is greater.[18] Further corroboratory evidence has been provided by Edwards, in work emanating from the Warwick survey, in which plant size appeared as the most significant determining factor in strike activity, though the nature of union organization had a slight influence too.[19] Obviously these are not the only contributory causes of strike activity, which will vary according to circumstances, but these are the factors which show up in statistical analysis. The conclusion to be drawn from this is not evident. Is it that we need a more rigidly enforced system of binding labour contracts which might serve to inhibit strike activity?

Counter-inflation Policies

The experience of a persistent and ever-increasing upward trend in the rate of price inflation during the 1960s and 1970s has led to a preoccupation on the part of successive British governments with measures aimed at controlling inflation. These have taken various forms, but could be categorized under the following headings: monetary policy, fiscal policy, and wages and price controls. We shall be concentrating on the policies, but before we turn to them we shall briefly consider the various hypotheses about the causes of inflation.

Theories about the causes of inflation may be roughly divided into two groups; demand-pull and cost-push. *Demand-pull theories of inflation* are based on the argument that the causes of inflation originate on the demand side of the market. If the aggregate demand for goods and services exceeds their supply this can cause a rise in the general price level as frustrated consumers bid up prices by competing for scarce supplies of goods and services. This will in turn lead to an increase in the derived demand for factors of production, including labour, and therefore money wages will tend to increase.

Under the *cost-push hypothesis* a variety of factors on the supply side might be the cause of inflation. Firms might decide to demand higher profit margins, or monopolistic trade unions might force up money wage rates. Producers, faced with increased costs, pass them on by marking up their prices and so the price level is forced up. The resultant increase in prices could lead to a fall in demand and a rise in unemployment if the supply of money is unchanged, or the authorities might seek to maintain demand by increasing the supply of money.

The picture is confused by the fact that an excess in the supply of money might be the root cause of demand-pull inflation—'too much money chasing too few goods'. Thus the money supply features in both analyses of the causes of inflation, but the suggested policy measures differ. If demand-pull is the basis of the problem, fiscal and monetary measures can be used to reduce excess demand without having too disastrous an effect on the level of activity in the economy. Whereas if cost-push factors are the cause—perhaps trade union aggressiveness in pushing up wages—then monetary and fiscal measures might be a very blunt weapon to use against this, in that it might require very high levels of unemployment and reduced activity levels before the unions temper their claims. For this reason successive administrations have been tempted into trying to control wage increases directly by a variety of incomes policies; however, there has been argument about the efficacy of these policies, and we shall consider some of the empirical evidence before considering them in detail.

In 1958 Phillips published an empirical investigation of the relationship between employment and the rate of change of money wage rates in the UK over the period 1861–1957.[20] The famous *Phillips curve* depicted a stable and inverse relationship between the level of employment and the rate of change of money wages, as shown in figure 14.12. Other things being equal, this seemed to show that, according to the remarkably consistent evidence from the data over this long period, if demand were kept to a level consistent with stable wage rates the associated level of unemployment would be about 5.5 per cent.

The analysis seemed to present the authorities with a trade-off between lower unemployment at the cost of higher inflation or vice versa. It provided the stimulus to a great deal of further theoretical and empirical work, and Phillips interpreted his findings as providing strong support for the demand-pull view of inflation. Then in the late 1960s and the 1970s the traditional Phillips curve began to be inconsistent with stagflation—the persistent combined high levels of unemployment and inflation which were experienced in the UK.

One of the first to highlight the theoretical deficiencies of this model was Milton Friedman. He formulated an expectations-augmented Phillips curve which related the rate of change of money wages not only to the level of unemployment but also to expectations of the future level of inflation.[21] This suggested that the higher the expected level of inflation at any given level of

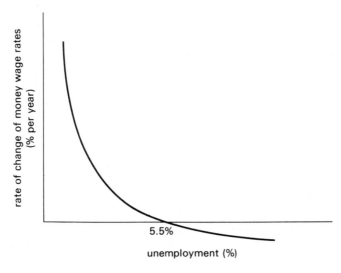

Figure 14.12 *The Phillips curve*

unemployment, the higher the rate of increases of the wage rate. Thus in figure 14.12 there would be a whole family of Phillips curves above the one shown, each corresponding to a different expected level of inflation. These would show the short-run trade-off between unemployment and inflation, but, suggested Friedman, in the long run there is only one level of unemployment—the natural rate—which is consistent with the absence of inflation.

Incomes policies of various forms have been a regular feature of post-war government. They could be interpreted either as attempts to deal with cost-push inflation or as a method of trying to shift the Phillips curve bodily to the left so that the inflation/unemployment trade-off is made available on more favourable terms. The term *incomes policy* covers a whole gamut of proposals from voluntary measures such as Cripps' 1948 wage standstill through to statutory policies.

In the early 1960s the Conservative Government of the period set up a National Incomes Commission as an alternative to demand management methods of dealing with inflation, but it was abolished in 1964 by the incoming Labour administration. That Government tried to introduce a 'voluntary' incomes policy—a tripartite statement of intent was signed by the government, the CBI and the TUC. The idea was to have a target norm for wage increases of 3.5 per cent. There are various political problems involved in setting the norm at an appropriate level, since once established it tends to be regarded as the minimum acceptable settlement. It could be argued that it distorts the price-allocatory mechanism in the labour market. Because of the perceived failure of a 'voluntary' policy the National Board for Prices and Incomes was set up to reinforce it, but to allow higher settlements where reallocation of labour was required. (In short, a formal incomes policy was in fact accepted by both political parties throughout the 1960s and much of the 1970s despite protestations to the contrary when each was in opposition.) The question of productivity-related deals proved difficult to handle and provided one of the major loopholes in the policy over the period 1964–69. It is also questionable whether all gains in productivity should be handed over to one factor of production. The policy proved fairly weak and in the second half of 1966 a statutory freeze of wage increases was adopted followed by a period of severe restraint. In the latter part of the Labour administration attention became focused more on dealing with strikes, and the resolution which lay behind the incomes policy, by then aimed at a ceiling of 3.5 per cent, weakened.

The Conservative Government which came to power in 1970 abolished the National Board for Prices and Incomes (as the Labour Party in 1964 had done with the National Incomes Commission). Unemployment was allowed to rise, though it did nothing to moderate the size of wage settlements; and in the public sector a 'nil' policy involved an attempt to reduce the size of each successive wage settlement, but this foundered on the miners' strike of 1972. A statutory incomes policy was then reintroduced with three stages. Stage one was a statutory freeze. Stage two was a norm of £1 plus 4 per cent, and a Pay Board and Price Commission to enforce it. Finally, stage three involved a threshold subject to various gateways, plus the promise of extra inflation-related adjustments should the rate of inflation exceed 7 per cent. Inflation did exceed this figure when stage three came into operation and resulted in wage promises which had to be kept by the incoming Labour administration in 1974.

The new government's approach was to initiate a 'social contract' between the government and the TUC which involved a commitment to moderation in wage claims. In its early years it was ineffective and though it was later stiffened there are numerous grounds for criticism. It would be more likely to succeed if bargaining were undertaken in the UK at a national or industry-wide level, but this is not the case. Individual bargaining units at single-employer level are much more likely to persuade themselves that they are a special case and are unlikely to be interested in the macro-economic consequences of their actions.

Conditions are different in the public sector, where industry-wide agreements are more common, extremely visible, and tend to set the pattern for the private sector to follow. Governments are here faced with the difficult task of reconciling the requirements of their macro-economic policy with the need to maintain an equitable and realistic pay structure within the public sector. Some sort of guidance on pay comparability was seen to be required. The government thus set up the Standing Commission on Pay Comparability which made several recommendations on public sector pay. These recommendations, made in 1978 and 1979, were honoured by the incoming Conservative Government. Like its Labour predecessor in 1974, the keeping of such promises posed a considerable macro-economic embarrassment to the administration. The Commission was also duly abolished. The new government provided for free collective bargaining in the private sector, and subsequently attempted to impose a blanket 6 per cent cash limit on public sector awards. The problem here is that this leads to further inequities; groups with industrial muscle, such as the miners, seem to have no trouble in exceeding the prescribed limits, whereas other groups, such as the nurses, are left standing on the sidelines. On the other hand, comparability claims can be used to justify leap-frogging wage increases.

The general efficacy of incomes policies thus remains in doubt. The attitude of the political parties appears to be totally ambivalent. It is frequently argued that incomes policies are temporarily successful in their stronger forms, but that as soon as they are relaxed a 'catching-up' phase undermines all that they have achieved. Yet some form of wage moderation may be required, if it is conceded that the free labour market is inadequate because of the monopoly powers of trade unions and the non-market responsiveness of the country's biggest employer, namely the state.

References

1 A. Smith, *The Wealth of Nations* (1776), Penguin, 1970, book 1, chapter 10.
2 K. Marx, *Capital: A Critique of Political Economy*, Penguin, 1978, vol. 2, part 2, chapter 10.
3 P. Sraffa, *The Production of Commodities by Commodities*, Cambridge University Press, 1960.
4 A. Marshall, *Principles of Economics*, Macmillan, 9th edn, 1961, vol. 1, book 6, chapter 1.
5 A. Marshall, *Principles of Economics*, vol. 1, book 5, chapter 6; Sir John Hicks, *The Theory of Wages*, Macmillan, 1968, p. 241.
6 A.C. Pigou, *Economics of Welfare*, 4th edn, London, 1962, book 4, chapter 5.
7 *Ibid.*
8 For a discussion of projections of the labour force see *Employment Gazette* Department of Employment (April 1981).
9 For further discussion of pay differentials and pay bargaining see F. Blackaby (ed.), *The Future of Pay Bargaining*, Heinemann, 1980.
10 Report of the Royal Commission on Trade Unions and Employers' Associations 1965–68, Chairman Lord Donovan, Cmnd 3623, HMSO, June 1968, p. 207.
11 *Employment Gazette* (Jan. 1981), p. 22.
12 A.M. Ross, *Trade Union Wage Policy*, University of California Press, 1948; J.T. Dunlop, *Wage Determination under Trade Unions*, Kelley, 1950.
13 Sir John Hicks, *The Theory of Wages*.
14 N.W. Chamberlain, *Collective Bargaining*, McGraw-Hill, 1951.
15 W. Brown (ed.), *The Changing Contours of British Industrial Relations*, Blackwell, 1981.
16 See 'Large industrial stoppages 1960–79', *Employment Gazette* (Sept. 1980).
17 H.A. Clegg, *Trade Unionism under Collective Bargaining*, Blackwell, 1976, p. 82.

18 S.J. Prais, 'The strike-proneness of large plants in Britain', *Journal of the Royal Statistical Society* 141 (1978).

19 P.K. Edwards, 'The strike-proneness of British manufacturing establishments', *British Journal of Industrial Relations* 19 (1981), pp. 135–48.

20 A.W. Phillips, 'The relationship between unemployment and the rate of change of money wage rates in the United Kingdom, 1861–1957', *Economica* 25 (1958).

21 M. Friedman, 'The role of monetary policy', *American Economic Review* 58 (1968).

15

Government Policy towards Industry

Government policy towards industry has two principal aims—monopoly and regional policies. Britain was one of the first nations to have an explicit regional policy but lagged several decades behind the USA in the establishment of a monopoly policy.

In addition there are other areas in which government is involved with industrial behaviour. We shall examine some of these below.

American Policy and the Structural Approach

American anti-monopoly (anti-trust) policy is often said to emphasize the structure of an industry. 'Unreasonable' and 'undue' concentrations of market power are discouraged either by merger prevention or by divestiture of assets (e.g. in 1982 American Telegraph and Telephone, AT & T, was compelled to sell off its interests in 22 regional telephone and cable companies). The objective is, therefore, to maintain a 'substantial' number of competing firms and hence to minimize monopolistic behaviour as such. In brief the rationale for the policy rests heavily on the traditional definitions of perfect competition (price takers) and monopoly (price searchers) rather than that of open and closed markets, either of which can have price takers or price searchers as we saw in tables 5.1 and 5.2.

The 1890 Sherman Act was the first manifestation of this approach. It was limited to two brief provisions:

1 It condemned as criminal every contract, combination in the form of trust or otherwise, or conspiracy in restraint of trade or commerce among the several states, or with foreign nations.
2 It condemned monopolies, or attempts or conspiracies to monopolize any part of that trade or commerce.

Although the Federal Trade Commission was established in 1914 to improve anti-trust enforcement it was not a court where infringements of the Sherman Act could be tried. As indicated above, by the use of the word 'criminal', the main enforcement agency was and remains the ordinary federal courts.

Until around 1920 almost all cases which reached as far as the Supreme Court were decided in favour of the government. During this period, however, the case experience, precedents and rulings which were accumulating were focusing on the word 'every'. In lower courts verdicts were being arrived at which bore little apparent consistency, because different judges interpreted the law in different ways. The controversy was resolved in a typical legal manner. 'Every' was to be interpreted 'reasonably'. This judgement was handed down from the Supreme Court in 1911 in the Standard Oil case. And since this the *rule of reason* has been used implicitly or explicitly in most anti-trust cases.

The rule of reason, although apparently riddled with potential for ambiguity, did attempt to move the law away from a purely structural approach to assessing monopoly (i.e. a sort of crude 'bigness is bad' *per se* attitude). In the 1911 case, the court said, both common law and statute were concerned with one question only. The question was 'does the restraint, viewed in its market setting, constitute a . . . significant limitation on competition?', or is the practice before the court 'clearly anti-competitive'? If so, the court's discretion under the rule of reason is exhausted. A restraint argued by the defendant to be justified in the public interest would not escape. To quote Rostow: 'In short, the Act did not forbid bad trusts, and condone good ones. It applied to all, by equating the public interest strictly with the elimination of substantial restraints on competition.'[1]

Thus offences under the Sherman Act came to be interpreted from an essentially economic viewpoint, albeit size and structure were still prime determinants of 'guilt' in the case of monopoly though no longer so in the case of restrictive practices. 'The monopolies of the turn of the century have (now) all disappeared, often in response to direct action under the anti-trust laws.'[2]

Why was American legislation some 60 years ahead of any equivalent activity in Britain? Rostow[3] argues that several reasons can be given:

1 There was no overt and dramatic merger movement in the UK in the 1880s and 1890s as there was in the USA. British buccaneering equivalents of Carnegie (steel), Rockefeller (oil) and Morgan (banking) did not exist. One trust which did come into being, the Players and Wills formation of Imperial Tobacco, was mainly a defensive move against the entry into the UK market by American Tobacco.
2 Competition in Britain was, in any event, far greater than in America. British firms had to compete in export markets, and against foreign imports. America, partly due to tariffs, partly to self-sufficiency, was far less exposed to foreign competition. There was thus a more overt 'need' for anti-trust laws.
3 The late nineteenth century depression was deeper and more prolonged in the USA. Big business there was regarded as a convenient scapegoat.
4 British political philosophy has never placed so strong an emphasis on the devolution of power as has the American tradition. The USA even

fought a civil war over the issue of states' rights. Thus the notion of a few large businesses controlling the economy and located in a few urban centres, such as New York, appeared more repellent to Americans than a similar situation would in Britain, which in any event is geographically only the size of many American states.

5 Politicians saw little mileage in Britain from anti-trust legislation. The Labour Party was more interested in reform through socialism than through competition. The Whig tradition of economic liberalism, which would have been interested, had been submerged in the Liberal and Conservative Parties, both of whom were concerned with other issues of public importance (social welfare spending, Imperial trade preferences, the 'Irish question' and the Boer War and its aftermath).

6 Academic economists, although they would have been favourably inclined towards the American legislation, were at the time more concerned with issues of international free trade or monetary policy.

In both Britain and the USA the 1930s was the nadir of anti-monopoly policy. The excess industrial capacity which existed was interpreted by many, rightly or wrongly, as a result of over-expansion due to excessive competition. The National Industrial Recovery Act of Roosevelt's New Deal authorized— and the tacit encouragement of *cartels* in Britain and Europe permitted— industries to fix prices and limit output. The rationale was that cartelization, by increasing profits, would induce production and investment and so stimulate employment. Certainly cartelization increases cartel members' profits, irrespective of general demand conditions, but profits do not induce investment *per se*. Investment is induced by the expectation that a high return will be obtained. If money is to be invested but *expected* profits are low (as they would be during a depression) then the investment will not take place. Instead of expanding, firms will: first take the increased profits due to cartelization out of the industry; second, reduce output from the competitive level to the monopolistic level; and third, increase price from the price-taking level to the closed market, price-seeking level. Although shareholders' income would be increased by government-encouraged cartelization, and so their spending power would rise, it seems unlikely that this would be sufficient to offset the reduced spending of consumers generally, owing to both the higher prices and the lower employment caused by the monopoly and the overall depression.

Why, then, did Britain eventually adopt and develop some form of competition policy?

British Policy and the Conduct Approach

To answer this question we again turn to Rostow.[4] During the 1920s and 1930s the Depression resulted in economic policy concentrating on mitigating the effects of the slump in world and domestic trade. The remedies selected were the abandonment of free international trade and the encouragement of industrial rationalization, including British participation in some existing continental cartels. Whether these remedies were right or wrong is irrelevant here: the time was not propitious for policies that discouraged monopolistic practices and encouraged competition.

The White Paper on Employment Policy in 1944, however, took a different view. It argued that competition would assist in mitigating any post-war inflation by encouraging firms to hold prices down. This argument was strengthened by the view that exhortation to the monopolists of labour, the trade unions, to hold down the price of labour and not press for excessive wage demands was unlikely to be successful if business was not also controlled in some fashion. It also argued that a competitive framework for industry was more likely to result in greater flexibility towards innovation and productivity-increasing technical change than a monolithic structure would be.

In the succeeding period, disillusion with nationalization in the Labour Government itself resulted in a swing towards a belief in the attractions of anti-monopoly legislation as an alternative. This resulted in a major Act being passed in 1948, with five later ones expanding, broadening the scope, consolidating or slightly amending their predecessors.[5] The six statutes were:

1   Monopolies and Restrictive Practices (Inquiry and Control) Act, 1948
2   Restrictive Trade Practices Act, 1956
3   Resale Prices Act, 1964
4   Monopolies and Mergers Act, 1965
5   Restrictive Trade Practices Act, 1968
6   Fair Trading Act, 1973.

It is often said that this legislation is conduct-oriented rather than structure-oriented, as is the Sherman Act (at least as far as monopolies are concerned). In other words a firm or group of firms will be condemned if its behaviour is deemed to result in some specific 'abuse' or poor performance detrimental to the public interest. Clearly 'abusive' or poor performance need not be associated automatically with market dominance. Thus, again, British policy is often alleged to be more pragmatic than its American equivalent.

Certainly the British approach emphasized, until recent years, the concept of the 'public interest', while the American rule of reason stressed the 'market setting' and 'competition'. Are the approaches conflicting? Is it fair to dub the American 'structural' and dogmatic and the British 'conduct'-oriented and pragmatic? These demarcation lines are probably too strict. Moreover, as noted below, the 'public interest' is difficult to determine. (So too is 'reasonableness', but it was then defined in the economic terminology of markets and competition, which even if interpreted variously by lawyers and judges does have clearer-cut meanings for economists.)

Monopolies and Restrictive Practices Act, 1948

As stated, British anti-monopoly legislation dates back to 1948, to the Monopoly and Restrictive Practices Act. This Act established the Monopolies Commission, and defined the scope of its jurisdiction in terms of situations in which either one seller or one buyer controlled one-third or more of a market, or there were agreements or arrangements which resulted in the non-supply of some market.

The Act offered as a guide to the public interest 'the need to achieve the production, treatment and distribution by the most efficient and economical means of goods of such types and qualities, in such volume and at such prices, as will best meet the requirements of home and overseas markets'.

The Commission first reported in 1951 on dental goods and disclosed practices which allowed manufacturers to make excessive profits; the government made an order prohibiting these practices. Since then the Commission has examined over 50 industries. In very few cases has another order been made. For the most part the government has preferred to obtain the 'voluntary' agreement of the industry to abandon any condemned practices.

Restrictive Trade Practices Act, 1956

A second piece of legislation came in 1956—the Restrictive Trade Practices Act. This Act set up the Restrictive Practices Court, composed of High Court judges helped by lay experts. The Court has to decide whether manufacturers' agreements restricting price competition and other forms of rivalry are against the public interest or not. All such agreements had to be registered with the Registrar of Restrictive Trading Agreements who brought them before the Court. (In passing it is interesting to compare the British and American systems of jurisdiction. Whereas the latter used ordinary Federal Courts, the British established the Monopolies Commission and the Restrictive Practices Court for explicitly defined functions. Implications of criminality, if not of litigiousness, were thus avoided.) In passing judgement on any agreement the Court presumed that these are against the public interest. This presumption of 'guilt' can be rebutted on one of six grounds—the six *gateways*:

1 The restriction is necessary to protect the public where the use of the goods requires special knowledge or skill.
2 The removal of the restriction would deprive buyers and users of substantial benefits.
3 The restriction is a necessary defensive measure against other restraints imposed on the trade by persons outside it.
4 The restriction is a necessary defensive measure against an outside monopoly.

5   The removal of the restriction is likely to have an adverse effect on the general level of employment in some area, or is likely to cause a substantial reduction in the export trade of the United Kingdom.

6   The restriction is necessary to maintain another restriction which the Court finds to be not contrary to the public interest.

There is an additional 'general' gateway through which all agreements must pass. The Court must be satisfied 'that the restriction is not unreasonable having regard to the balance between those circumstances and any detriment to the public or to persons not parties to the agreement resulting from, or likely to result from, the operation of the restriction'.

The pervasiveness of restrictive practices in industry can be gauged by the fact that, by June 1963, 2450 agreements had been registered. But most were subsequently abandoned by the firms concerned or were amended so as to be excluded from the Act. By June 1972, 35 cases had been contested in court; 11 were found not contrary to the public interest. Only a handful of agreements remained on the Register where the course of action had still to be decided.

Although the 1956 Act prohibited collective enforcement of *resale price maintenance* (RPM) it effectively increased the powers of manufacturers enforcing individual RPM (namely the practice whereby the manufacturer stipulates the resale prices by withholding supplies from retailers who do not adhere to his terms).

Resale Prices Act, 1964

The 1964 Resale Prices Act prohibited RPM on all but 'exempted' goods. Only pharmaceuticals, because of the special expertise and services provided by wholesalers and retailers, have been declared exempt. All other decisions have gone against the manufacturer (e.g. boots and shoes, toys, confectionery) and this has been accompanied by voluntary abandonment in many cases (e.g. cigarettes, domestic electrical appliances, wines and spirits).

Monopolies and Mergers Act, 1965

A fourth piece of legislation, the 1965 Monopolies and Mergers Act, empowered the Commission, at the direction of the government, to enquire into any proposed or recently completed merger which could result in a monopoly, or increase the power of an existing one. There were two alternative tests for deciding whether a merger should be investigated. First, did it establish or intensify a monopoly situation? Second, did the assets to be taken ever exceed £5m?

Between the passing of the Act and the end of 1972, sixteen merger reports had been issued by the Commission, including three on regional and one (*Times: Sunday Times*) on national newspapers. Only 6 of the 16 were deemed against the public interest. Generally, the Commission felt that the savings to be obtained through scale economies in the remaining mergers outweighed the costs of reduction in competition, provided that such savings were passed on to the consumer. Written assurances on such matters as pricing policy, access to supplies, and so on were obtained from three groups of companies before they were permitted to merge.

Restrictive Trade Practices Act, 1968

Experience since the 1956 Act, especially the possibility of operating unwritten price agreements, resulted in the Restrictive Practices Act, 1968, which amended the 1956 legislation in three ways. First, price exchange information, not registrable under the 1956 Act, can have much the same effect as a price-fixing agreement, although only the latter was registrable (and usually declared illegal). The 1968 Act empowered the Board of Trade to call up any such information agreements for registration (i.e. this would still not be compulsory). Second, an additional 'gateway' was added. A restriction can now be defended on the grounds that it 'does not directly or indirectly restrict or discourage competition'. Third, the government was permitted to make orders providing exemptions of certain agreements from registration, provided only that the agreement is necessary to promote efficiency in the national interest (this amendment was inserted to avoid embarrassment about the inter-firm discussions which often go on under the auspices of the National Economic Development Office) and which are reminiscent of the cartel encouragement of the 1930s.

Fair Trading Act, 1973

The Fair Trading Act, 1973, resulted in the total repeal, replacement and consolidation of the previous legislation. A Director General of Fair Trading was appointed. One of his main duties is 'to keep under review commercial activities with a view to becoming aware of, and ascertaining the circumstances relating to, monopoly situations or uncompetitive practices'. In most instances the Director General has the right (previously confined to a government minister) to make references to the (renamed) Monopolies and Mergers Commission. The Director General has also assumed the functions previously carried out by the Registrar of Restrictive Trade Practices.

There are two other major changes resulting from the passing of the Fair Trading Act. First, the definition of monopoly for purposes of investigation by the Commission has been widened from the 'one-third of a market' rule to embrace those situations where one firm or group of firms controls one-quarter or more of a market. Second, the guidelines provided to the Commission as to what is the public interest have been amended to emphasize the desirability of

1   Maintaining and promoting effective competition;

2 Promoting the interests of consumers, purchasers and other users of
   goods and services in respect of the prices charged for them and in
   respect of their quality and variety;
3 Promoting through competition the reduction of costs and the development and use of new techniques and new products, and of facilitating
   the entry of new competitors into existing markets;
4 Maintaining and promoting the balanced distribution of industry and
   employment in the United Kingdom;
5 Maintaining and promoting competitive activity in markets outside the
   United Kingdom on the part of producers in the United Kingdom.

Assessment of restrictive practices

The six gateways which the 1956 Act established and through one of which a
restrictive practice must pass before the Court will declare it legal have varying
degrees of support in economic logic. Gateways 1 and 2 are unexceptionable
in terms of economic theory. Similarly, gateways 3 and 4 both pertain to
countervailing power, and a restrictive practice allowed through either can
be justified on the grounds that the monopoly power so permitted is necessary
to offset monopoly power existing elsewhere. Gateway 5 relates to employment and exports. This is less easy to find an economic rationale for. It can
be argued that the general level of employment is a responsibility of macro-
government policy and not that of a group of firms operating a restrictive
agreement. Moreover, removal of a restriction generally has the effect of
raising output, not lowering it, so the presence of the gateway becomes even
less explicable. The inclusion of exports in gateway 5 could also be argued to
be a macro concern. It reflects political anxieties about the balance of
payments. Again such anxieties should probably not be expressed in industrial
legislation. Moreover, while this gateway is still extant under the 1973 Act,
even the main reason for it has gone now that floating exchange rates largely
self-correct the payments balance.

   The three additional provisions in the 1968 Act differ in their impact.
Bringing information agreements into the scope of the legislation strengthens
the 1956 provisions. The additional gateway, however, weakens the Act, and
the power given to the government to permit exemption from registration on
grounds of 'efficiency in the national interest' is symptomatic of the ambiva-
lence of government attitudes to the whole of competition policy. This particular clause was inserted after lobbying by the Chemicals Industry Economic
Development Committee (or 'little Neddy'). Its objective was to permit
discussion and agreement by large chemical firms on which of them should
construct new plants and which of them would, by implication, refrain from
doing so. Arguably, without such information exchange either over-capacity
would result, or all firms would hold back from net investment from fear of
such an outcome.

hours given their physical situation, and intimate knowledge of detailed customer wants.

Assessment of monopolies' policy

Professor G.C. Allen (a former member of the Monopolies Commission) has argued that the guidance provided by the 1948 Act as to the public interest 'consisted of a string of platitudes which the Commission found valueless, and it was left for the members themselves to reach their own conclusions by reference to the assumptions, principles or prejudices which their training and experience caused them to apply to economic affairs'. Only after the passing of the 1973 Act did anti-monopolies policy explicitly specify that the state of 'competition' should be regarded as a normative goal (points 1, 2, 3 and 5 in the earlier section on this Act). Even in the 1973 Act, however, the guidelines as to the public interest include as a preamble the need to take account of 'all matters which appear ... in the particular circumstances to be relevant'. There is also point 4, 'the balanced distribution of employment'. This is a guideline which would seem to be more relevant to an Act relating to regional than to monopolies policy. It can only confuse the workings of the Commission, and in certain circumstances may place it in a position where there is a need to take a decision favouring either more or less competition subject to providing less or more regional assistance. For reasons of both fairness and efficiency such decisions should be left to politicians, not their specialist advisers in unrelated areas.

It is often claimed that the strength of British monopolies' policy lies in its 'pragmatism' and flexibility (particularly in comparison with the 'dogmatic' approach of the American anti-trust laws, where size alone is often regarded as a sufficient ground on which to produce an unfavourable judgement). In Britain, market conduct has been examined rather than mere size. With the accumulation of case law over the years, charges of a lack of consistency have been made as often as has praise for the pragmatism of the Commission. In some cases, no doubt, this pragmatism had the advantage of providing flexibility and discretion which enabled the judgement to vary with the circumstances. In others, businessmen have been provided with judgements which must have been totally unexpected. This administrative capriciousness has *not* been removed, as had been hoped, by the rather more specific guidelines in the Fair Trading Act. Probably this is because, although 'competition' is in general the goal, the word 'competition', as we have seen, does have different interpretations according to whether the market under discussion is open or closed.

Assessment of mergers' policy

The Monopolies and Mergers Commission (it was renamed in the 1973 Act) must decide whether or not a monopoly is in the public interest. With merger vetting the task becomes more difficult still. The Commission must pass judgement on what it thinks might happen, not necessarily on what will happen, after the merger takes place. The Commission is allowed six months in which to make its prediction of the state of the post-merger market and to come to a judgement on the prediction. The merger can be subject to 'standstill' powers by the government until the report is issued. Enforced delays of this sort while awaiting judgement may well in themselves result in the firms calling off the merger. Either the possibility of a negative verdict or changed market conditions in the interim can explain such breakdowns. (The Allied Breweries: Unilever and Boots: House of Fraser proposed mergers are examples of this.)

The presence of scale economies has been a major reason for approving of mergers (British Motor Corporation: Pressed Steel) and their absence a major reason for withholding approval (United Drapery Stores: Montague Burton). The lack of scale economies, and the possible presence of diseconomies, in research, development and innovative activity resulted in the Beecham Group: Glaxo Group merger being halted. When all economies of scale have been reaped one of the few defences left for two companies wishing to merge is that the firm being acquired is on the verge of collapse and so can in no real sense be regarded as a competitor. This argument was accepted by the Commission in the case of the *Times: Sunday Times* merger.

By 1981–82 both the Monopolies and Mergers Commission and the Department of Trade were coming under widespread criticism for inconsistent and unpredictable verdicts. For example, the following reports have had questions raised about their logic or lack of logic.

S. & W. Berisford Ltd and the British Sugar Corporation Ltd (1981)

The Commission concluded that the sugar industry was in the hands of two main companies: Tate and Lyle and British Sugar (BSC). Berisford sold some Tate and Lyle products. 'Provided, therefore, that Berisford is required to give up its interests in selling Tate and Lyle products ... the proposed merger would have no effect on competition' in the market for sugar.

In the market for sugar beet BSC is the only UK purchaser (Tate and Lyle uses cane as an input). The Commission felt that competition would not be harmed here provided BSC was 'maintained as a separate subsidiary and (so) farmers ... had available full information on its operations'.

The Commission admitted it could not predict how market structure would develop whether the merger went ahead or not. With regard to efficiency the Commission examined management, capital and labour relations. As to the first it found that Berisford's business was not dissimilar, so even if some BSC personnel left the outcome would not be detrimental. Capital for continuing expansion was regarded by the Commission as important for BSC, but it found no case of a Berisford subsidiary suffering from lack of funds. On labour relations historical evidence gave no suggestion that Berisford would lack the necessary skills. None the less, using somewhat convoluted wording, the Commission disapproved of the merger: 'we find it hard to identify any way in which the proposed merger is likely to operate positively for the public benefit.' That is, the merger was presumably not in the public interest. It was, however, finally permitted by the Commission despite this conclusion.

Observer and George Outram & Co. Ltd (1980)

The take-over of the *Observer* by George Outram (owned by Lonrho Ltd) was referred to the Commission. The take-over was allowed to go ahead. Two factors are surprising here. Why was the referral made in the first instance? Lonrho owned no other national daily or Sunday newspaper, so an ultimate reduction (by in-house title merging) in the number of competitors or a reduction in editorial dispersion was not a possibility. Equally, the referral seemed to be unprecedented, since the take-over of the *Times* and *Sunday Times* earlier in the year by the Murdoch group of newspapers (which *did* already own both a national daily and a national Sunday paper) was not referred to the Commission. Second, as already noted, newspaper mergers have been permitted in the past when it was argued that if they did not occur competition would be reduced. This is so when the firm being acquired is about to collapse and so cannot be regarded as a competitor. This argument was accepted when the *Sunday Times* (then owned by the Thomson group) acquired the *Times* in the 1960s. Yet this 'failing company' argument, which is of extreme relevance to competition, was deliberately ignored. The *Observer* had accumulated losses in the period 1977–80 of £8.7 million but 'we have in our consideration of the public interest disregarded the possibility that the alternative to the proposed transfer might be closure.' No reason was given for this statement.

Lonrho Ltd and House of Fraser Ltd (1981)

This take-over was blocked by the Commission for one tangible reason only: the ownership by Lonrho of Brentfords (a textile supplier). It was feared that House of Fraser stores would come under pressure to buy from this supplier. The argument ignores the preferences of House of Fraser's ultimate customers who might well ensure that Fraser continued to stock a broad range. It ignores the fact that the textiles in question constitute only a small fraction of a department store's turnover anyway. And it ignores the possibility of removing the obstacle if it is indeed so regarded (namely requesting Lonrho to dispose of Brentfords: a course of action which Lonrho is now independently pursuing).

A comparison of Lonrho's dynamic profit growth and House of Fraser's unexciting figures make it difficult to disagree with the signatory of the Commission's minority report, who said 'the combination of Lonrho's wide business experience with the House of Fraser's retailing competence could well result in an enhanced performance' from Fraser.

The rejection of the bid is even more surprising given the fact that Lonrho owned 19 per cent of House of Fraser shares in 1979, and was permitted by the Commission to acquire Scottish and Universal Investments Ltd (SUITS) in that year. That merger increased Lonrho's holding to over 29 per cent since SUITS already held 10 per cent. In that report the Commission concluded that if the merger with SUITS took place 'a merger situation in respect of Lonrho and House of Fraser would be created' but this merger situation 'may be expected not to operate against the public interest'.

Royal Bank of Scotland, Standard Chartered Bank and the Hong Kong and Shanghai Banking Corporation

This was a contested bid by two different banks to take over the Royal. Standard is a British bank and Hong Kong is registered in the colony of that name. Neither bidder had a retail network of any significance in the UK. The Commission gave both bids a clean bill of health with regard to competition. It felt that either take-over would strengthen the competitive challenge of the Royal (under the Royal name in Scotland, and under the Williams and Glyn's name in England, both being subsidiaries of the Royal as a group) to the Big Four (Barclays, Midland, Lloyds and the National Westminster). Barclays, through the Bank of Scotland, and Midland, through its ownership of the Clydesdale, also had a presence in Scotland. It was felt that this would result in a significant 'fifth force' in British banking which would be impossible if the Royal remained independent. The resources of the bidding banks would permit expansion by the Royal, higher loan limits, more branches and a greater volume of lending.

Neither bid was opposed on the basis of competition. The Hong Kong bid was frowned upon mainly for chauvinistic British reasons. It is registered outside Britain and is not in the UK clearing system.

Both bids were opposed for still narrower chauvinistic (Scottish) reasons. Intense lobbying of the Commission was carried out by Scottish National Party MPs and other Scottish interests. The reasons were that career prospects for Scots would be threatened as would Edinburgh's dominance as Britain's second main financial centre after London.

Those arguments carried the day and both bids were found against the public interest. This decision was unpredictable and strange for several reasons. The 'public' whose interest the Commission was protecting was presumably not the British public who would have benefited from the 'fifth force'. Furthermore, in the SUITS/Lonrho case, the Scottish Council had put forward identical arguments about career prospects and the shift of control to London to counter the Lonrho take-over. That bid was allowed on the grounds that a large organization would remain in Scotland, and further-more that, if accepted, then any take-over of any firm in any part of Britain outside of London could put forward a similar defence. In that instance the Commission rejected such a defence; in this case it accepted it. Finally, if

Edinburgh is the second most important source of independently controlled capital finance outside of London (as it is), then if the dozens of Edinburgh-based financial institutions (unit trusts, investment trusts, merchant banks, insurance companies, pension funds, etc.) did not value the Royal as highly as an investment as did the bidders (since these institutions by definition must have been net sellers) then even the Scottish financial experts believed the bid should go ahead. The pressure group nous of Scottish politicians and the Scottish media lobby, however, was sufficiently potent to overrule any economic arguments and even the wider public interest considerations that the Commission may have examined.

Businesses attempting to predict the legislative environment which may arise if they cross the path of the Monopolies and Mergers Commission have every cause to feel that after 40 years Britain's competition policy still has neither rhyme nor reason.

Regional Policy

The regional 'problem' is based on regional inequalities or grievances. The United Kingdom was the first country to recognize that regional disparities were a matter for government action. Policy measures were first introduced in 1934. (It should, however, be pointed out that, in a global context, the UK is not an extreme example of a nation with regional inequalities. A.J. Brown has indicated that only Holland, Australia and New Zealand have a more uniform distribution of regional income.[7] And if we examine two other indicators of regional problems, unemployment and emigration, then unemployment in and emigration from poor regions is higher in the north of Sweden or the south of Italy than in north-east England or west-central Scotland.)

Regional difficulties are caused by structural or other factors. The structural explanation of the regional problem is that it arises out of changes in consumer and/or producer preferences.

Shifts in consumer preferences can result in industries facing decline in demand. If an area depends on a small number of such declining industries then the problem of unemployment, net emigration, relatively low income per head, and so on, will arise. Regions which have been heavily dependent on the coal, heavy engineering and shipbuilding industries have exemplified this.

Shifts in producer preferences have arisen in as much as firms in newer industries have located their factories closer to the major population centres of Birmingham and London. This has been made possible by the freedom of location which electric and oil or gas power provides *vis-à-vis* the lack of mobility when the fuel source is coal, so bulky and costly to transport. In like manner, the expansion of road transport has given firms the freedom to move from the fixed locations of railheads. Some of the newer industries have been in the consumer durable field, making goods with a high value relative to raw material weight and containing components from a wide variety of sources. Transport costs are consequently minimized by being near to the market. Other newer industries, such as electronics, manufacture products with a 'high brain content' and as a result the producer is more anxious to be liaising closely with the users and with specialist service suppliers than with raw material sources. Producer preferences have also changed in as much as foreign raw material producers have themselves commenced manufacturing as, for example, in the jute and cotton industries.

In the long run, however, if the malaise is solely structural there is no need for alarm, since either new indigenous sectors will be growing to replace the old ones and can be subsidized to help them grow faster if considered desirable, and/or new incoming industries can be attracted by some form of aid.

Another school of thought believes that the problem is structural in origin, as described above, but that other factors exist which will persistently keep a depressed area one of high costs and lagging economic activity. What reasons underlie this belief? A frequently proffered one is that labour costs are high because local wages tend to reflect national wage agreements, whereas local productivity per man is below the national average. Low local productivity will have arisen partly because trade unions are more militant in protecting staff differentials and 'soft' manning schedules, and partly because plant and equipment are, on average, relatively out of date. Another explanation could be unusually high transport costs. In addition to and partly because of this, depressed areas may be unattractive economically and psychologically to mobile companies, and indigenous growth is likely to be extremely limited since the mobile, entrepreneurial native will migrate to a more attractive area.

Table 15.1 highlights some indicators of the regional problem. Regional differentials in terms of per caput GDP narrowed slightly over the period 1966–74. The relative decline of the domestic car industry is possibly reflected in the West Midlands figures.

The general narrowing of spread may also partly be accounted for by the 'success' of trade unions in negotiating nation-wide agreements over this period. To the extent that regions have a more or less productive labour force this may or may not be desirable if it makes some regions still less attractive to industrialists in terms of unit labour costs. Unemployment rates followed the pattern of GDP per caput both in their disparity in one year and in their movement by region over a decade. Again some exceptions are noticeable, particularly Scotland, with North Sea oil and related developments having a not unpredictable impact. Nevertheless, this was also partly compensated for and explained by a net population decrease. Indeed, no matter how one examines table 15.1, the 'problem' areas are precisely those which existed in 1934 when regional policy was introduced. Similarly, the strongest area remains the South-East; this is reflected in the final column, which shows net output per employee (a proxy for productivity) in manufacturing industry.

Table 15.1 *Some indicators of the regional problem*

Region	Per caput GDP at factor costs (UK = 100)		Unemployment rates (GB = 100)		Population change (%)	Net output per employee in manufacturing industry (UK = 100)
	1966	1974	1965	1975	1965–1975	1971
North	84.1	90.1	179	144	0	96.9
Yorks, Humberside	96.7	93.0	79	98	2.2	90.9
East Midlands	96.5	95.6	64	88	7.5	89.4
East Anglia	96.0	93.4	93	83	14.6	103.1
South-East	114.7	116.6	57	68	2.0	110.2
South-West	92.0	93.1	107	115	9.1	100.8
West Midlands	108.2	99.3	50	100	5.5	93.3
North-West	95.7	94.5	114	129	0.9	98.8
Wales	84.2	83.9	179	137	2.9	101.6
Scotland	89.1	93.4	207	127	−0.1	102.8

Source: D. Maclennan and J.B. Parr (eds.), *Regional Policy*, Martin Robertson, 1979, pp. 117, 118, 121, 310

Table 15.1 provides support for the intuitive view that the regional problem is, at least partly, structural in character. That is, that the problem regions are heavily dependent on declining industries.

On the other hand, as indicated above, the differences are not enormous in magnitude (absolutely, and particularly in relation to other countries). However, the column relating to productivity does not embrace the effects, more difficult to capture, of the growing tertiary sector of the economy. Nor does it highlight which industrial sectors are responsible for the structural imbalance in any one region. One technique used to isolate the effects of industrial structures from other factors in a region is the *shift-share* approach.

Consider table 15.2. A hypothetical region is postulated. Employment change between years 1970 and 1980 is the indicator used. Assume a region is composed of only three industries, A, B and C, and that total employment nationally rose by 10 per cent. If industries A, B and C grew in the nation as a whole by 0, −40 and 20 per cent respectively, then, of these figures, −10, −50 and 10 per cent are due to growth or decline uniquely attributable to these industries themselves after deducting the national 10 per cent growth rate (the structural explanation). Any remaining difference is due to region-specific factors. Thus in our hypothetical region 450 jobs have been lost in

Table 15.2 *A hypothetical application of the shift-share technique in a given region*

Industry	Actual employment growth			Attributable to national growth (10%)	Attributable to industry growth (structure)		Change due to region-specific factors
	1970	1980	net				
A	1000	900	− 100	100	− 100	(− 10%)	− 100
B	500	150	− 350	50	− 250	(− 50%)	− 150
C	100	100	0	10	10	(10%)	− 20
Total	1600	1150	− 450	160	− 340		− 270

the decade. This is 160 more than would have been expected if the region had grown at the same rate as the national economy. Because the region is heavily reliant on declining industries, *A* and *B*, 340 jobs have been lost. But there are other peculiar factors in the region which are responsible for a further reduction in employment of 270. Had the economy as a whole not grown as it did, the region would have been still worse off than it actually is, namely by 160 jobs.

Current policy

The debates surrounding the causes of regional malaise and the effectiveness and appropriateness of any given regional policy have lasted as long as the perception of the problem itself. And they are probably no nearer to a resolution.

Since 1958 the problem regions have generally been defined on the basis of unemployment rates. The rate of 4.5 per cent was fairly rigidly applied and this led, especially after 1960, to a proliferation of 'black' and 'white' areas. This large number of small areas was reduced to a few very large areas in 1966 and, with a few modifications, that is the current position.

Policy has been subdivided into a carrot and a stick. The principal 'stick' is the *Industrial Development Certificate* which is required for most industrial buildings constructed outside the Development and Special Development Areas. The implicit hope of this negative control is that if an IDC is refused, the building will be constructed in the Development Areas. The 'carrot' has consisted and does consist of a range of grants, wage subsidies, loans, tax allowances on profits, and more recently 'selective assistance'.

Selective assistance can be obtained for a project if it satisfies one of three guidelines: it will create additional employment; it is necessary for modernization or rationalization in order to protect employment; or it is 'in the national interest'.

Work to the workers or workers to the work?

Those who favour taking the workers to the work stress mainly the loss of economic growth which is caused by interference with the location of industry. Only when businessmen are given a free choice will they select an optimal location. Choice restriction will lead to the plant not being established at all, or an inferior or overseas location being chosen. The result would be productivity losses and a lower national growth rate. Labour mobility does not incur such costs.

Supplementary arguments are based upon the practical difficulties of devising a policy to influence capital movement without encouraging inefficiency. For example, grants do not distinguish between the efficient firm and the inefficient. Moreover, both grants and tax allowances may be given to those who had decided to expand anyway.

Conversely, others argue that growth is little affected by locational interference. First, many industries' costs may vary very little by location. Second, firms may not choose optimum sites if left alone in any event. Third, the discussion should be about social costs, not pure economic or private costs, so the growth/productivity argument is not a relevant one. Such costs include diseconomies such as congestion and the over-utilization of existing social capital and infrastructure and the disappearance of local cultures. This last (cultural) reason is possibly the most honest and least disputable of all the reasons for having any type of regional policy.

The 'work to the workers' school goes still further and argues that labour migration is not only socially undesirable but also economically inefficient. First, migration depresses the donor region and has an expansionary effect on the host region. (Donor regional income is reduced; less is demanded of and so spent on social capital; the migrant tends to be the younger, more enterprising type.)

Most regional policy in the UK is of a 'work to the workers' type. However, it can be argued that both equipment grants and tax allowances on capital expenditure encourage capital—rather than labour-intensive industries to move towards the labour force. Moreover, while firms must be making profits to qualify for a tax allowance, any firm, efficient or inefficient (as measured by profits), can obtain a grant.

Growth points

The most that can be claimed for regional policy is a very modest degree of success. Critics of past policies argue that this may be because it was too piecemeal (from 1958–66 it was essentially a 'fire-fighting' policy applied to all employment exchange districts with 4.5 per cent unemployment), or because the aid provided was spread too widely over the country (as after 1966) to make a really perceptible impact on the problem areas.

As a consequence, the 'growth point' school of thought has attracted considerable support in recent years. Essentially, it implies that aid should not be distributed indiscriminately to whole regions but to those few critical points within them where it can do most good. Artificially stimulated growth points, like naturally occurring ones arising through the operation of market forces, will of course entail the costs of still further enhanced stagnation and decline in the other parts of the problem region.

As with all planning, a badly chosen growth point not only will require subsidies to establish itself but also may never grow up. The need for subsidies may never disappear. Several examples of the misguided application of growth point philosophy are the motor and lorry assembly plants of Rootes (subsequently Chrysler, then Peugeot) and BMC (now British Leyland) at Linwood and Bathgate respectively. The hopes that these would generate a plethora of supporting ancillary component industries were never realized.

Planning or laissez-faire?

The case for abolishing regional policy rests on the belief that in the long run a perfectly competitive market will lead to the optimum location of individual activity. 'Optimum' means the maximum production of goods and services desired by consumers. Any regional imbalances are corrected through the price mechanism. Where resources are scarce, their prices rise, demand falls and supply increases. The converse occurs if resources are under-utilized. But this situation need not hold in reality. Why?

First, factor prices need not reflect relative regional scarcities. For example, national wage negotiations may result in (relatively) uniform wage rates within the same occupational group. Second, even if prices truly reflect scarcities, factors may not be mobile and may not move to the high-reward area. Sociological and psychological barriers to labour mobility may deter workers from moving from a low-wage area and unemployment to a high-wage area with a job. Similarly, businessmen may have objectives which rank a pleasant environment and lower profits more highly than less sociable areas with higher profits. Moreover, even if the free market could be relied on, it is essentially a long-run solution.

The case for regional policy rests on the credo of all planners, namely that sensible planning will solve the regional problem. First, however, it is not at all obvious that civil servants or politicians know better where to locate a factory or a labour force than the factory owner or worker, whose full-time occupation it is to make such decisions. Second, the question must be raised as to how wise it is to encourage a belief in the population that industrial structure and location is static. Third, unless one postulates omniscience, it cannot be argued that planners can always take account of the fact that points of growth are constantly altering, new industries arising and new consumer needs developing. The benefits of the railway system would never have been realized had the canal, stage coach and land-owning interests had the power that such analogous lobbies possess today. Similar commercial misfortunes occurred with the British Aluminium smelter at Invergordon and the government-owned oil rig construction yard at Portavadie which was still not complete long after the oil rig construction boom was over and privately sponsored yards such as those at Ardyne had been put on a care and maintenance basis.

One of the few things that can be said with certainty is that the arguments for and against regional policy, its alleged success or failure, and the reasons for its paucity or plethora of achievements, will continue for some time to come.

Public Goods and Externalities

To this point we have restricted our discussion solely to private goods (i.e. goods which are scarce, or (what is the same thing) economic goods). When a good does not suffer from reduced availability due to consumption it is called a *public good*. As consumers increase in number the same given amount is available. National defence is a classic example; so too is the Thames flood barrage, a television broadcast or a football game. In addition, people often cannot be excluded from the benefits provided by the good. Thus if the authors' houses are saved (or not saved) from nuclear extinction by the effectiveness (or ineffectiveness) of Britain's defence forces the same result will also occur for our next-door neighbours. Similarly the Thames flood barrage provides flood protection equally to all inhabitants of that area. However, it becomes ever more possible to exclude outsiders as human ingenuity grows. In the simple case of the football game, the match is a public good until the point when someone decides to erect enclosures and stadia with only a few gates at which would-be spectators must pay. Similarly, cable-transmitted television (as opposed to wireless transmission) not only permits a wider choice of programmes but provides access to those programmes only if the viewer pays for the rental of the cable, or alternatively has a meter built into the set which registers the amount owing by the viewer to the broadcast company.

Another assumption we have made so far is that whenever a trade occurs all the costs and benefits from the exchange accrue only to the transactors. This need not be the case. For example, one consumer may heat his house with oil and pay the fuel company for the oil consumed. But the cost of his central heating may not be fully reflected in his fuel bill if the oil refinery produces a large amount of air pollution.

In effect, part of the cost of heating the consumer's house is being borne by others. They are subsidizing him. They may not use oil-fired central heating themselves but are involuntarily consuming dirty air. This is an external cost or *negative externality* (since it is external to the transaction which resulted in it). External benefits or *positive externalities* arise if, for example, a householder goes to his local garden nursery, purchases flowering shrubs for his garden, and makes his own property pleasant and appealing to look at.

Externalities only occur if property rights do not exist. When private property rights are well defined and easily enforced there is no cause for concern about externalities. We will examine first this situation, and second the problems of government policy when externalities persist.

The former proposition was first advanced by Ronald Coase and is now known as the *Coase theorem*.[8] The theorem states that efficiency will always be realized in the absence of transaction costs no matter how property rights are assigned. Consider an example used by Coase himself. There is a strip of unfenced, unowned land between the property of a grain farmer and a cattle farmer. The grain farmer would like to plant grain but the cattle would inevitably damage it in whole or in part, so he does not cultivate the land. This may or may not be socially optimal. If society values grain at the margin more highly than cattle it is certainly not optimal, since the grain farmer cannot or will not use the land, while the cattle farmer can graze more cattle at zero grazing cost (zero cost to himself: he gains an external benefit). Nevertheless society would prefer the land to be used for grain.

Now assume that we do not know which use is more efficient from society's point of view. But assume the grain farmer takes a chance that he can plant grain and get a profit from the sale of at least some undamaged portion of it. He also decides to sue the cattle farmer for damages to his crop. The law court will, of course, find it very difficult to decide whether or not to award damages. Both farmers had equal rights (i.e. no rights or only squatter's rights) to the land. The judge must make a value judgement. Let us assume he decides to award full private ownership of the land to one party or the other.

The important factor emerging from the Coase theorem is that once this award is made, irrespective of the direction of the judgement (in favour of the grain or the cattle farmer), the land will now be put to its most efficient, most socially highly valued use. Table 15.3 explains why, showing the outcome if the judgement is (a) in favour of the cattle farmer and (b) in favour of the grain farmer. It also considers the increased profits of each farmer if he secures legal access to the land relative to his profits if he had no such access.

Thus the Coase theorem is proved, and efficiency is realized no matter to whom the land is assigned by the legal authorities (albeit the wealth of the farmer to whom the land was awarded will increase). However, there are always transaction costs in real life. The Coase theorem, boldly stated, assumes them away. Rental agreements must be entered into between the farmers.

Negotiation expenses must be incurred; most obviously, in this example, fencing costs are necessary to keep the cattle off the grain. We see that, if transaction costs (on a yearly basis) amount to £400 or more then, even if situation (a) 2 occurs, cattle will be farmed. This is because the profits on farming grain less the transaction costs will be below £600, leaving no positive net profits with which to pay a rental to the cattle farmer. (Which party actually incurs the cost of fencing and other transaction expenses is not really relevant, it is the amount which matters. Once the property rights are

Table 15.3 *Property rights awarded to the farmer of (a) Cattle (b) Grain*

(a) Cattle	(b) Grain
1 *Additional profits per annum from use of the land*	
Cattle farmer £1000: the cattle farmer will farm cattle on the land and earn £1000 extra profit.	Grain farmer £600: the cattle farmer will farm cattle on the land, earn £1000, but pay a rental to the grain farmer which must be above £600 (or grain will be farmed) and below £1000 (or it will be unprofitable to graze cattle).
2 *Additional profits*	
Cattle £600: the grain farmer will grow crops, paying the cattle farmer a rent of over £600 but under £1000.	Grain £1000: the grain farmer will use the land, the profit of £1000 indicating that this is its most socially highly valued use.

assigned the grain farmer will always be able to claim damages from the cattle farmer if the land is assigned to him and he uses it for grain growing and not rental. Thus the cattle (grain) farmer will be motivated to fence in (out) the cattle to avoid paying for (losing) any grain. What it will affect obviously, will be the upper limit to the rental the grain farmer is willing and able to pay.)

The first main lesson from the Coase theorem is that externalities can often be 'internalized' if property rights can be established and means of charging devised. Thus public goods may not be so common as supposed. The classic lighthouse example is not necessarily a public good. In America it is provided by government. But in Britain, Trinity House in England and the Commissioners for Northern Lights in Scotland, plus other bodies, built substantial numbers of lighthouses in the nineteenth century, collecting tolls from ships when they entered the harbour. Cable TV has already been mentioned.

Another textbook example is that of beekeepers whose bees receive nectar free of charge from fruit tree owners (an external benefit) but provide cross-pollination services without charge (a negative externality to the beekeeper). In fact Steven Cheung has also dismissed this example.[9] He discovered that in California there were three groups of fruit orchards: those which provided nectar with a high honey potential; those with a moderate honey potential and those which provided little or no honey potential. All, however, required pollination and cross-fertilization by bees and other insects. Cheung found a well-developed market, contrary to the textbook writers. Orchard owners with fruit trees of the first type charged the apiary owners a site rental to leave their hives in the orchard. Those of the third type paid apiary owners to leave their hives in the orchards during the relevant seasons. The middle grouping came to more or less no-charge agreements because the respective alleged externalities cancelled out.

The second lesson from the Coase theorem is that externalities can still occur, and if property rights cannot be established or transaction costs minimized then market failure will arise. How can it be minimized? What does the demand curve look like for a public good? Unlike the market demand curve for a private good (obtained by adding each individual's demand curve horizontally), to obtain the market demand curve for a public good the addition is vertical. For private goods if one extra unit was made available only one individual could consume it (so we moved along the Q axis of the demand diagram) and this consumer would value the good at its market price (so we remained at the same position on the P axis). With public goods, however, everyone benefits if one extra unit is provided, so the value of that unit is the sum of the values all consumers place on it. To reflect this we must move up the P axis.

With this tool-kit we can now look at some of the problems of public good provision. What is the optimal provision of the public good? Figure 15.1 shows a three-citizen community where the demand curves D_1, D_2 and D_3 represent their relevant marginal valuation curves. Curve D is equal to $D_1 + D_2 + D_3$ added vertically at any given Q. MC is the marginal cost of providing the good. At output Q' social marginal benefits received equal social marginal costs; Q' is consequently the optimal output.

But here we encounter the next difficulty. Although output Q' is socially optimal, only one individual values the good sufficiently highly to pay a price for the first few units which will cover the marginal cost. This is individual 3. He will buy up to $Q*$ and then cease purchasing. In short, with public goods, everyone wants them, but few, and sometimes none, are prepared to pay for them.

In addition, if individual 3 does pay for $Q*$ units then the other two members of the community are *free-riding* at his expense. They are obtaining the benefits without incurring any costs. All three members of society would prefer Q' units, which would increase their net benefits to equal the area DPA, the maximum net benefit they can collectively obtain.

With three individuals a collective agreement could possibly be hammered out to ensure that Q' units were produced. With a large nation the solution to the problem is usually obtained by handing the task over to government who will fund the provision through taxation. Again figure 15.1 can be used to show the difficulties arising from this approach. People will still wish to free-ride, if they can. So they will attempt to conceal their preferences (in a private good situation the act of purchase reveals them). Thus although at Q'

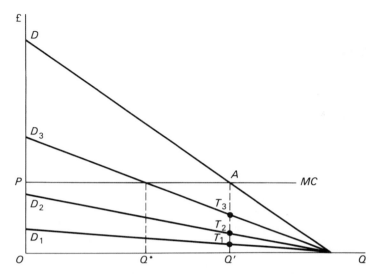

Figure 15.1 *Optimal provision of a public good under conditions of different marginal valuations*

the optimal solution is to raise marginal taxes of T_1, T_2 and T_3 from each individual respectively (where $T_1 + T_2 + T_3 = P$), and although Q' is the desired goal of all, it is clear that if people believe their share of total taxes will be based on their desire for the good then they will understate that desire to minimize their tax bills and hope, again, to free-ride. This difficulty may be viewed as real but practically insurmountable unless somehow the good can be privately supplied and the Coase theorem invoked.

Another, and more difficult case, is not only when people have genuinely different marginal valuations of the good, but also when agreement on the optimal quality and the optimal tax is impossible because of this (quite apart from any free-riding propensity or the practical difficulty of determining individual demand curves). This can occur with defence expenditures where pacifists would under no circumstances willingly support the military.

It can also occur with less obvious goods. Consider government expenditure on a new airport (this is not strictly a public good, but it has some of the characteristics; the provision of travel facilities for other people also results in their being provided for oneself). In figure 15.2 a two-consumer commodity has a demand for an airport as shown. Individual 2, a salesman, is a frequent traveller. Individual 1, an infrequent traveller but a keen gardener, with a house in the vicinity of the proposed airport, does not value the airport highly at all, given the noise and inconvenience it will cause him compared with the slight benefits which might accrue to him. Moreover, individual 1 has a much higher income than individual 2 and knows that, in reality, his marginal tax rate is related to his income and not to his preferences for public goods of whatever nature. If their marginal tax rates are T_1 and T_2 respectively then,

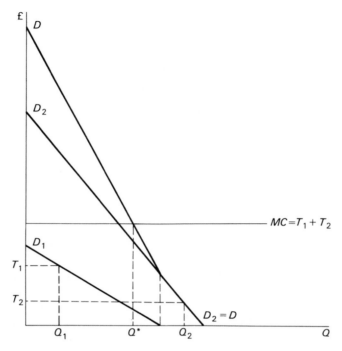

Figure 15.2 *Optimal provision of a public good under conditions
of lack of agreement on quality and tax*

given the two marginal valuation curves, the marginal values of the new
airport to individuals 1 and 2 exceed their marginal costs up to Q_1 and Q_2
units of airport (or flight arrivals or other subdivision).

Unfortunately, an airport is indivisible and both individuals must benefit
from and pay for the chosen size of airport. With normal tax structures
disagreement is inevitable, irrespective of preference distortion for public
relations purposes. Moreover, neither party would be satisfied with the
social optimum, Q^*, albeit that is the only output that both individuals
could desire and still collectively pay a tax covering the cost of the good.
Thus individuals 1 and 2 would desire the public good—airport, national
defence, industrial subsidies or whatever—up to the apparently, and probably
factually, irreconcilable levels of Q_1 and Q_2. This is a major advantage of
private goods and attempts to internalize so-called externalities; namely that
polarization of opinions and social disharmonies are minimized and individual
diversity is permitted and accommodated.

Environmental Pollution

With these basic principles about externalities and public goods in mind,
what can we learn about economic policy problems towards issues such as

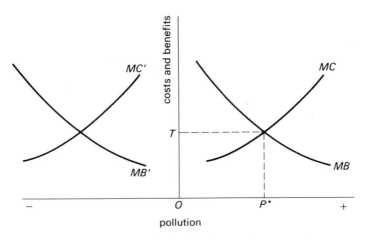

Figure 15.3 *Optimal level of pollution under a taxation system*

pollution? Private motorists pollute the atmosphere with their exhaust emissions; farmers do so with insecticides and weed killers; firms in heavy industry produce sulphur dioxide and other fumes from their factory chimneys.

Every activity we engage in, from breathing to steel production, generates a by-product discharged into the atmosphere. The pollution 'problem' could thus be easily solved by banning all of these activities, but the opportunity cost would be too great. We would die. The real issue is how much pollution we are prepared to accept in order to obtain the benefits we want simultaneously. How much of these benefits are we prepared to sacrifice to obtain a cleaner environment? What is the optimal level of pollution?

In principle the answer is given in figure 15.3. *MB* shows the marginal benefits from polluting. *MB* has a negative slope since the first few units provide enormous benefits (to individuals or firms); the last few units are near to irrelevant in the benefits they provide. The *MC* curve slopes up since the first few units of pollution impose negligible environmental costs, at higher levels an extra unit can impose extremely high additional costs. (Thus a little carbon monoxide in the atmosphere is almost harmless; a little more produces headaches; a little more still will result in death.)

The optimal level of pollution to society is P^*. This is positive, and will be so for most products. However, in some cases it either is or is presumed to be negative, as with curves *MC'* and *MB'*. When this occurs the government may ban the polluting activity altogether. Examples of such bans are the use of the drug thalidomide; the use of cyclamates, a very popular food additive in the 1960s as a sweetener; and the dumping of nuclear power station waste in unprotected heaps.

However, although the concepts of figure 15.3 are useful, they are difficult if not impossible to use. Moreover, the *MB* and *MC* schedules are society's valuations of the costs and benefits, and very few individuals in society are likely to agree over any average outcome even if it could be shown to be 'correct' in that statistical sense. What we can infer, however, is that pollution is likely to be in excess of the social optimum of P^*. Why? The reason lies in the frequent absence of property rights and resulting negative externalities.

A firm with a factory chimney emitting noxious fumes will (in figure 15.3) move from the origin rightwards. As the factory emits more and more pollution it earns more and more profit (represented by MB) but the firm will not stop at P^*. Other things equal, it could continue until MB hits the horizontal axis. Although MC is rising the firm itself is bearing none of the costs of the polluted air. The community as a whole is (hence the rising MC) but the firm is only one small part of the community. If the firm introduced pollution abatement procedures, the benefits to the community would be large, but the firm would bear the total cost of this abatement and there is thus a positive externality for pollution abatement. From our discussion of public goods we know that pollution abatement is a form of public good and as such is unlikely to be purchased.

What then is the appropriate policy response to the pollution problem? There are three alternatives. First, and probably best, is to bear in mind the Coase theorem, and look for ways to permit *trading between the polluter and polluted*. If the individuals or groups of individuals who suffer from the negative externalities can agree with the polluter on a price they should receive in compensation, or alternatively a price they will pay to make him cease or reduce polluting activities, then the optimal level of pollution is likely to be reached. Certainly this requires assignation of property rights in the atmosphere and a mechanism whereby the damaged can sue the damager (or pay the damager depending on how the courts assign the rights) but this permits variation in individual evaluation of the costs and benefits of pollution.

This flexibility is not so readily present in the second alternative, namely *taxation of the polluter*. Thus, in figure 15.3 a tax of T, levied on the polluter, would ensure he did not move down the MB curve beyond P^*. But the heights of the MB and MC curves can vary. Thus the demand for pollution (MB) is likely to be higher in cities and towns than in the country. (There are more people wishing to drive more cars; there are more firms wishing to be located close to their labour force and to their market.) Similarly the demand for a clean environment (i.e. the costs of pollution represented by the MC schedule) will be lower in country areas. This is because (a) there are fewer people anyway, and so the vertical aggregation of the curves results in a lower total schedule, and (b) the intensity of each individual's demand for anything, the height of the curve at a given quantity, is less the lower is his income. Country dwellers have a lower average per caput income than town dwellers, so the MC curve is again lower.

In short, even if the situation of figure 15.4 existed, where P^* is the same in both town and country, varying taxation levels (T and T') would be required to attain it. Given the extremely large numbers of alternative situations, it is unlikely that any one tax, or even any range of taxes, could possibly cover all the different situations in the way that individual contracting, under the Coase theorem assumptions, could.

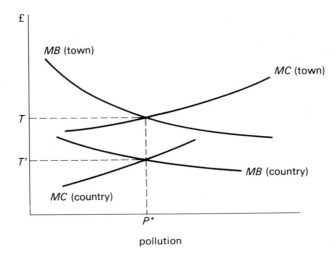

Figure 15.4 *Pollution and taxation in town and country*

Taxation, however, is probably a better policy tool than the third alternative, which is that of *setting standards*. Taxation will motivate the polluter to reduce pollution as cheaply as possible and to do so until the *MB* schedule equals the marginal tax rate. Even if the tax rate is not optimal or variable there are still significant advantages over the standards approach. The reason is due again to varying situations and therefore lack of complete information by the standard-setting authority.

For example, the typical anti-pollution law requires all polluters to reduce their emissions by a given percentage. Thus in figure 15.5 firms 1 and 2, which before the standard was set were polluting at P_1 and P_2 respectively (where their *MB* schedules equal zero, since they themselves assumed none of the costs of pollution), reduce their pollution levels by the same percentage to P_1' and P_2' after the law is passed. To do this each must incur a cost. This cost is represented by the sacrificed *MB* of the polluting activity and is achieved

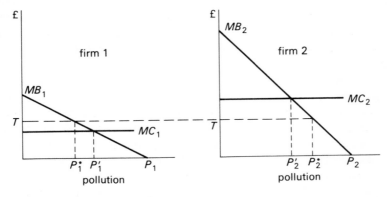

Figure 15.5 *Pollution under a standards system*

by installing pollution abatement machinery, adopting new processes, or most simply by reducing output. In any event the cost is still the opportunity cost of the sacrificed *MB*. These costs are represented by MC_1 and MC_2 respectively. For whatever reason, firm 1 is more efficient than firm 2 in reducing pollution levels ($MC_1 < MC_2$). Thus the same amount of pollution reduction could have been achieved at less social cost than it has been by the imposition of standards. For example, say MC_1 = £5 and MC_2 = £8, then if firm 1 is asked to restrict its output of pollution from P_1' by one further unit, the cost is £5. If firm 2 is permitted to produce one further unit of pollution above P_2' then the total pollution is unchanged, but £8 of pollution abatement expenditure has been saved, a net social gain of £3.

A uniform tax, for all its faults, is thus better than uniform standards. It encourages the lowest-cost pollution abaters more than the high-cost ones to reduce pollution. This is seen in figure 15.5 where a uniform marginal tax rate is imposed on both firms at *T*. Firms 1 and 2 will now alter output to P_1^* and P_2^* respectively. The total pollution reduction remains the same but the total cost of pollution abatement has been lowered.

Not only does a tax motivate reduction of pollution more cheaply than do standards, it also encourages still further reductions by motivating a search for new technologies, and does so in a way that the setting of standards fails to do. If the long run is important, this is a major advantage of the taxation approach. Consider figure 15.6. The *MB* schedules are identical in each. The pollution produced by the firm in figure 15.6(a) is identical to that in figure 15.6(b). The only difference is that in the first case the level of *P* achieved is accomplished by virtue of a tax, whereas in the second it is the result of a legal standard.

Now assume that a new technology becomes available which lowers the marginal costs of pollution abatement (i.e. it reduces the marginal benefits sacrificed by reducing the polluting activity). Diagrammatically *MB* shifts to *MB'*. In case (a) the firm subject to the tax is further motivated to reduce pollution to *P'*. There the *MB* of pollution (*MB'*) equals the marginal cost (*T*) of doing so. Any other position is not one of profit maximization. In case (b) the firm will continue to pollute up to the legal limit of *P* and any costs saved by the introduction of the new technology (*XYZ*) will simply be additional profits to the firm. (Furthermore, experience indicates that legislative changes are relatively infrequent and often lag behind technological improvements.)

But, of course, not only does the tax result in reduced pollution; somehow research into the new technology itself must be encouraged. The incentive to do such research is greater in case (a) than case (b). In case (b) the incentive to introduce the new technology is the additional profit *XYZ*. In case (a) the savings from introducing cheaper pollution abatement also include *XYZ*, but since the tax bill of the polluter is also reduced (by *P' WXP*) this must be added to *XYZ*; moreover, of course, the benefits forgone by reducing pollution from *P* to *P'* (*WYPP'*) must be deducted. Thus the tax-paying

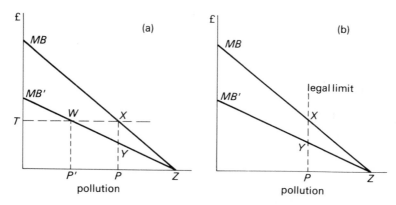

Figure 15.6 *Pollution and the search for new technology under systems of (a) taxation (b) standards*

polluter is better off by *WXY* as a consequence of introducing technology, *vis-à-vis* the regulated polluter. The tax-paying polluter thus has the stronger incentive to search for and introduce the new technology.

Resource Depletion

When a profit-maximizing firm has access to a finite resource it does not exhaust that resource as quickly as possible. Why? Consider a tin mine. Why would the owners conserve it and extract the tin gradually? The reason is that they realize that if they treble this year's production they may well treble income this year but they will be reducing their future income. This loss of future income would be reflected in the value (the share price) of the firm which owned the mine. The owner has to balance the advantages of immediate income against the loss in capital value (reflecting future income) of his shares.

Under some circumstances rapid depletion will be worthwhile (e.g. if the price of tin is expected to plummet in the future because it will be less highly valued then than it is now). Our discussion of speculation showed how markets in future goods could predict this. Such a future price fall could be due to anticipated new discoveries of tin ore or of substitutes for tin such as copper. Conversely, if the price of tin is expected to rise in the future then the incentive to conserve will be greater. This in turn will encourage a price rise in tin today and so an increase in tin exploration and a search by tin users for less expensive substitutes.

The two oil price rises of the 1970s were inflicted by the OPEC cartel of governments and not by the oil companies; nor did they reflect a geological change in oil's availability. They resulted in just such a search for new oil fields outside the cartel area, and for ways of using less oil, such as more fuel-efficient vehicles. It took some years for these efforts to produce results (the second laws of demand and of supply). But when Alaskan, Caribbean, North Sea and Far Eastern oil came on stream in the 1980s, and the motor manufacturers began to emphasize petrol-efficient engine designs, the oil price began to tumble; there was little OPEC could do to maintain the high real price it achieved in the 1970s by encouraging an 'artificial' shortage.

This was an example of output restriction caused by government interference. Excessive depletion of resources is generally brought about by absence of property rights. Thus property rights in the sea are ill defined. The consequence is over-fishing. There is no economic incentive to conserve the fish supply and every incentive to catch as much as possible as quickly as possible. And equally there is little incentive to engage in R & D to improve either the short-term or long-term productivity of fishing. Fish farming is an unknown occupation because no one can farm the seas. Yet in freshwater lakes, where property rights exist and can be policed fish farming is becoming ever more common. The blue whale may be a vanishing species, the rainbow trout is not.

Woodlands tend not to be depleted in Western Europe where private firms own the land. Firms have every incentive to cut down trees but also to replant intelligently in order to maintain or increase the capital value of their asset. In the USA the logic of property rights in forest land is not so well developed. Many forests are government owned and leased to firms. The timber company is then only interested in maximizing the annual value of its lease; that is, by felling the timber as rapidly as possible, it has no interest in reafforestation. In Britain, conversely, where much forest land is state owned, the tendency has been to plant excessive amounts of trees, usually of a visually homogeneous kind, and to consume resources which would be better employed (i.e. be more highly valued by society) elsewhere.

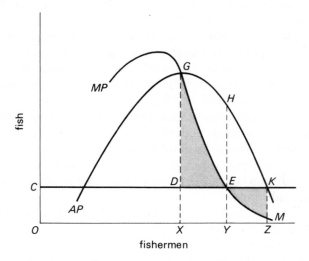

Figure 15.7 *Use of resources under three systems*

The theory behind these illustrations is given in figure 15.7. A fishing lake is operated under three alternative systems. First, the government owns it, with the objective of maximizing the apparent interests of identifiable fishermen (and hence of civil servants and politicians whose actions will be approved of or disapproved of by the fishermen). Second, the lake is privately owned, with profit maximization as an objective. Third, it is government owned, with the objective of providing free access to all citizens.

AP is the average product (or average catch) function. The more variable are the inputs awarded to a fixed input, the greater will be total output. At first *AP* will rise as the fixed input is used more effectively (say as more fishermen put in more bait in the water, so encouraging fish to congregate near the hooks). After a point diminishing returns will set in (the peak of *MP*, marginal product or the catch of the marginal fisherman), *AP* will rise less slowly and then at *G* turn over. *OC* is the opportunity cost of fishing (the output forgone elsewhere in the economy by undertaking a day's fishing, the cost of petrol to get to the lake, and so on).

Where the government wishes to maximize the apparent benefits to a particular interest group and so to itself it will ration access to the lake. *X* fishermen will be permitted to fish and each will catch *XG* fish, the maximum each individual could under any circumstances. Where government wishes to benefit its image by permitting free access to the lake, *Z* fishermen will voluntarily use this resource. Each fisherman will catch *ZK* fish, an amount equal to the (private) costs each such fisherman incurs.

But *X* is a situation of under-fishing and *Z* one of over-fishing from a *social* point of view. This is shown in two stages. First, it will be shown that a profit-maximizing owner will charge a fee resulting in *Y* fishermen. Second, it will be shown that any point below or above *Y* is suboptimal socially.

A profit maximizer will charge a fee for access in order to maximize his profits. What demand schedules face him? What fees *could* he charge, and what is the profit-maximizing fee? The demand schedule is obtained by deducting *OC* from *AP*. A fisherman will willingly pay a price equal to the value of his catch less his *OC*. Thus a fee of *DG* will attract *X* fishers, one of *HE* will attract *Y* fishers and so on. The lake owner will maximize profits when his *MR* equals his *MC*. When he permits an extra fisher he gains the fee from that extra fisherman, but since the fee (by definition) must now be lowered for all the previous fishermen too, he forfeits the amount by which he has had to lower the entrance fee, and forfeits it for all previous fishers.

Thus where $MR = MC$,

$$AP - OC = -\Delta APF$$

where *F* is the number of original fishermen. So in the profit-maximizing situation,

$$AP + \Delta APF = OC.$$

But it can be shown using calculus that, generally:

$$MP = \frac{\mathrm{d}TP}{\mathrm{d}F} = \frac{\mathrm{d}APF}{\mathrm{d}F} = AP\frac{\mathrm{d}F}{\mathrm{d}F} + \frac{\mathrm{d}APF}{\mathrm{d}F}$$

$$MP = AP + \Delta APF$$

Hence, under conditions of profit maximization $MP = OC$. So to obtain maximum profit $MP = OC$ at E, a fee of EH should be charged and Y fishermen will use the lake.

Why is this socially optimal? To the left of Y, say at X, movement towards X will result in a social cost of $DXEY$ but a benefit of $GEYX$. Society would gain in goods otherwise forgone by the shaded area DGE. (Benefits and costs are here measured in fish but this is for graphical convenience only; the costs, for example, that we already know include forgone output elsewhere of all society's goods or services.) To the right of Y, say at Z, a movement toward Z results in a cost increase of $YEKZ$, but a benefit loss of $YEMZ$. There is thus a net benefit loss, or social cost, of EKM.

Thus again we conclude that unless bureaucrats, civil servants and politicians behave irrationally, that is, against their own self-interest, it is more likely that private markets will produce socially optimal outcomes than will government regulations.

References

1 E.V. Rostow, 'British and American experience with legislation against restraints of competition', *Modern Law Review* 9 (1960), pp. 131–59.

2 *Ibid.*

3 *Ibid.*

4 *Ibid.*

5 The Restrictive Trade Practices Act, 1976, the Resale Prices Act, 1976, and the Competition Act, 1980, were simply Acts of consolidation and minor amendment and, in the last case, broadening of scope. (For example, agricultural product marketing boards, water authorities and some others were brought within the ambit of the legislation.)

6 B.S. Yamey, *Resale Price Maintenance and Shoppers' Choice*, Hobart Paper no. 1, Institute of Economic Affairs, 1960.

7 A.J. Brown, 'Regional economics with special reference to the United Kingdom', *Economic Journal* 79 (1969), pp. 759–96.

8 R.H. Coase, 'The problem of social cost', *Journal of Law and Economics* 4 (1961), pp. 1–49.

9 Steven Cheung, *The Myth of Social Cost*, Hobart Paper no. 82, Institute of Economic Affairs, 1978.

Index

It should be noted, however, that although the economist sees the rationale for anti-monopolies and restrictive practices legislation as being the promotion of competition, this is not the objective of the legislation as it stood, at least before 1973. The gateways may or may not facilitate the operation of a competitive market; that is not their objective. To a degree, such an outcome would be merely coincidental.

One case which was tried under the 1956 Act was the Net Book Agreement. This restrictive practice, which dates back nearly a century, permits publishers to make contracts with booksellers whereby the resale price is determined by the publisher. Judgement on the practice was passed in 1959 in favour of the restriction. The Court accepted that unrestricted competition among retailers would indeed lower the price of popular books. But this would allegedly reduce the number of specialist booksellers since they would lose sales of popular titles to any retailer who cared to stock them and undercut his prices. This in turn would reduce the number of outlets for serious titles, and so the number of 'quality' books themselves. Consequentially such books would also have to rise in price. Why the reader of 'less serious' books should cross-subsidize the buyer of 'quality' books was never fully explained. In retrospect, the experience of the musical recording trade, which has burgeoned since the 1950s, would seem to suggest that 'popular' and 'classical' records and cassettes can coexist without any price maintenance agreements to prevent competition, and can do so without suffering the harmful effects which allegedly would arise if the Net Book Agreement was to be abandoned.

Although, as mentioned above, *collective* enforcement of resale price maintenance (RPM) was banned by the 1956 Act, the Net Book Agreement survived (after a Court judgement) and RPM was still permitted on an *individual* basis. That is, a single supplier could still set and stipulate a price at or above which a retailer must resell his product. If the retailer did not comply the supplier could refuse to supply, but he could not call on fellow suppliers in the same industry to exercise such a sanction collectively.

Individual RPM remained strongly entrenched in goods accounting for approximately 50 per cent of consumer expenditure. These, according to Yamey,[6] included the following: bread, cereals, soap, matches, cigarettes, confectionery, cars, cycles, radios, TV and electrical goods, magazines, newspapers, preserves, beverages, manufactured and packeted foods, beer, wines and spirits, clothing and footwear, furnishings and carpeting. In 1964, consequently, the Resale Prices Act was passed banning the practice unless the manufacturer could prove to the Court that the public interest would suffer a net loss. Five 'escape clauses' were provided in the Act:

1 The quality and variety of goods would be substantially reduced.
2 The number of relevant retail outlets would be substantially less.
3 Retail prices would increase.
4 Goods would be sold under conditions likely to endanger health in consequence of their misuse by the public.

5   Any necessary services provided with or after the sale of the goods to the public would cease or be substantially reduced in provision.

As indicated earlier, the Act virtually ended RPM. The emergence of self-service retailing, supermarkets and discount stores was encouraged by the Act and facilitated its effective implementation (see chapter 13). None the less the argument and debate which surrounded its passing was heated and the major points are worth recalling both for their intrinsic interest and for a comparison with the marketing and distribution changes which have emerged over the last 25 years (chapter 13). The main points are summarized thus:

1   RPM widens retail and wholesale margins.
2   These margins are guaranteed.
3   Prices are uniform everywhere. Thus consumer choice is reduced; the consumer cannot choose a high-service, high-price shop *vis-à-vis* a low-service, low-price outlet. Discounts for quality purchasing are also precluded.
4   More efficient outlets cannot take advantage of their efficiency by offering lower prices to attract more custom to further increase profits; the stimulus to increase efficiency is thus removed and the ability of the more efficient to grow is stultified.
5   By similar reasoning, new and innovative forms of retailing are discouraged.
6   Competition between retailers is channelled into high-cost forms of rivalry rather than price cutting (credit, delivery, a wide selection of goods and so on): certainly such activities are desired by some consumers, but not by all.
7   Inefficient outlets are kept in being longer than they otherwise might, partly by guaranteed margins, partly by the inability of more efficient retailers to attract price-sensitive consumers. Average outlet turnover is therefore lower and costs are higher.
8   The number of outlets, particularly small shops, would decline if RPM was abandoned.
9   Services would be curtailed.

The last two points were the major arguments in favour of RPM. Certainly services have been reduced. But high-service stores (providing after-sales services, guarantees, a 'quality ambience', credit and delivery, etc.) have continued to survive alongside low-service, lower-priced equivalents. Consumers shop in the type of outlet they prefer. Small shops have tended to disappear, as was feared, but mainly from high-rent sites on high street and similar locations. There the guaranteed margins provided by RPM permitted their continued existence cheek by jowl with the multiples. On the contrary, however, small independent outlets have continued to flourish in residential areas, selling at higher prices but compensating for this by their competitive advantage in convenience of location, longer and more appropriate opening

16

Concluding Thoughts

A textbook does not lend itself readily to a climactic final chapter. But the following are put forward as suggestions for further thought by the reader:

Will reduced taxes and regulations foster the development of new products, new services, and new ways of using scarce resources? A few innovations, of course, will be introduced simply because reduced taxes and regulations will make labour and capital available. Some projects will now get the resources needed to carry them beyond the planning stage.

But labour and capital are needed only after a profit opportunity *has been perceived*. What, if anything, will stimulate the entrepreneurial process by which profit opportunities are *first perceived*? One way to stimulate entrepreneurship is to replace policies that discourage the search for profit opportunities. Lower tax rates and fewer regulations on industry's behaviour are obvious steps in this direction.

Reduced tax rates stimulate the search for profit opportunities by lowering the marginal tax on profits. Regulatory relief further encourages this search by freeing businessmen from paperwork, and by eliminating impediments to innovation and growth.

But not all profit opportunities are discerned through *deliberate search*. As Kirzner has shown in *Perception, Opportunity and Profit*,[1] entrepreneurship also embraces the *spontaneous perception* of profit opportunities. These are opportunities which have not been pursued, not because of prohibitive production costs, nor even because of search costs, but simply because no one has noticed them. The spontaneous perception of profit opportunities is the ultimate source of all entrepreneurial activity. Even if an innovation is introduced as a result of a long and deliberate analysis of market conditions, someone has to first decide to initiate the analysis. This original decision, which must precede any deliberate search, springs not from planning but from alertness. It springs from the spontaneous perception that profit opportunities may exist.

The best way to stimulate entrepreneurial alertness may simply be to guarantee that businessmen will be free to profit from their alertness.

Such increased alertness to profit opportunities would not necessarily mean an increase in the 'total alertness' in society. But with lowering of governmentally created barriers, people will become less alert to tax shelters, regulatory loopholes, opportunities for free-riding and the 'black economy' in general. At the same time, reductions in subsidies and special interest group activities will reduce the benefits available to those alert to such government behaviour. Such policies may not make firms more alert, but they will make them direct their attention and their efforts, to productive—that is, socially valued—activities.

References

1 Israel M. Kirzner, *Perception, Opportunity and Profit*, University of Chicago Press, 1978.